The Best Baby Names in the World
from Around the World

The Best Baby Names in the World
from Around the World

Edited by J. M. Congemi

☑®
Facts On File, Inc.

The Best Baby Names in the World from Around the World

Copyright © 2000 by LifeTime Media, Inc., 352 Seventh Avenue, New York, NY 10001; http://www.lifetimemedia.com

Checkmark Books
An imprint of Facts On File, Inc.
11 Penn Plaza
New York, NY 10001-2006

Library of Congress Cataloging-in-Publication Data

The best baby names in the world from around the world / by LifeTime Media, Inc.
  p.   cm.
  Includes index.
  ISBN 0-8160-4131-8 (acid-free paper).
  ISBN 0-8160-4132-6 (pbk. : acid-free paper)
  [1. Names, Personal—Dictionaries.] I. LifeTime Media, Inc.

CS2377.B47 2000
929.4'4—dc21   99-087420

Checkmark Books are available at special discounts when purchased in bulk quantities for businesses, associations, institutions or sales promotions. Please call our Special Sales Department in New York at (212) 967-8800 or (800) 322-8755.

You can find Facts On File on the World Wide Web at http://www.factsonfile.com

Text design by Cindy LaBreacht
Cover design by Nora Wertz

Printed in the United States of America

MP FOF 10 9 8 7 6 5 4 3 2 1
  (pb) 10 9 8 7 6 5 4 3 2 1

This book is printed on acid-free paper.

Contents

Foreword

What's in a name? Perhaps fortune? Fate? Personality? Identity? The importance of a name should not be underestimated and, indeed, demands careful consideration. Hence, choosing a suitable name for a child is never a simple task. The decision is further complicated by our multinational world, where borders are forever changing and advances in travel and communications are transforming the Earth into a global village.

When naming children, parents today often want to reach beyond the confines of the traditional names common to their community. Add to this the complexity of multicultural marriages, where the interests of varying heritages must be reconciled. The case of naming my half Russian, half Italian-American son—born in the Czech Republic, but now living in another part of Eastern Europe—offered numerous creative possibilities, as well as *headaches*.

My wife and I were first tempted by the idea of tossing some novelty into our son's life, perhaps naming him in honor of one of our Czech friends. However, family interests on both sides of the Atlantic—our relatives being entirely unfamiliar with Czech pronunciations—led us to abandon the idea with great regret. Instead, we decided to search for an international name, one easily recognizable in both Russian and English. Sitting in our apartment in Prague, with no book of names to be found, we sat up late at night compiling our own lists of familiar and favorite male names in both languages.

She proposed Nikita, a popular boy's name in Russia, but unfortunately one undone in an American context. Popular song and film have feminized the name, and we made special efforts to avoid cursing our child with a name that might encourage name-calling by his peers. Not many American boys aspire to be a femme fatale, as in the case of Nikita of celluloid fame.

Likewise, *my* first choice, Luke, met with my wife's immediate disapproval and laughter. In Russian, Luke sounds like the word *luc*, meaning "onion." My son, the little onion-head. Imagine the joy on his face. Hardly a way to earn your child's eternal love. My family in America pitched in, combing through countless baby name books for suggestions. But none of the books proved able to solve our cross-culture dilemma. Finally, less than one week before my son's birth, with no alternative, I thought enough to glance through the Bible, only to behold the Book of Daniel and hear the glowing description of a young prophet. At last, here was a powerful name to crown the family heir, one easily said and familiar in both languages.

How much easier the process would have been with the help of this unique reference book, with its extensive possibilities, variety, and cultural and anecdotal information. It is the closest thing to Divine Inspiration and an absolute must for every household—both those expecting and those already blessed with children.

—John Varoli

John Varoli is an American writer for the New York Times *living in St. Petersburg, Russia.*

Acknowledgments

This book was a team effort. LifeTime Media would like to acknowledge and thank the researchers and editors who contributed to the development of this book, particularly Richard Adler, John David Varoli, David Hart, Leah Ruggiero, Carlotta Dus, Artemis Christodulou, Melody Lin, Cecillia Lin, Carl Masthay, Paul Graves, Patsy Chen, Tim Longman, Neda Mollivalli, Jennifer Hansson, Meenal Pandya, Luanna Haraguchi, Isaac Meyers, Rina Ne'eman, and Joyce Kadzakumanja. Their efforts were invaluable to the completion of *The Best Baby Names in the World from Around the World*.

*T*he name you choose for your baby will be one of the most outstanding contributions that you, as parents, make to his or her well-being. Often before children have a chance to show off their unique and wonderful qualities, people will know them by name: family, friends, neighbors, schoolmates, teachers, employers, and so on. While browsing through the more than 10,000 names in this book, remember that the name you select will introduce your child to the world. Here are some issues you may want to consider.

ASSOCIATION

Your child's name should ultimately have pleasant associations for you. You might choose to name your baby after a much-admired close friend or relative; an historical figure or revered celebrity; an heroic character in literature or mythology; or perhaps a place that evokes special personal significance. An ancestral family name or a name that reflects your child's religious or ethnic heritage can represent a vital and fundamental connection between your child and his or her roots.

TRENDY VERSUS UNIQUE

Names can be subject to trends and the fashion of the times. A popular name has the potential of thrusting a child into shadows of anonymity, while a truly unusual name can perhaps attract too much attention to a little tyke who longs to fit in. A combination or hybrid name is a possible solution—you can create a unique name by uniting two already established and recognized ones.

HARMONY

The first and, if applicable, middle name you choose for your baby should blend nicely with your family name. Reading aloud and listening to the combined sound of potential first and middle names added to your last name should help you decide whether they match. Some widely followed suggestions are that you pick a first name that varies in length with your family name, and that the middle name should differ in length with the first name. Some people's ears are pleased by names that have the same beginning sound, as in the name of the latter-day singer and actress Dorothy Dandridge, while others prefer the same ending sound, as in the name of movie star Bruce Willis. Only by voicing and listening to different combinations will you decide what sounds best to you.

NICKNAMES AND VARIATIONS

Diminutive pet names and variations on names and spellings are endless. While an especially cutesy pet-name for a toddler may be endearing early on, it may be a great source of exasperation for a young adult. An exceptionally aberrant spelling of a common name may also prove frustrating to a school-aged child whose name is perpetually misspelled or mispronounced. A thoughtful parent needs to take these matters into account.

WATCH THOSE INITIALS

Take care that the child's initials do not spell out something embarrassing. The name "Richard Allen Thomas" sounds melodious enough, but to mischievous schoolmates, "R. A. T." spells an opportunity to make fun.

MAGIC

Throughout history, most cultures have believed that a person's name and how it is chosen have vital, even magical significance. The magic in the name you choose will be in the associations it brings of your loving relationship with your baby from birth onward, the pride you have in him or her, and the satisfaction you take in being a wonderful parent.

Part I:
The Best Baby Names in the World

Benin is a small but proud country in West Africa. It is here that the great ancient kingdoms of Benin and Dahomey flourished, gaining particular renown for their striking sculptural works of art. The Kingdom of Dahomey—the name of the country until 1975—was a well-organized and powerful state during the 17th century. Thus, children's names in Benin reflect various linguistic influences both European and African in nature. The traditional languages most widely spoken here are Fon and Yoruba, but French is also an official language. Beninese names are often structured around the root words *efe*, meaning "wealth," *osa*, meaning "God," and *omo*, meaning "this one can make a child."

BENIN: BOYS

Efosa (e-FO-sa)   A powerful name meaning "the wealth of God." Also spelled Efeosa.

Ehiogie (ahe-O-gehe)   Literally meaning "sent by God," it is a variation of *Osagie*.

Ewean (A-win)   Translated as "to be clever."

Idemudia (E-DA-mu-dee)   Meaning "bravery" or "a brave child." The name is given to a breech child who is considered brave for coming into the world feet first or "standing."

Omorogie (o-moro-GE-ha)   Believing life is more valuable than money. This name means "a child is richer than wealth."

Osagie (O-sa-ge-e)   Meaning "sent by God." A variation is *Ehiogie*.

Osazema (o-sa-za-MA)   For religious-minded families, this name means "the Lord has chosen this child for me." Often shortened to Osaze.

BENIN: GIRLS

Ehizokie (a-he-ZO-kea)   For parents who were hoping for a boy but are proud to receive a daughter this name means "the Lord has chosen the king."

Itohan (E-to-han)   Recognizing difficult times, this name means "to feel sorrowful" or "to have pity."

Izegbe (ih-ZEG-be)   For parents who waited a long time for a child to arrive, a name meaning "the long expected child."

Nehivena (na-HE-va-na)   "The one the lord has chosen for me."

Osarogre (o-sa-RO-gre)   For families that choose to follow the divine, above all others, this name is "God is king."

Ghana

Present-day Ghana is named after a West African empire that prospered along the Niger River from A.D. 400 to 1240. The country was part of Britain's Gold Coast colony for 113 years, and consequently children's names in Ghana reflect both African and English origins. While English is the official language, the indigenous tongues of Akan, Moshi-Dagomba, Ewe, and Ga hold sway in many parts of the country. Famous people from Ghana include Jerry Rawlings, Kwame Nkrumah, and United Nations Secretary General Kofi Annan.

GHANA: BOYS

Afram (ah-FRAM)   Meaning "a river in Ghana."

Ata (AH-ta)   This name, meaning "twin," can be given to multiple children.

Adika (ah-DEE-ka)   Meaning "the first child of a second marriage."

Adofo (ah-DO-fo)   Meaning "a courageous warrior."

Atsu (AH-tsoo)   Meaning "the younger of twins." Often shortened to *Tse*.

Atu (AH-too)   Meaning "born on Saturday." Also see Kwame.

Badu (BAH-doo)   A parent's perfect child can be given this name, meaning "the tenth."

Bodua (boh-DOO-ah)   Meaning "the tail of an animal."

Coffie (KO-fee)   Meaning "born on Friday," this name is popularly shortened to Fifi. See also Kofi.

Coujoe (KOO-joe)   Meaning "born on Monday," this name is often shortened to Jojo. Variations include *Kodwo* and *Kojo*.

Ebo (A-bo)   A name which means "born on Tuesday."

Fenuku (fen-OO-koo)   A name which means "born after twins."

Fifi (FEE-fee)   Meaning "born on Friday," this is short for Coffie.

Gyasi (GYAH-see)   Meaning "a wonderful baby."

Jojo (JO-jo)   Meaning "born on Monday." This name is short for Coujoe, Kodwo, or Kojo.

Kesse (KEH-seh)   Meaning "plump baby." Also *Kessie*.

Kizza (KEE-zuh)   Meaning "born after twins." Variations include *Kizzy* and *Twia*.

Kodwo (KO-dwo)   Meaning "born on Monday." See also Coujoe, Kojo, and Jojo.

Kofi (KO-fee)   Meaning "born on Friday." See also Coffie and Fifi. U.N. Secretary General Kofi Annan hails from Ghana, though he has worked in the United States most of his life.

Kojo (KO-jo)   Meaning "born on Monday." See also Coujoe, Jojo, Kodwo. Kojo Botsio was a government minister in Ghana's Nkrumah administration.

Kontar (KON-tahr)   Parents who want to have only one child may like this name, meaning "the only child."

Kpodo (k-PO-do)   Meaning "the elder of twins." See also Oko.

Kwakou (KWA-koo)   Meaning "born on Wednesday." See also Yooku. Kwakou is a name common to several Ashanti kings.

Kwame (KWA-may)   Meaning "born on Saturday." See also Atu. Author Kwame Anthony Appiah is a professor of African-American Studies at Harvard University and wrote *In My Father's House*.

Kwesi (KWAY-zee)   Meaning "born on Sunday." See also Sisi, Quaashie. Dr. Kwesi Dickson is the president of the Methodist Church of Ghana. A variation is *Kwasi*.

Lado (LAH-do)   "The second-born son." See also Manu.

Manu (MAH-noo)   Meaning "the second born." See also Lado. One famous Manu is pop musician Manu Dibango from Cameroon.

Mawuli (ma-WOO-lee)   Meaning "there is a God."

Mensah (MEHN-sah)   Meaning "the third son."

Minkah (MEEN-kah)   A family where one parent is a judge may like this name meaning "just" or "fair."

Msrah (m-SRAH)   Meaning "the sixth-born."

Nkrumah (n-KROO-mah)   Meaning "the ninth-born." Kwame Nkrumah was the founding president of Ghana.

Nsoah (n-SO-ah)   Meaning "the seventh-born."

Nyamekye (nya-MEH-kyeh)   Meaning "God's gift."

Oko (O-ko)   Meaning "the elder of twins." See also Kpodo.

Osei (o-SAH-ee)   Meaning "noble." Bafour Osei Akoto was chairman of the Asante Council. A variation is *Osee*.

Quaashie (KWAH-shee)   Meaning "born on Sunday." See also Kwasi or Sisi.

Sisi (SEE-see)   Meaning "born on Sunday." See also Kwasi or Quaashie.

Sono (SO-no)   Meaning "elephant."

Tse (TSAY)   Meaning "the younger of twins." A short form of Atsu.

Twia (TWEE-ah)   Meaning "born after twins." See also Kizza.

Yafeu (yah-FAY-oo)   Meaning "intrepid."

Yao (YAH-o)   Meaning "born on Thursday." See also Yawo, Yorkoo.

Yawo (YAH-wo)   Meaning "born on Thursday." See also Yao, Yorkoo.

Yoofi (YOO-fee)   Meaning "born on Friday." See also Coffie, Fifi, and Kofi.

Yooku (YOO-koo)   Meaning "born on Wednesday." A variation is *Kwakou*.

Yorkoo (YOR-koo)   Meaning "born on Thursday." Variations include *Yao* and *Yawo*.

GHANA: GIRLS

Aba (AH-bah)   Meaning "born on Thursday."

Ababuo (ah-BAH-boo)   Meaning "the child that keeps coming back."

Abam (a-BAHM)   Meaning "the second child after twins." Variations include *Dofi* and *Nyankomago*.

Abena (a-BAY-nah)   Meaning "born on Tuesday." See also Adowa.

Adowa (ah-DO-wah)   Meaning "born on Tuesday." See also Abena.

Afafa (ah-FAH-fah)   Meaning "the first child of second husband."

Afryea (ahf-RAY-ah)   Meaning "born into happiness."

Afua (ah-FOO-ah)   Meaning "born on Friday." See also Efua. Afua Sapon was queen mother of the Asante kingdom in the early 1880s.

Akosua (ah-ko-SOO-ah)   Meaning "born on Sunday." See also Esi.

Akua (ah-KOO-ah)   Meaning "born on Wednesday."

Akwete (ah-KWAY-tay)   Meaning "the elder of twins." See also Panyin, Ye.

Akwokwo (ah-KWO-kwo)   Meaning "the younger of twins." See also Kakra.

Ama (AH-mah)   Meaning "born on Saturday." Ama Ata Aidoo is the author of the play *Anowa*.

Antobam (ahn-TO-bahm) A child with this name will grow up to be a natural leader who is organized, friendly, pleasant, and sociable.

Baba (BAH-bah) Meaning "born on Thursday."

Boahinmaa (bo-ah-heen-MAH) Literally means "one who has left her community."

Do (DO) Meaning "the first child after twins." See also Tawiah.

Dofi (DO-fee) Meaning "the second child after twins." See also Abam, Nyankomago.

Efua (eh-FOO-ah) Meaning "born on Friday." Efua Sutherland is a Ghanaian playwright, author of *Foriwa*. Variations include *Efia* and *Afua*.

Enyonyam (eh-nyoYAHM) Meaning "it is good for me."

Esi (EH-see) Meaning "born on Sunday." See also Akosua and Jumapili under Kenya names.

Kakra (KAH-krah) Meaning "the younger of twins." See also Akwokwo.

Kunto (KOON-to) A name that means "the third child."

Mawusi (mah-WOO-see) Literally means "in the hands of God."

Morowa (mor-O-wah) A name that signifies "queen." See also Thema.

Nanyamka (nahn-YAHM-kah) Meaning "God's gift."

Nyankomago (nyahn-ko-MAH-go) Meaning "second child after twins." See also Abam, Dofi.

Ozigbodi (o-zeeg-BO-dee) Meaning "patience."

Panyin (PAHN-yihn) Meaning "the elder of twins." See also Akwete and Ye.

Serwa (SIR-wah) Meaning "noble one."

Tawiah (tah-WEE-ah) Meaning "the first child after twins." See also Do.

Thema (TAY-mah) Meaning "queen." See also Morowa.

Ye (YAY) A name signifying "the elder of twins." See also Akwete, Panyin.

**Kenya**

According to the most recent census figures, there are 42 tribes living in Kenya, as well as various non-African ethnic groups. Affairs of government and education are generally conducted in English—the official language—while the national language of Swahili is used for all other matters. In addition to these two languages, most of the people of Kenya also speak what they consider their mother tongues—the languages that they grew up speaking.

Although an increasing number of city-dwellers use English, most rural people continue to speak their tribal languages. More than 30 distinct languages or dialects exist in Kenya. One of Kenya's most renowned writers is Ngugi Wa Thiong'o, who was the first Kenyan author to write in his native Kikuyu.

KENYA: BOYS

Barasa (bah-RAH-sah)   A name that means "the meeting site."

Chilemba (chee-LEHM-bah)   Meaning "turban."

Chiumbo (chee-OOM-bo)   Meaning "a little creation."

Gakere (gah-KEH-ree)   Meaning "a small muscle." Variations include *Gakeri*.

Kamau (kah-MAH-oo)   Meaning "a quiet warrior." Daniel Kamau is a member of parliament from the Rift Valley.

Keanjaho (kay-ahn-JAH-o)   Meaning "a mountain of beans."

Lisimba (lee-SIHM-bah)   Meaning "a lion."

Makalani (mah-kah-LAH-nee)   Publishing parents may choose this name signifying "a writer."

Mpenda (m-PEHN-dah)   For romantic parents here is a name that means "a lover."

Okoth (O-kot)   Meaning "born when it is raining." See also Okot. Yona Okoth is the Anglican bishop of Bukedi in Uganda.

Otieno (o-tee-EH-no)   Meaning "born at night." Dalmas Otieno is minister of transportation and communication in the government under President Daniel arap Moi.

Thabiti (ta-BEE-tee)   Signifying "a true man."

Tumaini (too-mah-EE-nee)   A name that means "hope."

KENYA: GIRLS

Aluna (ah-LOO-nah)   Literally means "come here."

Gakeri (gah-KEH-ree)   Meaning "a small muscle." Wanguwa Gakeri is a popular Kenyan actor.

Jumapili (joo-mah-PEE-lee)   Meaning "Sunday." A name given to a girl born on Sunday.

Kainda (kah-EEN-dah)   Meaning "the hunter's daughter."

Kanika (kah-NEE-kah)   A child with this name will be naturally seen as the advice giver. She will possess an easy-going spirit that makes her approachable and sympathetic.

Kaweria (kah-weh-REE-ah)   Signifying "the loving one."

Makena (mah-KAY-nah)   A name that means "the happy one."

Nafula (nah-FOO-lah)   Meaning "rainy season," it's a name given to a baby born during the rainy season.

Ngina (n-GEE-nah)   Meaning "one who serves."

Njeri (n-JEH-ree)   Meaning "daughter of a warrior."

Wambui (wam-BOO-ee)   Meaning "the singer of songs." Wambui Otieno is a women's activist and opposition politician in Kenya.

*N*igeria With more than 100 million inhabitants, Nigeria is Africa's most populous nation. Early cultures in Nigeria, including the civilizations of the Ibo, Benin, Hausa, and Yoruba, date back to at least 700 B.C., with great cities at Ife, in the Yoruba area and in the country's northern region. Its size and location make Nigeria one of the continent's most diverse countries in terms of ethnic, religious, and cultural composition, which at times produced serious difficulties among the various factions. It is a nation that has produced many great artists, including Nobel laureate Wole Soyinka, musician Fela Kuti, and playwright Ken Saro Wiwa Ogoni.

NIGERIA: BOYS

Abayomi (ah-bah-YO-mee)   A name meaning "born to bring me joy."

Abiade (ah-bee-AH-day)   Meaning "born of royal parents."

Abiola (ah-bee-O-lah)   Meaning "born in honor." Mashood Abiola was a Yoruba chief and apparent winner of Nigeria's 1993 presidential election.

Ade (AH-day)   Meaning "royal" or "king." One notable Ade is Sunny Ade, a popular Nigerian singer.

Agu (AH-goo)   Meaning "leopard."

Ajala (ah-JAH-lah)   A name that means "potter."

Akins (AH-kins)   "Brave." Similar to the Japanese *Akira*, meaning "bright."

Ayinde (ah-YIHN-day)   Literally translated as "we praised him and he came." Sikiru Ayinde Barrister is a Fuji-style Nigerian singer.

Ayo (AH-yo)   Meaning "happiness."

Azi (AH-zee)   Meaning "youth."

Azikiwe (ah-ZEE-kee-way)   Meaning "full of vigor." Nnamdi Azikiwe, nationalist leader and president of Nigeria from 1963 to 1966.

Balogun (bahl-o-GOON)   Translated as "a general." Balogun Kuku, early Yoruba convert to Islam and leader of Ijebu.

Bandele (bahn-DEH-leh)   A name that signifies "born away from home."

Banjoko (bahn-JO-ko)   Meaning "stay with me and wander no more."

Bankole (bahn-KO-lay)   Meaning "help build our house."

Bem (BEHM)   A name suggesting "peace."

Boseda (bo-SAY-dah)   Meaning "born on Sunday." See also Danladi.

Chijioke (chee-jee-O-kay)   Translated literally, this name means "God gives talent."

Chike (CHEE-kay)   Meaning "the power of God." Chike Obi is a journalist known as "the Thomas Paine of Nigeria." He was arrested for sedition in 1961.

Chinelo (chih-NEH-lo)   Meaning "thoughts of God."

Chinua (CHIH-noo-ah)   Meaning "blessings from God." Chinua Achebe is a novelist best known for *Things Fall Apart*.

Chioke (chee-O-kay)   A name that signifies "God's blessing."

Dada (DAH-dah)   Meaning "curly haired." A variation is *Dadi*.

Danladi (dahn-LAH-dee)   Meaning "born on Sunday." See also Boseda.

Dibia (dih-BEE-ah)   A name that means "healer."

Diji (DEE-jee)   Meaning "a farmer."

Dunsimi (doon-SEE-mee) Translated literally, this name means "don't die before me."

Durojaiye (doo-ro-jah-EE-yay) Meaning "slow down and enjoy the world."

Ehioze (eh-hee-O-zay) Meaning "above the envy of others."

Ekon (AY-kon) Meaning "strong."

Ekundayo (ay-koon-DAH-yo) Meaning "sorrow becomes joy."

Enobakhare (ay-no-bah-KAH-ray) Meaning "the king's word."

Ewansiha (eh-wahn-SEE-ah) Meaning "secrets cannot be bought."

Eze (EH-zeh) Meaning "king." See also Tor.

Ezeamaka (eh-zeh-ah-MAH-kah) This name suggests "as magnificent as the king."

Ezenachi (eh-zeh-NAH-chee) Parents in a monarchy environment may enjoy this name, which means "the king rules."

Ezeoha (eh-zeh-O-ha) Meaning "a people's king."

Foluke (fo-LOO-kay) Meaning "given to God."

Gowon (go-WON) Meaning "a rainmaker." Yakubu Gowon was military ruler of Nigeria from 1966 to 1975.

Idogbe (ih-DOG-bay) Meaning "the second born after twins."

Idowu (ih-DO-woo) Meaning "born after twins."

Imarogbe (ih-mah-ROG-bay) Meaning "child born into a good family."

Iyapo (ee-YAH-po) Meaning "many trials; many impediments."

Jaja (JAH-jah) Meaning "a revered one." Ex-slave Jaja founded the Opobo state in the Niger River delta during the 1860s.

Jibade (jee-BAH-day) Meaning "of noble birth."

Jumoke (joo-MOH-kay) Meaning "everyone loves the child."

Kayin (KAH-yihn) A name that means "celebrated."

Kayode (kah-YO-day) Meaning "he brought joy." E.A. Kayode was an early Christian leader of the Yoruba.

Kehinde (keh-HIHN-day) Meaning "second born twin."

Kunle (KOON-lay) Meaning "much-honored home."

Madu (MAH-doo) Meaning "people."

Mazi (MAH-zee) Military parents will like this name, meaning "sir."

Modupe (mo-DOO-pay) Meaning "thank you." A name selected by parents who wish to show their great appreciation for the birth of their son.

Mongo (MON-go) "Famous." Mongo Beti is a novelist from Cameroon.

Ngozi (n-GO-zee) Meaning "a blessing."

Nika (NEE-kah) Meaning "ferocious." A name selected by parents who wish for their son to be seen as intimidating and powerful.

Nnamdi (NAHM-dee) Meaning "father's name lives on." Nnamdi Azikiwe was a nationalist leader and the former president of Nigeria. A variation is *Namdi*.

Nosakhere (no-sah-KEH-ree) Meaning "God's way."

Nwa (NWAH) Meaning "son."

Nwabudike (nwah-boo-DEE-kay) Meaning "his father's might."

Nweke (NWEH-kay) Meaning "born on market day." Chuba Nweke was a Nigerian poet and businessman. A variation is *Nwake*.

Oba (O-ba) Meaning "king."

Obadele (o-bah-DEH-leh) Meaning "the king arrives."

Obataiye (o-bah-tah-EE-yay) Meaning "king of the world."

Ode (O-day) Meaning "born along the road."

Odion (o-DEE-ahn)   Meaning "the first of twins." See also *Taiwo*.

Ogun (o-GOON)   Meaning "God of war." Variations include *Ogunkeye*, *Ogunsanwo*, and *Ogunsheye*.

Ojo (O-jo)   Meaning "a difficult birth."

Okpara (ok-PAH-rah)   A name that means "the first son."

Ola (O-lah)   Meaning "wealthy, rich."

Olajuwon (o-LAH-joo-wahn)   Meaning "wealth and honor are God's gifts." The center for the NBA's Houston Rockets is Hakeem "The Dream" Olajuwon. Variations include *Olaluan*, *Olajuwan*, and *Oljuwoun*.

Olamina (o-lah-MEE-nah)   Meaning "my riches."

Olatunji (o-lah-TOON-jee)   Meaning "honor reawakens." Percussionist and bandleader Baba Olatunji led the Drums of Passion.

Olu (O-loo)   Meaning "preeminent."

Olubayo (o-loo-BAH-yo)   Meaning "highest joy."

Olufemi (o-loo-FEM-ee)   Meaning "wealth and honor favors me."

Olujimi (o-loo-JEE-mee)   Meaning "God has given me this."

Olushola (o-loo-SHO-lah)   Meaning "God has blessed me."

Omolara (o-mo-LAH-rah)   Meaning "born at the right time."

Omorede (o-mo-REH-day)   A royal-toned name that means "prince."

Oriji (o-REE-jee)   Meaning "a sturdy tree."

Orunjan (o-ROON-jahn)   Meaning "born under the midday sun."

Osahar (o-sah-HAR)   Meaning "God hears."

Osayaba (o-sah-YAH-bah)   Meaning "God forgives."

Osaze (o-SAH-zay)   Meaning "whom God likes."

Ottah (O-tah)   Meaning "a thin baby." Isaac Rogana Ottah is a Nigerian High Life musician.

Rago (RAH-go)   Meaning "ram."

Segun (seh-GOON)   Meaning "conqueror." Parents who want their son to be a leader of men will favor this name.

Shangobunni (shan-go-BOO-nee)   Meaning "a gift from Shango."

Soja (SO-jah)   Meaning "soldier."

Sowande (so-WAHN-day)   Meaning "a wise healer sought me out."

Taiwo (tah-EE-wo)   Meaning "the first-born of twins." See also Odion.

Taliki (tah-LEE-kee)   A name that means "fellow."

Tobi (TOH-bee)   Meaning "great."

Tor (TOR)   Meaning "king." See also Eze, Ezeamaka, Ezenachi, and Ezecha.

Tyehimba (tyeh-HIM-bah)   Meaning "we are a nation." Parents who are nationalistic at heart may choose this name.

Uche (OO-chay)   Meaning "thoughtful."

Uzoma (oo-ZO-mah)   Meaning "born during a journey."

Wafor (WAH-for)   Meaning "born on Afor market day."

Weke (WAY-kay)   Meaning "born on Eke market day."

Worie (wo-REE-eh)   Meaning "born on market day." See also Nweke.

NIGERIA: GIRLS

Abagebe (ah-bah-GAY-beh)   Translates as "we begged to have this one to lift up."

Abayomi (ah-bah-YO-mee)   A name that suggests a "pleasant meeting."

Abebi (ah-BAY-bee)   Meaning "we asked for her." See also Abeni.

Abeje (ah-BAY-jay)   Meaning "we asked to have this one."

Abeni (ah-BAY-nee)   Meaning "we asked for her, and she is ours." See also Adebi and Ajebe.

Abeo (ah-BAY-o)   Meaning "her birth brings happiness."

Abidemi (ah-bee-DEH-mee)   Meaning "born during father's absence."

Abimbola (ah-BIHM-bo-lah)   Meaning "born to be rich." Wande Abimbola is a leader of the Yoruba religion.

Adanna (ah-DAH-nah)   Meaning "her father's daughter." A variation is *Adanya*.

Adebomi (ah-deh-BO-mee)   Meaning "a crown covered my nakedness."

Adedagbo (ah-deh-DAHG-bo)   Meaning "happiness is a crown."

Adedewe (ah-deh-DEH-way)   Translated literally, means "the crown is shattered."

Adedoj (ah-deh-DOJ)   Meaning "a crown becomes a thing of worth."

Adeleke (ah-deh-LEH-kay)   Meaning "a crown achieves happiness."

Adeola (ah-day-O-lah)   Meaning "a crown has honor."

Aderinola (ah-deh-ree-NO-lah)   Literally translated, "a crown walked toward wealth."

Adesimbo (ah-deh-SEEM-bo)   Meaning "of noble birth."

Adia (ah-DEE-ah)   A name that means "a gift." See also Isoka.

Aduke (ah-DOO-kay)   Meaning "much loved." Aduke Alakija was the president of the International Federation of Women Lawyers.

Aina (ah-EE-nah)   Meaning "difficult birth."

Aiyetoro (ah-ee-yay-TO-ro)   Meaning "peace on earth."

Akanke (ah-KAHN-kay)   Meaning "to meet her is to love her."

Alaba (ah-LAH-bah)   Meaning "the second child born after twins."

Alake (ah-LAH-kay)   Literally translated, "one to be petted and made much of."

Amadi (ah-MAH-dee)   Meaning "general rejoicing."

Arria (ah-REE-ah)   Meaning "slender."

Asabi (ah-SAH-bee)   Meaning "she is of choice birth."

Auta (ah-OO-tah)   Meaning "the last born."

Ayo (AH-yo)   Meaning "great joy."

Ayobami (ah-yo-BAH-mee)   Meaning "I am blessed with joy."

Ayobunmi (ah-yo-BOON-mee)   Meaning "joy is given to me." See also Bayo.

Ayodele (ah-yo-DEH-leh)   Meaning "joy come home."

Ayofemi (ah-yo-FEH-mee)   Meaning "joy likes me."

Ayoluwa (ah-YO-loo-wah)   Meaning "joy of our people."

Ayoola (ah-yo-O-lah)   Meaning "joy in wealth."

Baderinwa (bah-deh-REEN-wah)   Meaning "worthy of respect."

Bayo (BAH-yo)   Meaning "joy is found." See also Ayobunmi, Ayodele, and Dayo.

Bejide (beh-JEE-day)   Meaning "a child born in the rainy time."

Bolade (bo-LAH-day)   Meaning "honor arrives." See also Folade.

Bolanile (bo-lah-NEE-lay)   Meaning "the riches of this house."

Bunmi (BOON-mee)   Meaning "my gift."

Chinue (CHIH-noo-eh)   Meaning "God's blessing."

Dada (DAH-dah)   Meaning "a child with curly hair."

Danuwa (dah-NOO-wah)   Meaning "a close friend."

Daurama (dah-oo-RAH-mah) A name translated as "ninth in the succession of queens."

Dayo (DAH-yo) Meaning "joy arrives." See also Bayo.

Ebun (eh-BOON) Meaning "a gift."

Ekaghogho (ay-kah-GO-go) Meaning "born on an important day."

Enomwoyi (ay-no-MWO-yee) Meaning "graceful one."

Fabayo (fah-BAH-yo) Meaning "a lucky birth is joy."

Faraa (fah-RAH) Meaning "cheerful one."

Farih (FAH-ree) Meaning "bright and fair."

Fayola (fah-YO-lah) Literally translated, means "good fortune walks with honor."

Fayolla (fah-YO-kah) Meaning "lucky."

Femi (FEH-mee) Meaning "love me."

Fola (FO-kah) Meaning "honor."

Folade (fo-LAH-day) Meaning "honor arrives." See also Bolade.

Folami (fo-LAH-mee) Meaning "respect and honor me."

Folashade (fo-lah-SHAH-day) Meaning "honor confers a crown."

Folayan (fo-lah-YAHN) Translated literally, means "to walk in dignity."

Foluke (fo-LOO-kay) Meaning "placed in God's care."

Gerda (GER-dah) Meaning "charmer of serpents."

Gimbya (GIHM-byah) Meaning "princess."

Hanna (HAH-nah) A name that means "happiness."

Hazika (hah-ZEE-kah) Meaning "intelligent one."

Hembadoon (hehm-bah-DON) Meaning "the winner."

Idowu (ih-DO-woo) Meaning "the first child born after twins."

Ifama (ih-FAH-mah) Meaning "all is well."

Ife (EE-fay) Meaning "love."

Ifetayo (ee-fay-TAH-yo) Meaning "love brings happiness."

Ige (I-gay) Meaning "delivered feet first."

Ijaba (ih-JAH-bah) Meaning "a wish fulfilled."

Ikuseghan (ih-koo-seh-GAHN) Meaning "peace is greater than war."

Ina (EE-nah) Meaning "mother of the rains."

Isoke (ih-SO-kay) Meaning "a satisfying gift from God." See also Adia.

Iverem (ih-VEH-rehm) Meaning "blessings and favors."

Iyabo (ee-YAH-bo) Meaning "mother has returned."

Izegbe (ih-ZEHG-beh) Meaning "long-expected child."

Jumoke (joo-MO-kay) Meaning "everyone loves the child."

Kehinde (keh-HIN-day) Meaning "second-born of twins."

Kokumo (ko-KOO-mo) Meaning "this one will not die."

Lina (LEE-nah) A loving name that means "tender."

Lisha (LEE-shah) Meaning "mysterious."

Mbafor (m-BAH-for) Meaning "born on a market day."

Modupe (mo-DOO-pay) Meaning "I am grateful."

Monifa (mo-NEE-fa) Meaning "I have my luck."

Nayo (NAH-yo) Meaning "we have great joy." See also Olubayo and Olufunmilayo.

Ngozi (n-GO-zee) A religious-toned name that means "blessing."

Nneka (n-NAY-kah) Meaning "her mother is prominent."

Nnenaya (neh-NAY-yah) Meaning "like father's mother." Name given to a girl who looks like her grandmother. A variation is *Nnenia.*

Nourbese (noor-BAY-say) Meaning "a wonderful child."

Nwakaego (nwah-kah-AY-go) Translates as "more important than money."

Ode (O-day) Meaning "born along the road."

Olabisi (o-lah-BEE-see) Meaning "joy is multiplied."

Olabunmi (o-lah-BOON-mee) Translated literally, means "honor has rewarded me."

Olaniyi (o-lah-NEE-yee) Meaning "there's glory in wealth."

Olubayo (o-lah-BAH-yo) Meaning "greatest joy." See also Nayo and Olufunmilayo.

Olubunmi (o-loo-BOON-mi) Meaning "the highest gift is mine."

Olufemi (o-loo-FEH-mee) Meaning "God loves me."

Olufunke (o-loo-FOON-kay) Translated literally, means "God gives me to be loved."

Olufunmilayo (o-loo-foon-mee-LAH-yo) Meaning "God gives me joy." See also Nayo and Olubayo.

Oluremi (o-loo-REH-mee) Meaning "God consoles me."

Omolara (o-mo-LAH-rah) Meaning "born at the right time."

Omosede (o-mo-SAY-day) Translated literally, means "a child counts more than a king."

Omosupe (o-mo-SOO-pay) Meaning "a child is the most precious thing."

Oni (O-nee) Meaning "born in a sacred abode."

Oseye (o-SAY-yay) Meaning "happy one."

Sade (shah-DAY) Meaning "sweetly singing." African-born pop singer Sade, best known for her song "Sweetest Taboo." Also *Shade.*

Shiminege (shih-mee-NAY-gay) Meaning "let us perceive the future."

Taiwo (tah-EE-wo) Meaning "the first born of twins."

Titilayo (tih-tee-LAH-yo) Meaning "eternal happiness."

Torkwase (tor-KWAY-see) Meaning "a queen."

Uchefuna (oo-chay-FOO-nah) Translates as "I have my wits about me."

Urbi (OOR-bee) Meaning "princess."

Yahimba (yah-HIM-bah) Meaning "there is nothing like home."

Yejide (yeh-JEE-day) Meaning "the image of mother."

Yetunde (yeh-TOON-day) Meaning "mother returns." Francesca Yetunde Pereira was a folk singer and poet of Brazilian and Nigerian parentage.

Rwanda

The tiny landlocked East African nation of Rwanda was once a destination for many people seeking a peaceful encounter with the natural wonders of the continent. For centuries, the Tutsi tribe (an extremely tall people) dominated the Hutu, who composed 90 percent of the population. In 1959, a civil war erupted and many of the Tutsi were forced into exile. The country's present-day strife is primarily a continuation of this ongoing ethnic struggle. Although Swahili is widely used, many names in Rwanda reflect the influences of many years of Belgian rule as well as the dominant Kinyarwanda language. This is evident, for example, in the names of Prime Minister Pierre Claver Rwigema and President Pasteur Bizimungu.

RWANDA: BOYS

Gahiji (ga-HEE-jee) A name that means "the hunter."

Habimana (hah-bee-MAH-nah) Meaning "God exists." Kantano Habimana was a radio announcer in Rwanda.

Sebahive (seh-ba-HEE-vay) Meaning "bringer of good fortune."

Sentwali (sehn-TWAH-lee) Meaning "courageous."

RWANDA: GIRLS

Muteteli (moo-teh-TEH-lee) A name that means "dainty."

Uwimana (oo-wee-MAH-nah) Meaning "daughter of God."

South Africa

At the southern tip of the continent, South Africa boasts a land that is geographically diverse as well as enormously rich in natural resources—in particular, gold and gem diamonds. An historically attractive region for various European settlers, the nation's population is today composed of numerous multiethnic and multiracial groups, including black Africans, whites, Coloureds (people of mixed race), and Asians (predominantly Indians). Under apartheid, the political system of racial segregation, English and Afrikaans were considered the country's official languages. English currently continues to be used in most educational institutions; however, with the end of apartheid in 1994, an additional nine African languages have been officially recognized.

SOUTH AFRICA: BOYS

Ayize (ah-YEE-ay)   Translated as "let it happen."

Dingane (dih-NGAH-nay)   Meaning "searcher." Dingane succeeded his half-brother Shaka as king of the Zulu.

Ganya (GAHN-yah)   A name that means "clever."

Gogo (GO-go)   Meaning "like grandfather."

Nkosi (n-KO-see)   Meaning "ruler." Chicks Nkosi is a poet from Swaziland.

Nolizwe (no-LEE-zway)   Meaning "the nation."

Nonceba (no-NCHAY-bah)   Meaning "mercy."

Paki (PAH-kee)   Meaning "a witness."

Shaka (SHAH-kah)   Meaning "founder" or "first." Shaka was the founding king of the Zulu kingdom.

Sigidi (sih-GEE-dee)   Meaning "one thousand."

Sipliwo (sih-PLEE-wo)   Meaning "a gift."

Sipho (SEE-fo)   Meaning "present." Sipho Sepamla is a poet and novelist best known for *A Ride on the Whirlwind.*

Thandiwe (Tahn-DEE-way)   Meaning "beloved."

Themba (TEHM-bah)   Meaning "hope."

Uuka (oo-OO-kah)   Meaning "arise."

SOUTH AFRICA: GIRLS

Dziko (DZEE-ko)   A name that signifies "the world."

Mafuane (mah-foo-AH-nay)   Meaning "soil."

Mandisa (mahn-DEE-sah)   Meaning "sweet."

Nkosazana (n-ko-sah-ZAH-nah)   Meaning "princess."

Nombeko (no-m-BEH-ko)   Meaning "respect."

Nomble (no-m-BEHL)   Meaning "beauty."

Nomuula (no-moo-OO-lah)   Meaning "rain."

Sarafina (say-rah-FEE-nah)   Meaning "burning passion." Sarafina is the title character of a musical and film about children in the Soweto uprising. A variation is *Serafina.*

Thandiwe (tan-DEE-way)   Meaning "beloved."

Tanzania

Tanzania, a democratic country larger in surface area than Texas, is located on Africa's eastern coast, along the Indian Ocean. It was created through the union of Tanganyika and Zanzibar in 1964. Because of its numerous lakes, approximately 22,800 square miles of Tanzania's territory consists of inland water. It is in this country that Dr. Louis B. Leakey changed evolutionary theory with the discovery of a 1.75-million-year-old Zinjanthropus skull at Olducai Gorge.

The imposition of European rule, Arab influence, and the history of the movement and mixture of African ethnic groups for at least the last two millennia has implied adaptation to both new physical and human social arrangements for the native peoples in this country. For Tanzanians, kinship forms the basis for interpersonal relations and group formation, a pattern that persisted throughout the earlier period and continues to the present time. For individuals, kin ties through parents and by marriage define one's rights, obligations, and opportunities. For the last three decades, Tanzania has experimented with a cooperative socioeconomic system, Ujamaa, based on indigenous social structures and socialist economics and largely drafted by the country's first president, Julius K. Nyerere.

TANZANIA: BOYS

Ambokile (ahm-bo-KEE-lay)   A name that signifies "God has saved me."

Andwele (ah-n-DWEH-lay)   Meaning "God brought me."

Ipyana (ih-PYA-nah)   Meaning "grace."

Kami (KAH-mee)   The name of an east Tanzanian group with its own distinct culture.

Mposi (m-PO-see)   A child with this name has wonderful leadership skills. He is idealistic and inspiring to others.

Mwamba (MWAHM-bah)   Meaning "mighty."

Natron (nah-TRON)   The name of a Tanzanian lake.

Nikusubila (nee-koo-soo-BEE-lah)   Meaning "optimistic."

Rashid (rah-SHEED)   Meaning "well guided." Rashid Kawawa was vice president of Tanzania in the 1970s.

Tuponile (too-po-NEE-lay)   Meaning "we are afraid."

Vinza (VEEN-zah)   The name of a Tanzanian group with its own distinct culture.

Zaramo (zah-RAH-mo)   The name of a Tanzanian group with its own distinct culture.

TANZANIA: GIRLS

Bupe (BOO-pay)   Meaning "hospitality."

Kanoni (kah-NO-ni)   Meaning "little bird."

Ngabile (n-gah-BEE-lay)   Meaning "I have got it."

Sekelaga (seh-keh-LAH-gah)   Meaning "rejoice."

Sigolwide (see-gol-WEE-day)   Meaning "my ways are straight."

Syandene (syah-n-DAY-nay)   Meaning "punctual."

Tulinagwe (too-lee-NAH-gweh)   Meaning "God is with us."

Tumpe (TOOM-pay)   Meaning "let us thank God."

Tusajigwe (too-sah-JEEG-way)   Meaning "we are blessed."

Uganda

A lush and fertile country with a temperate climate, Uganda was once among the most ethnically diverse and prosperous countries in Africa. It is here that the kingdoms of Buganda, Karagwe, and Bunyoro once stood. Recently it has experienced several decades of economic and domestic crises. Following the notorious Idi Amin's military coup and eight-year reign, Yoweri Kaguta Museveni was sworn in as president in January 1986 and proclaimed a ten-point program through which the National Resistance Movement would "usher in a new and better future for the people of Uganda." English remains the nation's official language and exerts a strong influence in naming customs, although Islamic and indigenous names are certainly also popular. Native languages of Uganda include Luganda, Swahili, and Bantu, as well as Sudanic and Nilo-Hamitic dialects.

UGANDA: BOYS

Balondemu (bah-lo-n-DAY-moo) A name signifying "the chosen one."

Dembe (DEHM-beh) Meaning "peaceful." A variation is *Damba*.

Ejau (eh-JAH-oo) Meaning "we have received."

Gonza (GON-zah) An amorous name that means "love."

Gwandoya (gwan-DOH-yah) Meaning "met with unhappiness."

Irumba (ih-ROOM-bah) Meaning "born after twins."

Kabiito (kah-BEE-toh) Meaning "born while foreigners are visiting."

Kabonero (kah-bo-NEH-roh) Meaning "sign."

Kabonesa (kah-bo-NAY-sah) Meaning "difficult birth."

Kamoga (kah-MO-ga) The name of a royal Baganda family.

Kamuhanda (kah-moo-HAHN-dah) Translated literally, this name means "born on the way to the hospital."

Kamukama (kah-moo-KAH-mah) Meaning "protected by God."

Kamya (KAH-myah) Meaning "born after twin brothers."

Karutunda (kah-roo-TOON-dah) Meaning "little."

Karwana (kahr-WAH-nah) Meaning "born during wartime."

Kato (KAH-to) Meaning "second of twins."

Katungi (kah-TOO-ngee) Meaning "rich."

Kayonga (kah-YO-ngah) Meaning "ash." The name of a great Ankole warrior from the western part of Uganda.

Kibuuka (keEBoo- OO-kah) Meaning "brave warrior." The name of a celebrated warrior from Ugandan history.

Kigongo (kee-GONG-o) Meaning "born before twins."

Lutalo (loo-TAH-lo) A name that means "warrior."

Madongo (mah-DONG-o) Meaning "uncircumcised."

Magomu (mah-GO-moo) A name suggesting "the younger of twins."

Mayonga (mah-YONG-ah) Meaning "lake sailor."

Mpoza (m-PO-zah) A name that means "tax collector."

Mugisa (moo-GEE-sah) Meaning "lucky." Variations include *Mugisha* and *Mukisa*.

Mukasa (moo-KAH-sah) Meaning "God's chief administrator."

Mwaka (MWAH-kah) Meaning "born on New Year's Eve."

Mwanje (MWAHN-jay) Meaning "leopard."

Nakisisa (nah-kee-SEE-sah) Meaning "child of the shadows."

Nkunda (n-KOON-dah) Meaning "loves those who hate him."

Ojore (o-JO-ray) Meaning "a warrior."

Okot (O-kot) Meaning "born when it is raining." Okot p'Bitek is a popular Ugandan poet. A variation is *Okoth*.

Opio (o-PEE-o) Meaning "the first of twin brothers." See also Zesiro.

Sabiti (sah-BEE-tee) Meaning "born on Sunday."

Sanyu (SAHN-yoo) Meaning "happy."

Semanda (say-MAHN-dah) Meaning "cow clan."

Sempala (sehm-PAH-lah) Meaning "born in prosperous times."

Setimba (seh-TEEM-bah) Meaning "river dweller." The name of a river in Uganda.

Zesiro (zeh-SEE-roh) Meaning "the elder of twins." See also Opio.

UGANDA: GIRLS

Abbo (AH-bo) Meaning "a condiment."

Kissa (KEE-sah) Meaning "born after twins."

Mangeni (man-GEH-nee) Meaning "fish."

Masani (mah-SAH-nee) Translates as "has a gap between the front teeth."

Nabirye (nah-BEER-yay) Meaning "one who produces twins."

Nabulungi (nah-boo-LOONG-ee) Meaning "beautiful one."

Namono (nah-MO-no) Meaning "the younger of twins."

Nasiche (nah-SEE-chay) Meaning "born in the locust season."

Zesiro (zeh-SEE-ro) Meaning "the elder of twins."

More Favorite African Names

Africa is a vast continent encompassing a great diversity of nations, cultures, racial and ethnic groups, languages, and customs. The northern part of the continent is dominated by Arabic languages and culture, with various indigenous nomadic groups also found, such as the Berbers in Morocco, Algeria, and Mauritania. Naming traditions in this part of the continent are heavily influenced by Islamic codes, and often parents are obliged to select their children's names from a list of officially sanctioned names. However, Arabic parents often give children a second or third name relating to a personal attribute, such as "wise one," "benevolent one," etc. Central and southern Africa represent the continent's least homogeneous areas, with hundreds of ethnic groups all guarding their individual languages, customs, and cultures. Among the largest and most influential language groups are Yoruba in the western part of the continent (particularly in Nigeria), Swahili and Bantu (and their variants) in East Africa extending as far as South Africa, and Wolof in Senegal.

The colonial influence in Africa was very strong and in many countries has had an enduring effect, especially with regard to the naming of children. In the former French, Belgian, British, Portuguese, and Spanish colonies there is a tendency especially among urban dwellers to use European first names. While in some places parents feel that European names offer a certain cachet, many Africans eschew such names for political reasons and opt for traditional African names such as the names collected here.

MORE FAVORITE AFRICAN NAMES: BOYS

Bello (BELL-o) Meaning "helper or advocate for Islam." Bello was a leader of Sokoto in West Africa in the 1800s, the son of great Muslim ruler Usman dan Fodio.

Dumaka (doo-MAH-kah) Meaning "helping hand."

Kosey (KO-say) "Lion." Also spelled *Kosse*.

Liu (LEE-oo) A name that means "voice."

Moswen (MOHS-wen) Meaning "light in color."

Ohin (O-hin) Meaning "chief." A variation is *Ohan*.

Paki (PAH-kee) Meaning "witness."

Rudo (ROO-do) A name that means "love."

Senwe (SEHN-way) Meaning "dry as a stalk of grain."

Tuako (too-AH-ko) Meaning "the eleventh-born."

Ulan (oo-LAHN) Meaning "the first-born twin." See also Opio and Zesiro in Uganda section.

MORE FAVORITE AFRICAN NAMES: GIRLS

Adia (ah-DEE-yah) Meaning a "gift" as in the gift of a child or of life. A variation is *Adilla*.

Adimu (ah-DEE-moo) Translated literally, means "rare," for a special or treasured child.

Adin (ah-DEEN) Meaning "decorative" because children "adorn" a family.

Afi (AH-fee) "Born on Friday." See also Afua. Variations include *Affi*, *Afia*, *Efi*, and *Efia*.

Afiya (ah-FEE-yah) Meaning "health." Given to a child as an auspicious wish of good health.

Afua (AH-foo-ah) "Born on Friday." See also Afi.

Ahadi (ah-HAH-dee) Parents who believe anything is possible will choose this name signifying "with much promise."

Aisha (ah-EE-shah) Meaning "life" as a child signifies new life. A noteworthy Aisha is Egyptian writer Aisha Abd al-Rahman. A variation is *Asha*.

Akili (ah-KEE-lee) Scholarly families may choose this name meaning "intelligent."

Aleela (ah-lay-AY-lah) For a child who is born crying and doesn't seem to stop, this name means "she cries." Variations include *Aleelah*, *Alila*, or *Alile*.

Almasi (ah-MAH-see) Meaning "diamond." A name for a particularly precious child.

Amaziah (ah-mah-ZEE-ah) Meaning "extraordinary." Name given to children who seem unusually alert from birth.

Aminah (ah-MEE-nah) Parents putting faith in their newborn daughter will select this name meaning "she is trustworthy."

Aminifu (ah-mee-NEE-foo) Meaning "faithful," this name is given to a child who behaves dutifully.

Angavu (ah-n-GAH-voo) A daughter with brightly colored eyes is named "shining one."

Arusi (ah-ROO-see) For a child who arrives surprisingly early, this means "born at the time of a wedding."

Asali (ah-SAH-lee) Meaning "sweet honey," a child born of this name is sweet and delightful.

Asha (AH-sha) "Life." See also Aisha.

Asante (ah-SHAN-tee) Translated literally as "thanks," Asante reflects the parents' gratitude to God for the birth of their child. Variations include *Ashanta*, *Ashantae*, *Ashante*, *Ashantee*, or *Ashaunta*.

Asilia (ah-SEE-lee-ah) Meaning "honest."

Asya (AH-syah) Meaning "born at a time of grief."

Aziza (ah-ZEE-zah) A beautiful child can be named this, meaning "the child is gorgeous."

Bahati (bah-HA-tee) Parents' gratitude for the birth of a child is reflected in this name, meaning "my luck is good."

Batini (bah-TEE-nee) Philosophical parents may adopt this name meaning "inner thoughts."

Bimkubwa (bee-m-KOO-bwah) Meaning "great lady." A name reflective of the child's fate.

Bursar (boo-SAH-rah) Intelligent parents can pick this name, which means "wisdom."

Chausiku (cha-oo-SEE-koo) Meaning "born at night," a name given to a girl who is literally born at night.

Chiku (CHEE-koo) Translated literally, means "chatterbox."

Chinira (chee-NEE-rah) Means "one who receives God," it reflects the parents' desire for their child to be enlightened.

Chiwa (CHEE-wah) A name that means "death."

Chriki (CHREE-kee) Meaning "blessing."

Chuki (CHOO-kee) Meaning "hatred." A name given to a child born in the midst of animosity between neighbors or family.

Dalila (dah-LEE-lah) Meaning "gentleness is her soul."

Dalili (dah-LEE-lee) Meaning "sign." This name reflects the parents' belief that the birth of a child carries special meaning.

Dinka (DING-kah) Means "people." This name suggests the parents' hopes for their child to attain high social and occupational status.

Dofi (DOH-fee) Meaning "the second child after twins." See also Nyankomago.

Doto (DOH-fo) Meaning "the younger of twins." See Akwokwo and Kakra in Ghana names.

Eshe (EH-shay) Meaning "life." A variation is *Esha*.

Etana (eh-TAH-nah) Meaning "strong one."

Faizah (fah-YEE-zah) Meaning "victorious." The English version is Victoria. Also *Faiza*.

Fatima (fah-TEE-mah) Fatima was a daughter of the Prophet Muhammad. Fatuma was a queen of Zanzibar in the 1600s. Another variation is *Fauna*.

Fujo (FOO-jo) Meaning "born after a quarrel."

Goma (GO-mah) Meaning "joyful dance."

Habibah (hah-BEE-bah) Meaning "beloved," a name for a child dear to her parents' hearts.

Hadiya (hah-DEE-yah) Meaning "gift."

Halima (hah-LEE-mah) Meaning "gentle." Halima was the woman who cared for Muhammad after his mother's death.

Halla (HAH-lah) Meaning "unexpected gift." Variations include *Hala* and *Halle*. Hollywood actress Halle Berry is a noted person with this name.

Haoniyao (hah-o-nee-YAH-o) A name which means "does not see her own faults."

Hasana (hah-SAH-nah) Meaning "she arrived first." A name given to the first-born of female twins. Also *Huseina*.

Hasanati (hah-sah-NAH-tee) A name which means "good."

Hasina (hah-SEE-nah) Meaning "good." Variations include *Haseena*, *Hasena*, and *Hassina*.

Hawa (HAH-wah) Meaning "Eve" or "wife of Adam."

Huseina (huh-say-EE-nah) Meaning "good." An alternate form of Hasina.

Imani (ih-MAH-nee) A name that signifies "faith."

Imena (ee-MAY-nah) "Dream." Also *Imene*.

Jaha (JAH-hah) Meaning "dignified." Variations include *Jahaida*, *Jahaira*, *Jaharra*, *Lahayra*, *Jahida*, and *Jahira*.

Jamila (jah-MIH-lah) This name means "beautiful."

Jokha (JO-kah) Meaning "robe of adornment."

Kadija (kah-DEE-ja) This was the name of the wife of the Prophet Muhammad. Also spelled *Khadija*.

Kalere (kah-LAY-rah) "Short woman." Also spelled *Kaleer*.

Kaluwa (kah-LOO-wah) Meaning "forgotten one." Also spelled *Kalua*.

Kamaria (kah-mah-REE-ah) Meaning "moonlight." Variations include *Kamara* and *Kamarie*.

Kameke (kah-MAY-kay) Meaning "blind."

Kamilah (kah-MEE-lah) Parents that see their child without flaws can choose "perfection" with this name. Variations include *Kameela*, *Kameelah*, *Kami*, *Kammilah*, and *Kamili*.

Kanene (kah-NAY-nay) "A little important thing."

Kapuki (kah-POO-kee) "Firstborn daughter."

Karimu (kah-REE-moo) Philanthropic parents can choose Karimu for their child, which means "generous."

Kefilwe (keh-FEEL-weh) Meaning "I am given."

Kesi (KEH-see) Meaning "born at a time of father's troubles."

Kia (KEE-ah) Meaning "season's beginning."

Kianga (kee-AH-ngah) Meaning "sunshine."

Kijakazi (kee-kah-KAH-zee) Translated literally, means "your life is due to us"; highlights the importance of filial piety in the African culture.

Kipenzi (kee-PEHN-zee) Meaning "loved one."

Kisima (kee-SEE-mah) Meaning "spring." Perhaps reflective of the season in which the child was born.

Kizuwanda (kee-zoo-WAHN-dah) Meaning "the last-born child."

Kulwa (KOOL-wah) Meaning "the first of twins."

Layla (LAY-lah) Meaning "born at night."

Lulu (LOO-loo) Meaning "a pearl."

Madaha (mah-DAH-hah) Meaning "graceful."

Makini (mah-KEE-nee) Means "calm and serene."

Malaika (mah-lah-EE-kah) Translated literally, means "angel."

Mariamu (mah-ree-AH-moo) This is the Swahili name for the Virgin Mary.

Marini (mah-REE-nee) Means "healthy" or "pretty."

Marjani (mahr-JAH-nee) Parents with a baby born by the ocean can pick this name, meaning "coral."

Mashavu (mah-SHAH-voo) Translated literally, means "cheeks." A name given to a girl born with chubby cheeks.

Mashika (mah-SEE-kah) Means "rainy season." A name given to a girl born during the rainy season. Also Masika.

Mawusi (mah-WOO-see) Translated literally, it means "in the hands of God."

Morowa (mor-O-wah) Meaning "queen."

Mosi (MO-see) Meaning "first." A name given to the firstborn.

Murua (moo-ROO-ah) Meaning "elegant and refined."

Mwaka (MWAH-kah) Translated literally, means "year." A name given to a girl or a boy born at the beginning of the farming year.

Mwamini (mawh-MEE-nee) Meaning "honest one."

Mwanawa (mwah-NAH-wah) Meaning "first born of my children."

Mwasaa (mwah-SAH) A baby born as expected is "timely," as this name suggests.

Nadra (nahn-DRAH) Meaning "unique," a name for a child with special physical traits.

Nanyamka (nahn-YAHM-kah) "God's gift."

Ndege (n-DEH-gay) Meaning "bird."

Neema (ne-AY-mah) Meaning "prosperous." Name given to a baby born during prosperous times.

Niara (nee-AH-rah) A name which signifies "high purpose."

Nomalanga (no-mah-LAHNG-ah) A name that means "sunny."

Noni (NO-nee) Means "gift of God."

Nuru (NOO-roo) Meaning "daylight," a name given to a baby born during the day.

Nyankomago (nyahn-ko-MAH-go) Meaning "second child after twins." See also Dofi.

Paka (PAH-kah) Meaning "kitten." A name given to a child who is as sweet as a kitten. A variation is *Paca*.

Panya (PAHN-yah) Translated literally, means "mouse."

Pasua (pah-SOO-ah) A name typically given to a baby born by caesarean section.

Pili (PEE-lee) Meaning "second." A name given to a second born girl or boy.

Pita (PEE-tah) Meaning "the fourth daughter."

Poni (PO-nee) Meaning "the second daughter."

Radhiya (rah-DEE-yah) Meaning "agreeable."

Ramia (rah-MEE-ah) Meaning "fortune-teller." A variation is *Ramiah*.

Rashida (rah-SHEE-dah) Meaning "righteous." Variations include *Rahshea*, *Rahsheda*, *Rahsheita*, *Rashdah*, and *Rasheda*.

Raziya (rah-ZEE-yah) "Agreeable."

Rehema (reh-HAY-mah) Parents who are tender may choose this name, which means "compassionate."

Reta (RAY-tah) Meaning "shaken." Variations include *Reeta*, *Retta*, *Rheta*, and *Rhetta*.

Rukiya (roo-KEE-yah) Translated literally, means "she rises high."

Saada (sah-AH-dah) Meaning "helpful."

Safiya (sah-FEE-yah) Parents that are innocent to the spoils of the world may like this name, meaning "pure."

Salama (sah-LAH-moo) A name which means "peace."

Salma (SAHL-mah) Meaning "safe," it is a name for a healthy baby.

Sanura (sah-NOO-rah) A child named Snura is quick, intelligent, and very creative.

Sauda (sah-OO-dah) A child can be named Sauda, meaning "dark beauty" in celebration of her striking features.

Shafira (shah-FEE-rah) Meaning "defined."

Shani (SHAH-nee) Meaning "marvellous."

Sharifa (shah-REE-fah) Meaning "distinguished one." Sharifa M. Zawawi is a professor of Swahili and an expert on Swahili names at the City University of New York.

Sharik (shah-REEK) Meaning "a child of God."

Shukura (shoo-KOO-roo) Literally means "I am grateful."

Siboniso (see-bo-NEE-so) Meaning "a sign."

Siko (SEE-ko) Meaning "a crying baby."

Sikudhani (sih-koo-DAH-nee) Meaning "a pleasant surprise."

Siphiwe (si-FEE-way) Meaning "we were given."

Sisya (SEE-syah) Meaning "she of the Mfuu tree."

Siti (SEE-tee) Meaning a "respected woman."

Subira (soo-BEE-rah) This name signifies "the reward of patience."

Tabia (tah-BEE-ah) "Gifted."

Tatu (TAH-too) "Third." A name commonly given to a third-born child.

Themba (TEM-bah) A name that means "trusted."

Tisa (TEE-sah) "Ninth." A name given to a ninth-born child. Variations include *Tisah*, *Tysa*, and *Tyssa*.

Tulinagwe (too-lee-NAG-way) Meaning "God is with us."

Tuwalole (too-wah-LO-lay) Meaning "exemplary."

Waseme (wah-SAY-may) Meaning "let them talk."

Winda (WEEN-dah) A name meaning "hunter."

Winna (WIH-nah) Meaning "friend." A variation is *Winnah*.

Yiesha (yee-AY-shah) An alternate form of Aisha, this name signifies "life."

Zahra (ZAH-rah) Meaning "blossom."

Zainabu (zah-ee-NAH-boo) Meaning "beautiful."

Zakia (zah-KEE-ah) Meaning "smart." A variation is *Zakiya*.

Zalika (zah-LEE-kah) Meaning "born to nobility."

Zawadi (zah-WAH-dee) Meaning "gift."

Zuwena (zuh-WAY-nah) Meaning "good."

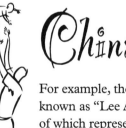

China

When it comes to naming children, the Chinese are among the most creative. Generally speaking, most Chinese names are arranged so the last name is first and the first name last. For example, the international film director known in English as Ang Lee would be known as "Lee Ang" in Chinese. Characters are based on individual symbols, each of which represents an idea or thing. Most names are either auspicious or symbolic in meaning. For example, *xing* (lucky) and *fu* (luck) are commonly used in boys' names, while *mei* (beautiful) and *li* (beauty) are often used in the naming of girls.

It is common practice for Chinese families to repeat a name among their children. One daughter, for instance, may be named Shiu Rei (elegant flower bud) while another is named Shiu Chun (elegant spring). The shared character, in this case *shiu*, symbolizes that the two girls are not only of the same family but also of the same generation. The following entries are based on a system of romanization known as Pinyin and are meant to serve merely as a guide to the characters most frequently used in name-giving.

Pronunciation: The Chinese language is tonal, so unaccented syllables should be pronounced softly and accented syllables should be short and hard.

CHINA: BOYS

An (ahn)   Meaning "peace" or "contentment." The Chinese character for peace and contentment is comprised of the written characters "woman" and "roof." Also *Ang*.

Bo (bow)   An aquatic name meaning "waves" or "ripples."

Cong (TSONG)   Meaning "intelligent" or "clever." The characters for "excitement" or "haste" are enhanced with the addition to the "ear" ideogram. This suggests quick hearing or a grasping of ideas.

De (DUH)   Meaning "virtue." The phonetic sound of the word denotes "a straight heart."

Di (DEE)   Meaning "younger brother," this name is not typically used as a child's given name, but rather as a nickname. The same is

true for the elder brother, elder sister, and younger sister. See also Ge.

Fu (fooh)   Meaning "rich and good fortune."

Gao (gaoh)   Meaning "high; tall." The pictograph depicts a high tower on a stable foundation. The character is meant to be auspicious of a "high position" in career and society.

Ge (GUH)   Meaning "older brother." Typically used as a nickname.

Guo (GUOH)   Meaning "country; nation."

Huo (HUOH)   A name that means "fire."

Jin (jin)   A name meaning "gold."

Jing (JIHNG)   Meaning "classic" or "already" or "pass through." Tradition is greatly treasured in the Chinese culture. One of the components of this character alludes to water currents running deep underground rather than superficially on the surface.

Lian (lee-ahn)   "Link" or "join" or "connect." The pictograph depicts carts moving continuously on an unbroken track.

Lei (lee)   Meaning "thunder."

Lin (LIHN)   A common family name meaning "forest."

Lu (LOO)   Meaning "high status; law; rule; discipline." The phonetic sound signifies written regulations; pictorially, it resembles a hand with a pen writing lines on a tablet.

Mai (my)   Parents who sail may elect this name, signifying "ocean."

Ming (mihng)   Meaning "clear and wise."

Mu (MOO)   A name that means "wood."

Nian (NEE-ahn)   Meaning "read" or "recite."

Ping (Pihng)   Meaning "peace and safety."

Quan (CHOO-ahn)   Meaning "complete" or "perfect." This character combines the character for "joined" with "work."

Sen (SEHN)   Meaning "forest." See also Lin.

Shi (SHUR)   Meaning "stone." The character reflects the image of a stone or rock falling from a high cliff. The rock is a symbol of strength, integrity, and stability.

Shui (shoo-WAY)   Meaning "water" which is vital to survival.

Si (se-eh)   Meaning "to think." This ideograph combines the "skull" with the "heart" to produce "thought."

So (soh)   Meaning "longevity" or "long life."

Tsai (SZAI)   Meaning "money" or "rich." A variation is *Chai*.

Tsong (TSZONG)   Meaning "intelligent." A variation is *Chong*.

Tu (TOO)   A name that means "earth."

Tzao (tszao)   Meaning "above and beyond." A variation is *Zhao*.

Tzong (tzhong)   Meaning "royalty" or "of royalty." A variation is *Zhong*.

Wen-Hsiung (woon shung)   Translated literally, means "scholastic hero." A variation is *Wu Xiong*.

Wang (WAHNG)   Meaning "king" or "ruler." Three horizontal planes make up the character and represent heaven, man, and earth, connected by a vertical structure. The written character represents the king, the one vested with the power to communicate between heaven and earth.

Wong (WOHNG)   Signifying "prosperity." A variation includes *Wang*.

Wu-Hsiung (WOO-shung)   Meaning "action hero." A variation is *Wu Xiong*.

Xiao (shao)   Meaning "respectful to the elders."

Xing (shing)   Meaning "to walk" or "go." The Chinese believe business thrives at cross roads; thus, this pictograph applies to all businesses and trade.

Yang (yahng)   A name that means "sun."

Yon (yawn)   Meaning "forever brave."

Yu (you)   Meaning "rain."

Zhen (szen)   Meaning "kind" or "merciful." A variation is *Ren*.

Zhu (zsoo)   Meaning "owner" or "master." The character is a pictograph of a lamp stand with a flame rising above it, symbolizing a master or lord who spreads enlightenment.

Zhuang (zoo-ang)   Meaning "strong."

CHINA: GIRLS

Ai (EYE)   A name that means "love."

Ching (CHING)   Meaning "clear weather day." A variation is *Qing*.

Chun (CHOON)   Meaning "spring." The character for spring signifies the budding and seemingly sudden growth of vegetation under the brilliance of the sun.

Ding (dihng)   Meaning "to fix" or "decide" or "certain." This character is comprised of a pictograph of a roof and the character for order. It signifies peace and order under one roof, thus asserting its fixedness or stability. The modern

Chinese writer Ding Ling, who wrote during the Chinese Cultural Revolution, has this name.

Fei (FAYE) A regal name meaning "empress."

Feng (fohng) Meaning "phoenix." The character relates the bird to wind in sound and symbol.

Hai (high) Meaning "sea" or "ocean." This character contains the root for "water" and depicts a woman with breasts nurturing a child.

Hong (hong) Meaning "red." Red is an auspicious color in the Chinese culture. Silk, a fabric used symbolically by Chinese royalty and officials, often contains red dye.

Hua (huah) Meaning "spectacular" or "flower."

Hui (hoo-eh) Meaning "wit" or "wisdom." This character is made of two leafy branches held in a single hand. It is meant to symbolize a broom placed over the heart to clear the way for wit and wisdom.

Jie (JEH) Meaning "elder sister." Typically this name is used among the immediate and extended family. It is often not a part of any person's formal name. See also Mei.

Lan (lahn) A flowery name meaning "orchid."

Li (lee) Meaning "pretty" or "beautiful" or "elegant." The character is of a graceful deer. Though the character stands for beauty, physical attractiveness is not considered a virtue. An example of a notable person with this name is internationally famed Chinese actor Gong Li of acclaimed films such as *Farewell My Concubine*.

Liang (lee-ahng) Meaning "kindness" or "bright."

Lien (LIEHN) Meaning "lotus."

Ling (lihng) Meaning "bell."

Mei (may) Meaning "younger sister." The pictograph suggests a tree in full leaf and branch yet still not fully mature, thus representing a younger sibling. Like Jei, meaning "older sister," this term is used only as a nickname and is not usually a part of one's formal name.

Mei (may) Meaning "beautiful." Though the sound is the same as "younger sister," the tone with which it is pronounced is different.

Mei-Gui (may-gueh) Meaning "rose."

Que (cheh) Meaning "sparrow." The sparrow as suggested through the ideograph, is a perfect symbol for something small and quick.

Ron (rohn) Meaning "glorified" or "glory."

Shuang (shoo-ahng) Meaning "a pair." The character is composed of two birds standing in one hand.

Su (sue) Meaning "understated" or "humble." A fair maiden.

Xi (shee) Meaning "fine," "tender," or "careful."

Xi (shee) Meaning "happiness" or "pleasure." This character is written and pronounced differently from the "xi" meaning "fine; tender; careful." It depicts the ancient drum on its stand with its stretched skin and an open right hand striking it. The character representing a mouth depicts the mouth singing.

Xian (shen) Meaning "fairy" or "recluse."

Xiang (shee-ahng) An aromatic name meaning "fragrance."

Xiao (shao) Meaning "dawn" or "small."

Xiu (shou) Meaning "outstanding."

Ya (yah) Meaning "elegant" and "graceful."

Yan (yahn) Meaning "swallow." Swallows abound in the northern hemisphere and are always a welcome sight in the spring. The pictograph reflects the bird flying across the waters with a stalk of grass in its mouth.

Yi (ee) Meaning "appropriate" or "comfortable."

Yin (yihn) Meaning "voice" or "music."

Ying (yihng) Meaning "smart."

Yue (YOO-eh) Meaning "moon."

Yun (yoohn) Meaning "cloud" or "melody."

India

Although there are hundreds of traditional Indian names, new names come into vogue every year. Each region of India has a distinctive naming pattern. For example, a South Indian name is easily discernible from a Bengali name. Authentic Hindu names usually come from a root word and then are modified or joined with another root word to create a special meaning. For example, the name Veda means "knowledge," derived from the word veed, meaning "to know." A land that has endured thousands of years of aggression waged by every race imaginable, from Greek and Roman to English and Arabic, India has adopted many names from various cultures.

INDIA: BOYS

Aakash (aah-KAA-sh) Meaning "sky." A variation is *Akasha*.

Agni (ah-g-NEE) Meaning "fire." The Hindu fire god symbolizes purity. Agni is believed to have a threefold composition—divine, human, and earthly—and is a witness to all Hindu Vedic ceremonies.

Ajay (ah-JA-y) Meaning "invincible."

Amandeep (ah-man-deep) Meaning "light of peace." Variations include *Amandip, Amanjit, Amanjot,* and *Amanpreet*.

Amar (a-MA-r) A name that means "immortal."

Amit (a-meet) Meaning "boundless," or "eternal," or "limitless."

Anand (AA-nun-d) Meaning "bliss." A variation is *Ananda*.

Anant (a-NUN-t) Meaning "eternal" or "without end." A variation is *Anantu*.

Anil (a-NEEL) Meaning "wind God." Also *Aneel*.

Arjun (ar-JUN) A child with this name is diligent and hardworking.

Arun (a-ROO-n) Meaning "the morning sun."

Ashwani (a-SHWA-nee) Meaning "first. It's the name of a Hindu month as well as that of a sage.

Ashwin (a-shwee-n) A name that means "star."

Bal (baal) Sanskrit for "child born with lots of hair." Bal Tilak is a scholar and the originator of the modern movement for the independence of India.

Balin (b-aa-lee-n) Meaning "mighty warrior." See also Valin.

Bhagwandas (bha-GWAAN-daa-s) Meaning "servant of God."

Braham (brah-um) Meaning "creator." Variations include *Braheim, Brahiem, Brahima,* and *Brahm*.

Chandan (ch-AN-dan) Meaning "fragrant wood used to offer in prayer." A variation is *Chandon*.

Chandaravth (ch-AN-dar-avth) Meaning "moonlike" or "similar to moon."

Chandra (cha-nd-re) Meaning "moon." Variations include *Chand* and *Chandara*.

Daksh (D-KSH) Meaning "intelligent."

Dandin (DAN-din) Meaning "holy man."

Darshan (DAR-shan) Meaning "vision." Usually a vision of God, as in visiting temple to have the *darshan* of God.

Deven (DEH-vehn) Meaning "God" or "Indra."

Ganesa (GAH-ne-saa) "Fortunate." The Hindu god of wisdom and good luck.

Gurpreet (GOOR-pree-t) Meaning "devoted to the guru" or "devoted to the prophet." Variations include *Gurjeet, Gurmeet,* and *Guruprit.*

Hansh (h-unsh) Meaning "God" or "god-like." Another name for the Hindu god Shiva.

Hara (ha-RAA) Meaning "seizer." Another name for the Hindu god Shiva.

Harpreet (har-PREET) Meaning "loves God." A variation is *Hardeep.*

Hasin (h-SEE) Meaning "smile" or "beautiful."

Hastin (has-TEEN) A name meaning "elephant."

Inay (in-NAY) Meaning "God" or "godlike." Another name for the Hindu god Shiva.

Inder (IN-der) Meaning "god of heaven" or "god of rain." The name of former prime minister of India, Inder Gujral. Variations include *Inderjeet, Inderjit, Inderpal, Indervir,* and *Indra.*

Ishan (e-SHA-n) A name signifying one direction out of the ten directions used by Hindus in their prayers and ceremonies.

Jalil (JA-leel) Meaning "God" or "godlike." Another name for the Hindu god Shiva. Variations include *Jahlee, Jahleel,* and *Jalal.*

Jaspal (JAS-paal) Meaning "living a virtuous life."

Jatinra (ja-teen-raa) Meaning "great Brahmin sage."

Jivin (jee-vee-n) Meaning "life-giver." A variation is *Jivanta.*

Josha (jo-shaa) A name that means "satisfied."

Kabir (ka-BEER) A famous Hindu mystic. Also *Kabar.*

Kakar (ka-kaar) Meaning "grass."

Kala (kaa-LAA) Meaning "black" or "time."

Kalkin (kal-keen) A name that means "tenth."

Kamal (ka-MA-l) Meaning "lotus," "waterlily," or "the flower that grows in the water." A famous Hindi film actor Kamal Hassan shares this name.

Kami (KAA-meeh) Meaning "loving" or "full of desires."

Karu (ka-ROO) Meaning "cousin." A variation is *Karun.*

Kavi (ka-VEE) Meaning "poet."

Kedar (KEH-daar) Meaning "mountain lord." Also the name of a famous peak of the Himalayas where Hindus go on pilgrimages.

Kesin (kay-SEE-n) Meaning "long-haired beggar."

Kintan (keen-TAAN) Meaning "crowned."

Kiran (KEY-run) Meaning "beam of light." From the Sanskrit.

Kiritan (KEE-ree-taan) Meaning "wearing a crown."

Krishnan (kree-SHNAN) Meaning "delightful" or "pleasurable." One of the human incarnations of the Hindu God. See also Kistna, Kistnah, Krisha, and Krishnah.

Krisna (kree-SHNAA) Meaning "sacred" or "holy." A sacred river in India. Also the name of one of the human incarnations of the Hindu god.

Kumar (KOO-maar) Meaning "prince." From the Sanskrit. See also Mehta.

Lal (L-AA-L) Meaning "beloved." The name of former prime minister Lal Bahadur Shastri, who died while on political mission to Russia.

Linu (LEE-noo) Meaning "lily." A variation is *Linus.*

Lusila (LOO-see-LAA) A name that means "leader."

Madhar (mah-DAHR) Meaning "God" or "godlike." Another name for the Hindu god Shiva.

Mahesa (mah-ESHA) Meaning "great lord." Another name for the Hindu god Shiva.

Malajitm (MAA-laa-jeet-um) Sanskrit for "garland of victory."

Mandeep (man-DEEP) Meaning "mind full of light" or "light of mind." A variation is *Mandieep*.

Manoj (mah-NOJ) A Sanskrit name that means "cupid."

Manu (maa-NU) Meaning "lawmaker," it is the name of the writer of the code of conduct for Hindus. The code is called *Manusmruti* and is often referred to by scholars and experts to this day.

Marut (maa-ROOT) Another name for Vayun, the Hindu god of the wind.

Mayon (maa-YAHN) An ancient name for Krishna meaning "God."

Mehta (meh-LEE-tah) A child with this Sanskrit name possesses the exemplary qualities of a prince. He is serious, responsible, but also good-natured and judicious. This is not a first name but a last name signifying a profession. For example, conductor Zubin Mehta. See also *Kumar.*

Mohan (MO-han) Meaning "delightful." Also the name for Lord Krishna because he is always pleasing. A notable person with this name is the freedom fighter Mahatma Gandhi.

Mukul (MOO-kool) Sanskrit for "bud" or "blossom" or "soul."

Murali (moo-RAA-lee) Meaning "God," it can also signify "flute." A name for the Hindu god Krishna, because he plays a flute. He is also called *Muralidhar,* "one who puts flute on his lips to create beautiful music."

Nadisu (na-DEE-soo) Meaning "beautiful river."

Nandin (nan-DEEN) Meaning "God" or "destroyer." Another name for the Hindu god Shiva.

Narain (NAA-raa-YAN) Meaning "protector." Another name for the Hindu god Vishnu. A variation is *Narayan.*

Natesa (NAH-te-saa) Meaning "destroyer." Another name for the Hindu god Shiva.

Navin (nah-VEEN) Meaning "new" or "novel."

Nehru (NEH-roo) Meaning "canal." The name of Jawaharlal Nehru, first prime minister of an independent India. A variation is *Neil.*

Onkar (OHN-kar) Meaning "pure being." Another name for the Hindu god Shiva.

Palash (puh-LAA-sh) Meaning "flowering tree."

Paramesh (par-ME-sh) Meaning "greatest." Another name for the Hindu god Shiva.

Pavit (Pa-VEET) Meaning "devout; pure."

Poshita (po-SHEE-taa) Meaning "cherished" in Sanskrit.

Puneet (poo-neet) A Sanskrit name that means "pure."

Purdy (PUHR-dee) Parents who prefer nature to society may choose this name meaning "recluse."

Qimat (CHEE-mut) Meaning "price."

Raheem (ra-HEEM) Meaning "compassionate God." This is not a Hindu or Sanskrit word, but an Urdu word used by Muslims to refer to God.

Rajah (RAA-JAA-h) Meaning "prince" or "chief." Variations include *Raj, Raja,* and *Rajae.*

Rajak (RAA-JAA-kah) Meaning "cleansing."

Raktim (rak-TEEM) Meaning "bright red," this is a rare name.

Ram (RAAM) Meaning "God" or "godlike." Another name for the Hindu god Shiva.

Ramanan (RAA-MAA-nan) Meaning "God" or "godlike." Another name for the Hindu god Shiva. Variations include *Raman, Ramandeep, Ramanlit, Ramanjot, and Ramiro.*

Ranjan (RAHN-jan) Meaning "delighted" or "gladdened." Variations include *Ravee* and *Ravijot.*

Ravi (ra-VEE) Meaning "sun." Another name for the Hindu sun god Surya. An example is sitar virtuoso Ravi Shankar has this name.

Rishi (REE-shi) Wise parents always like this name meaning "sage."

Rohan (RO-han)   Meaning "sandalwood."

Rohin (RO-heen)   Meaning "upward path."

Rohit (RO-heet)   Meaning "big and beautiful fish."

Sajag (sa-JAAG)   Meaning "vigilant" or "awakened."

Sanatan (sa-NAA-tan)   Meaning "ancient" or "eternal."

Sandeep (san-DEEP)   Meaning "enlightened."

Sani (sa-NEE)   Meaning "saturn."

Sanjiv (san-JEEV)   Meaning "long lived."

Sankar (SAN-kar)   Meaning "God." Another name for the Hindu god Shiva.

Santosh (san-TOSH)   Meaning "contented."

Sarad (sa-ra-D)   Meaning "autumn." One of the six seasons according to the Hindu calendar.

Sarojin (sah-ro-JEE-n)   Meaning "lotuslike." A variation is *Sarojun*.

Shalya (shah-LYA)   Meaning "royal seat."

Shiva (SHEE-vah)   Meaning "life and death." The most common name for the God of destruction and reproduction. Variations include *Shiv, Shivan,* and *Siva.*

Siddhartha (see-DH-AAR-thaa)   Meaning "one whose ambitions have been fulfilled." The original name of Buddha, an Indian mystic and founder of Buddhism. Variations include *Sida, Sidh, Sidharth, Sidhartha,* and *Sidhdharth.*

Vadin (vaa-DEEN)   Meaning "speaker."

Valin (vaa-LEEN)   Meaning "mighty warrior," this name refers to a mythological monkey king who fought with his own brother Sugriva. See also Balin.

Varun (va-ROON)   Meaning "rain god." A variation is *Varron.*

Vasin (va-SEEN)   Meaning "ruler" or "lord."

Venkat (VEN-kat)   Meaning "God" or "godlike." Another name for the Hindu god Shiva.

Vijay (VEE-JAH-y)   Meaning "victory."

Vikas (vee-KAAS)   Meaning "progress."

Vinay (vee-NAY)   Meaning "polite" or "courteous."

Vishnu (vee-SHNU)   Meaning "protector." Out of the three gods in Hindu mythology Vishnu is the protector, Brahma is the creator, and Shiva is the destroyer. Vishnu is also the husband of goddess Laxmi, the goddess of wealth and prosperity.

Vivek (vee-VEK)   Meaning "wisdom." Name of a famous sage, Vivekanand, who first came to America to represent Hinduism at a conference of world religion. A variation is *Vivekinan.*

Yogesh (YO-gesh)   Meaning "chief ascetic." Another name for the Hindu god Shiva.

INDIA: GIRLS

Aditi (adee-tee)   Meaning "unbound." The mother of Hindu gods.

Adya (aah-dyaa)   Meaning "ancient." A variation is *Adia.*

Aja (ah-jaa)   Meaning "goat." Variations include *Ajah, Ajaran,* and *Ajha.*

Amlika (am-LEE-kaa)   Meaning "mother." A variation is *Amlikah.*

Anala (A-na-LAA)   Meaning "fire."

Ananda (aah-NAN-daa)   Meaning "bliss."

Anila (ah-nee-laa)   A Hindu god of the wind.

Araxi   A child with this name is practical and well groomed.

Artha (ur-thaa)   Meaning "wealth." Variations include *Arti* and *Artie.*

Bakula (bah-KOO-LAA)   Meaning "flower."

Chakra (cha-KRAH)   Meaning "circle of energy." From the Sanskrit. Variations include *Chaka, Chakara, Chakaria, Chakeitha, Chakena, Chakira,* and *Chakrah.*

Chanda (CHAN-da)   Sanskrit for "great goddess or moon." The name assumed by the

Hindu goddess Devi. Variations include *Chandee, Chandey,* and *Chandi.*

Chandra (CHAN-dra) A Sanskrit name meaning "moon." Variations include *Chandre, Chandrea, Chandria,* and *Shandra.*

Deva (DEE-vaa) Meaning "divine" or "male god."

Devi (deh-VEE) Meaning "goddess." Any Hindu goddess is called Devi, not just the goddess of power and destruction.

Hara (HA-rah) Meaning "tawny." A name for Shiva the destroyer.

Indira (in-DEE-raa) Meaning "splendid." The Hindu god of heaven. Among the notable people with this name is former prime minister Indira Gandhi.

Jaya (JA-yaa) Meaning "victory." Variations include *Jaea, Jaia,* and *Jayla.*

Jivan (JEE-vahn) Meaning "life." A variation is *Jibon.*

Kalinda (KAA-lin-dah) A name that means "sun."

Kama (KAA-ma) Meaning "desire." The name for the Hindu god of love. From the Sanskrit.

Kamala (KAH-mlaah) Meaning "lotus." A variation is *Kamalah.*

Kanya (kan-YAA) Meaning "small girl."

Karma (KAR-maa) Meaning "action." According to Hindu philosophy destiny is based on one's actions; thus Karma also signifies "fate" or "destiny."

Karuna (ka-ROO-naa) Meaning "mercy" or "compassion."

Kasi (kaa-CEE) A holy Hindu city by the river Ganges. It is believed that if one dies in Kasi, his soul goes to heaven; consequently, many Hindus bring the ashes of their loved ones to Kasi after cremation.

Kaveri (kaa-VE-REE) One of the sacred rivers of India.

Kavindra (kah-VEEN-draa) Meaning "mighty poet" or "lord of poets."

Kusa (koo-saah) Meaning "sacred grass."

Lajila (lah-Jee-laa) Meaning "shy" or "coy."

Lalasa (laa-lsaa) Meaning "love," "desire," or "attachment."

Lalita (la-LEE-ta) Meaning "charming." A name for the Hindu goddess Shakti. From the Sanskrit.

Latika (la-TEE-kaa) Meaning "a small creeper."

Mahesa (ma-HEE-saa) Meaning "great lord" or "the name of Lord Shiva."

Mahila (ma-hee-LA) Sanskrit for "woman" or "lady."

Makara (mah-ka-raa) Meaning "born during the lunar month of Capricorn."

Malini (maa-lee-nee) Meaning "a gardener." The Hindu god of the earth.

Mandara (man-duh-raa) Meaning "calm." A mythical Hindu tree that dispels worries.

Matrika (maa-tree-kaa) Meaning "mother." A name for the Hindu goddess Shakti.

Maya (maa-yaa) Meaning "illusion" or "God's creative power." According to Hindu philosophy, God created this entire world, which is an illusion.

Meena (MEE-nah) A blue semiprecious stone.

Mehadi (me-HA-dee) Meaning "flower." Leaves of an herbal plant that are used to make henna design.

Mela (MEE-la) A country fair or any kind of get-together with friends and relatives usually for a festive occasion.

Mesha (me-shaa) Meaning "born in the lunar month of Aries." Also *Meshal.*

Mitra (MI-traa) Meaning "fiend." A name for the Hindu god of daylight.

Narmada (nar-m-dah) Name of a sacred river in western India.

Nata (na-TAA) Sanskrit for "dancer" or "actor." Lord Shiva is called Nataraaj, "the lord of dances."

Natesa (na-TE-shaa) Meaning "godlike" or "goddess." Another name for the Hindu goddess Shakti. A variation is *Natisa*.

Nila (NEE-laa) Meaning "blue." A cosmic color that is believed to be the skin color of God.

Nitara (NEE-tah-ra) Meaning "deeply rooted."

Opal (O-pal) Meaning "precious stone." Variations include *Opale*, *Opalina*, and *Opaline*.

Padma (pad-MAA) Meaning "lotus."

Pandita (pan-DEE-taa) Meaning "scholar." Educated parents might select this name for their children.

Pausha (PO-shaa) Signifying the lunar month of Capricorn. See also Tula.

Pinga (peen-GAAH) Meaning "bronze" or "dark." Another name for the Hindu goddess Shakti.

Pollyam (po-LEE-yam) Meaning "goddess of the plague." This is a Hindu name invoked to ward off bad spirits.

Priya (pree-YA) Meaning "beloved" or "sweet-natured."

Rani (RAA-NEE) A Sanskrit name that means "queen."

Ratri (RA-tree) Meaning "night."

Rekha (re-KHA) Meaning "thin line, usually straight."

Risha (REE-sha) Signifying the lunar month of Taurus. Variations include *Rishah* and *Rishay*.

Rohana (ro-HA-na) Meaning "sandalwood."

Rohini (ro-HEE-nee) Meaning "woman."

Roshan (RO-shun) Meaning "shining light." From the Sanskrit.

Ruchil (ROO-chil) Meaning "one who wishes to please."

Rudra (ROO-dra) Meaning "seeds of the rudraksha plant." Considered sacred, the plant's seeds are used to make necklaces for saints and others.

Sadhana (saa-DH-na) A loyal name that means "devoted."

Sagara (saa-GAH-ra) Meaning "ocean."

Sakari (saa-KA-ree) Meaning "sweet." A variant form is *Sakkara*.

Sakti (SA-ktee) Meaning "energy" or "power." An alternate form of *Shakti*.

Sala (SAA-la) Meaning "sala tree," the sacred tree under which Buddha died. Among notable people with this name is former congresswoman Sala Burton.

Sanya (SAN-yah) Meaning "born on Saturday." From the Sanskrit.

Saura (SAU-ra) Meaning "sun worshiper" or "born under the sign of Leo."

Shaka (SHA-ka) An alternate form of Shakti. Variations include *Shakah*, *Shakha*, and *Shikah*.

Shakti (SHA-ktee) Meaning "divine woman." The Hindu goddess of time and destruction. Variations include *Sakti*, *Shaka*, and *Sita*.

Sharan (SHA-run) Meaning "surrender." Variations include *Sharaine*, *Sharanda*, and *Sharanjeet*.

Sita (SEE-taa) An alternate form of Shakti. The wife of Lord Rama, she was kidnapped by the evil King Ravana, who was then killed by Rama to free her. Variations include *Sitah*, *Sitarah*, and *Sitha*.

Soma (SOH-maa) Signifying the lunar month of Cancer. A notable person with this name is author Soma Vira.

Sumati (soo-MAH-tee) Meaning "good intelligence and wisdom."

Taja (taa-jah) An Urdu word meaning "crown." The famous Taj Mahal means "the palace for the crown." Variations include *Taiajára*, *Taija*, *Teja*, and *Tejah*.

Taru (TAH-roo) Meaning "pine tree."

Tira (TEE-raa) Meaning "arrow." Variations include *Tirah*, *Tirea*, and *Tirena*.

Tirtha (TEER-thaa)   Meaning "a place of pilgrimage" or "a sacred place." A variation is *Tirza*.

Tula (TOO-laah)   Meaning "born in the lunar month of Capricorn." Variations include *Tulah*, *Tulla*, and *Tullah*. See also Pausha.

Tulsi (TOOL-see)   Meaning "basil," a sacred Hindu herb. Variations include *Tulsia*.

Usha (OO-shaa)   Meaning "sunrise." Parents who love the day may choose this name.

Veda (VEH-daa)   Meaning "wise" or "to know." The four Vedas constitute the sacred writings of Hinduism. Variations include *Vedad*, *Vedis*, *Veeda*, and *Veida*.

Vida (VEE-da)   An alternate form of the name Veda.

Yamuna (ya-MOO-naa)   Meaning "sacred river."

Zudora (ZOO-doh-rah)   A Sanskrit word meaning "laborer." This is not commonly used as a name in India. A variation is *Wellka*.

Japan

In Japan, girls and boys are conventionally given very different names. Boys' names identify their birth order or reflect traditionally male qualities such as power and courage. Girls' names express virtues long felt to be feminine, such as fidelity, refinement, purity, reserve, gentility, and beauty. In two respects the naming practice for girls and boys is quite similar. A character from the name of a grandparent or the child's father is often included in the child's name, in order to honor the elder relative. Names that refer to trees or their parts are often given because the tree is a symbol of longevity, strength, and success in Japan. In Japanese, written characters, known as ideograms, can have similar sounds but completely different meanings. The significance of each name offered in this section is only one of those possible.

JAPAN: BOYS

Akira (ah-KEE-rah) Meaning "bright." Legendary film director Akira Kurosawa bears this name.

Daichi (dah-EE-chee) A name that means "grounded."

Daiki (dah-EE-kee) Meaning "big tree."

Daisuke (dah-ee-SOOH-kee) A name that means "reliable."

Hideki (hee-DEH-kee) Meaning "bright tree." A notable Hideki is New York Yankees pitcher Hideki Irabu.

Kazuki (kah-ZOO-kee) Meaning "first or best tree."

Kenzaburo (kehn-zah-BOO-roh) Meaning "healthy third son." The name of Nobel Prize–winning novelist Kenzaburo Oe.

Kishi (KEE-shee) Meaning "long and happy life."

Kuma (KOO-mah) Meaning "bear."

Makoto (mah-KO-toh) Meaning "genuine." Name of baseball player Makoto Sasaki.

Masato (mah-SAH-toh) Meaning "commander." Name of baseball player Masato Yoshii.

Michio (MIT-chee-oh) Meaning "handsome, smart, and masculine." Among notable persons with this name is scientist Michio Kaku.

Misao (meh-SAY-oh) Meaning "fidelity."

Naoki (nay-OH-kee) Meaning "upright tree."

Naoto (nay-OH-toh) Meaning "honest person." Noteworthy for this name is Japanese political party leader Naoto Kan.

Ryou (REE-oh) A name meaning "good."

Ryouta (ree-OH-tah) Meaning "good and strong."

Ryutaro (ree-oo-TAH-roh) Meaning "strong, masculine dragon." Among notable persons, former Japanese prime minister Ryutaro Hashimoto bears this name.

Seiji (SAY-jee) Meaning "noble rule." Conductor Seiji Ozawa, for example.

Shou (SHO) Meaning "soaring."

Shouta (SHO-tah) Meaning "soaring and strong."

Shun (SHOON) Meaning "quick" or "smart."

Takumi (tah-KOO-mee) Meaning "skillful."

Takuya (tah-KOO-yah) Meaning "creative."

Taro (TAH-roh) Meaning "strong boy." Operatic tenor Taro Ichihara has the name.

Tatsuya (tat-ZOO-yah) Meaning "masculine dragon."

Tomiichi (toh-MEE-chee) Meaning "wealthy" or "best." Former Japanese prime minister Tomiichi Murayama has this name.

Toru (TOH-roo) Meaning "clarity." For example, composer Toru Takemitsu.

Toshiro (toh-SHEE-roh) Meaning "smart lad." The name is familiar to film audiences from the distinguished actor Toshiro Mifune.

Tsubasa (zoo-BAH-sah) Meaning "wings."

Yasuhiro (yah-soo-HEE-roh) Meaning "healthy and generous." Japanese martial artist Yasuhiro Yamashita is among the notable persons who share this name.

Yu (YOO) Meaning "masculine."

Yuki (YOO-kee) Meaning "brave spirit."

Yuta (YOO-tah) Meaning "masculine and strong."

JAPAN: GIRLS

Ai (EYE) A name that means "love."

Aiko (EYE-koh) Meaning "beloved."

Akako (ah-KAH-koh) A passionate name that signifies "red."

Akane (ah-KAH-neh) Meaning "Bengali madder," a family of flowers including the gardenia flower.

Aki (AH-kee) Meaning "born in autumn."

Akiko (ah-KEE-koh) Meaning "bright light." Among the notable people with this name is poet Akiko Yosano.

Amaya (ah-MAH-yah) A name that means "night."

Aneko (ah-NEH-koh) Meaning "older sister."

Asa (AH-sah) Meaning "born in the morning."

Asuka (ah-SOO-kah) An optimistic name that means "sweet future."

Aya (AH-yah) Meaning "bright."

Ayaka (ah-YAH-kah) Meaning "appealing."

Ayako (ah-YAH-koh) Meaning "pretty child." Golfer Ayako Okamoto, for example.

Ayano (ah-YAH-noh) Meaning "pretty and successful."

Chika (CHEE-kah) Meaning "near and dear."

Chikako (chee-KAH-koh) A shrewd name meaning "clever."

Chiyo (CHEE-yoh) Meaning "eternal." Also *Chiya*.

Cho (CHOH) A very light name, as it means "butterfly."

Dai (DYE) Meaning "great." Variations include *Dae*, *Daija*, *Daijon*, and *Day*.

Hachi (HA-chee) Meaning "eight thousand" and "good luck." Variations include *Hachiko* and *Hachiyo*.

Hama (HA-mah) Meaning "shore." A variation is *Hamako*.

Hana (HA-nah) A cheerful name that means "flower."

Hanako (ha-NAH-koh) Meaning "flower child."

Haru (HA-rooh) Meaning "spring."

Haruka (ha-ROO-kah) Meaning "fragrant springtime."

Haruna (ha-ROO-nah) Meaning "springtime child."

Haya (HA-yah) Meaning "quick" or "light."

Hisa (HEE-sah) Meaning "long-lasting." Variations include *Hisae*, *Hisako*, and *Hisay*.

Hoshi (HO-shee) Meaning "star." Variations include *Hoshie*, *Hoshiko*, and *Hoshiyo*.

Ima (EE-mah) Meaning "now." A variation is *Imako*.

Ishi (EE-shee) Meaning "stone." Variations include *Ishiko*, *Ishiyo*, and *Shiko*.

Ito (EE-toh) Meaning "thread."

Kaiyo (KYE-yoh) Meaning "forgiveness."

Kameko (kah-MEE-koh) Meaning "turtle child." In Japan, the turtle is a symbol of longevity.

Kana (KAH-nah) Meaning "beautiful" or "excellent."

Kane (KAH-neh) Meaning "two right hands."

Katsu (KAH-zoo) Meaning "victorious."

Kawa (KAH-wah) An aquatic name meaning "river."

Kei (KAYE) Meaning "happiness" or "reverence." Variations include *Keiana*, *Keikann*, and *Keikanna*.

Keiko (KAYE-koh) Meaning "happy child." Among the notable people with this name is author Keiko Ochiai. Also *Kei*.

Kiku (KEE-koh) Meaning "chrysanthemum." A variation is *Kiko*.

Kimi (KEE-mee) Meaning "righteous child." Among the notable people with this name is tennis player Kimiko Date.

Kioko (kee-OH-koh) Menaing "happy child." Variations include *Kiyo* and *Kiyoko*.

Kita (KEE-tah) Meaning "north" is commonly used as a last name.

Kiwa (KEE-wah) Meaning "borderline."

Koko (KOH-koh) Meaning "stork." A variation is *Coco*.

Koto (KOH-toh) Meaning "harp."

Kumiko (koo-MEE-koh) Meaning "girl with braids." A variation is *Kumi*.

Kuniko (koo-NEE-koh) Meaning "child from the country."

Kuri (KOO-ree) Meaning "chestnut."

Kyoko (kee-YOH-koh) Meaning "mirror."

Machiko (mah-CHEE-koh) Meaning "fortunate child." Also *Machi*.

Maemi (mye-EE-mee) Meaning "honest child." A variation is *Mae*.

Mai (MYE) Meaning "elegance."

Mari (MAH-ree) A name that means "ball."

Mariko (mah-REE-koh) A geometrical name that means "circle."

Maru (mah-ROO) A continuous name meaning "round."

Matsuko (mah-ZOO-koh) Meaning "pine tree."

Mayu (MAH-yoo) Meaning "truth."

Michi (MEE-chee) Meaning "righteous way." Variations include *Michiko*, *Miche*, and *Michee*. Michiko Shouda, the present Empress of Japan.

Midori (mee-DOH-ree) Meaning "green." Among notable persons with this name is ice skater Midori Ito.

Mieko (mee-EH-koh) Meaning "prosperous." A variation is *Mieke*.

Miho (MEE-hoh) Meaning "beautiful."

Mika (MEE-kah) Meaning "new moon." Among the notable people with this name is Mika Furukawa, CEO of Seisen Corporation that provides tea leaves, especially for formal tea ceremonies. Variations include *Miki*, *Mikia*, *Mikiala*, *Mikie*, *Mikita*, *Mikiyo*, *Mikka*, and *Mikki*.

Mio (MEE-oh) Meaning "three times as strong."

Misaki (mee-SAH-kee) Meaning "beautiful" or "blossom."

Mitsuko (meh-ZOO-koh) Meaning "bright child." Among the notable people with this name is concert pianist Mitsuko Uchida.

Miwa (MEE-wah) Meaning "far-sighted." A variation is *Miwako*.

Miya (MEE-yah) Meaning "temple." Variations include *Miyana* and *Miyanna*.

Miyo (MEE-yoh) Meaning "beautiful generation." Variations include *Miyoko* and *Miyuko*.

Miyuki (mee-YOO-kee) Meaning "snow."

Momoko (moh-MOH-koh) Meaning "peach child."

Mon (MOHN) Meaning "gate."

Morie (MOH-ree) Meaning "bay." Commonly used as a last name.

Mura (MOO-rah)   Meaning "village." Commonly used as a last name.

Nami (NAH-mee)   Meaning "wave." Variations include *Namika* and *Namiko*.

Nari (NAH-ree)   Meaning "thunder." Also *Nariko*.

Natsuki (nah-ZOO-kah)   Meaning "summer tree." Commonly used as a last name.

Natsumi (nah-ZOO-mee)   Meaning "summer beauty." Commonly used as a last name.

Nishi (NEE-shee)   Meaning "west."

Nyoko (nee-OH-koh)   A name of value that means "gem" or "treasure."

Oki (OH-kee)   Meaning "middle of the ocean."

Orino (oh-REE-noh)   Meaning "worker's field." A variation is *Ori*.

Raku (RAH-koo)   Meaning "pleasure."

Ran (RAHN)   Meaning "water lily."

Rei (RAY)   Meaning "polite" or "well behaved." A variation is *Reiko*.

Reina (RAY-nah)   Meaning "elegant" or "perfect."

Ren (REHN)   Meaning "arranger" or "water lily" or "lotus."

Rin (RIHN)   Meaning "park." Variations include *Rini* and *Rynn*.

Rina (REE-nah)   Meaning "just" or "honest."

Rui (ROO-ee)   "Meaning "affectionate."

Ruri (ROO-ree)   Meaning "emerald." A variation is *Ruriko*.

Ryo (REE-oh)   Meaning "dragon." Another version is *Ryoko*.

Sachi (SAH-chee)   Meaning "blessed" or "lucky." A variation is *Sachiko*.

Sada (SAH-dah)   Meaning "chaste." Among the notable people with this name is United Nations high commissioner for refugees Sadako Ogata.

Sai (SYE)   Meaning "talented." Also *Saiko*.

Sakae (sah-KYE)   Meaning "prosperous."

Saki (SAH-kee)   Meaning "blossom."

Sakura (SAH-koo-rah)   Meaning "cherry blossom." A symbol of prosperity; commonly used as a last name.

Sato (SAH-toh)   Meaning "sugar." Commonly used as a last name. A variation is *Satu*.

Sawa (SAH-wah)   Meaning "marsh."

Sayo (SAH-yoh)   Meaning "born at night."

Seki (SHE-kee)   Meaning "wonderful." Also *Seka*.

Sen (ZEHN)   Meaning "wood fairy."

Setsu (SEHT-zoo)   Meaning "fidelity." A variation is *Setsuko*.

Shika (SHEE-kah)   Meaning "gentle deer." A variation is *Shi*.

Shina (SHEE-nah)   Meaning "virtuous" or "wealthy."

Shino (SHEE-noh)   A name that means "bamboo stalk."

Shizu (SHEE-zoo)   Meaning "silent." Other versions are *Shizue*, *Shizuka*, *Shizuko*, and *Shizuyo*.

Sugi (SOO-gee)   Meaning "cedar tree."

Suki (SOO-kee)   A dear name that means "loved one."

Sumi (SOO-mee)   Meaning "elegant" or "refined." A variation is *Sumiko*.

Suzu (SOO-zoo)   Meaning "little bell."

Suzuki (soo-ZOO-kee)   Meaning "bell tree."

Taka (TAH-kah)   Meaning "honorable."

Takara (tah-KAH-rah)   Meaning "treasure." A variation is *Takra*.

Taki (TAH-kee)   Meaning "waterfall." Also *Tiki*.

Tama (TAH-mah)   Meaning "jewel."

Tamaka (tah-MAH-kah) Meaning "bracelet." Variations include *Tamaki*, *Tamako*, and *Timaka*.

Tamiko (tah-MEE-koh) Meaning "child of the people." Variations include *Tami*, *Tamica*, *Tamieka*, *Tamika*, *Tamike*, *Tamikia*, *Tamikka*, and *Tamiqua*.

Tani (TAH-nee) Meaning "valley."

Taree (TAH-ree) Meaning "arching branch." Variations include *Tarea*, *Tareya*, *Tari*, and *Taria*.

Tazu (TAH-zoo) Meaning "stork" or "longevity." Variations include *Taz*, *Tazi*, and *Tazia*.

Tetsu (THE-zoo) Meaning "strong as iron."

Toki (TOH-kee) Meaning "hopeful."

Tomi (TOH-mee) Meaning "riches." Variations include *Tomie* and *Tomilu*.

Tomo (TOH-moh) Meaning "intelligent." Variations include *Tomoko*.

Tora (TOH-rah) Meaning "tiger."

Tori (TOH-ree) Meaning "bird" or "chicken."

Toshi (TOH-shee) Meaning "year of plenty." Variations include *Toshie* and *Toshikyo*. Big band leader Toshiko Akiyoshi is one notable example.

Tsuna (ZOO-nah) Meaning "bond."

Urano (yu-RAH-noh) Meaning "coast."

Urneko (uhr-NEH-koh) Meaning "plum blossom child" or "patient." Variations include *Ume* and *Umeyo*.

Wakana (wah-KAH-nah) Meaning "plant."

Washi (WAH-shee) A soaring name that means "eagle."

Wattan (WAH-tahn) Meaning "homeland."

Yasu (YAH-soo) Meaning "calm." Variations include *Yasuko* and *Yasuyo*.

Yoko (YOH-koh) Meaning "generous child." Notable persons are avant-garde artist Yoko Ono and Yoko Shimazaki, the CEO of Shimazaki.

Yoni (YOH-nee) Meaning "wealth" or "rice."

Yori (YOH-ree) Meaning "reliable."

Yoshi (YOH-shee) Meaning "good" or "respectful."

Yuka (YOO-kah) Meaning "sweet smelling."

Yuki (YOO-kee) Meaning "snow."

Yukiko (yoo-KEE-koh) Meaning "snow child."

Yuri (YO-ree) Meaning "lily." Variations include *Yuriko* and *Yuriyo*.

Thailand

Thailand's official name of Muang Thai means "Free Land." The Thais pride themselves for being among the few countries in Asia to have successfully avoided colonial European intervention. This was largely due to a shrewd diplomatic approach on the part of Thai rulers, in particular King Mongkut and his son, King Chulalongkorn, who signed trade treaties with the British and French in the 19th century, established Thailand as a constitutional monarchy, and masterfully led their country on the road to modernization. The Thai language is a blending of various elements. Its elegant and intricate script is largely modeled on Indian Sanskrit, while many of the language's phonetic and grammatical elements are the result of Chinese influence. Names in Thailand tend to be long and elaborate, and many people are therefore referred to by pet names or nicknames.

Pronunciation: Because Thai is an inflectional language, voice pitch is indicated along with the pronunciation in this section.

' = glottal stop

ch, as in "Charles"

chh, as in "chicken" (aspirated)

kh = aspirated "k"

ph = aspirated "p" (not "f")

th = aspirated "t"

a = "a" as in "father," but short

â = "a" as in "father"

aw, as in "how"

e, as in "set"

ey, as in "hay"

eye, as in "I"

i, as in "ship"

ia, as in "yeah" (drawn out)

ee, as in "sheep"

u, as in "foot"

oh = short "o" (no equivalent in English)

o, as in "doe"

oo, as in "boot"

THAILAND: BOYS

Aran (A-ran) [low-even]   Meaning "forest."

Aroon (A-run) [low-even]   Meaning "dawn."

Atid (A-thit) [even-high]   Meaning "sun."

Chet (chheyt) [falling]   Meaning "elder brother."

Decha (dey-chhâ) [even-even]   Meaning "power."

Kasem (ka-seym) [low-rising]   Meaning "well-being."

Kiet (kiat) [low]   Meaning "honor."

Kovit (ko-wit) [even–high]   Meaning "expert."

Lek (lek) [high]   Meaning "small."

Niran (ni-ran) [high-even]   Meaning "eternal."

Pricha (pree-chhâ) [even-even]   Meaning "clever."

Rungrot (rung-rot) [falling-falling]   Meaning "prosperous."

Sakda (sak-dâ) [low-even]   Meaning "power."

Som (sohm) [rising]   Meaning "appropriate."

Virote (wi-rot) [high-falling]   Meaning "brilliant."

THAILAND: GIRLS

Daw (dow) [even]   Meaning "star."

Isra ('it-sa-ra) [low-low-low]   Meaning "free."

Kanya (kan-yâ) [even-even]   Meaning "girl" or "virgin."

Lawan (lâ-wan) [even-even]   Meaning "beauty."

Mali (ma-li)   Meaning "jasmine flower."

Mayuree (ma-yu-ree) [high-high-even] Meaning "peacock."

Phailin (pheye-lin) [even-even]   Meaning "sapphire." Phailin is the name of a Cambodian town near the Thai border where such precious stones are mined.

Ratana (rat-ta-nâ) [high-low-even]   Meaning "jewel."

Solada (so-la-da)   Meaning "listener." Also *Solana*.

Suchin (su-chin-dâ) [low-even-even]   Meaning "beautiful thought."

Sumalee (su-mâ-lee) [low-even-even] Meaning "flower" or "garland."

Tasanee (that-sa-nee) [high-low-even] Meaning "beautiful."

Tida (thi-dâ) [high-even]   Meaning "daughter."

Afghanistan

An ancient land whose history can be traced back to 50,000 B.C., Afghanistan was the site of one of the earliest cultures to domesticate plants and animals. The country has always distinguished itself by its heritage as a great crossroads of peoples, languages, and cultures. This is evidenced by the persistence of several spoken languages of which Pashtu, Dari, Farsi, Pahlawi, and Arabic predominate. Traditions in naming children were heavily influenced by the arrival of Islam in A.D. 652, and today there continues to be an overall tendency for parents to choose either religious or historical names.

AFGHANISTAN: BOYS

Ajmal (ADG-mal)   This name means "the most handsome" or "best looking."

Babur (BAAH-boor)   Derived from Old Persian meaning "joy."

Iskander (IS-kan-dur)   Iranian form of the Greek name Alexandros meaning "protection of men."

Matteen (MA-teen)   Meaning "well-disciplined; well-mannered."

Mirwais "noble ruler." The name of a tenth-century Afghani king.

Nadir (NAH-deer)   A Muslim name that means "dear" or "rare." Ralph Nader, the U.S. politician who is the leader of the Green Party, is one well-known person with this name.

Osman (OZ-man)   The name of the founder of the Ottoman Empire and the third Muslim Calif after Prophet Muhammad.

Yasir (yas-SEER)   A name that means "modest." This is the name of a Muslim hero and martyr contemporary to the prophet Muhammad.

AFGHANISTAN: GIRLS

Asman (ah-see-MAHN)   This name is derived from the Persian word "sky."

Badria (bad-ree-AH)   This name means "like the moon."

Fareiba (FA-ree-bah)   A name that means "beautiful" or "attractive."

Forogh (FO-rou-gh)   Meaning "brilliance" or "dawn."

Hebrew

Ashkenazic Jews of eastern Europe had a strong tradition mandating that a baby be named after a deceased relative. It is important to understand that this is a tradition and is not codified in Jewish law. No evidence of such a tradition appears in the Bible, in which most names are unique. The custom seems to have started in the first and second centuries and to have become entrenched by the 12th century. By the 12th century in Europe, we find given names repeating every other generation within families, as infants were named for grandmothers or grandfathers. Generally, a child was named for the closest deceased relative for whom no one else in that immediate family was already named.

Most Jewish males have two names, a religious name, called the *shem hakodesh*, and a secular name, called the *kinnui*. The religious name is a Hebrew name, and the secular name is in whatever vernacular language is in use. After immigration to a new country, a new secular name is often chosen in the secular language of the new country. Full Hebrew names do not exist per se. In Israel, for example, given names may be Hebrew and taken from biblical sources or Hebrew versions of Western names, but last names will be German, eastern European, Spanish, Arabic, or Indian, depending on the person's country of origin.

HEBREW: BOYS

Aba (A-ba) Aramaic, meaning "father" or "grandfather." Also used as a scholarly title. Aba in modern Hebrew means "dad." Notable men with this name include Abba Eban, Israel's delegate to the U.N. for many years and a spokesman for the State of Israel. Variations include *Abba, Abbah, Abin, Abinu, Abbas, Abbot,* and *Abbot.*

Adam (a-DAM) Meaning "earth." According to the Bible, the first man. "Son of Adam" means "person."

Adin (a-DIN) This name means "pleasant." Among famous individuals named Adin is Anglo-Jewish scholar Adin Steinsaltz.

Admon (ad-MON) Signifying "redness" or "health."

Aharon (a-ha-RON) The brother of Moses, the first High Priest. He was noted for loving peace; a "student of Aharon" is a peacemaker. Aaron Copeland was one of the greatest American composers. A variation is *Aaron.*

Akiva (a-KI-va) A great scholar of the Mishna.

Alon (a-LON) This name means "oak."

Ami (a-MI) A name that signifies "my people."

Amichai (a-mi-CHAI) Meaning "my people live." Among historical figures with this name is the great medieval Hebrew poet of Spain, Yehuda Amichai.

Amiel (a-mi-EL) Meaning "my people's God." A common surname.

Amitai (a-mi-TAI) Meaning "truthful." Author Amitai Etzioni is one celebrated person with this name.

Amos (a-MOS) Meaning "burdened." This is the name of an eighth-century prophet, as well as the contemporary author Amos Oz.

Amram (am-RAM) A name that signifies "great nation."

Arad (a-RAD) Meaning "bronze." One renowned individual with this name is soldier Ron Arad.

Ardon (ar-DON) This name means "bronzed."

Ari (a-RI)   A name that means "lion."

Ari'el (a-ri-EL)   Meaning "lion of God." Among well-known people with this name is general and politician Ariel Sharon.

Arye (AR-ye)   Meaning "lion."

Asa (a-SA)   Meaning "healers." In the Bible, a king of Judah.

Asaf (a-SAF)   A name that signifies "gathering." A singer of psalms. A variation is *Asaph*.

Asher (a-SHER)   Meaning "happy," "blessed," or "rich." The son of Jacob and patriarch of the tribe of Asher.

Avi (AV-i)   This name means "my father."

Avishalom (a-vi-sha-LOM)   Meaning "my father is peace."

Aviv (a-VIV)   A name meaning "Springtime." One popular Aviv today is bad-boy rock star Aviv Geffen.

Avner (av-NER)   Meaning "father of flame." King Saul's uncle and the commander of his army. A variation is *Abner*.

Avraham (av-ra-HAM)   Meaning "father of multitudes." The first patriarch, husband of Sarah, father of Isaac, grandfather of Jacob; at God's command he left his home in Ur and traveled to the land of Canaan, where he made a covenant with God. Famous and infamous Avrahams include U.S. president Abraham Lincoln, yippie Abbie Hoffman, and Yiddish playwright Avrom Goldfadn. Variations include *Abraham, Abe, Abey, Abbie, Avrohom, Avromi, Avroml,* and *Avromele*.

Avram (av-RAM)   Meaning "father of multitudes." Avraham's original name, which was changed by God by the insertion of the letter Hei, signifying God. Variations include *Abram, Avrom,* and all the diminutives of *Avraham*.

Avshalom (av-sha-LOM)   This name means "father of peace." King David's beloved but spoiled son, who led a revolt against his father. A variation is *Absalom*.

Azarya (a-ZAR-ya)   A name that has the significance. Meaning "God has helped."

Barak (ba-RAK)   Meaning "lightning." The biblical warrior who helped the judge Devorah; also the name of Israeli Prime Minister Ehud Barak.

Barukh (ba-RUCH)   This name means "blessed." Assistant and scribe of the prophet Jeremiah.

Ben-Ami (ben-a-MI)   This name means "son of my people."

Ben-Tziyon (ben-TZI-yon)   Meaning "son of Zion." A variation is *Ben-Zion*.

Benyamin (ben-ya-MIN)   Meaning "son of the right hand." Jacob's youngest son, patriarch of the tribe of Benjamin. A variation is *Benjamin*.

Beni (BE-ni)   A short form of Benyamin.

Betzalel (be-tza-LEL)   Meaning "in the shadow of God." The name for the Israelite artisan who built the Ark of the Covenant.

Bina (BI-na)   A famous scholar in the Gemara.

Bibi (BI-bi)   A familiar form of Benyamin.

Bizi (BI-zi)   A familiar form of Betzalel.

Boaz (BO-az)   A name that means "farmer" or "orange-grower." In the Bible the Israelite man who marries Ruth; also the ancestor of King David.

Dan (DAN)   Meaning "God has judged in my favor." The son of Jacob, patriarch of the tribe of Dan.

Dani (DA-ni)   A form of Dan and Daniel.

Daniel (da-ni-EL)   Meaning "God is my judge." A prophet during the Babylonian Exile.

Datan (da-TAN)   A son of Aaron.

David (da-VID)   A name that means "beloved," it is the name of the second and greatest king of Israel. A variation is *Davi*.

Dekel (DE-kel)   This name has a meaning "palm tree."

Dor (DOR)   A name that means "generation."

Dov (DOV) A name that means "bear." A familiar form is *Dovi*.

Dror (DROR) Meaning "freedom," or "swallow; sparrow."

Efrayim (e-FRAY-im) The younger son of Joseph; patriarch of the tribe of Ephraim; often used by prophets to mean "Israel." A variation is *Ephraim*.

Ehud (e-HUD) Which means "union." A descendent of Benjamin. Among noteworthy individuals with this name are Prime Minister Ehud Barak.

Elazar (el-a-ZAR) Meaning "God has helped."

Eli (E-li) A name that means "up" or "light."

Eliazar (e-li-a-ZAR) Meaning "my God has helped." A variation is *Eleazar*.

Eli'ezer (e-li-EZ-er) Meaning "my God is a shelter."

Elihu (e-LI-hu) This name means "He is my God" or "my God lives."

Elisha (e-LI-sha) Meaning "God saves." Eliyahu's assistant and successor.

Eliyahu (e-li-YA-hu) Meaning "my God is God." The name for a major prophet and harbinger of the Messiah. Also *Elijah*.

Elkhanan (el-kha-NAN) Which means "God has been gracious." Variations include *Elchanan* and *Elhanan*.

Enosh (e-NOSH) One of the first people, according to the Bible. In Hebrew, used to mean "human being" (like "guy" in English). A variation is *Enos*.

Eshkol (esh-KOL) A name meaning "grape cluster."

Etan (e-TAN) Meaning "strong." A variation is *Ethan*.

Even (EV-en) Meaning "rock." One noteworthy individual with this name is old-time Israeli politician Abba Eban. A variation is *Eban*.

Evenezer (e-ve-NE-zer) Meaning "rock of shelter." Also *Ebenezer*.

Eykhavod (ey-kha-VOD) Meaning "Where is glory?" A variation is *Ichabod*.

Eyli (ey-LI) Meaning "my God." High priest, mentor of Samuel.

Ezer (E-zer) Meaning "shelter," or "help." Former Israeli president Ezer Weitzman.

Ezra (ez-RA) Meaning "shelter" or "help." The name of a post-exilic prophet and the poet Ezra Pound.

Gad (GAD) A name that means "kid." Son of Jacob and patriarch of the tribe of Gad.

Gadi (GA-di) A familiar form of Gad.

Gamli'el (gam-li-EL) Meaning "God is my rescue." The name of the great Mishnaic scholar.

Gavri'el (ga-vri-EL) Meaning "God is my might." The name of an archangel. A variation is *Gabriel*.

Gershom (ger-SHOM) "A stranger there." Moses' first son.

Gidyon (gi-DYON) A judge and war-chief of the early Israelites, noted for his continence and bravery. A variation is *Gideon*.

Gil (GIL) Signifying "joy." Musician Gil Dor is one notable individual with this name.

Gili (gi-LI) Meaning "my joy."

Givon (gi-VON) A name that signifies "hill" or "height."

Go'el (go-EL) Meaning "redeemer."

Gomer (go-MER) Meaning "completed."

Gur (GUR) Meaning "young lion." a short form of Guryon.

Guryon (gur-YON) This name means "young lion." One noteworthy person with this name is Prime Minister David Ben-Gurion.

Hadar (ha-DAR) This name means "grandeur."

Hanokh (ha-NOKH) Meaning "learned." Varitions include *Enoch*.

Heman (he-MAN) Meaning "faithful."

Hilel (hi-LEL) Meaning "praise." Celebrated individuals with this name include great Talmudic scholar Rav Hillel, and modern author and commentator Hillel Halkin.

Hosheya (ho-SHE-ya) Signifying "salvation." The name of a prophet. A variation is *Hosea*.

Ilan (i-LAN) This name means "tree."

Immanu'el (im-man-u-EL) Meaning "God is with us." Variations include *Emmanuel* and *Manuel*.

Issakhar (is-sa-KHAR) A son of Jacob and partriarch of the tribe of Issachar. A variation is *Issachar*.

Itamar (I-ta-mar) In the Bible, the name of a great artisan. A variation is *Ithamar*.

Itzik (ITZ-ik) A familiar form of Yitzkhak.

Jacob (JAY-cub) Meaning "the supplanter."

Kalev (ka-LEV) This name means "loyal." Leader of the spies in the Land of Canaan sent by Moses while the Israelites were wandering in the desert. Also spelled *Caleb*.

Karmi (kar-MI) Meaning "my vineyard."

Khavakuk (kha-va-KUK) The name of a prophet.

Khaggai (khag-GAI) Meaning "my festivals." The name of a prophet. A variation is *Haggai*.

Khayyim (khay-YIM) or (KHAY-yim) This name means "life." Israeli president Chaim Weitzman and poet Chaim Nachman Bialik share an English variation of this name. Variations include *Haim*, *Chaim*, and *Hayam*.

Khanan (kha-NAN) A name that means "he has been gracious." The name of a shepherd in the popular children's song "Khanan v'Aliza." Variations include *Chanan* and *Hanan*.

Kheyn (KHEYN) Meaning "grace."

Khever (KHE-ver) Meaning "ally; partner."

Khiram (khi-RAM) A Tyrian artisan who helped construct Solomon's Temple. Variations include *Hiram* and *Khirom*.

Khizkiyahu (khiz-ki-YA-hu) Meaning "God is my strength." Good king of Judah. A variation is *Hezekiah*.

Khoni (KHO-ni) This name means "gracious." Variations include *Choni* and *Honi*.

Lev (LEV) Meaning "heart."

Levi (ley-VI) A son of Jacob and patriarch of the tribe of Levi, the priestly tribe.

Malakhi (ma-la-KHI) Meaning "my messenger; my angel." The name of a prophet. A variation is *Malachi*.

Matan (ma-TAN) Meaning "gift."

Mati (MA-ti) A familiar form of Mordekhai.

Matityahu (ma-tit-YA-hu) Meaning "God is a gift." The leader of the revolt against the Hellenistic king Antiochus; father of Judah Maccabee. Variations include *Matthias*, *Matthew* and *Matt*.

Menashe (me-na-SHE) The elder son of Joseph and the patriarch of the tribe of Menashe.

Mikha'el (mi-kha-EL) Meaning "Who is like God." The name of an archangel. Variations include *Michael*, *Mike*, *Mickey*, and *Mick*.

Misha (MI-sha) A form of Mikha'el.

Mordekhai (mor-de-KHAI) Related to the Persian war god Marduk. The name of Queen Esther's cousin (or uncle), who became grand vizier of Persia, noted for his piety. Among contemporary people with this name is Mordecai Richler, Canadian Jewish novelist.

Moshe (mo-SHE) Meaning "drawn out (of the water)." The greatest prophet, leader of the Children of Israel through the desert; he brought the Torah from God to the Jewish people. Noted for his great modesty. Among renowned individuals with this name Moshe ben Maimon, also known as Rambam or Maimonides, the great medieval Torah scholar; and Moshe Dayan, Israeli general and politician. Variations include *Moses* and *Mose*.

Moti (MO-ti) A familiar form of Mordekhai.

Na'aman (na-a-MAN) Meaning "delighter." In the Bible, Assyrian general and proselyte to Judaism.

Nadav (na-DAV) This name means "noble."

Naftali (naf-ta-LI) A son of Jacob and patriarch of the tribe of Naphtali. Variations include *Naphtali* and *Naftule*.

Na'im (na-IM) Signifying "pleasant."

Nakhman (nakh-MAN) A name that means "comforter."

Nakhum (na-KHUM) Meaning "comfort." A prophet. Also *Nahum*.

Nakhshon (nakh-SHON) Meaning "serpent." In legend, the first Israelite to step into the Red Sea.

Nekhemya (ne-KHE-mya) Meaning "God has comforted." The last prophet. A variation is *Nehemiah*.

Natan (na-TAN) Meaning "he gave." A prophet, King David's advisor. Among notable people with this name is Russian immigrant politician Natan Sharansky. Variations include *Nathan*, *Nate*, and *Nat*.

Noakh (NO-wakh) A name that means "rest." The builder of the ark that preserved every species of animal during the Flood. Noted for his humility and love of God.

Noam (no-WAM) Signifying "pleasance."

Ofer (O-fer) A name that means "fawn" or "kid."

Ofir (o-FIR) A legendary land producing fine gold. A variation is *Ophir*.

Ovadya (o-VAD-ya) Meaning "servant of God." A prophet. The name of the chief Sephardi rabbi of Israel. Also *Obadiah*.

Paz (PAZ) Meaning "fine gold."

Peretz (pe-RETZ) This name means "breach." Among those who share this name is former Israeli prime minister Shimon Peres.

Pesakh (pe-SAKH) This name means "passover."

Petakhya (pe-TAKH-ya) Meaning "God has opened."

Pinkhas (pin-KHAS) The name of a zealous priest in the Bible. A variation is *Phineas*.

Rami (RA-mi) A name that means "my exalted one."

Re'uven (re-u-VEN) Meaning "behold" or "a son." Eldest son of Jacob and patriarch of the tribe of Reuben. Variations include *Reuben* and *Ruben*.

Ron (RON) This name means "song."

Roni (RO-ni) A familiar form of Ron.

Roni (ro-NI) A name that means "my song."

Sa'adya (sa-A-dya) Sa'adya Gaon was a famous and revered medieval Torah scholar.

Sha'ul (sha-UL) This name signifies "answered." First king of Israel. A variation is *Saul*.

Shimon (shim-'ON) A son of Jacob and patriarch of the tribe of Simon. Also *Simeon*.

Shimshon (shim-SHON) Meaning "sun." the name of a judge with incredible physical strength. Also *Samson*.

Shlomo (shlo-MO) This name means "peace." Son of King David the king of Israel at the time of its greatest size and power. Noted for his wisdom and wealth. Variations include *Solomon* and *Sol*.

Shmu'el (shmu-EL) Meaning "God has heard." The name of a judge, mentor of Kings Saul and David. Variations include *Samuel* and *Sam*.

Shmuli (SHMU-li) A familiar form of Shmuel.

Sivan (si-VAN) The name of a spring month.

Thomas (TAH-mus) Meaning "twin."

Tzakhi (TZA-khi) A familiar form of Yitzkhak.

Tzefanya (tze-FA-nya) Meaning "God has hidden." A prophet. A variation is *Zephaniah*.

Tzidkiyahu (tzid-ki-YA-hu) Meaning "God is my righteousness." A king of Judah. Variations include *Tzidkiya*, *Zed*, and *Zedekiah*.

Tzvi (TZVI) Meaning "gazelle," this name signifies grace and beauty.

Uri (u-RI) Meaning "my light."

Ya'akov (ya-a-KOV) Meaning "he has supplanted" or "he will supplant." The name for Isaac's second-born son, a patriarch. Variations include *Jacob* and *Jake*.

Yarden (yar-DEN) Signifying "the river Jordan." A variation is *Jordan*.

Yared (ya-RED) Meaning "he will descend." Also *Jared*.

Yaron (ya-RON) This name means "he will sing."

Yehu (ye-HU) Meaning "He is God (God is eternal)." The name of several biblical figures. A varitation is *Jehu*.

Yedidya (Y'-DID-ya) Meaning "beloved of God." Variations include *Jedidiah* and *Jed*.

Yehoshua (ye-ho-SHU-wa) Meaning "God saves." Moses' deputy. Variations include *Joshua*, *Jesus*, and *Yeshua*.

Yehoyakim (ye-ho-ya-KIM) Meaning "God will establish; God will raise." Variations include *Joachim* and *Joaquin*.

Yehuda (ye-hu-DA) A son of Jacob and patriarch of the tribe of Judah, and hence ancestor of most modern Jews.

Yekhi'el (ye-khi-EL) Meaning "God lives."

Yigal (yi-GAL) Meaning "He will redeem."

Yirmiyahu (yir-mi-YA-hu) Meaning "God is my exaltation." Major prophet. Variations include *Jeremiah*, *Jeremy*, *Jerry*, *Jem*, and *Yirmiya*.

Yishai (yi-SHAI) A name that means "wealthy" or "a gift." A variation is *Jesse*.

Yishaiyahu (yi-shai-YA-hu) Meaning "God is salvation." A great prophet. Variations include *Isaiah* and *Yishaiya*.

Yishma'el (yi-shma-EL) Meaning "God has heard." The name of Abraham's son by Hagar and the ancestor of the Arabs. Variations include *Ismael* and *Isma'il*.

Yisra'el (yis-ra-EL) Meaning "God has wrestled." An alternate name given by God to Jacob. Often used in the Bible to refer to the Jewish people and the name of the modern Jewish state. A variation is *Israel*.

Yitro (yi-TRO) Meaning "increase." Moses' father-in-law. A variation is *Jethro*.

Yitz (YITZ) A short form of Yitzkhak.

Yitzkhak (yitz-KHAK) Meaning "she has laughed" or "he will laugh." The name of the son of Abraham. One notable individual with the name is the assassinated Israeli prime minister Yitzhak Rabin, who tried to bring about an Israeli-Palestinian peace. Variations include *Isaac*, *Issac*, *Izak*, *Ike*, *Ikey*, and *Izzy*.

Yo'av (yo-AV) Meaning "God is father." Variations include *Joab*.

Yo'el (yo-EL) Meaning "God is God (God is eternal)." A familiar form is *Yo'eli*.

Yokhanan (yo-kha-NAN) Meaning "God has been gracious." The name of the father of Moses. Variations include *Jochanan*, *Johannes*, *John*, *Johnny*, and *Jack*.

Yona (yo-NA) Meaning "dove." The name of a prophet. A variation is *Jonah*.

Yonatan (yo-na-TAN) Meaning "God has given." David's bosom companion, son of Saul. Variations include *Jonathan*, *Johnathan*, *Jonathon*, *Jon*, and *Yehonatan*.

Yoni (YO-ni) A familiar form of Yonatan and Yona.

Yoram (yo-RAM) Meaning "God is exalted." Variations include *Joram*.

Yosef (yo-SEF) Meaning "he will increase; he shall add." A son of Jacob and Rachel. Variations include *Joseph* and *Joe*.

Yosi (YO-si) A familiar form of Yosef.

Zekharya (ze-KHAR-ya) Meaning "God has remembered." The name of a prophet. Also spelled *Zechariah*.

Zimri (zim-RI) This name has the meaning "my song."

Zvulun (zvu-LUN) A son of Jacob and patriarch of the tribe of Zvulon. A variation is *Zebulon*.

HEBREW: GIRLS

Abigail (a-vi-GAIL) Meaning "father's joy." Abigail was a wife of King David. Among notable people with this name are former first ladies Abigail Adams and Abigail Fillmore, as well as advice columnist Abigail van Buren. Variations include *Abagael, Abagail, Abagale, Abagil, Abbegail, Abbe, Abbegale, Abbegayle, Abbey, Abbi, Abbigale, Abbie, Abby,* and *Abbye*.

Abira (a-bi-RA) A name that means "my strength."

Abra (a-VRA) "Mother of many." A feminine form of Abraham. Variations include *Abame Abree,* and *Abri*.

Adah ('A-da) "Adornment." A variation is *Ada*.

Adena (a-DE-na) "Ornament." Variations include *Adeana, Adeen, Adeena,* and *Aden*.

Adina ('a-DI-na) An alternate form of Adena. Variations include *Adiana, Adiena, Adinah,* and *Adinna*.

Adira (a-di-RA) Meaning "powerful." A variation is *Adirah*.

Afra (af-RA) Meaning "young doe."

Ahava (a-ha-VA) Meaning "beloved." A variation is *Ahivia*.

Aleeza ('a-LI-za) A form of Aliza. Variations include *Aleezah, Alieza,* and *Aliezah*.

Aliya (a-li-YA) Meaning "ascender." Variations include *Alea, Aleah, Alee, Aleea, Aleia, Aleya, Alia, Aliyah,* and *Alya*.

Aliza (a-LI-za) Meaning "joyful." Variations include *Aleeza, Aleezah, Alieza, Aliezah, Alitza,* and *Alizah*.

Amaris (a-ma-RIS) Meaning "promised by God." Variations include *Amarissa, Amarit,* and *Maris*.

Amira (a-MI-ra) This name signifies "speech."

Amissa (a-mi-SA) A name that means "friend." A variation is *Amissah*.

Amita (a-mi-TA) A name that signifies "truth." A variation is *Amity*.

Anais (a-na-IS) Meaning "gracious." Among notable people with this name is author Anais Nin.

Aphra (af-RA) Meaning "dust." Variations include *Afra, Affera,* and *Aphrah*.

Ardi (ar-DI) A short form of Ardith. A variation is *Ardie*.

Ardice (ar-DIS) An alternate form of Ardith. Variations include *Ardis, Artis, Ardiss,* and *Ardys*.

Ardith (ar-DITH) Meaning "blossoming field." Variations include *Ardath, Ardi, Ardice,* and *Ardyth*.

Arella (ar-E-la) Meaning "angel" or "God's messenger." Variations include *Arela* and *Arelle*.

Ariel (ar-i-EL) Meaning "lioness of God." The name of the mermaid princess in *The Little Mermaid*. Also *Aeriale, Aeriel, Aeryal, Aireal,* and *Airial*.

Arin (ar-IN) This name means "enlightened."

Atara (a-TA-ra) A name that has the significance "crown." Variations include *Atarah* and *Atera*.

Atira (a-ti-RA) Meaning "prayer."

Aviva (a-VI-va) Meaning "springlike." Variations include *Avivah, Avivi, Avivice, Avni, Avnit,* and *Avrit*.

Aya (A-ya) This name means "bird."

Ayla (a-ya-LA) Which means "oak tree." Variations include *Aylana, Aylee,* and *Ayleen*.

Barra (BA-ra) Meaning "select." Variations include *Bara* and *Bari*.

Basia (BAT-ya) Meaning "daughter of God." Variations include *Basya, Bathia, Batia,* and *Batya.*

Bathsheba (bat-SHE-va) Meaning "daughter of the oath." Bathsheba was a wife of King David and the mother of Solomon. Variations include Sheba.

Becca (BE-ka) A short form of Rebecca. Variations include *Becka* and *Bekka.*

Bess (BE-si) A familiar form of Elizabeth. Renowned individuals with this name include former first lady Bess Truman, former Miss America Bess Myerson, "Empress of the Blues" Bessie Smith, and aviator Bessie Coleman. Variations include *Bessi, Bessie,* and *Bessy.*

Beth (BETH) Meaning "house of God." A short form of Bethany and Elizabeth. Singer Beth Orton. Variations include *Betha, Bethe,* and *Bethia.*

Bethany (BE-tha-ni) Meaning "house of figs." According to the Christian scriptures, this is the name of the village near Jerusalem where Lazarus lived. Variations include *Beth, Bethane, Bethanee, Bethaney, Bethani, Bethania,* and *Bethanie.*

Betty (BE-ti) A short form of Elizabeth, which means "pledged to God." Former First Lady Betty Ford and actress Betty Garrett are among well-known individuals with this name.

Betula (be-tu-LA) Meaning "girl" or "maiden."

Beulah (be-'u-LA) Meaning "married." A biblical name for the land of Israel. Variations include *Beula, Beulla,* and *Beullah.*

Bina (BI-na) This name means "perception" or "understanding."

Blum (BLUM) Meaning "flower." A variation is *Bluma.*

Cali (KA-li) Meaning "hill" or "fountain" or "spring." Variations include *Calice* and *Calie.*

Carmela (kar-ME-la) Meaning "garden" or "vineyard." The Mount Carmel of the Bible. A variation is *Carmella.*

Cayla (KAY-la) An alternate form of Kayla, which means "crown." Variations include *Cailee, Cailey, Cailie, Caily, Calee, Caly,* and *Caylee.*

Chai (KHAY) This name signifries "life." Variations include *Chae, Chaela, Chaeli,* and *Chaena.*

Chana (KHA-na) An alternate form of Hannah.

Chava (KHA-va) Meaning "life." Among notable people with this name is singer Chava Alberstein. Variations include *Chabah, Chaya,* and *Chayka.*

Chavon (kha-VON) An alternate form of Jane. Variations include *Chavonn* and *Chavonne.*

Daliah (DAL-ya) A name that means "slender branch." Variations include *Dahlia, Dalia,* and *Dalialah.*

Danelle (da-NEL) An alternate form of Danielle. Among notable people with this name is romance author Danelle Harmon. Variations include *Danel, Danele, Danell,* and *Danella.*

Danica (DA-ni-ka) An alternate form of Danielle. One famous Danica is actor Danica McKellar. A variation is *Danika.*

Danielle (da-ni-EL) Meaning "God is my judge." A feminine form of Daniel. Author Danielle Steel is a giant is the romance genre. Variations include *Daneal, Daneala, Daneale, Danee, Daneil, Daneille, Dani, Dania, Daniah, Danial, Danialle, Danie, Daniele, Danielka, Daniella, Danna, Danne, Dannee, Danni,* and *Danya.*

Danit (da-NIT) An alternate form of Danielle. Variations include *Danett, Danis, Danisha, Daniss,* and *Danita.*

Davida (da-VI-da) Meaning "beloved." A feminine form of David. Variations include *Daveta, Davetta, Davette, Davika, Davisha,* and *Davita.*

Deborah (DVO-ra) Meaning "bee." Deborah was a great Old Testament judge. Well-known actresses with this name include Deborah Kerr, who lit up the screen in a bygone era. Variaions include *Debbey, Debbi, Debbie, Debi,* and *Debie.*

Delilah (dli-LA)   This name means "flirt." Also *Dalilah*.

Dena (DE-na)   An alternate form of Dinah.

Denae (de-NEY)   An alternate form of Dena. Variations include *Denaé*, *Denay*, *Deneé*, and *Dene*.

Devora (DVO-ra)   An alternate form of Deborah. Variations include *Deva*, *Devorah*, *Devra*, and *Devrah*.

Dinah (DI-na)   Meaning "justified." The name of a daughter of the biblical patriarch Jacob. Among famous Dinahs are singers Dinah Shore and Dinah Washington. Variations include *Dina*, *Dyna*, and *Dynah*.

Diza (DI-tza)   Meaning "joy." Variations include *Ditza*, *Ditzah*, and *Dizah*.

Edna (ED-na)   Meaning "enjoyment." Noteworthy individuals with this name include poet Edna St. Vincent Millay, actor Edna Mae Oliver, as well as novelist and playwright Edna Ferber. Variations include *Ednah*, *Edneisha*, and *Ednita*.

Eleora (el-i-O-ra)   Meaning "the Lord is my light." A variation is *Eliora*.

Eliana (el-i-A-na)   Meaning "the Lord is my God." A feminine form of Eli and Elijah. Variations include *Elianna*, *Elliane*, *Ellianna*, *Iliana*, *Liana*, and *Liane*.

Elicia (e-LIS-ya)   An alternate form of Eliza. A variation is *Ellicia*.

Eliza (e-LAY-za)   A short form of Elizabeth, meaning "consecrated to God." Among notable people with this name are former first lady Eliza Johnson (wife of Andrew Johnson) and poet Eliza Acton. Variations include Aliza, Elizalina, Elize, and Elizea.

Elizabeth (e-LI-za-beth)   Meaning "consecrated to God." This is the name of the mother of John the Baptist. A wildly popular name and there are many celebrated women who share this name, including former first ladies Elizabeth Kortright Monroe, Elizabeth Virginia Wallace Truman; and actress Elizabeth Taylor, queens Elizabeth I and II. Variations include *Bess, Beth, Betsy, Betty, Eliabeth, Elisa, Elisabet,*

Elisabeta, Elisabeth, Elisabethe, Elisabetta, Elisabette, Elise, Elisebet, Elsa, Ilse, Libby, Liese, Liesel, Lisa, Lisette, Lissa, Lissie, Liz, Liza, Lizabeta, Lizabeth, Lizzy, and *Yelisabeta*.

Elsa (EL-sa)   A short form of Elizabeth. Among notable people with this name are actor Elsa Lanchester and author Elsa Maxwell.

Emmanuelle (e-ma-nu-EL)   Meaning "God is with us." A feminine form of Emmanuel. One famous person with this name is actress Emmanuelle Béart. Variations include *Emmanuela* and *Emmanuella*.

Ethana (e-THA-na)   This name signifies "strong" or "firm." A feminine form of Ethan.

Eve (IV)   An alternate form of Chava, which signifies "life." According to the Hebrew Scriptures, this is the name of the first woman created by God. Noteworthy Eves include actor Eve Arden and photographer Eve Arnold.

Gada (GA-da)   Meaning "fortunate." A variation is *Gadah*.

Gail (GAYL)   A short form of Abigail. Famous athletes with this name are track and field Olympic great Gail Deevers and golfer Gail Graham.

Ganya (GAN-ya)   Meaning "garden of the Lord." The name of a character in Dostoyevsky's *The Idiot*. Variations include *Gana*, *Gani*, and *Gania*.

Gavriella (gav-ri-E-la)   Meaning "God is my strength." Variations include *Gavila*, *Gavilla*, *Gavriela*, *Gavrielle*, *Gavrila*, and *Gavrilla*.

Geela (GI-la)   This name means "joyful." Among notable people with this name is sociologist Gila Hayim. Variations include *Gela* and *Gila*.

Geva (GE-va)   Meaning "hill." A variation is *Gevah*.

Gilana (gi-LA-na)   A name that means "joyful." Variations include *Gilah*.

Gisa (GI-sa)   Meaning "carved stone." Variations include *Gazit* and *Gissa*.

Gurit (gu-RIT)   This name has the significance of "innocent baby."

Hadara (ha-DA-ra) Meaning "adorned with beauty." Variations include *Hadar* and *Hadarah*.

Hadassah (ha-DA-sa) Meaning "myrtle tree."

Hagar (ha-GAR) Meaning "forsaken" or "stranger." The name of Sarah's handmaiden, the mother of Ishmael. Variations include *Haggar*.

Hania (HAN-ya) A name that signifies "resting place." A variation is *Haniya*.

Hannah (KHA-na) Meaning "grace." In the Hebrew Scriptures, this is the name of the mother of the prophet Samuel. Noteworthy individuals named Hannah include former first lady Hannah Van Buren and writer Hannah Bat-Shahar. Variations include *Hana, Hanna, Hanneke, Hannele,* and *Hanni*.

Hava (KHA-va) See Chava.

Haviva (kha-VI-va) Meaning "beloved." Variations include *Hava, Havah, Havelah,* and *Havvah*.

Hinda (HIN-da) This name means "doe." Variations include *Hindey, Hindie,* and *Hindy*.

Ikia (IK-ya) A name that means "God is my salvation."

Ilana (i-LA-na) Meaning "tree." Among notable people with this name is artist Ilana Raviv. Variations include *Elana, Eleana, Ilane, Illani,* and *Ilainie*.

Ilisha (i-LI-sha) An alternate form of Alisha, meaning "truth." Variations include *Illishia, Illycia, Ilysha, Illyshia,* and *Lisha*.

Ivria (iv-ri-YA) Meaning "from the land of Abraham." Variations include *Ivriah* and *Ivrit*.

Jacobi (ya-KO-bi) Meaning "supplanter." A feminine form of Jacob. Variations include *Coby, Jacoba, Jacobette,* and *Jacobina*.

Jael (ya-'EL) This name means "mountain goat." Variations include *Jaelee, Jaelle, Jaelynn, Jayel,* and *Yael*.

Jaffa (YA-fa) An alternate form of Yaffa. Variations include *Jaffice, Jaffit,* and *Jafit*.

Jamie (JEY-mi) Meaning "supplanter" or "substitute." One popular Jamie is actress Jamie Lee Curtis who went from horror movies to comedies. A variation is *Jami*.

Jane (JEYN) Meaning "God is gracious." A feminine form of John. Renowned Janes include novelist Jane Austen; former first lady Jane Pierce; actresses Jane Fonda and Jane Seymour; frontierswoman Martha (Calamity) Jane Burke; and film director Jane Campion. Variations include *Jaine, Jan, Jayne,* and *Jean*.

Janice (JA-nis) An alternate form of Jane. A notable individual with this name was soul singer Janis Joplin. Variations include *Janess, Janessa, Janesse, Jenice,* and *Jenise*.

Janna (YA-na) A short form of Johana, meaning "God's gracious gift." Tennis player Janna Kandar is one popular Janna.

Jardena (yar-DE-na) An alternate form of Jordan.

Jayna (JEY-na) An alternate form of Jane. A variation is *Jaynae*.

Jem (JEM) A short form of Jemima. Variations include *Gem, Jemi,* and *Jemie*.

Jemima (je-MAY-ma) This name has the significance of "dove."

Jemma (JE-ma) A short form of Jemima.

Jerusha (ye-ru-SHA) Meaning "a possession." The name of the wife of King Uzziah, whose story is found in the Hebrew Scriptures. Variations include *Jerushah* and *Yerusha*.

Jessica (JE-si-ka) Meaning "she sees." A feminine form of Jesse. A name adapted from the Hebrew by Shakespeare for a character in his *The Merchant of Venice*. One notable Jessica is actress Jessica Tandy, who certainly played Shakespearean roles, but is better known for acting in modern works, the original Broadway production of *A Streetcar Named Desire* among them. Variations include *Gessica Jesica, Jesika, Jessa, Jessah, Jessca, Jesscia, Jesseca, Jessia,* and *Yessica*.

Jessie (JE-si) A short form of Jessica. Among notable people with this name is opera star Jessye Norman. Variations include *Jesse, Jessia, Jessey,* and *Jessye*.

Jésusa (khe-ZU-sa)   This name means "God is my salvation."

Jimi (JI-mi)   A feminine form of Jacob, which means "he will supplant."

Joan (JON)   An alternate form of Jane, which means "God is gracious." Illustrious Joans include Joan of Arc, saint and warrior for France; Hollywood actresses Joan Crawford and Joan Fontaine; and folk singer Joan Baez. Variations include *Jean, Joane, Joanel, Joanelle, Joanie, Joann, Joanne, Juanita,* and *Siobahn.*

Joaquina (khua-KI-na)   "God will establish." Also *Joaquine.*

Joby (JO-bi)   A name that means "afflicted." A feminine form of *Job.*

Joella (yo-E-la)   Meaning "the Lord is willing." Variations include *Jola.*

Joelle (yo-EL)   Meaning "the Lord is God." A feminine form of Joel. Among notable people with this name is performance artist "Joelle." Variations include *Joelee, Joeleen, Joeline,* and *Joell.*

Jolene (jo-LIN)   Meaning "God will increase." One distinguished Jolene is former congresswoman Jolene Unsoeld. Variations include *Jo, Jolaine, Jolean, Joleen, Jolena,* and *Joline.*

Jonina (yo-NI-na)   This name means "dove." A feminine form of Jonah. Variations include *Jona, Jonika, Joniqua, Jonita, Jonnina,* and *Yonina.*

Jora (YO-ra)   A name that signifies "autumn rain." Also *Jorah.*

Jordan (yar-DEN)   Meaning "descend." Supermodel Jordan follows the trend of single names among celebrities. Variations include *Jordain, Jordana, Jordane, Jordanna, Jorden, Jordenne,* and *Jordi.*

Jordana (jor-DA-na)   An alternate form of Jordan. Variations include *Jordann, Jordanne, Jourdana, Jourdann, Jourdanna,* and *Jourdanne.*

Jori (JO-ri)   A familiar form of Jordan. Variations include *Jorai, Jorea, Joree, Jorie, Jorey, Jorian, Jorin, Jorina, Jorine, Jorita, Jorrian, Jorrie, Jorry,* and *Jory.*

Josie (JO-si)   A familiar form of Josephine. Variations include *Josee, Josey, Josi,* and *Josy.*

Judith (ye-hu-DIT)   Meaning "Jewish woman." A feminine form of Judah. Judith is the name of a legendary Hebrew warrior whose existence has not been proven. Variations include *Giuditta, Jodi, Jody, Judana, Judine, Judit, Judita, Juditha, Judithe, Judy, Yehudit,* and *Yudita.*

Judy (JU-di)   A familiar form of Judith. Among celebrated people with this name are entertainer Judy Garland, folk singer Judy Collins, and congresswoman Judy Biggert. Variations include *Judi, Judie,* and *Judye.*

Kaela (ka-E-la)   A name that signifies "beloved sweetheart." Variations include *Kaelah, Kayla,* and *Kaylah.*

Kaila (KAY-la)   Which means "laurel; crown." Variations include *Kailah, Kailee, Kailey,* and *Kayla.*

Karmell (kar-MEL)   An alternate form of Carmela, which menas "garden" or "vineyard." Variations include *Karmeita, Karmela, Karmelina,* and *Karmella.*

Katriel (ka-tri-EL)   Meaning "God is my crown." Variations include *Katri, Katrie, Katry,* and *Katryel.*

Kayla (KAY-la)   An alternate form of Kaela and Kaila, meaning "laurel" or "crown." Variations include *Kaela, Kaila,* and *Kayle.*

Kayleen (kay-LIN)   An alternate form of Kayla, which means "beloved" or "sweetheart." Variations include *Kaeleen, Kaelen, Kaelene* and *Kaylene.*

Kelila (kli-LA)   Meaning "crown" or "laurel." Variations include *Kelula.*

Kenya (KEN-ya)   Meaning "an animal is born." Kenya is also the name of a country in East Africa. Variations include *Keenya, Kenia, Kenja.*

Keren (KE-ren)   Meaning "animal's horn." Variations include *Kerrin* and *Keryn.*

Keziah (KHEZ-ya)   A cinnamon-producing shrub. The name of one of the daughters of Job.

Variations include *Kazia, Kaziah, Ketzi, Ketzia, Ketziah, Kezi,* and *Kezia.*

Kitra (kit-RA)   This name has the meaning "crowned."

Laela (la-E-la)   An alternate form of Leila. Variations include *Layla* and *Laylah.*

Layla (LAY-la)   An alternate form of Leila. Variations include *Layli* and *Laylie.*

Leah (LE-a)   Meaning "weary." One of Jacob's two wives. Among well-known individuals with this name is writer Leah Goldberg. Variations include *Lea, Lee, Leea, Leeah, Leia,* and *Leigh.*

Leeza (LI-za)   Meaning "joyful." A short form of Aleeza. One popular Leeza is television personality Leeza Gibbons, who came to fame on *Entertainment Tonight.*

Leila (LEY-la)   Signifying "dark beauty" or "night."

Levana (le-VA-na)   Meaning "the moon." Variations include *Lewana* and *Livana.*

Levia (le-VI-ya)   A name that means "joined" or "attached."

Levona (le-VO-na)   Meaning "spice, incense." Variations include *Leavonia, Levonat,* and *Livona.*

Lewana (le-VA-na)   An alternate form of Levana. Variations include *Lebhanah* and *Lewanna.*

Liana (li-A-na)   A short form of Eliana, which means "the Lord is my God." Variations include *Liane* and *Lianne.*

Libby (LI-bi)   A familiar form of Elizabeth, meaning "consecrated to God."

Liora (li-O-ra)   This name means "light."

Liron (li-RON)   Meaning "my song." Variations include *Leron, Lerone,* and *Ikone.*

Lisa (LI-za)   A form of Elizabeth. Actress Lisa Bonet was one of Cosby's kids.

Lisha (LI-sha)   A short form of *Alisha, Efisha,* and *Ilisha.*

Liviya (le-vi-YA)   Meaning "brave lioness" or "regal crown." Variations include *Leviya, Levya,* and *Livya.*

Luann (lu-AN)   Meaning "graceful woman warrior." Among notable people with this name is actress Luann Lee.

Magdalene (mag-da-len)   This name means "from magdala." In the Bible, Mary Magdalene is a repentant prostitute, befriended by Jesus. A variation is *Magdalen.*

Mahira (me-HI-ra)   Meaning "energetic." A variation is *Mahri.*

Malina (ma-LI-na)   A name that means "tower."

Malka (MAL-ka)   Meaning "queen." Singer Malka Spigel is one of today's popular Malkas.

Mangena (man-gi-NA)   Meaning "song" or "melody." A variation is *Mangina.*

Maria (ma-RI-ya)   Meaning "bitter" or "sea of bitterness." Educator Maria Montessori, opera singer Maria Callas, and prima ballerina Maria Tallchief are among distinguished women with this name. A variation is *Marie.*

Mariah (ma-RI-ya)   An alternate form of Maria. One famous Mariah is singer Mariah Carey. Variations include *Maraia, Maraya, Mariyah, Marriah,* and *Moriah.*

Mariam (MAR-yam)   An alternate form of Miriam. Variations include *Maryam, Mariem,* and *Meryam.*

Marilla (ma-RI-la)   A form of Mary. Variations include *Marella* and *Marelle.*

Marilyn (MA-ri-lin)   Meaning "Mary's descendents." Among extremely popular Marilyns of the 20th century is actress Marilyn Monroe, who brought comedy and vulnerability to a pretty face and baby voice.

Marit (ma-RIT)   This name means "lady." A variation is *Marita.*

Marnina (mar-ni-NA)   A name that means "rejoice."

Mary (ME-ri)   Meaning "bitter" or "sea of bitterness." Distinguished Marys inlcude author Mary Shelley, former first lady Mary Todd Lincoln, astronomer Mary Somerville, first-century chemist Mary Hebraea, and singer Mary O'Brien (better known as Dusty Springfield). Variations include *Maire, Mare, Mari, Maria, Marie, Marika, Marita, Marlo, Miriam,* and *Mirjam.*

Matana (ma-ta-NA) Meaning "gift." A variation is *Matat.*

Mathena (ma-ta-NA) Meaning "gift of God."

Mattea (ma-te-A) Meaning "gift of God." Variations include *Matea, Mathea, Mathia, Matia, Matthia,* and *Mattia.*

Mazel (ma-ZAL) This name signifies "lucky."

Mehira (me-hi-RA) Meaning "speedy" or "energetic." Also *Mahira.*

Mehitabel (me-khi-ta-BEL) Meaning "benefited by trusting God." Archy the cockroach's feline friend in Don Marquis's *Archy and Mehitabel.* Variations include *Mehetabel, Mehitabelle, Hetty,* and *Hitty.*

Meira (me-I-ra) A name that has the significance "light." Also *Meera.*

Micah (MI-kha) A short form of Michaela. The name of one of the prophets from the Hebrew Scriptures. Variations include *Meka, Mica, Mika, Myca,* and *Mycah.*

Michaela (mi-kha-E-la) Meaning "Who is like the Lord?" A feminine form of Michael. Variations include *Machaela, Makayla, Meecah, Mia, Micaela, Michael, Michaila, Michal, Michala,* and *Micheal.*

Mikaela (mi-kha-E-la) An alternate form of Michaela. Variations include *Mekaela, Mekala Mekayla, Mickael, Mickaela, Mickala, Mickalla,* and *Mikail.*

Milena (mi-LE-na) A form of Magdalene. The name of author Franz Kafka's sister, to whom he wrote a series of letters that were later published.

Mireil (mi-ri-EL) This name means "God spoke."

Miriam (mi-ri-YAM) The original form of the name Mary, which means "bitter" or "sea of bitterness." Among famous people with this name is singer Miriam Makeba. Variations include *Mariame, Maruca, Mimi, Miriama, Mirian, Mirjam, Mirriam, Miryam,* and *Myriam.*

Moriah (mo-ri-YA) Meaning "God is my teacher."

Moselle (mo-ZEL) This name means "drawn from the water." A feminine form of Moses.

Nagida (na-gi-DA) Meaning "prosperous." Variations include *Nagda* and *Nageeda.*

Naomi (ne-o-MI) Signifying "pleasant" or "beautiful." The name of the mother-in-law of Ruth from the Hebrew Scriptures. Celebrity Naomis include supermodel Naomi Campbell, who personifies beauty, while author Naomi Wolf comments upon it. Variations include *Naoma, Naomia, Naomie, Naomy, Neomi, Noami,* and *Noemi.*

Nasya (NAS-ya) A name that has the significance of "miracle." Variations include *Nasia.*

Natania (na-tan-YA) Meaning "gift of God." A feminine form of Nathan. Variations include *Natie, Nathania, Nathenia,* and *Netania.*

Nava (NA-va) A name that signifies "beautiful" or "pleasant." Variations include *Navah, Naveh,* and *Navit.*

Neta (NE-ta) Meaning "plant" or "shrub." Variations include *Netia, Netta,* and *Nettia.*

Nima (ni-MA) This name means "thread."

Nina (NI-na) A familiar form of Hannah, which means "grace." Among the notable people with this name is actress Nina Foch.

Nirel (nir-EL) A name that signifies "light of God."

Niria (nir-YA) This name has the meaning "plow."

Nissa (NI-sa) Meaning "sign" or "emblem."

Nita (NI-ta) Meaning "planter." One distinguished Nita is congresswoman Nita Lowey, a rising star in Democratic Party circles.

Nitza (NI-tza) A name that means "flower bud." Variations include *Nitzah, Nitzana, Nitzanit, Niza,* and *Nizah.*

Nizana (ni-TZA-na) An alternate form of Nitza. Variations include *Nitzana*, *Nitzania*, and *Zana*.

Noemi (no-e-MI) An alternate form of Naomi. Variations include *Noemie*, *Nohemi*, and *Nomi*.

Noga (NO-ga) This means "morning light."

Noya (NO-ya) Meaning "ornament."

Nura (NU-ra) A name signifying "light." Variations include *Noor*, *Nour*, *Noura*, and *Nur*.

Nuria (nur-YA) Meaning "the Lord's light." Variations include *Nuri*, *Nuriel*, and *Nurin*.

Nurita (nu-RIT) Signifies a flower with red and yellow blossoms. A varitation is *Nurit*.

Odeda (o-DE-da) This name means "strong" or "courageous."

Odera (o-DE-ra) A name that has the significance of "plough."

Ofira (o-FI-ra) Meaning "gold. " Variations include *Ofarrah* and *Ophira*.

Ofra (OF-ra) This name means "young deer." A variation is *Ofrat*.

Ohanna (o-KHA-na) Meaning "God's gracious gift."

Oma (O-ma) A name that means "reverent."

Oprah (OF-ra) An alternate form of Orpah. One of today's enormously popular Oprahs is actress, talk-show host Oprah Winfrey. Variations include *Ophra*, *Ophrah,* and *Opra*.

Oralee (o-RA-li) This means "the Lord is my light." Variations include *Orali*, *Orlee*, *Orli*, and *Orly*.

Orinda (o-RIN-da) A name that has the meaning "pine tree."

Ornice (or-NIS) Meaning "cedar tree."

Orpah (or-PA) Meaning "a fawn." Variations include *Orpa*, *Orpha*, and *Orphie*.

Oz (OZ) This name means "strength."

Ozara (o-ZA-ra) Signifying "treasure" or "wealth."

Pazia (paz-YA) Meaning "golden." Variations include *Paz*, *Paza*, *Pazice*, and *Pazit*.

Poria (po-ri-YA) Meaning "fruitful." Also *Pora*.

Rachel (ra-KHEL) This name has the meaning "innocence of a lamb." The name of the wife of the biblical patriarch Jacob. Among renowned Rachels are Rachel Carson and former first lady Rachel Jackson. Variations include *Rae*, *Racha*, *Rachael*, *Rachaele*, *Rachaell*, *Rachal*, *Rochelle*, and *Shelley*.

Raizel (RAY-zel) A form of Rose. Variations include *Rayzil* and *Razil*.

Rama (RA-ma) Meaning "lofty" or "exalted."

Ranita (ra-NI-ta) Meaning "song." Variations include *Ranit* and *Ranice*.

Raphaela (re-fa-E-la) A name that signifies "healed by God." The name of one of the four archangels. A variation is *Rafaella*.

Raya (RA-ya) Meaning "friend." Variations include *Raia*, *Raiah*, *Ray*, and *Rayah*.

Razi (RA-zi) "Secretive."

Reba (RI-ba) A short form of Rebecca. One of today's popular Rebas is country singer Reba McIntyre. Variations include *Rabah*, *Reeba*, *Rheba Reva*, and *Riva*.

Rebecca (riv-KA) Meaning "bound" or "servant of God." The wife of the biblical patriarch Isaac. Among notable people with this name are author Rebecca West, actress Rebecca de Mornay, and model Rebecca Romijn. Variations include *Becca*, *Becky*, *Reba*, *Rebbecca*, *Rebeca*, *Rebeccah*, *Riva*, and *Rivka*.

Rebi (RE-bi) A familiar form of Rebecca. Variations include *Rebbie*, *Rebe*, and *Reby*.

Rena (RI-na) Meaning "melody." A familiar form of Irene, Regina, Renata, Sabrina, and Serena. Pro wrestler Sable's given name is Rena Mero. Variations include *Reena*, *Rina*, and *Rinna*.

Reubena (re-u-VE-na) This name means "behold a daughter." A feminine form of

Reuben. Variations include *Reubina, Reuvena, Rubena,* and *Rubenia.*

Rimona (ri-MO-na) Meaning "pomegranate." Variations include *Mona.*

Rinah (RI-na) Meaning "joyful." A variation is *Rina.*

Rishona (ri-sho-NA) A name that means "first."

Riva (RI-va) A short form of Rebecca.

Rivka (riv-KA) A short form of Rebecca. Variations include *Rivca, Rivcah,* and *Rivkah.*

Rochelle (ra-KHEL) An alternate form of Rachel.

Ronli (RON-li) This name signifies "joyful."

Ruth (RUT) This name means "friendship." The biblical Ruth was a model of loyalty. Illustrious women with this name are actress and writer Ruth Gordon, actress Ruth Roman, and Supreme Court Justice Ruth Bader-Ginsberg. Variations include *Ruthi, Ruthie,* and *Ruthy.*

Sabra (SAB-ra) This name signifies "fruit of the thorny cactus." Native Israelis are sometimes known as Sabras—like the thorny cactus, rugged on the outside, sweet on the inside.

Sade (SHA-dey) An alternate form of Chadee and Sarah. Contemporary popular singer Sade is one of those people who can get away with one name. A variation is *Sadee.*

Sadia (SEY-di) A familiar form of Sarah. Among notable people with this name is actor Sada Thompson. Variation include *Sada, Sadah, Sady, Sadye, Saidee,* and *Saydie.*

Samala (sa-MA-la) This name means "asked of God." Variations include *Samale* and *Sammala.*

Samantha (sa-MAN-tha) Meaning "listener." Among well-known individuals with this name is actress Samantha Eggar.

Sameh (sa-ME) Meaning "listener."

Sami (SA-mi) A short form of Samantha and Samuela.

Samuela (shmu-E-la) Meaning "told by God." A feminine form of Samuel. Variations include *Samala, Samelia, Samella,* and *Samielle.*

Sanne (SA-ne) A name that means "lily." A variation is *Sanneen.*

Sapphira (sa-FI-ra) A form of Sapphire. Variations include *Safira, Saphira,* and *Sephira.*

Sarah (SA-ra) This name means "princess." The name of the wife of Abraham and mother of Isaac. Distinguished individuals with this name include former first lady Sarah Polk, astronomer Sarah F. Whiting, as well as actresses Sarah Bernhardt and Sarah Michelle Gellar. Variations include *Sally, Sara, Saree, Sharai, Shari, Zara,* and *Zarita.*

Sarina (sa-RI-na) A familiar form of Sarah. Variations include *Sareen, Sarena,* and *Sarene.*

Sarita (sa-RI-ta) A familiar form of Sarah. Variations include *Saretta, Sarette,* and *Saritia.*

Selima (sa-LI-ma) A name that means "peaceful." A feminine form of Solomon. Variations include *Selerna, Selemah,* and *Selimah.*

Serafina (se-ra-FI-na) Signifying "burning" or "ardent." From Seraphim, the highest order of angels in heaven. Variations include *Sarafina, Serafine, Seraphe, Seraphin, Seraphina,* and *Seraphine.*

Shaina (SHEY-na) Meaning "beautiful." Variations include *Shainah, Shaine, Shainna, Shanie, Shayna, Shayndel, Sheina,* and *Sheindel.*

Shamira (sha-MI-ra) Meaning "precious stone." A feminine form of Shamir.

Shara (SHA-ra) A form of *Sharon.* Variations incluse *Shaara, Sharal, Sharala,* and *Sharalee.*

Sharai (sa-RAI) Meaning "princess." An alternate form of Sarah. Variations include *Sharae, Sharah,* and *Sharaiah.*

Sharna (SHAR-na) An alternate form of Sharon. Variations include *Sharnae, Sharnay, Sharne, Sharnea,* and *Sharnee.*

Sharon (sha-RON) Meaning "desert plain." One of today's popular Sharons is actor Sharon Stone who has gone from ingenue to sophisticate in the movies. Variations include *Shaaron, Shara, Sharai, Sharan, Shareen, Sharen,* and *Shari.*

Sharonda (sha-RON-da) An alternate form of Sharon. Variations include *Sharronda, Sheronda,* and *Sherrhonda.*

Sharrona (sha-RO-na) An alternate form of Sharon. Variations include *Sharona, Sharone, Sharonia,* and *Sharony.*

Shayna (SHEY-na) Meaning "beautiful." Well-known people with this name include television journalist Shaina Alexander. Variations include *Shaina, Shayne, Shaynee, Shayney,* and *Shayni.*

Sheba (SHI-ba) A short form of Bathsheba, which means "daughter of the earth." Variations include *Saba, Sabah, Shebah,* and *Sheeba.*

Sheena (SHI-na) Meaning "God is gracious." Singer Sheena Easton is one popular Sheena from the 1980s.

Shera (SHI-ra) Meaning "light." Variations include *Sheera, Sheerah, Sherae, Sherah, Sheralee, Sheralle,* and *Sheralyn.*

Shifra (SHIF-ra) A name that means "beautiful." Variations include *Schifra* and *Shifrah.*

Shilo (shi-LO) Meaning "God's gift." A site near Jerusalem where the Ark of the Covenant was kept. A variation is *Shiloh.*

Shira (SHI-ra) Meaning "song." A noteworthy individual with this name is author Shira Gorshman.

Shoshana (sho-SHA-na) An alternate form of Susan, meaning "lily." Among notable people with this name is Shoshana Lonstein, who caught the public eye as girlfriend of Jerry Seinfeld and stayed in the eye with a line of lingerie. Variations include *Shosha, Shoshan, Shoshanah,* and *Shoshanha.*

Shulamith (shu-la-MIT) Meaning "peaceful." Among notable people with this name is author Shulamith Hareven. Variations include *Shulamit* and *Sulamith.*

Sidonia (si-DON-ya) A name that means "enticing."

Simcha (SIM-cha) Meaning "joyful."

Simone (si-MON) Meaning "God heard." Well-known Simones are pioneering feminist, author Simone de Beauvoir and actress Simone Signoret.

Sue (SU) A short form of Susan and Susanna. Among women who share this name are mystery writer Sue Grafton and fashion designer Sue Rowe. Variations include *Suann* and *Suanna.*

Sula (SU-la) A short form of Shulamith and Ursula.

Susan (SU-zan) This name means "lily." Noteworthy Susans include feminist Susan B. Anthony who was immortalized on a dollar coin, as well as actresses Susan Hayward, Susan Sarandon, and Susan Dey. Variations include *Shoshana, Sosanna, Sue, Suesan, Sueva, Suisan, Suke,* and *Susann.*

Susanna (su-ZA-na) An alternate form of Susan. Among notable people with this name is philosopher Susanne Langer. Variations include *Sue, Suesanna, Susana, Susanah, Susanka, Susanne, Susette,* and *Susie.*

Tabitha (TA-bi-tha) A name that means "gazelle." The name of a little girl in the Christian Scriptures whom Jesus raised from the dead. Distinguished individuals with this name include Tabitha Soren, a journalist who came to fame working for MTV. Variations include *Tabatha, Tabbee, Tabbetha, Tabbey, Tabbi, Tabble,* and *Tabbitha.*

Takenya (ta-KEN-ya) Meaning "animal horn."

Tamara (ta-MA-ra) Meaning "palm tree." Among the noteworthy people with this name are artist Tamara De Lempicka and film director Tamara Jenkins. Variations include *Tamar, Tamarii, Tamarah,* and *Tamaria.*

Tameka (ta-ME-ka) A name that means "twin." Variations include *Tameca, Tamecia, Tamecka, Tameeka,* and *Tamekia.*

Tamma (TA-ma) This name signifies "perfect."

Tammy (TA-mi) A familiar form of Tamara. Famous Tammys include country singer Tammy Wynette and congresswoman Tammy Baldwin.

Tamra (TAM-ra)   A short form of Tamara. Variations include *Tammra* and *Tamrah*.

Tara (TA-ra)   Meaning "throw" or "carry."

Temira (TMI-ra)   A name that signifies "tall." Variations include *Temora* and *Timora*.

Thirza (TIR-tza)   Signifying "pleasant." Variations include *Therza*, *Thirsa*, *Thirzah*, *Thursa*, and *Thurza*.

Thomasina (to-ma-SI-na)   Meaning "twin." A feminine form of Thomas. Variations include *Tamassa*, *Tammy*, *Thomasa*, *Thomasia*, *Thomasin*, *Thomasine*, and *Thomazine*.

Tivona (ti-VO-na)   This name means "lover of nature."

Tobi (TO-bi)   Meaning "God is good." A feminine form of Tobias. Variations include *Tobe*, *Tobee*, and *Tobey*.

Tommie (TO-mi)   A short form of Thomasina. Variations include *Tomme*, *Tommi*, *Tommia*, and *Tommy*.

Tovah (TO-va)   Meaning "good." Among famous people with this name is actress Tovah Feldshuh. Variations include *Tova* and *Tovia*.

Urit (u-RIT)   Meaning "bright." Variations include *Urice*.

Urk (URK)   This name means "poetic" or "lyrical."

Varda (VAR-da)   This name means "rose." Variations include *Vadit*, *Vardia*, *Vardice*, *Vardina*, and *Vardis*.

Yachne (YAKH-ne)   Meaning "hospitable."

Yael (ya-'EL)   A name signifying "strength of God." Among distinguished Yaels is Yael Dayan, an Israeli parliament member and author. Variations include *Jael*, *Vaella*, *Yaeli*, and *Yeala*.

Yaffa (YA-fa)   Meaning "beautiful." Variations include *Jaffa* and *Yaffit*.

Yarkona (yar-KO-na)   Signifying "green."

Yehudit (ye-hu-DIT)   An alternate form of Judith. Among notable people with this name is author Yehuudit Hendel. Variations include *Yudit*, *Yudita*, and *Yuta*.

Yeira (ye-i-RA)   This name means "light."

Yessica (YE-si-ka)   An alternate form of Jessica. Variations include *Yessika* and *Yesyka*.

Yoanna (yo-A-na)   An alternate form of Joanna. Variations include *Yoana*, *Yohana*, *Yohanka*, *Yohanna*, and *Yohannah*.

Yonina (yo-NI-na)   An alternate form of Jonina. Variations include *Yona* and *Yonah*.

Yosepha (yo-SE-fa)   A feminine form of Joseph, which means "he will increase." Variations include *Yosefa*, *Yosifa*, and *Yuseffa*.

Yovela (yo-VE-la)   Meaning "rejoicing."

Zacharie (za-KHA-ri)   Meaning "remembered by God." A feminine form of Zachariah. Variations include *Zacari*, *Zacceaus*, and *Zacchaea*.

Zahar (za-HAR)   This name means "daybreak" or "dawn."

Zahavah (ze-HA-va)   Meaning "golden." Variations include *Zahava*, *Zehuva*, and *Zehavit*.

Zara (ZA-ra)   An alternate form of Sarah. Variations include *Zaira*, *Zarah*, *Zaree*, *Zareen*, and *Zareena*.

Zayit (ZA-yit)   This name has the meaning "olive."

Zemirah (zmi-RA)   A name that means "song of joy."

Zera (ZE-ra)   Meaning "seeds."

Zilla (TZI-la)   Meaning "shadow." Variation includes *Zila*, *Zillah*, and *Zylla*.

Zilpah (zil-PA)   Meaning "dignified." Variations include *Zilpha* and *Zylpha*.

Zimra (zim-RA)   Meaning "song of praise." Variations include *Zamora*, *Zemira*, and *Zemora*.

Zipporah (tzi-PO-ra)   Signifying "bird." The name of the wife of Moses. Variations include *Zipora*, *Ziporah*, and *Zipporia*.

Ziva (ZI-va)   Meaning "splendour" or "radiance." Variations include *Zeeva*, *Ziv*, *Zivanka*, and *Zivit*.

Zohar (ZO-har)   Meaning "shining" or "brilliant." Variations include *Zoheret* and *Zohra*.

Iran

In this territory once known as Persia lives an Indo-European group related to the Aryans of India, having supplanted an earlier agricultural civilization, and having emigrated from the East during the second millennium B.C. In 549 B.C., Cyrus the Great united the Medes and the Persians to form the Persian Empire; and in 538 B.C., he succeeded in conquering Babylonia and restored Jerusalem to the Jews. Colonizing Arabs from Damascus brought Islam to Persia in the seventh century of this millennium, replacing the indigenous religion of Zoroastrianism.

Names in Iran reflect the unique nature of the predominant language, Farsi (or Persian), which despite its use of Arabic script is not related to the Semitic group of languages. Children's names in Iran are derived from religious or historical sources, and, as in many Islamic countries, must be officially sanctioned, such as Muhammad, Ebrahim, Kourosh, Farhad, or Hamid. Among well-known Iranians is the internationally acclaimed filmmaker Abbas Kiarostami.

IRAN: BOYS

Aban (AH-bahn)   This name is for a mythological figure associated with water. Also, the eighth month in modern Persian calendar: second month in autumn.

Arman (AR-mahn)   Meaning "desire" or "goal." A variation is *Armaan*.

Bahram (BAH-rahm)   Meaning "he who is of a good disposition" or "nice." Ancient Persian king from the Sassani dynasty, who was famous for his hunting skills. He died in a swamp while pursuing his hunt too far.

Casper (KAS-par)   Meaning "treasurer." Former defense secretary Caspar Weinberger is one distinguished person with this name. Jasper and Casper are two forms of the same Zarathoustrian name: Gaspar, a name often visited in Avesta, Zarathoustrians' holy book. A variation is Caspar.

Cyrus (SYE-rus)   "Sun." Cyrus the Great, the first king of the Achaemenion dynasty, the first Persian dynasty, who expanded the Persian boundaries from today's India to Egypt. Cyrus Vance, former secretary of state, Cyrus McCormick, inventor of a harvesting machine. Variations include *Ciro, Cy, Cyris,* and *Kir*.

Dara (DAH-rah)   "Wealthy. " Popular Persian name during the 1950s, somewhat quaint today. A variation is *Darell*.

Feirouz (FEE-ruz)   "Fortunate." Firouz is the Arabic pronunciation of the Persian name Pirouz. A variation is *Ferran*.

Jamsheed (jahm-SHEED)   From old Persia signifying "From Persia." The name of a mythical prehistoric savvy king of Persia who possessed incredible courage and justice, based on the national epics called *Shahnameh*. He pretended to be God toward the end of his reign.

Jasper (JAS-per)   Meaning "treasurer." One of the Magi. A variation is *Jaspar*.

Kaveh (KAAH- vay)   The name for the heroic mythical Persian ironsmith. He is Persia's first independence leader based on the epics of *Shahnameh*.

Mehrdad (MEHR-dahd)   A name the signifies "gift of the sun." A legendary name from the Zarathoustrian tradition; *mehr*, meaning the sun, is a holy entity in the Old Persian tradition, because of its relationship to fire.

Nasim (NA-seem)   Meaning "breeze" or "fresh air." Boxer Prince Naseem Hamed is one notable individual with this name. A variation is *Naseem*.

Pirouz (PEE-ruz) Meaning "victory" or "prosperous." See also Feirouz.

Sohrab (So-rAAHB) The name of a legendary hero in the national epics of *Shahnameh*.

Soroush (SO-rush) A name that means "happiness." The name is derived from Old Persian.

IRAN: GIRLS

Esther (ETHS-ter) This name means "star." According to the Bible, Esther was a Hebrew woman who became the queen of Persia and played a leading role in preventing genocide against Persian Jews.

Jasmine (JAZ-mihn) or (JAZ-meen) This name means "jasmine flower." Variations include *Jazman, Jazmen, Jazrninn, Jazrnon, Jazmyn, Jazmyne, Jazzmin, Jazzmin, Jazmin,* and *Jazmine.*

Laleh (LAH-lay) This name means "tulip." Variations include *Lalah.*

Mehri (MEH-ree) Meaning "kind" or "lovable" or "sunny."

Nahid (NAAH-heed) The Persian name for Venus, the goddess of love and beauty.

Pari (PAH-REE) A name that means "fairy" or "angel."

Roxanne (roks-ANNE) Means "sunrise." Rocsana was the Persian princess (Darius III's daughter) who, after the invasion of Persia by the Greeks, married Alexander, the Greek emperor. Also the name of the heroine of Edmond Rostand's play *Cyrano de Bergerac.* Variations include *Rocxann, Roxana, Roxane, Roxanna, Roxianne,* and *Roxy.*

Soraya (so-RA-ee-a) Meaning "princess." This is the name of the second queen of Iran's last king, Mohammad Reza Shah. She was the daughter of Bakhtiari tribe's main chief and was famous for her incredible beauty. A variation is *Suraya.*

Souzan (SU-zen) Meaning "burning fire," "fire's hottest point," or "flame." A Persian form of Suzan.

Taraneh (TAR-ah-nay) A name meaning "melody."

Yasmin (YAH-sa-meen) or (YAh-sa-man) A Persian form of Jasmine. Variations include *Yashmine, Yasaman, Yasmeen, Yasmene, Yasmina, Yasmine, Yasmyn, Yazmin, Yazmina, Yazmine, Yesmin, Yesmina, Yesmine,* and *Yesmyn.*

Bulgaria In the middle of the second millennium B.C., the Thracian civilization dominated what is today known as Bulgaria. Like Turkey and Afghanistan, Bulgaria has distinguished itself as a crossroads of peoples. The cultural identity of modern Bulgaria began to emerge following two victories over the Byzantine Empire in A.D. 680 and 681. Bulgarian is a Slavic language that continues to use the Cyrillic alphabet. Since the fall of communism, the general trend for many parents is to select more traditional Christian names for their children.

BULGARIA: BOYS

Andrei (an-DRAY) Meaning "manly." A form of the Greek name Andreas or Andrew. Variations include *Andreian, Andej, Audrey, Andreyan, Andrie,* and *Aundrei.*

Foma (foh-MA) Which means "twin." A form of the name Thomas. A variation is *Fomka.*

Gedeon (GID-ee-on) Meaning "tree cutter." Variations include *Gida, Gideon,* and *Gidyon.*

Grigori (GREH-goh-ree) Meaning "vigilant." Variations include *Grigori, Girgor Grigorios,* and *Grigory.*

Ioan (YO-ahn) Meaning "God is gracious." Variations include *Ioane, Ioann, Ioannes, Ioannikios, Ioannis, Inoel,* and *John.*

Iustin (I-UUS-tin) Meaning "just." Variations include *Justin* and *Justinus.*

Kir (k-EER) Meaning "sun."

Matai (mat-AI) Meaning "God is a gift." Variations include *Matei, Matityahur,* and *Matey.*

Mladen (MLA-den) A name meaning "young." Variations include *Matthew, Mlado,* and *Mladcho.*

Mihail (MI-ha-eel) Which means "who is like God." Variations include *Mihailo, Mihal, Mihalls,* and *Mikha'el.*

Petr (PETR) Meaning "rock." Variations include *Petyo* and *Petko.*

Piotr (pee-OTR) A form of Peter. Variations include *Piotrek.* Among notable people with this name is Piotr Fijas, holder of the ski jump world record.

Veniamin (VEN-ya-meen) A form of Benjamin, which means "son of the right hand." Variations include *Venyo* and *Venya.*

Zhivoin (zh-EE-vo-in) Meaning "warrior." Variations include *Zhivko* and *Zhivan.*

BULGARIA: GIRLS

Cecillia (SE-see-lya) A name inspired by the feminine form of the Latin name Cecil, meaning "blind."

Fidanka (FEE-dan-ka) Translated literally, means "sapling."

Devora (DE-vo-ra) A form of Deborah which means "bee." Variations include *Devka* and *Dora.*

Igilka (EE-gil-ka) A name that means "primrose."

Kira (KEE-ra) Meaning "throne."

Liliana (LEE-lee-ana) Meaning "lily," as in the flower. This name finds its roots in the Latin name Lilian. A variation is *Lilianka.*

Lucine (LOO-see-na)   A name that means "to glitter" or "to shine." Variations include *Lucia, Lucia,* and *Lucy.*

Marketa (MAR-ki-ta)   A form of Margaret, a name that means "pearl." Variations include *Marka.*

Radka (RAD-ka)   A name that means "happiness." Variations include *Rada, Radha,* and *Raina.*

Rahil (RA-heel)   A form of the Hebrew name Rachel, which means "innocence of a lamb."

Snezhana (sne-ZHA-na)   A name that means "snowflake."

Temenuzha (te-me-NU-zha)   A name inspired by the "violet," a purple flower. Variations include *Violeta.*

Violeta (VEE-o-let-a)   A name inspired by the beautiful violet flower. Variations include *Temenuzha.*

Czech Republic

Czech is part of the western Slavonic family of languages. Although it resembles Latin in many ways, it is closely related to the Baltic languages. The most recent ancestor of Old Czech is Old Church Slavonic. Czech uses the Roman alphabet. The Czech people have been greatly affected by long years of occupation and the political influence of the Germans, Austrians, and, most recently, the Russians.

Dialectic differences can be found in this relatively small country, most notably in the two major geographical regions of Moravia (the eastern third of the country), which prides itself in correct, precise pronunciation, and Bohemia (the western part of the country), where there is often a tendency to shorten vowel sounds. With the fall of communism, there has been a tendency toward giving children names that are variants of western European or American names.

CZECH REPUBLIC: BOYS

Adamec (ad-AM-ek)   A form of the Hebrew name Adam, which has the root meaning "earth." Variations include *Adamek, Adamik, Adamka, Adamko,* and *Adamok.*

Alois (AL-o-yeez)   A form of Aloysius, which means "famous warrior." A famous Alois is Czechoslovakian writer Alois Irasek.

Arno (AR-no)   A short form of Ernest, which means "intense" or "driven." Variations include *Arnou* and *Arnoux.*

Bedrikh (BED-rzhih)   Meaning "comrade." A notable Bedrikh is classical Czech composer Bedrikh Smetana.

Bela (BAY-la)   Translated literally, means "white." Famous Czechs with this name include composer Bela Bartok and actor Bela Lugosi, the man who breathed life into the infamous Count Dracula.

Bobek (BO-bek)   A Czech form of Robert, which means "bright" or "famous." This name is commonly shortened to Bob. A variation is *Rubert.*

Bohuslav (BO-hu-slav)   Literally means "glory to God." A notable person with this name is Czech musician and composer Bohuslav Chernogorsky.

Dano (DA-no)   A form of the Hebrew name Daniel, which means "judge." A variation is *Danko.*

Durko (DUUr-ko)   A Czech variation of the name George, is Greek for "farmer." See also Jiri and Jur.

Dushan (DUU-shan)   A name that means "heartfelt," or "sincere."

Edo (ED-o)   A Czech alternative to the name Edward, which means "happy" or "fortunate."

Eman (EM-an)   Translated literally, means "God is with us." A variation on the Hebrew name *Emmanuel.*

Erich (ERR-ik)   Meaning "popular." A form of the popular German name Eric. A noteworthy person with this name is Erich Maria Remarque, the author of *All Quiet on the Western Front.*

Ezven (IZ-ven)   Meaning "born well." A form of the Greek name Eugene. Variations include *Esven* and *Esvin.*

Frantisek (FRAN-tee-shek)   Meaning "free man." A variation on the name Francis, which finds its linguistic roots in Latin. A variation is *Franta.*

Hanus (HA-nuus)   Meaning "God is kind." A popular form of the Hebrew name John. Variations include *Honxa* and *Janco*.

Holic (HO-lik)   A name that means "barber."

Honxa (HON-za)   Meaning "God is kind." A common form of the Hebrew name John. Variations include *Hanus* and *Janco*.

Imrich (EEM-rih)   Meaning "home ruler." A form of the German name Emery. Variations include *Imrus*.

Izak (IZ-ak)   Meaning "he laughs." A popular variation of the Hebrew name Isaac. Variations include *Isaak*, *Izak*, *Izeke*, and *Izsak*.

Janco (YAN-ko)   Meaning "God is kind." A common form of the Hebrew name John. Variations include *Hanus*, *Honxa*, and *Jancsi*.

Jaroslav (YA-ro-slav)   Translated literally, means "glory of spring." Nobel Prize winners with this name include Jaroslav Seifert for literature and Jaroslav Heyrovsky for physical chemistry.

Jindra (YIN-dra)   Meaning "commander" or "leader." A form of the German name Harold.

Jiri (YI-ri)   Meaning "farmer." A form of the Greek name George. Variations include *Durko*, *Jirka*, and *Jur*.

Josef (YO-sef)   Meaning "he will increase," or "add." A form of the Hebrew name Yosef or Joseph. Famous Josefs include architect Josef Zitek and Josef K., Franz Kafka's blighted protagonist in his famed 1925 novella *The Trial*.

Jur (YUR)   Meaning "farmer." A popular form of the Greek name Giorgos or George. Variations include *Durko*, *Jiri*, *Juraz*, *Jurek*, *Jurik*, *Jurko*, and *Juro*.

Klement (KLE-ment)   Meaning "gentle" or "kind." Based on the Latin name Clement. Klement Gottwald was once the Czech communist leader. Variations include *Klema*, *Klemenis*, *Klemens*, and *Klimek*.

Kuba (KUU-ba)   Meaning "supplanter." A form of the Hebrew name Yaokov or Jacob. Variations include *Kubo* and *Kubus*.

Ladislav (la-DEE-slav)   Meaning "ruler." A form of the old German name Walter, which is translated "army of power." Variations include *Laco*, *Lada*, *Ladislaus*, and *Waltr*.

Lukas (LUU-kas)   Meaning "light." A form of the Latin names Luke and Lucius. Variations include *Loukas*, *Lukash*, *Lukasha*, *Lukass*, and *Lukasz*.

Matus (MA-tus)   Meaning "gift of God." A form of the Hebrew names Matthew and Mathias.

Maxi (MA-ksi)   Meaning "greatest" or "best." A familiar form of the Latin name Maximilian. Variations include *Maximo* and *Makszi*.

Milan (MEE-lan)   Meaning "beloved." Variations include *Miko* and *Milko*. Novelist Milan Kundera wrote *The Unbearable Lightness of Being*.

Miloslav (MEE-lo-slav)   Translated literally, means "lover of glory."

Miroslav (MEE-ro-slav)   Meaning "peace" and "glory."

Noe (nOy)   Meaning "peaceful." A form of the Hebrew name Noah.

Ondro (ON-droh)   Meaning "manly." A form of the Greek name Andreas or Andrew. Variations include *Ondrek* and *Ondre*.

Ota (O-ta)   This is an auspicious name meaning "prosperous." Variations include *Otik* and *Otko*.

Rostislav (ROS-tee-slav)   Translated literally, means "growing glory."

Rubert (RUU-bert)   Meaning "bright." A form of the German name Robert. Variations include *Bobek*.

Ruda (RUU-da)   Meaning "ginger." A form of Rudolph. Variations include *Rude*, *Ruda*, and *Rudek*.

Salman (SAL-man)   Meaning "perfect." A form of the Arabic name Salim. Variations include *Solomon*, *Salmaine*, and *Salmon*.

Sarno (SAR-no)   Meaning "heard by God." A form of the Hebrew name Samuel. Variations include *Samho* and *Samko*.

Slane (SLAIN)   Meaning "salty." A variation is *Sian*.

Tonda (TON-da)   Meaning "priceless." A form of the Greek and Latin name Anthony. Commonly shortened to Tony. A variation is *Tonek*.

Tynek (TEE-nek)   Meaning "warrior." The French variation is Martin and the Latin version is Martinus. Another Czech variation is *Tynko*.

Vaclav (VA-slav)   Meaning "wreath of glory." A variations is *Vacek*. Czech Vaclav Havel was a dissident and avant-garde writer before ascending to the presidency.

Villiam (VEE-lee-am)   A form of the popular name William, which means "protector." The French version of Villiam is Guillaume, and the German version is Wilhelm. Czech variations include *Vila, Viek, Vilim, Vilko,* and *Vilous*.

Waltr (vol-tr)   Meaning "ruler." A form of the German name Walter. Variations include *Ladislav*.

CZECH REPUBLIC: GIRLS

Anezka (an-EZH-ka)   A form of Hannah, which means "gracious."

Anika (AN-ee-ka)   Meaning "full of grace." A familiar form of Anna. Variations include *Anaka, Aneeky, Aneka, Anekah, Anica,* and *Anik*.

Anna (AN-na)   A form of Hannah, which means "gracious." Among notable people with this name are Russian ballerina Anna Pavlova.

Bela (BE-la)   Meaning "white."

Eva (EE-va)   A form of the Hebrew name Eve, which means "life."

Fiala (FEE-a-la)   Meaning "violet flower."

Gizella (GEE-ze-la)   A form of Giselle, which means "pledge." Variations include *Gizelle* and *Gizi*.

Iolanta (YO-lan-ta)   Meaning "glorious" and "notable." Variations include *Iola, Lana,* and *Lanta*.

Jenka (YEN-ka)   Meaning "God's gracious gift." A form of Jane, the female form of the Hebrew name John.

Jirina (YI-ree-na)   A form of the Latin name Georgia, meaning "farmer." Among the notable people with this name are authors Jirina Fikejzova and Jirina Fuchsova.

Juliana (YUU-lee-ana)   A form of the Latin name Julia, which means "youthful."

Katarina (KA-ta-rzhee-na)   A form of the Greek name Katherine, meaning "chaste." A variation is *Kata*.

Kirystin (KEE-R-uh-steen)   A form of the Scandinavian name Kristin, meaning "follower of Christ."

Krista (kr-EES-ta)   A form of the popular name Christina, the feminine form of the Greek name Christina, which means "anointed." Variations include *Khrissa, Khrista, Khryssa, Khrysta, Krissa, Kryssa,* and *Krysta*.

Magda (MAG-dah)   A form of Magdalen, which means "high tower." Among the notable people with this name is actress Magda Szubanski. Also *Magdelena*.

Markita (mar-KEE-ta)   A form of the name Margaret, which is derived from Greek and Latin and means "pearl." Variations include *Marka, Markeda, Markee, Markeeta,* and *Marketa*.

Milada (mee-LA-da)   A name that means "my love." Variations include *Mila* and *Milady*.

Milka (MEEL-ka)   A form of the Latin name Amelia, meaning "hard worker."

Ondrea (OHN-dree-a)   A form of the Latin name Andrea, meaning "womanly." Variations include *Ohndrea, Ohindreea, Ohndreya,* and *Ohndria*.

Otillie (o-TEE-lee-a)   Meaning "lucky heroine." Variations include *Otila, Otka,* and *Ottili*.

Pavia (PA-vee-ya)   A form of the Latin name Paula, which means "petite." Variations include *Pavlina* and *Pavlinka*.

Reza (RE-za) A form of the Greek name Theresa, meaning "harvester." Variations include *Rezi* and *Rezka*.

Rusalka (RUU-zal-ka) Meaning "wood nymph." Antonín Dvořák's opera *Rusalka*, which is about a nymph, is considered his masterpiece.

Ruza (RUU-za) Meaning "rose." Variations include *Ruzena, Ruzenka, Ruzha,* and *Ruzsa*.

Ryba (REE-ba) Meaning "fish." A variation is *Rylee*.

Teodora (TEO-do-ra) A form of Greek name Theodora, meaning "God's gift." A variation is *Teadora*.

Trava (TRAV-a) Meaning "spring grasses." The famous Czech bluegrass band is named Druha Trava.

Vondra (VON-dra) Meaning "loving woman." Variations include *Vonda* and *Vondrea*.

Zusa (ZUU sa) A form of the Hebrew name Susan, which means "lily." Author Zuzana Kocova is among notable Czechs with a form of this name. Variations include *Zuzana, Zmanka, Zuzia, Zuzka,* and *Zuzu*.

Estonia

Until the 12th century the marshes and forest lands along the eastern coast of the Baltic Sea were in the undisturbed possession of a number of non-Christian tribes. The Esths and the Livs in the northern regions (present-day Estonia and Latvia) belonged to the Finnish branch of the Ural-Altaic family, which derives from Central Asia. Hungarian, Finnish, and Estonian all share this Asian heritage. Contrary to common belief, Estonian uses the Roman alphabet and not the Cyrillic alphabet. In addition to the standard alphabet, some diacritical marks are used. On letters for certain sounds, these are pronounced similarly to those in German.

ESTONIA: BOYS

Aleksander (AL-ksan-der) A form of the Greek Alexandros or Alexander, which means "defender of mankind." A popular diminutive form is *Leks*.

Jaan (YA-an) Meaning "follower of Christ." A form of the popular Greek and Latin name Christian. Jaan Tonnison is the former Estonian prime minister.

Kristjan (KRIS-tyan) Meaning "follower of Christ." A form of the popular Greek and Latin name Christian.

Matt (Mat) A form of the Hebrew name Matityahu or Matthew, meaning "God's gift."

Mikk (MEEk) Meaning "Who is godlike?" Derived from the Hebrew name Mikha'el, or Michael.

Nikolai (NEE-ko-lai) Meaning "victory." A form of the Greek name Nikolaus or Nocholas. Variations include *Kolya, Nikolais, Nikolas, Nikolah, Nikolay, Nikoli*, and *Nikolia*.

Peeter (PE-ter) A form of *Peter* from the Greek and Latin names, meaning "stone."

Riki (REE-kee) Meaning "mighty ruler." See also Richart in German names. Variations include *Rikki* and *Riks*.

Rolli (ROL-lee) Meaning "famous throughout the land." A form of the German name Roland.

Toomas (TO-mas) Meaning "twin." A form of the Aramaic name Thomas. A variation is *Toomis, Tuomas*, and *Tuom*.

ESTONIA: GIRLS

Betti (bet-TEE) Meaning "joined with God." Variations include *Elts, Elizabeth*, and *Liis* under Hebrew names.

Daggi (DAG-ee) A short form of the Hebrew name Dagania, which is related to the corn grain.

Elts (ELLts) Meaning "joined with God." Variations include *Betti, Elizabeth*, and *Liisi*.

Hele (HEY-le) Meaning "light" or "enlightened." Variations include *Helene*.

Kati (KA-tee) Meaning "pure." A form of the Greek based name Kate. Variations include *Katia, Katya*, and *Katye*.

Leena (LEE-na) Meaning "light" or "enlightened." A form of the Greek name *Helene*. Variations include *Hele* or *Helen*.

Liisi (LEE-see) Meaning "joined with God." Variations include *Betti, Elts*, and *Elizabeth*.

Marga (MAR-ga) Meaning "pearl," it is a form of Margaret.

Mari (MA-ree) A variant of the Hebrew name Mary, which means "bitter."

Olli (O-lee) Meaning "pious." In German this name is Helga.

Reet (REEt) A form of the name Margaret, which is derived from Greek and means "pearl." Variations include *Reatha, Reta*, and *Retha*.

Tilda (TIL-da) Meaning "chaste." Actress Tilda Swinton starred in *Orlando*.

Ulli (UL-lee) A variation of the Latin based name Ursula, which means "she-bear."

Hungary

Hungarian is one of four Asiatic languages spoken in Europe. It bears no resemblance to the languages spoken in surrounding countries, i.e., German, Czech, Slovak, or Romanian. In the fifth century the Hungarian tribes left the area of the Ural Mountains in Central Asia. The tribes passed along the Volga River and Caspian Sea and after several hundred years of wandering, reached the Carpathian Basin. This small country is one of the great survivors of history: States and empires emerged, expanded, or disintegrated around it.

Hungarians are a "people torn by fate," as suggested by their national anthem. They have survived the devastation of invasions by the Tartars, Turks, Hapsburgs, Germans, and Russians. Renowned Hungarians have included photographer László Moholy-Nagy, philosopher György Lukács, Denis Gabor (the inventor of holography), and composers Franz (Ferenc) Liszt and Béla Bartók, as well as many Hungarian-Americans such as the Gabor sisters, Milos Forman, Elie Wiesel, and George Soros.

HUNGARY: BOYS

Andor (AN-door) Meaning "love" or "manly." A form of the name Andrew. Variations include *Andreas*.

Andros (AN-drohsh) Meaning "love" or "manly." A form of the name Andrew. See also Andreas under Greek names. Variations include *Andri*, *Andris*, *Andrius*, *Andriy*, *Aundras*, and *Aundreas*.

Antal (AN-tahl) Meaning "priceless." A form of the Latin based name Anthony. Variations include *Antek*, *Anti*, and *Antos*.

Domokos (DO-mo-kohs) Meaning "belonging to the Lord." A form of the Latin name Dominic. Variations include *Dedo*, *Dome*, *Domek*, *Domok*, and *Domonkos*.

Elek (EL-ek) A form of the Greek name Alexandros which means "protection of man." Variations include *Elec*, *Elic*, and *Elik*.

Endre (YEN-dr) Meaning "love" or "manly." See also Andreas in Greek names. A variation is *Ender*.

Erno (YEH-rno) A form of Ernest, meaning "sincere" or "earnest."

Ferenc (FE-rens) A form of the Latin based names Francis and Francisco, which literally mean "from France." Among the notable people with this name are composer and pianist Ferenc (better known as Franz) Liszt, playwright and novelist Ferenc Molnár, and conductor Ferenc Friesay. Variations include *Feri*, *Ferke*, and *Ferko*.

Gabor (GA-bor) Meaning "God is my strength." Gabor was king of Hungary in the 17th century. Variations include *Gabbo*, *Gabko*, and *Gabo*.

Gellert (GEL-lert) A form of the German name Gerald. Variations include *Gelo*, *Gelko*, and *Gerko*.

Gyula (GYU-la) Meaning "youth." Variations include *Gyala* and *Gyuszi*.

Imre (IM-ray) A form of the German name Emery, which means "home ruler." A variation is *Imri*.

Ince (IN-say) A name that means "innocent."

Istvan (ISH-tven) A form of the Greek name Stefanos or Stephan, which means "crowned." An English version is Stephen. Istvan Gyungyusi is a celebrated poet. Variations include *Isti* and *Istvin*.

Janos (YAN-nosh)   A form of the name John, which means "God's gracious gift." Janos Sylvestert invented the first Hungarian alphabet. Variations include *Jancsi*, *Jani*, and *Jankia*.

Jenu (YEN-u)   A form of the Greek name Eugene which means "high born." Variations include *Jenci*, *Jency*, *Jence*, *Jensi*, and *Jensy*.

Kelemen (KAY-le-men)   A name that means "gentle" or "kind."

Lajos (LA-yosh)   Meaning "renowned" or "sacred." Lajos Dula was a medieval Hungarian noble prince. Variations include *Lajcsi*, *Laji*, *Lail*, and *Laco*.

Laszly (LAS-lee)   Meaning "famous leader." Laslo Tomashy was a prominent Hungarian poet. Variations include *Lad*, *Lacko*, *Laslo*, and *Lazio*.

Lyrand (LEE-rand)   A form of the German name Roland, which means "renowned land."

Lyront (LEE-rant)   A form of the name Lawrence which means "crowned with laurel." A variation is *Lorant*.

Maco (MA-ko)   A form of the Hebrew name Emmanuel, which means "God is with us." Variations include *Macho* and *Matsko*.

Maks (Maks)   Meaning "superior." A form of the Latin name Maximilian. See also Maxi and Miksa. A variation is *Makszi*.

Marcilko (MAR-sil-ko)   A form of Marcellus, which means "warlike." Variations include *Marcil* and *Marchilki*.

Maxi (MAK-see)   A familiar form of Maximilian, which means "superior." See also Maks and Miksa. Variations include *Makszi*, *Maxey*, *Maxiev*, and *Maxy*.

Micu (MEE-kuu)   A form of the Greek name Nikolaos, which means "victory." Variations include *Niki*.

Miksa (MEEK-sa)   A familiar form of the name Maximilian, which means "superior." See also Maks and Maxi. A variation is *Miks*.

Natan (NA-than)   Meaning "God has given." Variations include *Nataneal* and *Nataniel*.

Niki (NEE-kee)   Meaning "victory" or "triumph." A familiar form of Nicholas. See also Micu. Variations include *Nikia*, *Nikiah*, *Nikki*, *Nikko*, and *Niko*.

Odon (OD-ahn)   Meaning "wealthy protector." A variation is *Odi*.

Orbon (OR-ban)   Meaning "born in the city."

Pol (Pohl)   A form of the name Paul, which means "small." Variations include *Pali* and *Palika*.

Pista (PEESH-ta)   A familiar form of Istvan, a popular name in Hungary, it means "crowned." Variations include *Pisti* and *Pishto*.

Rendor (REN-dar)   A name that means "peace officer."

Sandor (SHAN-dar)   A short form of the Greek name Alexandros or Alexander, which means "protector of man." Sandor Kisfaludy is a poet and song writer; Sandor Wekerle was a late 19th-century Hungarian leader.

Szygfrid (ZIG-freed)   A form of the German name Siegfried, which means "victorious peace."

Tibor (TEE-bar)   Meaning "hallowed place." Tibor Jannoshy was a famous Hungarian sculptor. A variation is *Tiburclo*.

Vencel (VEN-tsel)   Meaning "necklace of glory." A short form of Wenceslas, originating from the old Slavic language. Variations include *Vend* and *Vencie*.

Vidor (VEE-dar)   A delightful name that means "cheerful."

Viktor (VEEK-tor)   A form of the Latin name Victor, meaning "victorious." Variations include *Viktoras* and *Viktors*.

Vili (VEE-lee)   A form of William, which means "determined guardian." Also *Vilmos*.

Vinci (VEEN-see)   A form of the Latin name Victor, which means "victorious." Variations include *Vinci*, *Vinco*, and *Vincze*.

Zako (ZA-koh)   Meaning "God has remembered." See also Zekharya under Hebrew names.

Zoltin (ZOHL-than) Meaning "life." Filmmaker Zoltán Korda and composer Zoltán Kodály are two famous Hungarian Zoltans. Variations include *Zoltan*.

Zsigmond (ZEEG-mand) Meaning "successful defender." A form of the German name Sigmund. Variations include *Ziggy*, *Zigmund*, and *Zsiga*.

HUNGARY: GIRLS

Anci (AN-tsee) Meaning "grace." See also Hannah under Hebrew names. Variations include *Annus* and *Anushka*.

Aniky (an-EE-kee) Meaning "grace." Variations include *Any* and *Anky*.

Bella (BEL-la) Meaning "noble" or "bright." U.S. Congresswoman Bella Abzug was a major figure in the feminist movement. Variations include *Bela* and *Belle*.

Buzsi (BUU-see) Meaning "consecrated to God." From the Hebrew name Elizabeth.

Darda (DAR-da) A name whose literal meaning is "a dart."

Eszter (ES-ter) Meaning "star." The French version is Esperance; another variation is *Ezsti*.

Etel (E-tehl) A name that means "noble." A variation is *Etilka*.

Franci (FRAN-tsi) A familiar form of Francine, which is a feminine form of Francis, meaning "free" or "from France." Variations include *Francey*, *Francie*, and *Francy*.

Ilona (EEL-on-a) Meaning "light." See Helene under Greek names. Actress Ilona Massey is among the notable people with this name. Variations include *Ila*, *Ilka*, *Ilken*, *Illona*, *Illonia*, *Illonya*, and *Illomka*.

Juci (YUU-tsi) Meaning "Hebrew woman" or "praised." See Judith under Hebrew names.

Lenci (LEN-tsi) Meaning "light." See Helene under Greek names.

Malika (MA-lee-ka) A name that means "industrious."

Margit (MAR-geet) A form of the name Margaret, which means "pearl." Notable people with this name include authors Margir Kaffka and Margita Figuli. A variation is *Margita*.

Neci (NET-see) Meaning "fiery" or "intense." Variations include *Necia* and *Nede*.

Nusi (NUU-see) Meaning "grace." See Hannah under Hebrew names.

Onella (AN-el-la) Meaning "light." See Helene under Greek names.

Rezi (REH-zee) A form of Theresa, which means "reaper."

Sarlota (SHAR-lo-tah) Meaning "princess." See Sarah under Hebrew names.

Sasa (SA-sa) Meaning "princess." See Sarah under Hebrew names

Teca (THE-kah) A form of Theresa, which means "reaper." Variations include *Teka*, *Tica*, and *Tika*.

Tsigana (SEE-gana) An alternate form of Zigana, which means "Gypsy girl." Variations include *Tsigane*, *Tigana*, and *Tzigane*.

Vica (VEE-ka) Meaning "life." See Eve under Hebrew names. A notable person with this name is Hungarian poet Vica Eger.

Zigana (ZEE-ga-na) Translated literally, means "Gypsy girl." A variation is *Zigane*.

Zizi (ZEE-zee) A familiar form of Elizabeth, which means "consecrated to God." Variations include *Zsi* and *Zsi Zsi*.

Zsa Zsa (ZAH-zah) A familiar form of Susan, which means "lily." A famous person with this name is celebrity-actress Zsa Zsa Gabor. A variation is *Zha Zha*.

Zsusanna (SUU-san-na) Meaning "lily." See Susanna under Hebrew names. The name of Hungarian actress Zsuzsanna Tibor. Variations include *Zsuska*, *Zsuzsa*, *Zsuzsi*, and *Zsuzsilka*.

**Latvia** Latvia is a relatively flat country with low undulating hills on the eastern edge of the Baltic Sea. The Latvians constitute a prominent division of the ancient group of peoples known as the Balts, who were documented as having had an extensive trade with the Romans as early as the first century A.D. During the 10th and 11th centuries Latvian lands were subject to military threats from both sides. From the east there was Slavic penetration; from the west came the Swedish push toward the shores of western Latvia. During the Crusades, Latvia began to fall under German dominance, which would continue until the 18th century, when the prevalent power then became Russia. Although it did enjoy a brief period of independence in the early part of the 20th century, Latvia remained a constituent republic of the U.S.S.R. from 1940. It finally declared its independence in 1991.

Despite the country's repeated foreign occupation, Latvian identity has managed to survive. Amateur art thrives in Latvia. Clubs and individual enterprises have drama groups, choirs, ensembles, orchestras, and dance companies. Latvia has a conservatory of music, an academy of arts, and a number of specialized secondary educational establishments for students of music, painting, and the applied arts. Noted Latvian composers include Jazeps Medins, Janis Medins, and Emilis Melngailis. Janis Raninis, who died in 1929, is generally considered Latvia's most important writer.

LATVIA: BOYS

Aigars (I-gars)   A name of honor that means "brave."

Brencis (BREN-tsees)   Meaning "joyful" or "delightful."

Girts (DYErts)   Meaning "forest." The name of Latvian film actor Girts Jakoviev.

Indulis (IN-doo-lees)   Meaning "gift." Variations include *Indi*, *Induls*, and *Indis*.

Janis (YA-nees)   From the Hebrew name John, which means "God is gracious." Janis Rainis was an outstanding Latvian poet of the 19th century. Variations include *Ansis*, *Jancis*, and *Zanis*.

Juris (YUR-ees)   Meaning "sea." Juris Podnieks was a Latvian filmmaker who was killed in January 1990 during the nation's struggle for political independence. Variations include *Juri* and *Jurens*.

Karklens (KARK-lens)   The equivalent to the Teutonic name Charles, meaning "man."

Margots (MAR-gohts)   "Margo's son." Margots was an ancient Latvian prince.

Martins (MAR-teensh)   A form of the name Martin, which means "warlike."

Niklavs (NEEK-lavs)   The equivalent of the Greek name Nikolaus, meaning "victory of the people." A variation is *Niklaas*.

Olgerts (OL-gerts)   Meaning "prosperous." Variations include *Ole* and *Gerts*.

Raimonds (RAY-monds)   Meaning "happy" and "lucky." Raimonds Pauls is a prominent contemporary Latvian pop music composer.

Ritvars (REET-vars)   Translated literally, means "morning." Ritvars Berzinsh was a contemporary Latvian poet. Variations include *Rits* and *Ritus*.

Taiivaldis (TA-iee-cal-dees)   A name that means "prompt," "quick," or "fast." Taiivaldis Skuinsh is a prominent Latvian architect and sculptor.

Uldis (Uul-dees)   A name that means "kind" or "dear."

Zigfrid (ZEEG-freed)   The equivalent to the German name Siegfried, which means "victorious peace." Variations include *Aigfrieds*, *Ziggy*, and *Zyga*.

LATVIA: GIRLS

Agatha (AH-gah-tah)   Meaning "wealthy." Agatha Christie was an English writer whose detective novels were often turned into films. Variations include *Agatinya*, *Gata*, and *Gatynya*.

Aija (I-ya)   Meaning "song." Aija Kukule is a Latvian singer.

Asnate (AS-na-te)   Meaning "fresh" or "new wave."

Aspazija (AS-pah-zee-ya)   Meaning "sublime." Aspazija Rainis is a poet and the wife of Latvia's most famous writer and poet, Janis Rainis.

Baiba (EI-bah)   Meaning "cheerful." Variations include *Baybe*, *Bayb*, *Baybyna*, and *Baybite*.

Beatrise (BEE-a-tree-se)   Which means "bringer of joy." A form of the Latin name Beatrice.

Benita (BEH-nee-ta)   A name that means "lovely" or "pretty."

Biruta (BEE-ruu-ta)   A name that means "giving joy."

Dagmara (DAG-ma-rah)   Meaning "sublime soul." Variations include *Daggy* and *Dagniete*.

Eizenija (AYE-zhe-nee-ya)   Meaning "of noble birth."

Gerda (GER-dah)   Meaning "tiller of the soil." Gerda Lerner is a noted historian. Variations include *Gerdynya* and *Gerdite*.

Grieta (GREE-eta)   A short form of the name Margarita, a variation on Margaret, meaning "pearl."

Karlene (KAR-leneh)   A feminine equivalent of the name Charles, which means "strong" or "manly."

Lelde (LEL-de)   Meaning "peace." The name of Latvian actress Lelde Vickmane. Variations include *Leldyna* and *Leldite*.

Liene (LEE-yeney)   Meaning "light," from the Greek name Helene.

Mara (MA-rah)   A form of the Hebrew name Mary, which means "bitter." Variations include *Marita* and *Maryna*.

Regina (RE-gee-na)   Meaning "queen." Variations include *Gina*, *Regite*, and *Regynya*.

Snaige (SNI-geh)   A name that means "snow."

Varaviksne (VA-ra-veeks-neh)   Meaning "rainbow." Varaviksne Melte is a contemporary Latvian actress. Variations include *Varava*, *Varve*, and *Vike*.

Vija (VEE-ya)   Meaning "beautiful" or "fascinating." Vija Artmane is an outstanding contemporary Latvian actress.

Zanna (ZHAN-nah)   Translated literally, means "God has been gracious."

Lithuania

Lithuania is the southernmost and largest of the three Baltic nations, which also include Estonia and Latvia. The earliest known mention of the name "Lithuania" is found in the German (Teutonic) chronicles of 1009. Lithuania emerged as a larger state in the middle of the 13th century through a union of Baltic territories with Mindaugas becoming the state's first grand duke. The country, however, did not adopt Christianity until 1387 and was, for the most part, under constant military attack by the Germanic Livonian and Teutonic Orders for the first 200 years of its existence as a united territory. Not only did the Teutonic and Livonian Orders fail to conquer Lithuania, however, but by the end of the 14th century Lithuania became one the most powerful states in eastern Europe. In 1410, a joint Lithuanian, Polish, Russian, Tatar, and Czech army under the leadership of Lithuanian Grand Duke Vytautas crushed the Teutonic Order once and for all at the Battle of Tannenberg.

The power of the Lithuanian state began to decline following the death of Grand Duke Vytautas in 1430. In 1569, Lithuania agreed to be governed as an independent part of a joint Lithuanian-Polish state, but later become merely one of Poland's provinces. The life of this joint state ended with the eventual total annexation of its territories by Russia, Austria, and Prussia. Russian domination characterized most of Lithuania's history thereafter, until the country achieved independence in 1991.

LITHUANIA: BOYS

Adomas (A-do-mas) A name that has the root meaning "earth." See Adam under Hebrew names.

Bernandas (BER-nahr-das) A form of the German name Bernard, which means "brave as a bear."

Danukas (DA-nuu-kahs) A form of the Hebrew name Daniel, which means "God is my judge." Variations include *Danu* and *Dano*.

Donatas (DO-na-tas) Meaning "giving hand." Donatas Banionis is a prominent Lithuanian actor.

Gedeminas (GEH-de-mee-nas) Gedeminas was an ancient Lithuanian prince. Variations include *Gedemino*, *Gede*, *Gedo*, and *Gedeus*.

Jecis (YE-cees) A form of the Hebrew name Jacob, which means "supplanter."

Jonas (YOH-nas) A form of the Hebrew name John, which means "he accomplishes."

Jurgis (YUUR-gees) A form of the name George, which means "farmer." Variations include *Jurgi* and *Juri*.

Liutas (LEE-uu-tas) A form of the Hebrew name Moshe or Moses, which means "drawn out (of the water)."

Moze (MOH-zeh) See also Moses under Hebrew names. Variations include *Mozes* and *Mose*.

Petras (PET-ras) A form of Peter, which means "rock." Variations include *Peterlis*, *Pete*, *Peti*, and *Petra*.

Raulas (RA-u-las) A form of the English name Ralph, which means "wolf counselor." Variations include *Rollo* and *Raul*.

Vacys (VAH-ises) A form of the German name Walter, which means "army of power." Variations include *Valters*, *Valther*, and *Valtr*.

LITHUANIA: GIRLS

Ale (AH-lee) Meaning "light." See Helene under Greek names.

Annze (AN-tse) Meaning "grace." See Hannah under Hebrew names.

Dorota (DO-ro-tah) A form of the name Dorothy, which means "gift of God."

Elzbieta (ELZ-bee-e-ta) Meaning "consecrated to God." See Elizabeth under Hebrew names. Variations include *Ele* and *Bety*.

Jadvyga (YAD-vee-gah) A name that means "refuge in battle."

Janina (YA-nee-na) Translated literally, this name means "God has been gracious."

Jurate (YUU-ra-the) Meaning "amber." Variations include *Jure*, *Jura*, *Jute*, and *Juta*.

Kofryna (KOHF-ree-nah) A form of the name Katherine, which means "pure."

Marija (MA-ree-ya) Meaning "bitter." See also Mary under Hebrew names.

Niele (NEE-ye-leh) Meaning "spring flower." The name of Lithuanian actor Niele Savichenko.

Rasa (RAH-sa) Meaning "dew."

Salomeya (SAH-lo-me-ya) Meaning "strong." Salomeya Neris was a 19th-century writer and poet.

Viktorija (VEEK-toh-ree-ya) A form of the Latin name Victoria, which means "victorious."

Zuzane (ZUU-za-neh) Meaning "lily." See also Susan in Hebrew names.

Poland

Poland has a proud history that politically extends back to the 10th century when Mieszko I founded the first Polish state. During the Renaissance, Poland achieved great power, but was later at the mercy of the Germans, Tatars, Swedes, and Turks. The country was partitioned several times, and from the 18th to the 20th centuries was continually suppressed by its neighbors. One of the largest of the countries of eastern Europe, Poland was the first of these countries to liberate its government from the communist domination endured for 45 years. It was the relegalization of the trade union Solidarity and the agreement to hold partially free parliamentary elections that appeared to have opened the floodgates of radical reforms that spilled over into other countries of the Soviet bloc. In 1989, a year of drama unmatched in modern history, government after government collapsed in eastern Europe and politically transformed not only Poland but also East Germany, Hungary, Czechoslovakia, Bulgaria, Romania, and the Soviet Union itself. Famous Poles include Nicolaus Copernicus; Thaddeus Kosciusko; Frederic Chopin; Ignace Paderewski, a pianist who became Poland's prime minister in 1918; and Cselaw Milosz, who won the Nobel Peace Prize in 1980.

POLAND: BOYS

Andros (AN-drohs) Meaning "sea." Andros is a mythological sea god. Variations include *Andris, Andrius,* and *Andrus.*

Aurek (AUU-rek) Meaning "golden-haired." Variations include *Auro* and *Aurek.*

Bronislaw (BRO-nee-slav) Meaning "weapon of glory." Bronislaw Malinovski was a distinguished anthropologist.

Crystek (KREES-tek) A form of the name Christian, which means "follower of Christ." Variations include *Christe, Christo,* and *Khrist.*

Dobry (DOH-bree) Meaning "good" or "kind." Variations include *Dobrek, Dobra,* and *Dobr.*

Fil (FE-el) A form of the name Phil, short for Philip, which means "love of horses." A variation is *Filipek.*

Garek (GAH-rek) A form of the English name Edgar, which means "wealthy spearman."

Genek (GEH-nek) A form of the name Gene, short for Eugene, which means "high-born." A variation is *Genko.*

Gerck (GEH-rek) A form of the English name Gerard, which means "chief spearman."

Gerik (GE-reek) A form of the English name Edgar, which means "wealthy spearman."

Gwidon (gy-EE-dohn) A name that means "life."

Heniek (HEN-ek) A form of the German name Henry, which means "estate ruler." A variation is *Henier.*

Holleb (HOL-ep) Meaning "dove." Variations include *Hollub, Holub,* and *Holco.*

Honok (HO-nok) A form of the German name Henry, which means "estate ruler."

Ignace (IG-nah-tsus) A form of the name Ignatius, which means "fiery." Ignace Jan Paderewski was a concert pianist and Polish statesman.

Iwan (EE-van) A form of the name John, Iwan Gilkin is a poet and playwright. Variations include *Iwko, Iva,* and *Ivo.*

Janek (YAN-ek)   A form of the name John, which means "God is gracious." Variations include *Janik*, *Janka*, *Jankie*, and *Janko*.

Jas (Yas)   A form of the name John, which means "God is gracious."

Jeorek (YED-rek)   Meaning "strong; manly." Variations include *Jedrik* and *Jedrus*.

Jetzy (YER-zhee)   A form of the name George, which means "farmer." Polish expatriate author Jerzy Kozinski wrote *The Painted Bird*. A variation is *Jurek*.

Kazio (KA-zho)   A form of the name Casimir or Kasimir, which means "peacemaker." Variations include *Kazho*.

Koby (KOH-bee)   A familiar form of the Hebrew name Jacob, which means "supplanter." A variation is *Kobi*.

Krystian (KREES-tee-an)   A form of the name Christian, which means "follower of Christ." Variations include *Krys*, *Krystek*, and *Krysto*.

Liuz (LEE-uus)   Meaning "light." Variations include *Lius*, *Loosha*, *Luza*, and *Liu*.

Lubomir (LUU-beh-mear)   Meaning "lover of peace." Lubomir Strona was an ancient Polish chronicler.

Machas (MA-has)   A form of the name Michael, which means "Who is like God."

Maksym (MAK-seem)   A form of the name Maximilian, which means "greatest." Variations include *Maksimus*, *Maksim*, and *Maksymilian*.

Mandek (MAN-dek)   A form of the name Armand, or Herman, which menas "noble." Variations include *Mandie*, *Mando*, and *Mandzek*.

Marcin (MAR-tseen)   A form of the name Martin, which means "warlike." Marcin Bielski is a well-known Polish historian and poet. Variations include *Marco*, *Marto*, and *Marte*.

Marian (MAH-ree-ahn)   A form of the Latin name Marcus, or Mark, which means "warlike." Variations include *Maro*, *Marek*, *Marco*, and *Mar*.

Marke (MARK)   A form of the Latin name Marcus, or Mark, which means "warlike." Variations include *Mark* and *Marco*.

Mateusz (MAH-tee-uush)   A form of the Hebrew name Matitayahw, or Mathew, which means "God is a gift." Variations include *Matheus* and *Mathels*.

Miron (MEE-ron)   A name that means "peace."

Mashe (MASH-ee)   A form of the name Moses or Mosheh, which means "drawn out (of the water)."

Natan (NA-tan)   Meaning "God has given." Variations include *Nataneal* and *Nataniel*.

Nelck (NE-lek)   A form of the Greek name Cornelius, which means "cherry tree" or "horn colored." Variations include *Nelo* and *Nelko*.

Nikolai (NEE ko lai)   A form of the Greek name Nicolaua, or Nicholas, which means "victory."

Olus (OL-uus)   A familiar form of Alexander, which means "protector of man."

Onufry (ON-uuf-ree)   A form of the German name Humphrey, which means "protector of man."

Otek (OT-ek)   A form of the German name Otto, which means "rich."

Patek (PA-tek)   A form of the name Patrick, which means "nobleman." Patek Philippe makes watches.

Paulin (POW-leen)   A form of the name Paul, which means "small."

Pawel (PA-vel)   A form of the name Paul, which means "small." Variations include *Pawelek* and *Pawl*.

Radoslaw (RA-do-slav)   Meaning "happy, glory." Variations include *Radik*, *Rado*, *Radzmir*, and *Slawek*.

Rafal (RA-fahl)   A form of the name Raphael, which means "God has healed."

Rufin (RUU-feen)   A fiery name that means "redhead."

Slawek (SLA-vek)   A short form of the names Stanislaw, Radoslaw, and Luboslaw.

Stasio (STA-see-oh)   A form of the name Stanislaus, which means "stand of glory." Variations include *Stas*, *Stasiek*, and *Stuasius*.

POLAND: GIRLS

Anna (AN-na)   A familiar form of the Hebrew name Hannah, which means "grace."

Beata (BEE-a-tah)   Meaning "she blesses."

Bodgana (BOG-da-na)   A name that means "God's gift." A variation is *Bogna*.

Bryga (BREE-ga)   A form of the Irish name Bridget, which means "strong." Variations include *Brygid*, *Brygida*, and *Brygitka*.

Dominika (do-MEE-na-ka)   A name that means "of the Lord."

Dorota (DO-re-tah)   Meaning "God's gift." See also Bogdana.

Ela (EL-a)   A form of the German name Adelaide, which means "noble and serene."

Elizaveta (ELZH-be-ta)   A form of the name Elizabeth, which means "consecrated to God." Variations include *Elisavet*, *Elisaveta*, *Elisavetta*, *Elisveta*, and *Elizavet*.

Elka (el-KA)   A form of the name Elizabeth, which means "consecrated to God." A variation is *Ilka*.

Ewa (EV-a)   Meaning "life." Well known are authors Ewa Hoffman and Ewa Kuryluk.

Florentyna (flo-ren-TEE-na)   A name that means "flowering."

Filomena (FEE-lo-me-na)   Meaning "lover of mankind."

Grazyna (GRA-zhee-na)   Meaning "grace."

Gutka (GOOT-ka)   Meaning "good."

Halina (HA-lee-na)   Meaning "light."

Hilaria (HEE-la-ree-ya)   A name that means "cheerful."

Hortensia (HOR-ten-sya)   Meaning "gardener." A variation is *Tesia*.

Jasia (YA-sya)   A form of the name Jane, a feminine version of John. Meaning "God's gracious gift."

Joanka (YO-han-ka)   A feminine version of John, meaning "God's gracious gift." Variations include *Nina*, *Joanna*, and *Janka*.

Jula (YO-la)   A form of the name Julia, which is a feminine version of Juluis, meaning "youthful." Variations include *Juica*, *Julcia*, and *Juliska*.

Jolánta (YO-lan-tah)   Meaning "violet blossoms." A variation is *Jola*.

Justyna (YU-stee-na)   A fair name that means "just."

Kasia (KA-sya)   A form of the name Katherine, which means "pure." Variations include *Kasha*, *Kashia*, *Kasienka*, and *Kasia*.

Krysta (KREE-sta)   A form of the name Krista, which means "anointed." A variation is *Krystka*.

Lechsinska (LESH-een-ka)   Meaning "woodland spirit."

Lilka (LEEL-ka)   Meaning "celebrated warrior maiden." Variations include *Ludka*, *Lucwika*, and *Luisa*.

Macia (MA-tsya)   A form of the Hebrew name Miriam, which means "bitter." Variations include *Macelia*, *Macey*, *Machia*, and *Macy*.

Magda (MAG-da)   A form of the name Magdalen, which means "high tower."

Morelia (MOR-el-ya)   Meaning "apricot."

Pela (PEH-la)   A short form of Penelope, which means "weaver."

Tola (TOH-la)   A form of the name Antoinette, which means "flourishing." A variation is *Tolsia*.

Waleria (VA-ler-ee-ya)   A form of the name Valerie, which means "strong." A variation is *Wala*.

Wera (VEH-ra)   A form of the name Vera, which is Latin for "true." Variations include *Wiera*, *Wiercia*, and *Wierka*.

Weronika (VEH-ro-nee-ka)   Meaning "true image." A form of the name Veronica. A variation is *Weronikra*.

Wicktoria (VEEK-tor-ee-ya)   A form of the name Victoria, which means "victorious." Variations include *Wicktorja*, *Wiktoria*, and *Wiktorja*.

Wira (YEE-ra)   A form of the name Elvira, which means "victorious." Variations include *Wiria* and *Wirke*.

Wisia (VEE-see-ya)   A form of the name Victoria. Variations include *Wicia* and *Wikta*.

Zocha (ZO-ha)   An alternate form of the Greek name Sophia, which means "wise."

Zusa (ZUU-sa)   A form of the name Susan, which means "lily." Variations include *Zuzana*, *Zmanka*, and *Zuzia*.

Zytka (ZEET-ka)   A fragrant name meaning "rose."

 **Romania**

Romania is a mountainous country with a considerable coastline along the northwestern Black Sea. Ancient Romania was inhabited by Thracian tribes. The Greeks called them Getate and the Romans called them Dacians, but they were actually a single Geto-Dacian people. From the seventh century B.C. the Greeks established trading colonies along the Black Sea at Callatis (Mangalia), Tomis (Constanta), and Histria. In the first century B.C., a Dacian state was established to meet the Roman threat. The last king, Decebalus, consolidated this state but was unable to prevent the Roman conquest in A.D. 105–6. From the 15th to the 19th centuries, Romania offered strong resistance against the expansion of the Turkish Byzantine and Ottoman empires. For much of this period the country paid tribute to maintain its autonomy. Romania later fell under the influence of Russia, and suffered considerably during the communist regime of the notorious Nicolae Ceausescu.

Most of present Romania brought their civilization and mixed with the conquered tribes to form a Daco-Roman people speaking a Latin tongue. Romanian remains the only Romance language in eastern Europe. Famous Romanians include Vlad Tepes ("Vlad the Impaler"); the writers Tristan Tzara, Mircea Eliade and Eugene Ionesco; the sculptor Constantin Brancusi; and musicians Radu Lupu and Angela Georghiu.

ROMANIA: BOYS

Andrei (AN-drey) A form of the name Andrew, which means "strong" or "manly."

Artur (AR-toor) A form of the name Arthur, meaning "noble."

Dic (DEEk) A form of the name Richard, which means "rich" and "powerful ruler."

Enric (EN-reek) A form of the name Henry, which means "estate ruler."

Godoired (GO-do-fred) A form of the name Gottfried, which means "God's peace."

Ioan (YO-an) A form of the name John, meaning "God is gracious."

Noe (NOY) A form of the Hebrew name Noah, meaning "to rest."

Petar (PE-tar) Meaning "rock." A form of the name Peter. Poet Petar Hektorovic.

Reimond (REY-mond) Meaning "mighty." A form of the name Raymond.

Simion (SEE-mee-on) A form of the name Simon, which means "he heard."

Vasile (VA-see-ly) A form of the name Basil, which means "royal." Vasile Alecsandri is a Romanian diplomat.

ROMANIA: GIRLS

Amalia (AM-al-ee-ya) A form of the name Amelia, which means "hardworking."

Alina (AL-ee-na) A name that means "to soothe."

Anicuta (an-ee-KU-ta) A form of the Hebrew name Hannah, which means "grace."

Dol (DOL) Meaning "gift of God." A form of the name Dorothy.

Elica (EL-ee-ka) A form of the German name Adelaide, which means "noble and serene."

Ema (EM-a) Meaning "beloved." A form of the name Amy.

Francise (FRAN-see-se)   Meaning "free" or "from France." A form of the name Frances, which is a feminine form of Francis.

Irini (EAR-ee-nee)   A form of the Greek name Irene, which means "peaceful."

Jenica (YEN-ee-ka)   Meaning "God is gracious." A form of the name Jane, which is a feminine version of John. Variations include *Jenika*, *Jennica*, and *Jennika*.

Lacrimioara (LAK-ree-mee-oa-ra)   Meaning "little tear."

Luminita (LU-mee-nee-ta)   Meaning "little light."

Maricara (MA-ree-ka-ra)   A form of the Hebrew name Miriam, which means "bitter" or "sea of bitterness."

Nadia (NA-dya)   Meaning "hope." Nadia Comaneci was an Olympic champion gymnast. Variations include *Nada*, *Nadea*, *Nadenka*, *Nadezhda*, *Nadie*, *Nadine*, *Nadiya*, and *Nadja*.

Rada (RA-da)   A happy name that means "joy."

Reveca (RE-ve-ka)   A form of the Hebrew name Rebecca, which means "bound" or "servant of God."

Ursule (OAR-soo-le)   A form of the name Ursula, which means "she-bear."

Viorica (VEE-o-ree-ka)   Meaning "flower."

 Until the Russian Revolution of 1917, Russian names were limited to those sanctioned by the Orthodox Church. After 1917, naming became a revolutionary endeavor. The communists encouraged people to give their children names reflecting the new order, its ideals and its goals. Some of them were quite imaginative and innovative, such as Rem (an acronym for revolution, Engels, and Marx), Traktor (tractor), Elektrifikatsiya (electrification), and Vladlen (Vladimir Lenin). Some of these names are still heard today among those older than 50. Rem Vyakhirev, for instance, is the chief executive officer of Russia's largest and most powerful corporation, Gazprom.

Since the 1980s, Russian nationalist and Orthodox religious feelings have enjoyed a comeback, and many parents are choosing traditional Church-sanctioned names, especially ancient ones not commonly heard in this century. Some of the most popular boys names for Russia are Nikita, Daniil, and Grigori, while those for girls include Darya or Dasha, Anastasia, and Ksenya. Nevertheless, many people in both countries prefer to give international and Western names to their children, and it is not unusual to hear a young Russian boy named Robert, or girl called Christina.

RUSSIA: BOYS

Aleksandr (al-eks-AN-dr) Meaning "to protect." Notable persons with this name include poet Aleksandr Pushkin, as well as the 13th century Russian hero Aleksandr Nevsky. Variations include *Sasha, Sanya, Sanochka, Shura,* and *Sanok.*

Aleksei (alek-SAY) Meaning "to protect." Variations include *Lyesha* and *Lyeshinka.*

Anatoli (a-na-TOL-ee) Meaning "sunset." Writer Anatoli Rybakov is among the notable people with this name. Variations include *Tolya* and *Tolik.*

Andrei (an-DREY) Meaning "brave." Film director Andrei Konchalovsky has this name in common with medieval icon painter Andrei Rublev. Also *Andrusha.*

Anton (an-TON) Translated literally, means "to go into battle." A variation is *Antosha.*

Arkady (ar-KA-dee) Derived from the name of the ancient Greek city Arkadii. A variation is *Arkasha.*

Artem (ar-TYEM) Meaning "healthy, vigorous." A variation is *Tyema.*

Afansy (af-an-AS-ee) Meaning "immortal." Variations include *Afanas, Fasya,* and *Fonya.*

Bogdan (bog-DAN) Meaning "given by God." Also *Bogdasha.*

Boris (boar-HES) Meaning "to fight." Writer Boris Pasternak and former Russian president Boris Yeltsin share this name. Variations include *Borya* and *Borichka.*

Daniil (dan-YEEL) Meaning "divine judge." Variations include *Danichka* and *Danya.*

Dmitri (dam-EET-ree) Derived from the Greek god Demeter, god of fertility and farming. Notable persons with this name include composer Dmitri Shostakovich. Variations include *Mitya, Dima,* and *Dimochka.*

Gennadi (gen-NAD-ee) Meaning "noble." This is the name of Communist Party leader Gennadi Zyuganov. Variations include *Gena* and *Genchik.*

Giorgi (gee-OR-gee) Meaning "farmer." Variations include *Goga, Yegor, Gosha,* and *Zhorya.*

Grigori (gree-GOR-ee) Meaning "alert." Notable persons with this name include liberal leader Grigori Yablinsky. Variations include *Grisha*.

Igor (EE-gor) Derived from the name of the Scandinavian god of abundance. Notable persons with this name include composer Igor Stravinsky. Variations include *Gosha* and *Igorka*.

Ilya (eel-YA) Meaning "God is my fortress." Painter Ilya Repin has this name. Variations include *Ilukha* and *Ilushya*.

Ivan (ee-VAN) Meaning "God has mercy." Notable persons include the infamous Ivan the Terrible. Variations include *Vakya*, *Vanochka*, and *Vanya*.

Kirill (keer-EEL) Meaning "ruler." Variations include *Kirusha* and *Kirucha*.

Konstantin (kon-stan-TEEN) Meaning "firmly established." Variations include *Kostya* and *Kostinka*.

Lev (LEV) Meaning "lion." Notable persons include the great writer Lev Tolstoi. Variations include *Lyeva*, *Lyenya*, and *Lyeka*.

Leonid (leo-NEED) Meaning "son of a lion." Soviet leader Leonid Brezhnev was among the notable people with this name. Variations include *Lyenya* and *Lyeka*.

Maksim (mak-SEEM) Meaning "the greatest." The Russian author of *Dead Souls* and other novels wrote under the pen name Maksim Gorky. Variations include *Maks* and *Maksimochka*.

Mikhail (mik-hi-EEL) Meaning "Who is like God." Ballet dancer Mikhail Baryshnikov has found a way to create dances for himself into his fifties, well beyond the usual age of retirement for dancers. Variations include *Misha*, *Micha*, and *Mishinka*.

Nikita (nik-EE-ta) Meaning "to be victorious." Film director Nikita Michailkov is among the notable people with this name. Variations include *Kita* and *Nikitichka*.

Nikolai (nik-o-LIE) Meaning "the victorious nation." Nikolai II was the last Russian tsar. Other variations include *Kolya* and *Kolinka*.

Oleg (ol-EG) Meaning "holy." A notable Oleg is Hollywood fashion designer Oleg Cassini, who courted many stars in his day. Variations include *Olegushka*, *Lyesha*, and *Olik*.

Pavel (PAA-vel) Meaning "small." Notable persons include the Russian Tsar Pavel I. Variations include *Pavlik*, *Pava*, and *Pasha*.

Pyotr (PYE-tya) Meaning "rock." Czar Peter I, or Pyotr Alekseyvich, is known as Peter the Great. Another famous Russian with this name is romantic composer Pyotr Ilich Tchaikovsky. Also *Petr* and *Pyeta*.

Sergei (sir-GAY) Meaning "exalted one." Film director Sergei Eisenstein produced films, including *Battleship Potemkin*. Sergey Rachmaninoff was a formidable Russian composer, pianist, and conductor. Variations include *Sergey*, *Seryega*, and *Seryeshka*.

Fyodor (FYO-door) Meaning "gift of God." The Russian form of the Greek Theodore. Fyodor Dostoyevsky wrote *The Brothers Karamazov* and other important novels. Variations include *Fedya*.

Vadim (vad-EEM) Meaning "to accuse." Variations include *Vadik*.

Valentin (val-en-TEEN) Meaning "healthy" or "vigorous." A variation is *Valya*.

Valeri (va-LEAR-ee) Meaning "healthy" or "vigorous." Orchestra director Valeri Gergiev is a notable contemporary. Variations include *Valya* and *Lyeka*.

Vasili (va-SEAL-ee) Meaning "tsar" or "ruler." Abstract painter Wassili Kandinsky is among the notable people with versions of this name. Variations include *Wassili*, *Vasya*, *Vasik*, *Vasilka*, and *Vasha*.

Viktor (VICK-tor) Meaning "conqueror as the victor." Variations include *Vitya* and *Vitusha*.

Vitali (vi-TA-lee) Meaning "life." Variations include *Vitya* and *Vitenka*.

Vladimir (vlad-EE-mear) Meaning "ruler of the world." Bolshevik leader Vladimir Lenin led the Soviet revolution. Variations include *Vlad*, *Vladik*, *Volodya*, *Volodechka*, *Vova*, and *Vovichka*.

Vladislav (vlad-ee-SLAV)   Meaning "full of glory." Variations include *Vlad, Vladik, Vladichka, Slava, Slavka,* and *Slavochka.*

Vsevolod (VSE-vol-od)   Meaning "to own everything." Variations include *Vseva, Seva, Sevishka,* and *Vova.*

Vyacheslav (vyach-e-SLAV)   Meaning "the most prominent." Vyacheslav Ekimov has been Russia's greatest cyclist. Variations include *Slava* and *Slavichka.*

Yevgenie (yev-GEN-iya)   From the Greek, meaning "noble" or "previous." Pushkin's literary hero was Yevgenie Onegin. Variations include *Zhenya, Zhenka,* and *Zhenichka.*

Yuri (YOUR-ee)   Meaning "farmer." The first man in space was Yuri Gagarin. Variations include *Yurichka.*

RUSSIA: GIRLS

Agrippina (a-grip-EE-na)   An old Roman family name derived from the Latin for "wild horseman." Also *Agripa.*

Aleksandra (a-leks-AN-dra)   From the Greek for "to protect." Variations include *Sasha, Asya, Shusya,* and *Shura.*

Alena (AYE-leen-a)   Meaning "light." Variations include *Aleen, Aleena, Alenah, Alene, Alenka, Allene,* and *Alyna.*

Anastasijia (an-na-STA-see-ya)   From the Greek, meaning "resurrection." Anastasia Romanova was the youngest daughter of Tsar Nicholas II, who some believe escaped execution by the Bolsheviks in 1918. Variations include *Nastya, Nastinka, Stasya,* and *Nastuka.*

Angelika (an-zhe-LEE-ka)   Meaning "angel" or "messenger." An alternate form of Angela. Among notable people with this name is actress Angelika Neovlina. Variations include *Lika* and *Anzehl.*

Antonina (an-ton-EE-na)   From the name of the Roman emperor Antonii. Variations include *Tonya, Tonichka, Nidochka, Nina, Ninochka, Ina,* and *Inochka.*

Anya (ANN-ya)   From the Hebrew word for "divine gift." Among notable people with this name is writer Anya Martin. Variations include *Anjin, Annichka,* and *Anusya.*

Darya (DA-rya)   From the Persian meaning "owning." Among notable people with variations of this name are teenage artist Dasha Lukina and model and actress Dasha Pastoukhova. Variations include *Dasha, Dashenka,* and *Dasia.*

Galina (ga-LEE-na)   From the Greek, meaning "calm" or "serene." The name of a notable person is ballerina Galina Ulanova. Variations include *Galya, Galayna,* and *Galichka.*

Inna (EEN-a)   From the Latin, meaning "innocent." Variations include *Innochka, Innya,* and *Inka.*

Irina (ir-EE-na)   Meaning "peace." Notable people with this name are actor Irina Alferova and Ukrainian pop singer Irina Bilyk. Variations include *Ira, Irena, Irenka, Irin, Irinia,* and *Irinka.*

Ivana (EE-va-na)   From the Hebrew, meaning "God is gracious." Model and actress Ivana Trump became famous for her marriage to Donald Trump, then made a name for herself.

Ksenya (ks-YEN-a)   From the Greek meaning "guest" or "foreigner." This is the name of Saint Ksenya of St. Petersburg. Variations include *Ksusha, Ksush, Sushinka,* and *Sush.*

Lada (LAA-da)   Derived from the ancient Slavic god of marriage and love. Variations include *Ladka* and *Ladushka.*

Lubov (lu-BOFF)   Meaning "love." Variations include *Luba* and *Lubichka.*

Ludmila (lud-MEE-la)   From the ancient Slavic meaning "lover of people." Variations include *Luda, Ludichka,* and *Mila.*

Marina (mar-EE-na)   Meaning "sea." Variations include *Marichka, Marusya, Marinichka,* and *Marochka.*

Maya (MY-ya)   In Greek mythology, Maya is the mother of Hermes. Also *Mayichka.*

Mariya (MA-ri-ya)   From the Hebrew, meaning "exalted." Variations include *Masha, Mashenka, Marochka,* and *Marusa.*

Milena (me-LEN-a)   From the Slavic, meaning "kind." Variations include *Milenichka* and *Milen*.

Nadezhda (na-DEZH-da)   From the Russian, meaning "hope." Variations include *Nadya*, *Nadichka*, and *Nadinka*.

Natasha (na-TASH-a)   A name that derives from the Latin name Natalie, meaning "child of Christmas." Among famous Natashas are actress Natasha Henstridge and Russian Olympic gymnastics coach Natasha Matveena. Variations include *Natashenka*, *Natash*, and *Tasha*.

Nika (NEE-ka)   From the Greek meaning "victory." Also *Nichka*.

Nina (NEE-na)   The founder of the ancient Assyrian state. Variations include *Nin*, *Ninka*, *Ninochka*, *Ninula*.

Olga (OL-ga)   A version of the name Helga from the Old Scandinavian meaning "holy." A famous Olga is author Olga Shapir. Variations include *Olya*, *Olinka*, and *Olichka*.

Raisa (rye-EES-a)   From the Greek, meaning "light." Raisa Gorbachev, married to former Soviet president Mikhail Gorbachev. Variations include *Sonja* and *Sonichka*.

Sonja (SON-ya)   Meaning "wise."

Svetlana (svet-LA-na)   From the Slavic, meaning "bright light." Olympic gymnastic champion Svetlana Boguinskaia and Svetlana Alulyeva, daughter of Soviet political leader Josef Stalin share a name and a homeland. Variations include *Sveta*, *Svetochka*, *Lana*, and *Lanichka*.

Tatiana (TAT-ya-na)   From the Greek meaning "to appoint." Variations include *Tanya* and *Tanichka*.

Valentina (val-en-TEE-na)   From the Latin meaning "strong." Variations include *Valeria*, *Valya*, *Valichka*, *Lera*, and *Lerichka*.

Varvara (var-VAR-a)   From the Greek meaning "rude foreigner." Variations include *Varya*, *Varochka*, and *Varka*.

Vera (VEER-a)   From the Slavic meaning "faith." A variation is *Verochka*.

Yekaterina (ye-kat-er-EE-na)   From the Greek meaning "pure." Ballet dancers Yekaterina Geltzer and Yekaterina Maximova, Olympic gold medalist biathlete Yekaterina Dafovska. Variations include *Katya*, *Katinka*, and *Katusha*.

Yelena (ye-LEN-a)   From the Greek name Helene meaning "light." Among the notable people with this name is gymnast Yelena Grosheva. Variations include *Lena* and *Lenichka*.

Yelisabeta (ye-liz-a-BET-a)   See also Elizabeth under Hebrew names. From the Hebrew phrase for "God is my oath." The wife of Tsar Alexander I of Russia was Tsarina Yelizaveta Alekseyevna von Baden Romanova. Variations include *Liza* and *Lizichka*.

Yevdokiya (yev-do-KEE-ya)   From the Greek meaning "reverence." Variations include *Yevdosha*, *Yevdosya*, *Yevda*, and *Yeva*.

Yulia (YOU-ly-a)   From the Greek meaning "youthful." Among the notable people with this name is skater Yulia Soldatova. Variations include *Yula*, *Yulenka*, *Yulinka*, *Yulka*, and *Yulichka*.

Yyevgenia (yev-GEN-iya)   From the Greek meaning "noble" or "previous." Variations include *Zhenya*, *Zhenka*, and *Zhenichka*.

Zoya (ZOI-ya)   From the Greek meaning "life." Variations include *Zoika* and *Zosya*.

Ukraine

Like names in the languages of most European nations, Ukrainian names have been greatly influenced by Christianity. By the close of the 10th century, when the eastern Slavic tribes who were ancestors to both Russians and Ukrainians accepted Greek Orthodoxy as the state religion, many Greek names had entered the local language. Despite this strong outside influence, however, genuine Slavic names remained in the culture. Since Russia and Ukraine are linguistic as well as geographic neighbors, names of the two nations are similar when written and pronounced, the difference often being a matter of one letter. For instance, where there is a letter "a" in Russian, Ukrainians will say "o," and where there is a hard "g" in Russian, Ukrainians will say "h."

UKRAINE: BOYS

Adrian (ad-ree-AN)   From the name of the ancient city of Adria. Variations include *Adrya*, *Ariasha*, and *Yasha*.

Bohdan (boh-DAN) Meaning "given by God."

Danylo (dan-YEEL-o) Meaning "divine judge."

Dmitro (DMEE-tro) Masculine version of the name Demeter, the Greek goddess of fertility and farming.

Ihor (EE-hoar)   From the Scandinavian god of abundance.

Ivan (ee-VAN) Meaning "God has mercy." Variations include *Vanya* and *Vanko*.

Josyp (YO-sip)   Meaning "God multiplies." A variation is *Josya*.

Kosma (kos-MA) Meaning "order" or "peace." Variations include *Kuzya*.

Luka (lu-KA) Meaning "light."

Maksym (mak-SEEM) Meaning "the greatest." Also *Maks*.

Marko (MAR-ko) Meaning "hammer." A variation is *Marik*.

Matviy (mat-VAY) Meaning "gift of God." A variation is *Matya*.

Mykola (mik-OL-a)   Meaning "Who is like God."

Myron (meer-ON)   Meaning "sweet smelling oil." Variations include *Mirosha* and *Mosha*.

Oleh (ol-EH)   Meaning "holy."

Oleksander (oleks-AN-dr)   Meaning "to protect." Variations include *Sasha* and *Sana*.

Ondrij (on-DREY)   Meaning "brave." A variation is *Ondrusha*.

Orest (or-EST)   Meaning "mountain." A variation is *Ora*.

Pavlo (PAHV-low)   Meaning "small."

Petro (PYE-ter)   Meaning "rock." Also *Petya*.

Roman (ro-MAN)   Meaning "Roman citizen." Variations include *Roma* and *Romichka*.

Serhiy (sir-HAY)   Meaning "exalted one."

Stanislav (stan-ee-SLAV) Meaning "to establish glory." Variations include *Stanya* and *Slava*.

Stepan (step-AN) Meaning "crown." Variations include *Stefan*, *Styepa*, and *Styesha*.

Taras (tar-AS) Meaning "to unsettle." A notable person with this name is poet Taras Shevchenko. Also *Tarasha*.

Yaroslaw (ya-ro-SLAV) Meaning "bright glory." Variations include *Yaro* and *Slava*.

Youri (YOUR-ee) Meaning "farmer." A form of George.

Wasyl (va-SEAL-ee) Meaning "tsar" or "ruler." Variations include *Vasya*, *Vasik*, *Vasilka*, and *Vasha*.

Wolodymyr (vlad-EE-mear) Meaning "ruler of the world." A notable person with this name is Prince Wolodymyr.

Zenon (zen-ON) Meaning "like Zeus." A variation is *Zena*.

UKRAINE: GIRLS

Anna (ANN-ya) Meaning "divine gift."

Halyna (ha-LEE-na) Meaning "calm" or "serene."

Iryna (ir-EE-na) Meaning "peace."

Lada (LA-da) Meaning "dear" or "beloved." A variation is *Ladka*.

Lubov (lu-BOFF) Meaning "love." Also *Luba*.

Maria (MA-ri-ya) Meaning "exalted." Variations include *Marika* and *Masha*.

Mikayla (mik-hi-ELL) Meaning "Who is like God."

Natalka (na-TASH-a) Meaning "natural." A variation is *Natasha*.

Oksana (ok-SA-na) Meaning "guest" or "foreigner." Oksana Baiul of Ukraine won the 1994 Olympic gold medal for figure skating. A variation is *Ksusha*.

Olha (ol-HA) Meaning "holy."

Stefania (stef-AN-iya) Meaning "wreath." Variations include *Stefa* and *Fanya*.

Tamara (tam-AR-a) Meaning "date leaf." Tamara McKinney U.S. Olympic skiier. A variation is *Tama*.

Tatiana (TAT-ya-na) Meaning "to appoint."

Valentyna (val-en-TEE-na) Meaning "strong." A variation is *Valya*.

Vera (VE-ra) Meaning "faith." Also *Verichka*.

Vita (VEE-ta) From the Latin, meaning "life." A variation is *Vitka*.

Yekaterina (ye-kat-er-EE-na) Meaning "pure." Variations include *Katya* and *Katusha*.

Zenovia (zen-OV-iya) Meaning "like Zeus." Also *Zenya*.

 **England** One of the most remarkable facts about English naming practices is that a relatively small stock of modern English names have been popular for hundreds of years. In the records of male baptisms between 1550 and 1800, William, John, and Thomas accounted for 50 to 60 percent of all given names. Records of the baptisms of female infants during the same years show that the names Elizabeth, Mary, and Ann were chosen 46 to 57 percent of the time. In England today, these names are still among the most popular.

ENGLAND: BOYS

Ackerley (ACK-er-lee) Meaning "oak meadow." Variations include *Accerley, Ackerlea, Ackerleigh, Ackersley, Acklea, Ackleigh, Ackley,* and *Acklie.*

Acton (AC-ton) Meaning "oak-tree settlement."

Addison (ADD-is-un) Meaning "son of Adam." Addison Verrill is a celebrated zoologist. Variations include *Addis, Adison,* and *Adisson.*

Adney (AD-nee) Meaning "noble's island."

Afton (AF-ton) A person from Afton, England. Also *Affton.*

Alcott (AL-cot) Meaning "old cottage." Variations include *Alcot, Alkot, Alkott, Allcot, Allcott, Allkot,* and *Allkott.*

Alden (AL-din) Meaning "old friend." See also Aldwin. Variations include *Aldin, Aldous,* and *Elden.*

Aldred (AL-dread) Meaning "old counselor." Variations include *Alldred* and *Eldred.*

Aldrich (AL-dritch) Meaning "old leader." Variations include *Aldric, Aldrick, Aldridge, Aldrige, Aldritch, Alldric, Alldrich, Alldrick, Alldridge,* and *Eldridge.*

Aldwin (ALD-win) Meaning "old friend." See also Alden. Variations include *Aldwyn* and *Eldwin.*

Alford (AL-ford) Meaning "old river ford."

Alfred (ALL-frid) Meaning "counsel from elves." Romantic poet Alfred, Lord Tennyson and filmmaker Alfred Hitchcock. Variations include *Ailfrid, Ailfryd, Alf, Alfeo, Alfie, Alfredo,* and *Alured.*

Algernon (AL-jer-nohn) Meaning "bearded" or "moustached." Among the famous people with this name is poet Algernon Swinburne. Variations include *Algenon, Alger, Algie, Algin,* and *Algon.*

Alistair (AL-ih-stir) See Alexandros under Greek names. Notable persons with this name include American-born Alistair Cooke, a journalist and television host whose fame was British-based. Variations include *Alisdair, Alistaire, Alistar, Alister, Allister,* and *Allistir.*

Allard (AL-lurd) Meaning "well-born" or "courageous." Variations include *Alard* and *Ellard.*

Alston (AL-stun) Meaning "noble's settlement." A variation is *Allston.*

Alton (AL-tun) Meaning "old town." A variation is *Alten.*

Alvin (AL-vin) Meaning "noble friend" or "elf friend." Variations include *Al, El, Elvin, Elvyn, Elwin, Elwyn,* and *Elwynn.*

Arledge (AR-ledj) Meaning "lake with the hares." Variations include *Arledge* and *Arlidge*.

Arley (AR-lee) A diminutive form of Harley. Variations include *Arleigh*, *Arlie*, and *Arly*.

Arnette (AR-net) Meaning "little eagle." Variations include *Arnat*, *Arnet*, *Arnot*, and *Arnott*.

Ashford (ASH-ford) Meaning "ash-tree ford." Variations include *Ash* and *Ashtin*.

Ashley (ASH-lee) Meaning "ash-tree meadow." Variations include *Ash*, *Asheley*, *Ashelie*, *Ashely*, *Ashlan*, and *Ashleigh*.

Ashton (ASH-tun) Meaning "ash-tree settlement." A variation is *Ashtin*.

Aston (AS-tun) Meaning "eastern town." Variations include *Asten* and *Astin*.

Atherton (ATH-ur-tun) Translated literally, means "town by a spring."

Atley (AT-lee) Meaning "meadow." Variations include *Atlea*, *Atlee*, *Atleigh*, *Atli*, and *Attley*.

Atwell (AT-well) Meaning "at the well."

Atworth (AT-wurth) Meaning "at the farmstead."

Audric (AUD-ric) Meaning "noble ruler."

Avery (AY-vuh-ree) A variation on the more popular name Aubrey, which means "elf-ruler." Longtime Olympic Committee president Avery Brundage. Variations include *Avary*, *Aveary*, *Averey*, *Averie*, and *Avry*.

Ayers (A-urs) Meaning "heir to a fortune."

Baker (BAY-kur) A variation of the name Baxter, which means "the baker."

Bancroft (BAN-kroft) Meaning "field of beans." Variations include *Ban*, *Bancrofft*, *Bank*, *Bankroft*, *Banky*, and *Binky*.

Barclay (BAR-klay) Meaning "place where birches grow."

Barker (BAR-kur) Meaning "lumberjack" or "carnival hawker."

Barlow (BAR-lo) Meaning "bare hillside." Variations include *Barlowe*, *Bardow*, and *Barrlowe*.

Barnaby (BAR-nah-bee) Meaning "son of comfort." Famous fictional Barnaby is T.V. sleuth Barnaby Jones. Variations include *Barnabe*, *Barnabee*, *Barnabey*, *Barnable*, *Bernabi*, and *Burnaby*.

Barnes (BARNZ) Meaning "bear" or "son of Barnett."

Barney (BAR-nee) A familiar form of Barnabas and Barnett. See also Barnaby. Race car driver Barney Olfield and the enormously popular purple dinosaur "Barney." Variations include *Barnie* and *Barny*.

Barric (BAR-ick) Meaning "grain farm." Variations include *Barrick* and *Beric*.

Bartlet (BART-let) A variation on the Hebrew name Bartholomew, which means "farmer" or "son of the furrows." Variations include *Bartlett* and *Bartley*.

Barton (BAR-tun) Meaning "barley farm" or "Bart's town." The eponymous writer in the movie *Barton Fink*. Variations include *Barrton* and *Bart*.

Bartram (BAR-tram) An alternate form of Bertram, meaning "bright raven." A variation is *Barthram*.

Bassett (BASS-set) Meaning "little person." Variations include *Basett* and *Basset*.

Baxter (BAX-tur) An alternate form of Baker. Variations include *Bax*, *Baxie*, and *Baxy*.

Bayard (BAY-yard) Meaning "russet-haired." Civil rights leader Bayard Rustin. Variations include *Baiardo*, *Bay*, *Bayerd*, and *Bayrd*.

Beaman (BEE-man) Meaning "beekeeper." Variations include *Beamann*, *Beamen*, *Beeman*, and *Beman*.

Beamer (BEE-mur) Meaning "trumpet player."

Beasley (BEEZ-lee) Meaning "meadow of peas."

Beaver (BEE-vur) Meaning "beaver." Variations include *Beav*, *Beavo*, *Beve*, and *Bevo*.

Beck (BECK) Meaning "brook." Variations include *Beckett*.

Benton (BENT-tun) Meaning "rough grass." Variations include *Bent*.

Berkeley (BUR-kuh-lee) Meaning "from the birch meadow." An alternate form of Barclay. "Bloom County" cartoonist Berkeley Breathed. Variations include *Berk, Berkie, Berkley, Berklie, Berkly,* and *Berky*.

Bernard (ber-NARD) Meaning "brave as a bear." Variations include *Barn, Barnard, Barnhard,* and *Barnhardo*.

Berry (BAIR-ee) Meaning "berry" and "grape."

Berton (BUR-tun) Meaning "bright settlement." Variations include *Bert*.

Bertram (BUR-tram) Meaning "bright raven."

Berwyn (BUR-win) Meaning "powerful friend." A name for babies born under the astrological signs of Virgo, Capricorn, and Taurus. Variations include *Berwin, Berwynn,* and *Berwynne*.

Bickford (BIK-ford) Meaning "axman's ford."

Birch (BURCH) Meaning "birch tree." Senator Birch Bayh. Variations include *Birk* and *Burch*.

Birkey (BUR-kee) Meaning "island with birch trees." Variations include *Birk, Birkie,* and *Birky*.

Birkitt (BUR-kit) Meaning "birch coast." Variations include *Birk, Birket, Birkit, Burket, Burkett,* and *Burkitt*.

Birney (BUR-nee) Meaning "island with a brook." Variations include *Birne, Birnie, Birny, Burney, Burnie,* and *Burny*.

Blake (BLAYK) Meaning "attractive" or "dark." Film director Blake Edwards. Variations include *Blakely, Blakeman,* and *Blakey*.

Bond (BOND) Meaning "man of the earth." Variations include *Bondie, Bondon, Bonds,* and *Bondy*.

Booker (BOO-ker) Meaning "bookmaker," "book lover," or "Bible lover." A notable person with this name is American educator Booker T. Washington. Variations include *Bookie, Books,* and *Booky*.

Booth (BOOTH) Meaning "dwelling place." A famous Booth is American author Booth Tarkington.

Bosley (BOZ-lee) Meaning "meadow near the woods."

Brad (BRAD) A short form of Bradford or Bradley. Variations include *Bradd* and *Brade*.

Bradburn (BRAD-burn) Meaning "broad stream."

Bradford (BRAD-ford) Meaning "broad river ford." Variations include *Brad, Braddford,* and *Ford*.

Bradley (BRAD-lee) Meaning "broad meadow." Variations include *Brad, Bradlay, Bradlea, Radlee, Bradleigh, Bradlie, Bradly, Bradney,* and *Bradly*.

Bradon (BRAY-dun) Meaning "broad hill." Variations include *Braedon, Braidon,* and *Braydon*.

Bradshaw (BRAD-shaw) Meaning "broad forest."

Brainard (BRAY-nurd) Meaning "bold raven" or "prince." A variation is *Brainerd*.

Bramwell (BRAM-well) Meaning "bramble-bush well." Variations include *Brammel, Brarnmell, Bramwel,* and *Brarnwyll*.

Branden (BRAN-den) Meaning "beacon valley."

Brandon (BRAN-dun) Meaning "beacon hill." Variations include *Bran, Brand, Brandan, Branddon, Brandin, Brandone,* and *Brandonn*.

Brant (BRANT) Meaning "proud." Variations include *Brandt, Brannt, Brantley,* and *Brantlie*.

Braxton (BRAX-tun) Meaning "Brock's town."

Brennan (BREN-nun) An alternate form of Brendan (see Irish names). Variations include *Bren, Brennin,* and *Brennon*.

Brent (BRENT)   A short form of Brenton. A notable Brent is Brent Scowcroft, U.S. Navy admiral and former national security advisor. Variations include *Brendt* and *Brentson.*

Brenton (BREN-tun)   Meaning "steep hill." Variations include *Brent, Brentan, Brenten, Brentin, Brentton,* and *Brentyn.*

Brewster (BREW-stir)   Meaning "brewer." Was the main character of Spalding Gray's autobiographical novel *Impossible Vacation* Brewster North.

Bridger (BRIDJ-ur)   Meaning "bridge builder." Variations include *Bridd, Bridgeley,* and *Bridgely.*

Brigham (BRIG-hum)   Meaning "village by the covered bridge." Brigham Young was the Mormon leader who took Joseph Smith's movement west.

Brock (BROC)   Meaning "badger." Variations include *Broc, Brocke, Brockett, Brockie, Brockley,* and *Brockton.*

Bromley (BROM-lee)   Meaning "brushwood meadow."

Bronson (BRON-son)   Meaning "son of Brown." Actor Bronson Pinchot who played Balki on the TV series *Perfect Strangers.* Variations include *Bransen, Bransin, Branson, Bron,* and *Bronnie.*

Brook (BROOK)   Meaning "brook" or "stream." Variations include *Brooke, Brooker, Brookin,* or *Brooklyn.*

Brooks (BROOKS)   Meaning "son of Brook." Critic Brooks Atkinson and baseball player Brooks Robinson. Variations include *Brookes* and *Broox.*

Brown (BROWN)   Meaning "brown."

Buckminster (BUCK-min-stir)   Meaning "preacher." Geodesic dome creator Buckminster Fuller.

Bud (BUHD)   Meaning "herald" or "messenger." Bud Abbott of the comedy team Abbott and Costello. Variations include *Budd* and *Buddy.*

Buford (BEW-ford)   Meaning "ford near the castle." A variation is *Burford.*

Burgess (BUR-gess)   Meaning "town dweller" or "shopkeeper." Actor Burgess Meredith. Variations include *Burg, Burges, Burgh, Burgiss, Burr,* and *Burris.*

Burne (BURN)   See Bourne in French section. Variations include *Beirne, Burn, Burnell, Burnett, Burney, Byrne, Bryne,* and *Burnes*

Burney (BUR-nee)   A familiar form of Rayburn, signifying "island of the brook."

Burton (BUR-tun)   Meaning "fortified town." Actor Burt Lancaster started his career as a circus acrobat. Variations include *Berton* and *Burt.*

Butcher (BUTCH-ur)   Meaning "butcher." A variation is *Butch.*

Byford (BYE-ford)   Meaning "by the ford."

Calvert (CAL-vurt)   Meaning "calf herder." Variations include *Cal, Calbert,* and *Calvirt.*

Carlisle (CAR-lyle)   A name that means "Carl's island." Variations include *Carlyle* and *Carlysle.*

Carlton (CARl-tun)   Literally means "Carl's town." Variations include *Carl, Carleton, Carliton, Carlston, Carltonn, Cartton,* and *Charlton.*

Carnell (CAR-nell)   Meaning "defender of the castle."

Carson (CAR-sun)   Literally means "son of Carr." MTV vee-jay Carson Daly. Also spelled *Carrson.*

Cater (CAY-tur)   Meaning "caterer."

Cedric (SED-ric)   An alternative form of Kedrick, which means "war leader." Actor Sir Cedric Hardwicke. Variations include *Cad, Caddaric, Ced, Cedrec, Cedrick, Cedryche, Sedric, Cederick, Cedirick,* and *Cedrik.*

Chad (CHAD)   From the Celtic meaning "warrior" or "battle." The name of a country of north-central Africa. Among notable people with this name are actors Chad Everett and Chad Lowe. Variations include *Ceadd, Chaad, Chadd, Chaddie, Chaddy, Chade, Chadleigh,*

Chadier, Chadley, Chadlin, Chadlyn, Chadmen, Chado, Chadron, and *Chady.*

Chadwick (CHAD-wic)   A name that signifies "warrior's town." Variations include *Chadwyck* and *Chadvic.*

Chance (CHANTZ)   A short form of Chancellor or Chauncey. Variations include *Chanc, Chancey, Chancy, Chanse, Chansy, Chants, Chantz,* and *Chanz.*

Chauncey (CHAWN-see)   Meaning "chancellor" or "church official." Composer Chauncey Olcott; Chauncey Gardner, name of protagonist in the film *Being There.* Variations include *Chan, Chance, Chancey, Chaunce, Chauncei,* and *Chauncy.*

Chester (CHES-tur)   A short form of Rochester. Chester Allan Arthur was the twenty-first president of the United States. Variations include *Ches, Cheslay, Cheston,* and *Chet.*

Chilton (CHILL-tun)   A name that means "farm by the spring." Variations include *Chil, Chill,* and *Chilt.*

Clayborne (KLAY-born)   Meaning "brook near the clay pit." Variations include *Claiborn, Claiborne, Clay, Clayborn, Claybourne,* and *Clayburn.*

Clayton (KLAY-tun)   Meaning "town built on clay." Actor Clayton Moore played the *Lone Ranger* on TV. A variation is *Clay.*

Cleavon (KLEE-von)   Meaning "cliff." Actor Cleavon Little, the star of *Blazing Saddles.* Variations include *Cleaveland, Cleavland, Cleavon, Cleve, Clevelend, Clevelynn, Clevey, Clevie,* and *Clevon.*

Clifford (KLIFF-ford)   Meaning "cliff at the river crossing." Playwright Clifford Odets and actor Cliff Robertson. Variations include *Cliff, Cliford,* and *Clyfford.*

Clifton (KLIFF-tun)   Literally. "cliff town." Among famous people with this name is actor Clifton Webb. Variations include *Cliff, Cliffton, Clift, Cliften,* and *Clyfton.*

Clinton (KLIN-ton)   Meaning "hillside town." Among famous people with this name

are country singer Clint Black and actor Clint Eastwood. Variations include *Clint, Clinten, Clintton,* and *Clynton.*

Clive (KLIVE)   Meaning "a steep bank." An alternate form of Cliff. Among notable people with this name is movie and theater critic Clive Barnes. Variations include *Cleve, Clivans, Clivens,* and *Clyve.*

Colley (KOLL-lee)   Meaning "dark-haired." Variations include *Collie* and *Collis.*

Collier (CALL-e-ur)   Meaning "cool miner." Variations include *Colier, Collayer, Collie, Collyer,* and *Colyer.*

Colt (KOLT)   Signifying "a young horse" or "frisky." A short form of Colter or Colton.

Connie (KON-nee)   A familiar form of Conan, Conrad, Constantine, or Conway. Among the famous people with this name is country musician Conway Twitty. Variations include *Con, Conn, Conney,* and *Conny.*

Crandall (KRAN-doll)   Meaning "crane's valley." Variations include *Cran, Crandal, Crandell,* and *Crendal.*

Crawford (KRAW-ford)   Literally meaning a "ford where crows fly." Variations include *Craw, Crow,* and *Ford.*

Creighton (KRAY-tun)   Meaning "rocky spot." Variations include *Cray, Crayton, Creighm, Creight,* and *Crichton.*

Cromwell (KROM-well)   This name means "winding stream."

Dagwood (DAG-wood)   Meaning "shining forest." A well-known Dagwood is Dagwood Bumstead, husband of ditsy comic strip heroine Blondie.

Dale (DALE)   Meaning "dale" or "valley." Noteworthy people with this name include pioneering self-help expert Dale Carnegie. Variations include *Daelan, Daelen, Daelin, Dallin, Dalan, Dalian, Dalibor, Dalin, Dalione, Dalian, Dalyn, Daylan, Daylen, Daylin,* and *Daylon.*

Dalton (DAWL-tun)   Meaning "town in the valley." Academy Award–winning screenwriter Dalton Trumbo was a victim of blacklisting.

Variations include *Dal, Dallton, Dalt,* and *Dalten.*

Dane (DAIN) Meaning "from Denmark." Variations include *Daine, Danie, Dayne,* and *Dhane.*

Danforth (DAN-forth) An alternate form of the Hebrew name Daniel, which means "God is judge."

Darnell (DARN-ell) A name that means "hidden place."

Darton (DAR-tun) Meaning "deer town." Variations include *Dartel* and *Dartrel.*

Dayton (DAY-tun) A name that literally means "day town" or "bright, sunny town." Variations include *Daeton, Daiton,* and *Deyton.*

Delbert (DEL-burt) A name that means "bright as day." Variations include *Bert, Dalbert, Del,* and *Dilbert.*

Dell (DELL) Meaning "small valley." A short form of Udell.

Delvin (DELL-vin) Meaning "proud friend" or "friend from the valley." Variations include *Del, Delavan, Delvyn, Delwin, Dalwin, Dalwyn, Del, Dellwin, Dellwyn, Delwyn,* and *Delwynn.*

Denham (DEN-him) Meaning "village in the valley."

Denley (DEN-lee) Meaning "meadow, valley." Variations include *Denlie* and *Denly.*

Dennison (DEN-nis-sun) Meaning "son of Dennis." A unique combination of the names Dyson and Tennyson. Variations include *Den, Denison, Denisson,* and *Dennyson.*

Denton (DEN-tun) A name that means "settlement in the valley." Variations include *Dent, Denten,* and *Dentin.*

Derward (DUR-ward) Literal meaning is "deer keeper."

Dixon (DICKS-sun) Meaning "son of Dick." Variations include *Dickson* and *Dix.*

Dudley (DUD-lee) Meaning "common field." British comic actor Dudley Moore will

be remembered for his role in *Arthur.* Variations include *Dudd* and *Dudly.*

Dunley (DUN-lee) A name signifying "hilly meadow."

Dunton (DUN-tun) Meaning "hill town."

Durward (DUR-ward) Meaning "gatekeeper." Variations include *Dur* and *Ward.*

Dustin (DUST-in) Meaning "strong-hearted leader." Academy Award–winning actor Dustin Hoffman. Variations include *Dusty* and *Dustyn.*

Dwight (DWHYT) Which means "light." Former U.S. president Dwight David Eisenhower.

Dyer (DIE-ur) A name that means "fabric dyer."

Dyke (DIEK) Meaning "ditch." A variation is *Dike.*

Earnest (UR-nest) Literally meaning "earnest" or "sincere." An alternate form of Ernest. Variations include *Earn, Earnesto, Earnie,* and *Ernest.*

Edbert (ED-burt) Meaning "wealthy" or "bright." A variation is *Ediberto.*

Edgar (ED-gur) Meaning "wealthy spearman." Famous people with this name include poet Edgar Allen Poe, who wrote "The Raven," and ventriloquist Edgar Bergen. Variations include *Ed, Eddie, Edek, Edgard,* and *Edgars.*

Edison (ED-is-sun) Literally meaning "son of Edward." Variations include *Eddison, Edisen,* and *Edson.*

Edmund (ED-mund) Which means "prosperous protector." Among notable people with this name are former Senator Edmund Muskie of Maine and Mount Everest explorer Sir Edmund Hillary, the first person to summit and survive. Variations include *Eadmund, Eamon, Edmon, Edmond, Edmonde, Edmondson, Esmond, Edmundo,* and *Edmunds.*

Edward (ED-word) Meaning "prosperous guardian." Noteworthy Edwards include senator Edward Moore Kennedy of Massachusetts and playwright Edward Albee, and actor Edward G. Robinson. Variations include *Ed, Edd, Eddie, Edik, Edko, Edo, Edoardo, Edorta, Edouard, Eduard, Eduardo, Edus, Ted,* and *Teddy.*

Edwin (ED-win) Meaning "prosperous friend." Journalist and TV news commentator Edwin Newman. Variations include *Eadwinn, Edik, Edlin, Eduino,* and *Edwyn.*

Egbert (EGG-burt) A name that means "bright sword." One famous Egbert is the first English king in recorded history.

Egerton (EGG-er-tun) Literally means "Edgar's town." Variations include *Edgarton, Edgartown, Edgerton,* and *Egeton.*

Elbert (EL-burt) See Albert under French names.

Elden (EL-den) See Alden. A variation is *Eldin.*

Elder (EL-dur) A name that means "dweller near the elder trees."

Eldon (EL-dun) Meaning "sacred hill."

Eldred (EL-dread) An alternate form of Aldred. A variation is *Eldrid.*

Eldridge (EL-dridge) An alternate form of Aldrich. Radical civil rights activist Eldridge Cleaver. Variations include *El, Eldred,* and *Eldredge.*

Eldwin (EL-dwin) An alternate form of Aldwin. Variations include *Eldwinn, Eldwyn,* and *Eldwynn.*

Elgin (EL-gin) Meaning "noble" or "white." Variations include *Elgan* and *Elgen.*

Ellery (ELL-uh-ree) A name that means "elder tree island." Fictional detective Ellery Queen. Variations include *Ellary* and *Ellerey.*

Elliot (EL-lee-ot) Form of Eli and Elijah. Crime fighter Elliot Ness and actor Elliot Gould. Variations include *Elio, Eliot, Eliott, Eliud, Eliut, Elliott, Elyot,* and *Elyott.*

Ellison (EL-iss-sun) Literally means "son of Ellis." Variations include *Elison, Ellson, Ellyson,* and *Elson.*

Ellsworth (ELS-wurth) Meaning "nobleman's estate." Variations include *Ellswerth* and *Elsworth.*

Elmer (EL-mur) Meaning "noble" or "famous." Film music composer Elmer Bernstein and Sinclair Lewis's title character in *Elmer Gantry* are well-known Elmers. Variations include *Aylmer, Ellmer, Elmir,* and *Elmo.*

Elmore (EL-more) This name means "moor where the elm trees grow."

Elston (EL-stun) Meaning "noble's town." A variation is *Ellston.*

Elton (EL-tun) Meaning "old town." Composer, performer Elton John has rocked the house for three decades. Variations include *Alton, Eldon,* and *Ellton.*

Elwood (EL-wood) Meaning "old woodland." An alternate form of Wood and Woody.

Emerson (EM-mur-sun) Literally "son of Emery." Among noteworthy Emersons is Indy 500 winner Emerson Fittipaldi. Variations include *Emmerson* and *Emreson.*

Erland (UR-land) Meaning "nobleman's land." A variation is *Erlend.*

Ernest (UR-nest) Meaning "earnest" or "sincere." Actor Ernest Borgnine, author Ernest Hemingway, and comedian Ernie Kovacs. Variations include *Arne, Earnest, Ernestino, Ernesto, Ernestus, Ernie, Erno,* and *Ernst.*

Errol (ERR-uhl) From the Latin *erroneus,* meaning "to wander." A popular Errol was actor Errol Flynn.

Ervin (UR-vin) Alternate form of Irwin, which means "sea friend." Variations include *Earvin, Ery, Erven,* and *Ervyn.*

Esmond (ES-mund) Meaning "protected by grace."

Evan (EV-an) A form of Hebrew John, meaning "God's gracious gift."

Everett (EV-ur-ett) A form of Eberhard. Senator Everett Dirksen. Variations include *Ev, Evered, Everet, Everette, Everitt, Evert,* and *Evrett.*

Everley (EV-ur-lee) A name that means "boar meadow." Variations include *Everlea* and *Everlee*.

Everton (EV-er-tun) This name signifies "boar town."

Ewert (EWE-urt) Meaning "ewe herder" or "shepherd." A variation is *Ewart*.

Ewing (EWE-ing) Meaning "friend of the law." Variations include *Ewin* and *Ewynn*.

Fairfax (FAIR-fax) From the Anglo-Saxon meaning "blond."

Farley (FAR-lee) Meaning "bull meadow" or "sheep meadow." Among famous people with this name is actor Farley Granger. Variations include *Fairlay, Fairlee, Fairleigh, Fairley, Fairlie, Far,* and *Farlay*.

Farnell (FAR-nell) Meaning a "fern-covered hill." Variations include *Farnall, Fernald, Fernall,* and *Furnald*.

Farold (FAR-old) Meaning "robust traveler."

Felton (FELL-tun) Literally "field town." Variations include *Felten* and *Feltin*.

Fenton (FEN-tun) Meaning "marshland farm." A noteworthy Fenton is educator Fenton Keyes. Variations include *Fen, Fennie,* and *Fenny*.

Fielding (FEELD-ing) From "feld" meaning "field" or "field-worker." Variations include *Field* and *Fields*.

Filbert (FILL-burt) Meaning "brilliant." Type of nut named for a seventh-century monk, Saint Filbert. Variations include *Bert, Filberte, Filberto,* and *Philbert*.

Filmore (FILL-more) Meaning "famous." Variations include *Fillmore, Filmer, Fyllmer,* and *Fylmer*.

Firth (FURTH) Signifying "woodland."

Fiske (FISK) Meaning "fisherman." A variation is *Fisk*.

Fitch (FITCH) Meaning "weasel" or "ermine." A variation is *Fitche*.

Fitz (FITZ) Meaning "son." A variation is *Filz*.

Fitzgerald (FITZ-jerr-old) Literally meaning "son of Gerald," this name is usually a surname.

Fitzhugh (FITZ-you) Literally, "son of Hugh."

Fitzpatrick (FITZ-pat-rick) This name means "son of Patrick."

Fleming (FLEM-ing) Derived from Middle Dutch for "from Flanders." Variations include *Flemming, Flemmyng,* and *Flemyng*.

Fletcher (FLET-chur) From the Old French, meaning "arrow featherer" and "arrow maker." Jazz great Fletcher Henderson. Variations include *Flecher* and *Fletch*.

Flint (FLINT) Meaning "stream" or "flintstone." Also *Flynt*.

Floyd (FLOYD) A form of Lloyd. Among notable Floyds is former heavyweight boxing champion Floyd Patterson.

Ford (FORD) Meaning "river crossing." Among those who share this name is Ford Madox Ford, author of *The Good Soldier*.

Frank (FRANK) A short form of Francis, which means a "free man." Notable Franks are premier singer Frank Sinatra and architect Frank Lloyd Wright. Variations include *Franc, Franck, Franek, Frang, Franio, Franke, Frankie, Franko,* and *Franky*.

Franklin (FRANK-lin) Meaning "free landowner." Persons with this name include two former U.S. presidents, Franklin Delano Roosevelt and Franklin Pierce. Variations include *Fran, Francklin, Francklyn, Frank, Frankin, Franklinn, Franklyn,* and *Franquelin*.

Garfield (GAR-field) Meaning "field of spears; battlefield."

Garman (GAR-mun) Meaning "spearman." Variations include *Garmann* and *Garrman*.

Garrett (GAR-reht) Meaning "gentle."

Garrick (GAIR-rick) Meaning "spear command." Variations include *Gaerick, Garek, Garick, Garik, Garreck, Garrek, Garrik, Garryck, Garryk, Gerreck,* and *Gerrick*.

Garrin (GAIR-rin) An alternate form of Garrett, which means "gentle." Variations include *Garran, Garren, Garron,* and *Garyn.*

Garson (GAR-sun) Literally means "son of Gar." Notable persons with this name include playwright and screenwriter Garson Kanin.

Garvin (GAR-vin) Meaning "comrade in war." Variations include *Gar, Garvan, Garven, Garvyn, Garwen, Garwin, Garwyn,* and *Garwynn.*

Garwood (GAR-wood) Meaning "evergreen forest." Variations include *Garrwood, Wood,* and *Woody.*

Gary (GAIR-ree) Meaning "spear fighter." Famous persons with this name include actors Gary Cooper, Garry Shandling, and *Different Strokes'* Gary Coleman. Variations include *Garry, Garrey, Garri, Garrie,* and *Garrin.*

Geffrey (JEFF-ree) An alternate form of Geoffrey. Variations include *Geff, Geffery,* and *Geffrard.*

Geoffrey (JEFF-ree) Meaning "divinely peaceful." Famous Geoffreys include *Canterbury Tales* author Geoffrey Chaucer. Variations include *Geffrey, Geoff, Geoffery, Geoffre, Geoffrol, Geoffroy, Geoffry, Geofrey, Geofri,* and *Gofery.*

George (JORJ) patron saint of England.

Geraint (jer-AYNT) A name that means "old."

Gerald (JER-ald) Meaning "spearman." Variations include *Geri, Gerre, Gerri, Gerrie, Gerry, Gerryson,* and *Jerry.*

Gerard (jer-RARD) Meaning "chief spearman." French film actor Gérard Depardieu. Variations include *Jerard* and *Jerry.*

Gifford (GIF-ford) Meaning "brave giver." Variations include *Giff, Giffard, Gifferd, Giffie,* and *Giffy.*

Gig (GIG) A name signifying a "horse-drawn carriage." Among notable people with this name is actor Gig Young.

Gilbert (GIL-burt) Meaning "brilliant pledge" or "trustworthy." Author Gilbert Chesterton. Variations include *Gib, Gil, Gilberto, Gilburt, Giselbert, Giselberto,* and *Gulibert.*

Gordon (GORD-un) Meaning "triangular hill." Photographer and movie director Gordon Parks. Variations include *Geordan, Gord, Gordain, Gordan, Gorden,* and *Gordy.*

Graham (GRAHM) Meaning "grand home." English novelist Graham Greene. Variations include *Graeham, Graehame, Graehme, Graeme, Grahame, Grahme,* and *Gram.*

Grant (GRANT) Meaning "great." Painter Grant Wood. Variations include *Grand, Grantham, Granthem,* and *Grantley.*

Grover (GROW-vur) Meaning "grove." Among celebrated people with this name are Grover Cleveland, both the 22nd and 24th president of the United States, and baseball pitcher Grover Cleveland Alexander, who won 374 games. A variation is *Grove.*

Guilford (GILL-ford) Meaning "ford with yellow flowers." A variation is *Guildford.*

Hadley (HAD-lee) Meaning "heather-covered meadow." Variations include *Had, Hadlea, Hadlee, Hadleigh, Hadly, Lee,* and *Leigh.*

Hadwin (HAD-win) Meaning "wartime friend." Variations include *Hadwinn, Hadwyn, Hadwynn,* and *Hadwynne.*

Hagley (HAG-lee) Meaning "enclosed meadow."

Halbert (HAL-burt) Meaning "shining hero." Variations include *Bert* and *Halburt.*

Hall (HALL) Literally means "manor" or "hall."

Halley (HAIL-lee) Meaning "meadow near the hall" or "holy."

Halsey (HALL-see) Meaning "Hal's island."

Hamilton (HAM-il-tun) Meaning "proud estate." Hamilton Jordan worked in President Jimmy Carter's administration. Variations include *Hamel, Hamelton, Hamil, Hamill,* and *Tony.*

Hanley (HAN-lee) Meaning "high meadow." Variations include *Handlea, Handleigh, Handley, Hanlea, Hanlee, Hanleigh, Hanly, Henlea, Henlee, Henleigh,* and *Henley.*

Harden (HAR-din)   This name means "valley of the hares." A variation is *Hardin*.

Harlan (HAR-lan)   "Hare's land" or "army land." Among notable Harlans is Harlan Stone, former Chief Justice of the U.S. Supreme Court. Variations include *Harland, Harlen, Harlenn, Harlin, Harlon, Harlyn,* and *Harlynn.*

Harley (HAR-lee)   Meaning "hare's meadow" or "army meadow." Variations include *Arley, Harlea, Harlee, Harleigh,* and *Harly.*

Harlow (HAR-low)   Meaning "hare's hill" or "army hill."

Harmon (HAR-mon)   A form of Herman, which means "army man." Baseball great Harmon Killebrew played for the Minnesota Twins. Variations include *Harm, Harman, Harmond,* and *Harms.*

Harper (HAR-pur)   Literally means "harp player." Variations include *Harp* and *Harpo.*

Harrison (HAHR-riss-sun)   Literally meaning "son of Harry." Actor Harrison Ford. Variations include *Harris* and *Harrisen.*

Harold (HAHR-old)   Famous persons with this name include former U.S. president Harry S. Truman, magician Harry Houdini, and Clint Eastwood's "Dirty" Harry. Variations include *Harray, Harrey, Harri,* and *Harrie.*

Hartley (HART-lee)   Meaning "deer meadow." Variations include *Hart, Hartlea, Hartlee, Hartleigh,* and *Hartly.*

Heathcliff (HEETH-cliff)   Meaning "cliff near the heath." Protagonist of Emily Brontë's *Wuthering Heights.* Variations include *Heathe* and *Heith.*

Hedley (HEAD-lee)   Meaning "heather-filled meadow." Variations include *Headley, Headly,* and *Hedly.*

Henderson (HEN-dur-sun)   Literally, the "son of Henry." Variations include *Hendrie, Hendries, Hendron,* and *Henryson.*

Holden (HOLE-din)   Meaning "hollow in the valley." One popular Holden is *Catcher in the Rye* protagonist Holden Caulfield, allegedly based on author J.D. Salinger. Variations include *Holdin* and *Holdun.*

Hollis (HOLL-liss)   Meaning "grove of holly trees." Other versions are *Hoille* and *Holly.*

Horton (HOR-tun)   Meaning "garden estate." Reverend Horton Heat is an innovator in the music subgenre known as psycho-billy, a tripped-out version of rockabilly. Variations include *Hort, Horten,* and *Orton.*

Houghton (HAW-tun)   A name meaning "settlement on the headland." A variation is *Hough.*

Howard (HOW-wurd)   Which means "watchman." Notable Howards are eccentric millionaire Howard Hughes and comedian Howie Mandel. Variations include *Howie, Howey,* and *Ward.*

Hubie (HUE-bee)   A familiar form of Hubert. Former NBA coach Hubie Brown led many teams, including the New York Knicks. Variations include *Hube* and *Hubi.*

Huey (HUE-ee)   A familiar form of Hugh. Notable persons with this name are Black Panther leader Huey P. Newton and Huey Long, former governor of Louisiana. Variations include *Hughey, Hughie,* and *Hughy.*

Hugh (HUE)   A short form of Hubert. Notable persons with this name include Supreme Court Justice Hugo Black and actor Hugh Grant. Variations include *Fitzhugh, Hew, Hiu, Huey, Hughes, Hugo,* and *Hugues.*

Hunter (HUN-tur)   Meaning "hunter." Among famous Hunters is gonzo journalist Hunter S. Thompson who wrote *Fear and Loathing in Las Vegas.* A variation is *Hunt.*

Huntington (HUNT-ing-tun)   Which means "hunting estate." Millionaire Huntington Hartford was heir to the A&P fortune. Variations include *Hunt* and *Huntingdon.*

Hyatt (HI-at)   Meaning "high gate."

Ingram (ING-rum)   Meaning "angel." Variations include *Inglis, Ingra, Ingraham,* and *Ingrim.*

Irwin (UR-win)   Meaning "sea friend." See also Ervin. A well-known Irwin is American author Itwin Shaw. Variations include *Irwinn* and *Irwyn*.

Isam (ISH-um) Literally means "home of the iron one."

Ives (EYE-vez) or (IVES) Means "young archer." Variations include *Ive, Iven, Ivey,* and *Yves.*

Jackson (JACK-sun) Literally meaning "son of Jack." Famous Jacksons are abstract painter Jackson Pollack and singer Jackson Brown. Variations include *Jacson* and *Jakson.*

Jayme (JAY-mee) An alternate form of Jamie. Variations include *Jaymes* and *Jayrns.*

Jaymes (JAY-mes) An alternate form of James. A variation is *Jayms.*

Jefferson (JEFF-ur-sun) Meaning "son of Jeff." Jefferson Davis was the president of the Confederate States of America. Variations include *Jeferson* and *Jeff.*

Jeffrey (JEFF-ree) Meaning "divinely peaceful." Variations include *Geffrey, Geoffrey, Godfrey, Jeff, Jefferies, Jeffery, Jeffree, Jeffrery,* and *Jeffrie.*

Jerald (JER-ald) See Gerald. Variations include *Jeraldo, Jerold, Jerral, Jerrald, Jerrold,* and *Jerry.*

Jeremy (JER-em-ee) Meaning "exalted by the Lord." Actor Jeremy Irons. Variations include *Jaremay, Jaremi, Jaremy, Jem, Jemmy, Jerahmy, Jeramle, Jeramy, Jere, Jereamy, Jereme, Jeremee, Jeremey, Jeremle, Jirimle, Jeremry, Jeremye, Jereomy,* and *Jeriemy.*

Jerome (jer-OME) From the Greek for "sacred name." Also *Gerome.*

Kedrick (KED-rick) An alternate form of Cedric. Variations include *Keddrick* and *Kedric.*

Kendall (KEN-doll) "Valley of the river Kent." Variations include *Ken, Kendal, Kendale, Kendaii, Kendel, Kendell, Kendrall, Kendrell,* and *Kendryll.*

Kenrick (KEN-rick) Meaning "bold ruler, royal ruler." Variations include *Kenric* and *Kenricks.*

Kenton (KEN-tun) Literally signifies from Kent, England. Variations include *Kent, Kenten, Kentin,* and *Kentonn.*

Kim (KIM) A short form of Kimball. Variations include *Kimie* and *Kimmy.*

King (KING) Meaning "supreme ruler." Among celebrated men with this name is director King Vidor, famous for *Duel in the Sun* and King Camp Gillette, inventor of the disposable safety razor.

Kingsley (KINGS-lee) Meaning "king's meadow." For example Bristish novelist Kingsley Amis. Variations include *King, Kingslea, Kingslie, Kingsly, Kinslea, Kinslee, Kinsley, Kinslie,* and *Kinsly.*

Kipp (KIP) Meaning "pointed hill." Variations include *Kip, Kippar, Kipper, Kippie,* and *Kippy.*

Kirkley (KIRK-lee) Meaning "church meadow."

Kirkwell (KIRK-well) Meaning "church well, church spring."

Kirton (KUR-tun) Meaning "church town."

Knowles (NOLZ) Meaning "grassy slope." Variations include *Knolls* and *Nowles.*

Knox (NOX) Signifies "hill."

Kyle (KY-lur) Meaning "a narrow piece of land." A variation is *Kyler.*

Lane (LAIN) Meaning "narrow road." American character actor Lane Smith and labor organizer Lane Kirkland.

Langston (LANGS-tun) Meaning "long, narrow town." Poet Langston Hughes is a celebrated person with this name.

Lathrop (LATH-rop) "Farmstead." Variations include *Lathe, Lathrope,* and *Lay.*

Latimer (LAT-i-mur) Meaning "interpreter." Variations include *Lat, Latimor, Lattie, Latty,* and *Latymer.*

Lee (LEE) A short form of Farley. Actor Lee Marvin led *The Dirty Dozen.* A variation is *Leigh.*

Leland (LEE-land) Signifies "meadow-land." A famous Leland was theatrical agent Leland Hayward. Variations include *Lealand, Lee, Leeland, Leigh, Leighland, Lelan, Lelann,* and *Leyland.*

Leonel (LYE-nel) "Little lion." A variation is *Lionel.*

Lewis (LEW-iss) "Famed battler." The pen name of author of *Alice in Wonderland* is Lewis Carroll.

Lincoln (LIN-con) Signifies "settlement by the pool." American author Lincoln Child wrote the bestseller *The Relic.* Variations include *Linc* and *Lincon.*

Lindsey (LIND-zee) "Linden tree island." Variations include *Lind, Lindsay, Lindsee, Lindsy, Linsey, Lyndsay, Lyndsey, Lyndsie,* and *Lynzie.*

Linford (LIN-ford) Suggesting "linden tree ford." A variation is *Lynford.*

Locke (LOCK) "Forest." Variations include *Lock* and *Lockwood.*

Lyman (LY-men) "Meadow dweller." Variations include *Leaman* and *Leeman.*

Lyndal (LIN-dall) "Valley of linden trees." Variations include *Lyndale, Lyndall, Lyndel,* and *Lyndell.*

Lyndon (LIN-dun) Suggests "linden tree hill." Lyndon B. Johnson, former U.S. president. Variations include *Lin, Lindon, Lyden, Lydon, Lyn, Lynden,* and *Lynn.*

Manfred (MAN-fred) Signifies "man of peace." Singer Manfred Mann had his Earth Band. Variations include *Manfrid, Manfried, Mannfred,* and *Mannfryd.*

Marlin (MAR-lin) Meaning "deep-sea fish." Marlin Fitzwater, former White House press secretary. A variation is *Marlion.*

Marlow (MAR-low) Meaning "hill by the lake."

Marston (MARS-tun) Meaning "town by the marsh."

Martell (MAR-tell) Meaning "hammerer." A variation is *Martel.*

Marvin (MAR-vin) Meaning "lover of the sea." Famous Marvins include soul singer Marvin Gaye and prodigious composer Marvin Hamlisch. Variations include *Marv, Marvein, Marven, Marwin, Marwynn,* and *Mervin.*

Maxwell (MAX-well) "Great well." Variations include *Max, Maxwell, Maxwill,* and *Maxy.*

Mayhew (MAY-hue) A form of Matthew, which is Hebrew for "God is a gift."

Maynard (MAY-nurd) Meaning "powerful, brave." Variations include *May, Mayne, Maynhard, Manard,* and *Meinhard.*

Merlin (MUR-lin) Meaning "falcon." The wizard in King Arthur's court was Merlin. Variations include *Marion, Merle, Merlen, Merlinn, Merlyn,* and *Merlynn.*

Mick (MIK) A short form of Michael, Mickey. One notable Mick is rocker Mick Jagger of the Rolling Stones. A variation is *Mickerson.*

Milborough (MILL-bur-oh) Meaning "middle borough." A variation is *Milbrough.*

Milford (MIL-ford) Meaning "mill by the ford."

Miller (MIL-lur) Meaning "miller; grain grinder." Former New York Yankees general manager Miller Huggins. Variations include *Mellar, Millard,* and *Millen.*

Mills (MILZ) "Mills."

Milton (MILL-tun) "Mill town." Comedian Milton "Uncle Miltie" Berle. Variations include *Milt, Miltie, Milty,* and *Mylton.*

Mitchell (MITCH-ull) A form of Michael. Variations include *Mitch, Mitchael, Mitchall, Mitchel, Mitchele, Mitchelle, Mitchem, Mytch,* and *Mytchell.*

Montgomery (MONT-gum-uh-ree) Meaning "rich man's mountain." Actor Montgomery Clift was an icon of the 1950s. Variations include *Monte, Montgomerie,* and *Monty.*

Morley (MORE-lee) Meaning "meadow by the moor." *60 Minutes* correspondent Morley Safer. Variations include *Moorley, Moorly,*

Morlee, Morleigh, Morlon, Morly, Morlyn, and *Morrley.*

Morton (MOR-tun)   Literally "town near the moor." Political commentator Morton Kondrake. A variation is *Mort.*

Ned (NED)   A familiar form of Edward. Variations include *Neddle, Neddym,* and *Nedrick.*

Nelson (NELL-sun)   Literally "son of Neil." South African freedom fighter and President Nelson Mandela. Variations include *Neilson, Nellie, Nels, Nelsen, Nilson,* and *Nilsson.*

Nicholson (NIK-ols, NIK-ol-sun)   Literally, the "son of Nicholas." Variations include *Nicols, Nicolls, Nickelson,* and *Nickoles.*

Nick (NIK)   A short form of Dominic, Nicholas. Variations include *Nic* and *Nik.*

Niles (NI-ulz)   Meaning "son of Neil." A well-known Niles is TV sitcom character Niles Crane from Frasier. A variation is *Nilesh.*

Northrop (NORTH-rup)   "Northern farm." Literary critic Northrop Frye is among the notable people who share this name. Variations include *North* and *Northup.*

Norton (NOR-tun)   Literally meaning "northern town."

Norvin (NOR-vin)   Meaning "northern friend." Variations include *Norvyn, Norwin, Norwinn, Norwyn,* and *Norvynn.*

Norward (NOR-wurd)   Signifies "protector of the north." A variation is *Norwerd.*

Ogden (OG-den)   Meaning "oak valley." Humorous poet Ogden Nash. Variations include *Ogdan* and *Ogdon.*

Olin (O-lin)   Meaning "holly." Variations include *Olen, Olney,* and *Olyn.*

Onslow (ONZ-low)   Meaning "enthusiast's hill." A variation is *Ounslow.*

Ormond (OR-mund)   Meaning "Bear mountain."

Orrick (OR-rik)   Signifying "old oak tree."

Orrin (OR-rin)   "River." Senator Orrin Hatch represents Utah. A variation is *Orin.*

Orton (OR-tun)   Meaning "shore town."

Orvin (OR-vin)   Meaning "spear friend." Variations include *Orwin* and *Owynn.*

Osbert (OZ-burt)   Meaning "divine" or "bright."

Osgood (OZ-good)   Meaning "divine goth."

Osmar (OZ-mar)   Meaning "divine" or "wonderful."

Osmond (OZ-mund)   Meaning "divine protector." Variations include *Osmand, Osmonde, Osmont, Osmund, Osmunde,* and *Osmundo.*

Osric (OZ-rik)   Meaning "divine ruler." Variations include *Osrick.*

Oswald (OZ-wald)   Meaning "God's power." Variations include *Osvaldo, Oswaldo, Oswall, Oswell, Oswold, Oz,* and *Ozzie.*

Oswin (OZ-win)   Meaning "divine friend." Variations include *Osvin, Oswinn, Oswyn,* and *Oswynn.*

Paige (PAGE)   Alternate form of the French name Page, which means "servant to the royal court."

Parker (PAR-kur)   Meaning "little Peter." Variations include *Perkin, Perka, Perkins, Perkyn,* and *Perrin.*

Perry (PER-ree)   A familiar form of Peregrine and Peter. Singer Perry Como; TV D.A. Perry Mason; fashion designer Perry Ellis. Variations include *Parry* and *Perrie.*

Peyton (PAY-tun)   An alternate form of Patton and Payton. Football player Peyton Manning might yet become the next hero of the NFL. A variation is *Peyt.*

Philbert (PHIL-burt)   An alternate form of Filbert. Variations include *Philibert* and *Phillbert.*

Pierce (PEERSS)   A form of Peter. Variations include *Pearce, Pears, Pearson, Pearsson, Peerce, Peers, Peirce, Plercy, Piers, Pierson,* and *Piersson.*

Pitney (PIT-nee)   "Island of the strong-willed man." A variation is *Pittney.*

Pitt (PIT)   Meaning "pit" or "ditch."

Preston (PRESS-tun) "Priest's estate." Film director and screenwriter Preston Sturges. Also *Prestin*.

Radburn (RAD-burn) Meaning "red brook." Variations include *Radborn, Radborne, Radbourn, Radbourne,* and *Radburne*.

Radcliff (RAD-cliff) "Red cliff." Variations include *Radcliffe* and *Radclyffe*.

Radford (RAD-ford) Meaning "red ford" or "ford with reeds."

Radley (RAD-lee) Meaning "red meadow" or "meadow with reeds." Boo Radley, the mysterious neighbor of the children in Harper Lee's *To Kill a Mockingbird*. Variations include *Radlea, Radlee, Radleigh,* and *Radly*.

Radnor (RAD-nor) Meaning "red shore."

Rafe (RAYF) A short form of Rafferty and Ralph. Rafe Rackstraw, a humble seaman, became the captain of Gilbert and Sullivan's *H.M.S. Pinafore*. A variation is *Raff*.

Raine (RAIN) Meaning "lord" or "wise counsel." Variations include *Rain, Raines,* and *Rains*.

Ralph (RALF) Meaning "wolf counselor." Among persons who share this name are Sir Ralph Richardson and poet-philosopher Ralph Waldo Emerson. Variations include *Radolphus, Rafe, Ralf, Ralpheal, Ralphel, Ralphie, Ralston, Raoul, Raul,* and *Rolf*.

Ralston (RALL-stun) Meaning "Ralph's settlement."

Ramsden (RAMZ-den) Meaning "valley of rams."

Ramsey (RAMZ-ee) Meaning "ram's island." Former U.S. attorney general Ramsey Clark served during the Carter administration. Variations include *Ram, Ramsay, Ramsy, Ramzee,* and *Ramzi*.

Rance (RANCE) A short form of Laurence and Ransom. Actor Rance Howard is also the father of actor-director Ron Howard.

Randolph (RAN-dolf) Meaning "shield-wolf." Actor Randolph Scott, author Randolph

Churchill. Variations include *Randall, Randol, Randolf, Randolfo, Randolpho, Randy,* and *Ranolph*.

Randy (RAN-dee) A familiar form of Rand, Randall, Randolph. Variations include *Randey, Randi, Randle,* and *Ranndy*.

Rayburn (RAY-burn) Meaning "deer brook." Variations include *Burney, Raeborn, Raeborne, Raebourn,* and *Ray*.

Raymond (RAY-mund) Meaning "wise protector." Actor Raymond Burr of *Perry Mason* fame. Variations include *Radmond, Raemond, Raemondo, Raimondo, Raimundo, Ramón, Ramond, Ramonde, Ramone,* and *Ray*.

Reading (RED-ing) Meaning "son of the red-haired wanderer." Variations include *Redding, Reeding,* and *Relding*.

Redford (RED-ford) "Red river crossing." Variations include *Ford, Radford, Reaford, Red,* and *Redd*.

Redpath (RED-path) Literally a "red path."

Reed (REED) An alternate form of Reid. Variations include *Raeed, Read,* and *Reyde*.

Reginald (REHJ-in-uld) Meaning "king's advisor." An alternate form of Reynold. Actor Reginald Owen; baseball great Reggie "Mr. October" Jackson. Variations include *Reg, Reggie, Reggis, Reginal, Reginaldo, Reginale, Reginalt, Reginauld, Reginault, Reginel, Regnauld,* and *Ronald*.

Remington (REM-ing-tun) "Raven estate." TV action character Remington Steele. A variation is *Rem*.

Renfred (REN-frid) Signifies "lasting peace."

Renshaw (REN-shaw) Meaning "raven woods." A variation is *Renishaw*.

Renton (REN-tun) Meaning "settlement of the stag."

Richard (RIH-chard) Means a "rich and powerful ruler." Among notable Richards are composer Richard Rodgers, former U.S. president Richard Nixon, and actor Richard Burton. Variations include *Aric, Dick, Juku, Likeke, Reku, Ricardo, Rich, Richar, Richards, Richardson, Richart, Richer, Richerd, Richie, Richshard, Rick, Rickard, Rickert, Rickey, Ricky,* and *Rico.*

Ridley (RID-lee) Meaning "meadow of reeds." Film director Ridely Scott. Variations include *Riddley, Rldlea, Ridleigh,* and *Ridly.*

Rigby (RIG-bee) Meaning "ruler's valley."

Robert (RAAB-urt) Signifies "bright fame." Among famous people with this name are American poet Robert Frost and television journalist Robert MacNeil. Variations include *Bob, Rab, Rabbie, Raby, Riobard, Riobart, Rip, Rob, Robars, Robart, Robbie, Robby, Rober, Robers, Roberto, Roberts, Robin,* and *Robinson.*

Robin (RAAB-in) A short form of Robert. Popular Robins include the legendary Robin Hood and comedian/actor Robin Williams. Variations include *Robben, Robbin, Robbins, Robbyn, Roben, Robinet, Robinn, Robins,* and *Robyn.*

Robinson (RAAB-in-sun) Literally, the "son of Robert." Daniel Defoe's stranded hero was *Robinson Crusoe.* Variations include *Robbinson, Robson,* and *Robynson.*

Rockwell (ROCK-well) Meaning "rocky spring." A notable Rock was popular film and television actor Rock Hudson. Variations include *Rock.*

Rod (ROD) A short form of Penrod, Roderick, or Rodney. Rocker Rod Stewart. Variations include *Rodd* and *Roddy.*

Rodney (ROD-nee) Meaning "island clearing." Comedian Rodney Dangerfield. Variations include *Rhodney, Rod, Rodnee, Rodni, Rodnie,* and *Rodnne.*

Rollo (RO-lo) A familiar form of Roland. Psychologist author Rollo May. Variations include *Rolla* and *Rolo.*

Roper (ROPE-ur) Signifies "rope maker."

Rowan (ROW-an) Meaning "tree with red berries." British comedian Rowan Atkinson,

also known as Mr.Bean. Variations include *Roan, Rowe, Rowen,* and *Rowney.*

Rowell (ROW-ull) Meaning "roe deer well."

Rowley (ROW-lee) Meaning "rough meadow." Variations include *Rowlea, Rowlee, Rowleigh,* and *Rowly.*

Royce (ROYS) Meaning "son of Roy." Variations include *Roice* and *Roy.*

Royden (ROY-dun) Meaning "rye hill." Variations include *Royd* and *Roydan.*

Rudolph (RUE-dolph) Meaning "famed wolf." Silent film idol Rudolph Valentino and New York City mayor Rudolph Giuliani share this name. Variations include *Ruddy, Ruddie,* and *Rudey.*

Rudyard (RUD-yard) Meaning "red enclosure." Author Rudyard Kipling wrote tales of exotic places. A variation is *Rudd.*

Ruford (RU-ford) Meaning "red ford" or "ford with reeds." A variation is *Rufford.*

Rugby (RUG-bee) Meaning "rook fortress." This name is inspired by the famous British school and the game named after it.

Rutherford (RUTH-ur-ford) "Cattle ford." Former U.S. president Rutherford Birchard Hayes. A variation is *Rutherfurd.*

Scott (SCOT) Meaning "from Scotland." Ragtime music king Scott Joplin, author Scott Turow, NBA Chicago Bulls star Scotty Pippin. Variations include *Scot, Scotto,* and *Scotty.*

Seldon (SELL-dun) Literally means "willow tree valley." Variations include *Selden, Sellden, Shelden,* and *Sheldon.*

Selwyn (SELL-win) Meaning "friend from the palace." Variations include *Selvin, Selwin, Selwinn, Selwynn, Selwynne,* and *Wyn.*

Shattuck (SHA-tuck) Meaning "little shad fish."

Sheldon (SHELL-dun) Meaning "farm on the ledge." A well-known Sheldon is children's poet Shel Silverstein, who wrote *The Giving Tree.* Variations include *Shel, Shelden, Sheldin, Shell, Shelley, Shelly,* and *Shelton.*

Sherill (SHERR-ill) Meaning "shire on a hill." Opera singer Sherrill Milnes. Variations include *Sheril*, *Sherril*, and *Sherrill*.

Sherlock (SHUR-lock) Meaning "light-haired." A name made popular by fictional detective Sherlock Holmes. Variations include *Sherlocke*, *Shurlock*, and *Shurlocke*.

Sherman (SHUR-man) Meaning "sheep shearer" or "resident of a shire." Actor Sherman Hemsley of *The Jeffersons*. Variations include *Scherman*, *Schermann*, *Sherm*, *Shermann*, *Shermle*, and *Shermy*.

Sherrod (SHUR-rod) This name means "clearer of the land." Variations include *Sherod*, *Sherrad*, *Sherrard*, and *Sherrodd*.

Sidwell (SID-well) Meaning "wide stream."

Sinjon (SIN-gin) Meaning "Saint John." Broadway producer Sinjon Terrell. Variations include *Sinjun* and *Sjohn*.

Skeeter (SKEE-tur) A popular nickname meaning "swift." Actor Skeet Ulrich. Variations include *Skeat*, *Skeet*, and *Skeets*.

Slade (SLAYED) Meaning "valley." U.S. senator Slade Gorton represents the state of Washington. Variations include *Slaide* and *Slayde*.

Slater (SLAY-tur) Meaning "roof slater."

Smedley (SMED-lee) Meaning "flat meadow." Variations include *Smedleigh* and *Smedly*.

Sonny (SON-nee) Familiar form of Grayson, Madison, and Orson. Jazz musician Sonny Rollins; singer and former congressman Sonny Bono. A variation is *Sonnie*.

Spalding (SPALL-ding) Meaning "divided field." Monologist Spalding Gray. A variation is *Spaulding*.

Spark (SPARK) Meaning "happy." Boston Red Sox manager Sparky. Variations include *Sparke*, *Sparkle*, and *Sparky*.

Spear (SPEER) Meaning "spear carrier." Variations include *Speare*, *Spears*, *Speer*, *Speers*, and *Splers*.

Spencer (SPEN-sir) Meaning "dispenser of provisions." Actor Spencer Tracy. Variations include *Spence*, *Spencre*, and *Spenser*.

Spike (SPYK) Meaning "ear of grain." Famous Spikes include film director Spike Lee and musician and bandleader Spike Jones.

Spurgeon (SPUR-gen) Meaning "shrub."

Squire (SKWY-ur) Meaning "knight's assistant."

Stancliff (STAN-cliff) Meaning "stony cliff." Variations include *Stanclife* and *Stancliffe*.

Stanfield (STAN-field) Meaning "stony field." Stansfield Turner was CIA director in the Carter administration. Variations include *Stansfield*.

Stanford (STAN-ford) Signifies "rocky ford." Variations include *Sandy*, *Stamford*, *Stan*, *Standford*, and *Stanfield*.

Stanley (STAN-lee) Meaning "stony meadow." Film director Stanley Kubrick and Laurel and Hardy's Stan Laurel. Variations include *Stan*, *Stanlea*, *Stanlee*, *Stanleigh*, and *Stanly*.

Starbuck (STAR-buck) Meaning "challenger of fate." A character in Herman Melville's novel *Moby Dick*.

Starling (STAR-ling) A kind of bird. Also *Sterling*.

Steadman (STED-man) Meaning "owner of a farmstead." Oprah Winfrey's longtime beau, Steadman Graham. Variations include *Steadmann*, *Stedman*, and *Steed*.

Steven (STEE-ven) From the Greek, meaning "a crown." Among notable men with this name is Hollywood director Steven Spielberg. Variatons include *Stevan*, *Steve*, and *Stevie*.

Sterling (STIR-ling) An alternate form of Starling, meaning "valuable." Actor Sterling Holloway

Stewart (STEW-art) An alternate form of Stuart. Film actor Stewart Granger. Variations include *Steward* and *Stu*.

Sting (STING) Meaning "spike of grain." A celebrity with this unique name is rock musician Sting, although he was born Gordon Sumner.

Stoddard (STOD-dard) Meaning "horse keeper."

Stone (STONE) Literally "stone." Television journalist Stone Phillips. Variations include *Stoney* and *Stony*.

Storm (STORM) A familiar form of Norman, which means "tempest" or "storm." Meteorologist Storm Field. Variations include *Stormi* and *Stormy*.

Stuart (STEW-urt) Signifying "caretaker" or "steward." The name of a Scottish and English royal dynasty. Variations include *Stewart*, *Stu*, and *Stuarrt*.

Styles (STYLZ) Meaning "stairs put over a wall to help cross it."

Sutton (SUT-tun) Meaning "southern town."

Talcott (TAL-cot) Meaning "cottage near the lake." Sociologist Talcott Parsons.

Tanner (TAN-nur) Meaning "leather tanner." Variations include *Tan*, *Tanery*, *Tann*, *Tannor*, and *Tanny*.

Tanton (TAN-tun) Meaning "still river town."

Ted (TED) A short form of Edward or Theodore. Well-known Teds include television journalist Ted Koppel; Massachusetts Senator Ted Kennedy; *Amateur Hour* host Ted Mack. Variations include *Tedd*, *Tedek*, *Tedik*, and *Tedson*.

Tedmund (TED-mund) Meaning "protector of the land." Variations include *Tedman* and *Tedmond*.

Teller (TELL-ur) Literally "storyteller." One popular so-named person is the silent half of the magic duo Penn and Teller. Variations include *Tell* and *Telly*.

Templeton (TEMPULL-tun) Meaning "town near the temple." The name of the rat in E.B. White's *Charlotte's Web*. Variations include *Temp* and *Templeten*.

Tennant (TEN-ant) Literally "tenant" or "renter." Variations include *Tenant* and *Tennent*.

Terrence (TER-ree) Literally means "tender," or "good," or "gracious." Playwright Terrence McNally and film writer and director Terry Gilliam. Variations include *Tarry*, *Terence*, *Terrance*, *Terrey*, *Terri*, *Terrie*, and *Terry*.

Thane (THAIN) Meaning "attendant warrior." Variations include *Thain*, *Thaine*, and *Thayne*.

Thatcher (THAT-chur) Meaning "roof thatcher," or "repairer of roofs." Variations include *Thacher*, *Thatch*, and *Thaxter*.

Theodore (THEE-o-dorr) American novelist Theodore Dreiser, art dealer Theo Van Gogh, brother of Vincent.

Thomas (TOM-as) Meaning "twin." Well-known people with this name include British authors Thomas Carlyle and Thomas Hardy; inventor Thomas Alva Edison. Variations include *Teo*, *Thom*, *Tom*, *Tommey*, *Tommie*, and *Tommy*.

Thorndike (THORN-dike) Has the meaning "thorny embankment." Variations include *Thorndyck*, *Thorndyke*, and *Thorne*.

Thorne (THORN) Meaning "thorn grove." Variations include *Thorn*, *Thornie*, and *Thorny*.

Thornley (THORN-lee) Meaning "thorny meadow." Variations include *Thorley*, *Thorne*, *Thornlea*, *Thornleigh*, and *Thornly*.

Thornton (THORN-tun) Meaning "thorny." *Our Town* playwright Thornton Wilder.

Thurlow (THUR-lo) Meaning "Thor's hill."

Tiger (TIGH-gur) Affectionate term, meaning "playful as a tiger." Golfer Eldrick "Tiger" Woods.

Todd (TOD) Meaning "fox." Variations include *Tod*, *Toddle*, and *Toddy*.

Tomlin (TOM-lin) Signifying "little Tom." Variations include *Tomkin* and *Tomlinson*.

Torr (TOR) Signifying "tower." A variation is *Tory*.

Travis (TRAV-iss) Meaning "at a crossroad." Country singer Travis Tritt. Variations include *Traves, Traveus, Traviss, Travus, Travys,* and *Trevais.*

Trayton (TRAY-tun)   Meaning "town full of trees."

Trey (TRAY)   Meaning "three" or "third." *South Park* creator Trey Parker. Variations include *Trae, Tral,* and *Tray.*

Trip (TRIP)   Signifies "traveler." A variation is *Tripp.*

Trot (TROT)   Meaning "trickling stream."

Truman (TRUE-man)   Meaning "honest." Fictional character Truman Burbank of the film the *Truman Show*; writer Truman Capote. Variations include *Trueman, Trumaine,* and *Trumann.*

Trumble (TRUM-bull)   Meaning "strong" or "bold." Variations include *Trumball, Trumbell,* and *Trumbull.*

Trustin (TRUS-tin)   Meaning "trustworthy." Variations include *Trustan, Trusten,* and *Truston.*

Tupper (TUP-pur)   Meaning "ram."

Turk (TURK)   Signifying "from Turkey."

Tyler (TIE-lur)   Meaning "tile maker." Variations include *Tiler, Ty, Tyel, Tylar, Tyle, Tyller,* and *Tylor.*

Tyrus (TIE-russ)   A form of Thor, a name of Scandinavian God of thunder. Variations include *Ty* and *Tyruss.*

Upton (UP-tun)   Literally, "upper town." American novelist and journalist Upton Sinclair.

Vail (VALE)   Meaning "valley." Variations include *Valle, Vaill, Vale,* and *Valle.*

Vance (VANTZ)   Meaning "thresher." Vance Packard was a demystifier of advertising strategies.

Vian (VIE-an)   Meaning "full of life." A masculine short form of Vivian.

Vinson (VIN-sun)   Literally "son of Vincent." A variation is *Vinnis.*

Wade (WAYD)   Meaning "ford" or "river crossing." Baseball player Wade Boggs. Variations include *Wadie, Waide, Wayde,* and *Waydell.*

Wadley (WAHD-lee)   Meaning "ford meadow." Variations include *Wadleigh* and *Wadly.*

Wainwright (WAIN-right)   Signifies "wagon maker." Variations include *Wain, Wainright, Wayne, Wayneright,* and *Wright.*

Walker (WALL-kur)   Signifies "cloth-walker" or "cloth cleaner." Among those who share this name are photographer Walker Evans and author Walker Percy. Variations include *Wallie* and *Wally.*

Wallace (WALL-ass)   Meaning "from Wales." Notable men with this name include actor Wallace Berry and playwright and actor Wallace Shawn. Variations include *Wallach, Wallas, Wallie, Wallis, Wally, Walsh,* and *Welsh.*

Ward (WARD)   Signifies "watchman, guardian." Well-known Wards include Hollywood actor Ward Bond, as well as Ward Cleaver, the television father of Beaver Cleaver. Variations include *Warde, Warden,* and *Worden.*

Wardell (WAR-dell)   Meaning "watchman's hill."

Wardley (WARD-lee)   Meaning "watchman's meadow." Variations include *Wardlea* and *Wardleigh.*

Ware (WARE)   Meaning "wary" or "cautious."

Watson (WATT-son)   Literally "son of Walter." Sherlock Holmes's sidekick Dr. Watson is one famous Watson, although it's a surname for him.

Wayne (WAIN)   Meaning "wagon maker." A short form of Wainwright. Hockey great Wayne Gretzky. Variations include *Wain, Wayn, Waynell,* and *Wene.*

Wentworth (WENT-worth)   Meaning "pale man's settlement."

Wesley (WESS-lee)   Meaning "western meadow." Action actor Wesley Snipes. Variations include *Wes, Weslee, Wesleyan, Weslie, Wesly, Wessley, Westleigh,* and *Westley.*

Westbrook (WEST-brook)   Meaning "western brook." Variations include *Brook, West,* and *Westbrooke.*

Whitcomb (WIT-come) Meaning "white valley." Poet James Whitcomb Riley. Variations include *Whitcombe* and *Whitcumb*.

Whitey (WHITE-ee) Meaning "white skinned" or "white haired." New York Yankees pitcher Whitey Ford.

Whitley (WIT-lee) Meaning "white meadow." Variations include *Whitlea*, *Whitlee*, and *Whitleigh*.

Whitney (WIT-nee) Meaning "white island." Variations include *Whit*, *Whittney*, *Widney*, and *Widny*.

Whittaker (WIT-a-kur) Meaning "white field." Among notable people with this name is cold war figure Whittaker Chambers. Variations include *Whitacker*, *Whitaker*, and *Whitmaker*.

Wilbur (WILL-bur) Meaning "wall fortification" or "bright willows." Well-known Wilburs are pioneer aviator Wilbur Wright; the name of the pig saved by *Charlotte's Web*. Variations include *Wilber*, *Wilburn*, *Wilburt*, *Willbur*, and *Wilver*.

Wiley (WHY-lee) Meaning "flood meadow." Famous men with this name include aviator Wiley Post. Variations include *Wildy*, *Willey*, and *Wylie*.

Wilford (WILL-ford) Signifying "willow tree ford."

Wilkie (WILL-kee) A familiar form of Wilkins. A variation is *Willkie*.

Wilton (WILL-tun) Meaning "farm by the well." Variations include *Will* and *Wilt*. A well-known Wilt is basketball star Wilt Chamberlain, who defined the position as center.

Winchell (WIN-chill) Meaning "bend in the road" or "bend in the land."

Winfield (WIN-field) A name signifying "friendly field." U.S. general and presidential candidate Winfield Scott. Variations include *Field*, *Winifield*, *Winnfield*, *Wynfield*, and *Wynnfield*.

Winslow (WINZ-low) Meaning "friend's hill." Famous Winslows include painter Winslow Homer.

Winston (WINZ-tun) Meaning "friendly town." English statesman Winston Churchill. Variations include *Win*, *Winsten*, *Winstonn*, *Winton*, *Wynstan*, and *Wynston*.

Winward (WIN-ward) Meaning "friend's guardian."

Wolcott (WALL-cot) Meaning "cottage in the woods." A famous writer with this name is Wolcott Gibbs. Variations include *Walcott*, *Wallcott*, and *Wallcot*.

Woodrow (WOOD-row) Meaning "passage in the woods." Thomas Woodrow Wilson is a former U.S. president. Variations include *Wood*, *Woodman*, and *Woody*.

Woodruff (WOOD-ruff) Meaning "forest ranger."

Wycliff (WHY-cliff) Meaning "white cliff." A variation is *Wycliffe*.

Wylie (WHY-lee) Meaning "charming." Variations include *Wiley* and *Wye*.

Yardley (YARD-lee) Signifies "enclosed meadow." Variations include *Lee*, *Yard*, *Yardlea*, *Yardlee*, *Yardleigh*, *Yardly*, and *Yarom*.

Zane (ZAIN) A form of John, which means "God's gracious gift." Novelist of the American west Zane Grey. Variations include *Zaln* and *Zayne*.

ENGLAND: GIRLS

Adeline (AA-de-line) A form of Adelaide, meaning "noble and serene." "Sweet Adeline" is a barbershop quartet standard. Variations include *Adalina*, *Adaline*, *Addie*, *Adelina*, *Adelita*, *Adeliya*, *Adeele*, *Adelyn*, *Adelynn*, and *Adilene*.

Adele (a-DELL) A short form of Adelaide and Adeline. Variations include *Adel*, *Adela*, and *Adelle*.

Adriane (AYE-dree-en) Meaning "rich." A variation is *Adrianne*.

Afton (AF-ton) Indicating "from Afton, England." Variations include *Aftan*, *Aftine*, and *Aftyn*.

Agate (AA-get) A semiprecious stone. A variation is *Aggie*.

Alberta (al-BER-ta) A feminine form of Albert, meaning "noble or bright." One well-known Alberta is blues singer Alberta Hunter.

Alice (AA-lis) Meaning "noble" or "kind." Among notable people with this name are authors Alice McDermott and Alice Walker. Variations include *Alicia, Alison*, and *Allyce*.

Alicia (a-LEE-sha) A form of Alice which means "noble" or "bright." *Clueless* star Alicia Silverstone. Variations include *Alecia, Aleecia, Ali, Alicea, Alicha, Alichia, Alicya, Alycea, Alycia*, and *Lycia*.

Alison (AA-li-son) A form of Alice meaning "noble" or "bright." Among notable people with this name are actress Allison Janney and country singer Allison Moorer. Variations include *Ali, Alicen, Alicyn, Alisann, Alisanne, Alisen, Alisson, Alisun, Alisyn, Allison, Allyson, Allysen, Alyson*, and *Allyson*.

Alonza (a-LON-za) A feminine form of *Alonzo*, which means "noble" or "eager."

Alvina (al-VEE-na) Suggests "noble friend" or "friend to all." A feminine form of *Alvin*. Variations include *Alveanea, Alveen, Alveena, Alveenia, Alvenea, Alvie, Alvincia, Alvine*, and *Alvinea*.

Amy (AYE-mee) Meaning "beloved." Among notable people with this name are poet Amy Lowell, author Amy Tan, singer Amy Grant, gymnast Amy Chow, and actress Amy Irving. Variations include *Aimee, Ami*, and *Esme*.

Anice (AA-nis) An alternate form of Agnes, which means "pure." Variations include *Anesse, Anis, Anise, Anisha, Annes, Annice Annis, Anisa*, and *Annissa*.

Anne (AAHN) A form of Hanna, meaning "grace." Among notable people with this name are champion of religious freedom Anne Hutchinson; authors Anne Sexton, Anne Brontë, Anne Rice, Anne McCaffrey; actresses Anne Heche, Ann Bancroft, and photographer Anne Geddes. Variations include *An, Ana, Anelle,* *Anika, Anissa, Anita, Annalie, Annchen, Ann, Annette, Annie, Annik, Annika, Annze, Anouche,* and *Anouk*.

Annabel (AA-nu-bell) A combination of Anna, which means "grace" and Belle, meaning "beautiful." Variations include *Amabel, Anabel, Anabela, Anabella, Anabelle, Anabal, Annabell, Annabella,* and *Annabelle*.

Annelisa (AA-nuh-LEE-sa) A combination of Anne, meaning "grace" and Lisa, which signifies "consecrated unto God." Variations include *Analiese, Anallsa, Analise, Anelisa, Anallse, Annalise, Annallsa,* and *Annalise*.

Annemarie (AAHN-muh-REE) Combinations of Ann, meaning "grace" and Marie, which means "bitter." Variations include *Annamaria, Anna-Maria, Annamarie, Anna-Marie, Anne-Marie, Annmaria,* and *Annmarie*.

Annie (AAH-nee) A familiar form of Anne. Among notable people with this name is actress Annie Potts. Variations include *Anni*, and *Anny*.

Anon (a-NON) Meaning "pineapple."

Arden (AR-den) Meaning "burning with enthusiasm." The name of a mystically beautiful forest in Shakespeare's *As You Like It*. Variations include *Ardeen, Ardeena, Ardena, Ardene, Ardi, Ardenia, Ardin,* and *Ardine*.

Arleigh (AR-lee) An alternate form of Harlet, which signifies "long field." Variations include *Arlea, Arlee, Arley,* and *Arlie*.

Arlette (ar-LET) A form of *Arlene*, meaning "pledge." Variations include *Arleta* and *Arletta*.

Ashley (ASH-lee) Which means "ash tree meadow." Among notable people with this name are playwright Ashley Dukes and actress Ashley Judd. Variations include *Ashalee, Ashalei, Ashaley, Ashelee, Ashelei, Asheleigh, Asheley, Ashely, Ashlay, Ashlea,* and *Ashleah*.

Ashlyn (ASH-lin) Meaning "ash tree pool." A variation is *Ashlynn*.

Aspen (ASS-pin) Signifying "aspen tree." A variation is *Aspin*.

Aster (ASS-ter) A form of Astra, which means "star." Also *Astera, Asteria,* and *Astyr*.

Audrey (AU-dree) Meaning "noble strength." Among notable people with this name are actresses Audrey Hepburn and Audrey Meadows. Variations include *Audra, Audray, Audre, Audree,* and *Audri.*

Avril (a-VRIL) Meaning "born in April."

Bailey (BAY-lee) Meaning "bailiff." Variations include *Bailee, Bailley, Bailly, Baily, Baylee, Baylie,* and *Bayly.*

Berlynn (bur-LIN) A combination of Bertha, meaning "shining" or "bright," and Lynn signifying "waterfall." Variations include *Berla, Berlinda, Berline, Berlyn, Berlyne,* and *Berlynne.*

Berni (BUR-nee) A familiar form of Bernadine or Bernice, which means "brave as a bear." Variations include *Bernie* and *Berny.*

Berti (BUR-tee) A familiar form of Gilbert or Bertina, meaning "shining" or "bright." A variation is *Bertine.*

Bethann (BETH-ann) A combination of Beth, meaning "house of God" and Anne. Variations include *Beth-Ann, Beth, Bethan, Bethanne,* and *Beth-Anne.*

Beverly (BEHV-ur-lee) Meaning "beaver stream." Well-known Beverlys include opera singer Beverly Sills and actress Beverly Garland. Variations include *Bev, Bevalee, Beverle, Beverlee,* and *Beverley.*

Binnie (BIG-nee) A familiar form of Benedicta, meaning "blessed," Bianca, meaning "white," and Bina, meaning "kind." Among notable people with this name is actress Binnie Barnes. Variations include *Binnee, Binne, Binnie,* and *Binny.*

Blake (BLAKE) Signifies "dark."

Bliss (BLIS) Literally, "happy" or "joyful." Variations include *Blisse, Blyss,* and *Blysse.*

Blossom (BLAH-sum) Meaning "flower."

Blythe (BLY-th) Meaning "happy" or "cheerful." Stage and film actress Blythe Danner, mother of actress Gwyneth Paltrow. Variations include *Blithe* and *Blyth.*

Bonnie (BON-nee) Meaning "beautiful." Among notable people with this name are actresses Bonnie Franklin and Bonnie Bedelia. Variations include *Bonn.*

Britany (BRIT-ah-nee) Means literally "from Britain." Singer Britney Spears and actress Britt Ekland. Variations include *Britanee, Britanny, Britenee, Briteny, Britianey, Britani, Brittanie, Brit, Britanie, Britanii, Britanni, Britatani, Britia, Britini, Brittanni, Britaney, Britani, Britanie, Britney, Britt, Brittainny, Brittainy, Brittyne, Brityn, Brityne,* and *Bryton.*

Brooke (BROOK) Literally signifies "brook" or "stream." A feminine form of Brook. Actress Brooke Shields. Variations include *Brookie, Brooks,* and *Brooky.*

Cady (KAY-dee) A form of Catherine. Variations include *Cade, Cadee, Cadey, Cadi, Cadie,* and *Cadye.*

Carlene (CAR-leen) A form of Caroline. Variations include *Carlaen, Carlaena, Carleen, Carleena, Carlena, Carline, Carlyne,* and *Karlene.*

Carly (CAR-lee) A familiar form of Caroline and Charlotte. Singer Carly Simon. Variations include *Carlee, Carley, Carli, Carlie,* and *Carlye.*

Carole (CAHR-ol) A form of Carol. Carole Lombard star of screwball comedy. Variations include *Carolee, Karole,* and *Karrole.*

Carolyn (CAHR-o-lynn) A form of Caroline. Among notable people with this name is New York Congresswoman Carolyn McCarthy. Variations include *Caralyn, Caralynn, Caralynne, Carilyn,* and *Carilynn.*

Carrie (CAHR-ree) A familiar form of Carol and Caroline. Carrie Fisher starred in *Star Wars* as Princess Leia. Variations include *Carree, Carri,* and *Carry.*

Chanel (SHA-nell) Literally means "channel." A variation is *Shanel.*

Charlene (SHAR-leen) Signifies "little and womanly." A form of Caroline. Variations include *Charla, Charlaine, Charlane, Charlanna, Charlayne, Charleen, Charlena, Charlesena, Charline, Charlyn,* and *Charlyne.*

Charlie (CHAR-lee) Meaning "strong and womanly." A feminine form of Charles. Variations include *Charle, Charlea, Charlee, Charleigh, Charley, Charli, Sharli,* and *Sharlie.*

Chelsea (CHELL-see) Meaning "seaport" or "landing." First daughter Chelsea Clinton. Variations include *Chelese, Chellesia, Chelsa, Chelsae, Chellse, Chelsee, Chellsei, Chelsey, Chellsie, Chesea, Chellsay, Chellsy, Chesley, Chelcy, Chelcie, Chelsi, Cheslee,* and *Cheslie.*

Cherilyn (SHER-a-lynn) A combination of Cheryl and Lynn. Among notable people with this name is actress and singer Cher, who started as a Cherilyn but shortened it. Variations include *Cher, Cherallyn, Cherillynn, Cherrallyn, Cherrillynn, Cherryllyn, Cherylin,* and *Sherillyn.*

Cherish (CHAIR-ish) Signifies "precious." Variations include *Charish, Charisha, Cheerish, Cherise, Cherishe,* and *Cherrish.*

Cherry (CHER-ree) Meaning "cherrylike."

Chrissy (KRIH-see) A familiar form of Christina, meaning "Christian." Variations include *Chrisie, Chrissee, Chrissie,* and *Khrissy.*

Christine (KRIS-teen) A form of Christina, meaning "fair Christian." Variations include *Chrisa, Christeen, Christen, Christene, Christi, Christie, Christin, Christy, Chrys,* and *Chrystine.*

Christy (KRIS-tee) A short form of Christina and Christine, meaning "fair Christian." Supermodels Christie Brinkley and Christy Turlington.

Chrys (KRIS) A form of Chris, which is short for Christine or Christina. A variation is *Krys.*

Cicely (SIS-eh-lee) A form of Cecilia. Among notable people with this name is actress Cicely Tyson. Variations include *Cicelie, Cicilie, Cicily, Cile, Cilka, Cilia, Cilli, Cillie,* and *Cilly.*

Cinderella (SIN-dur-el-lah) Meaning "little ash-girl." The name of a fairy-tale heroine.

Clara (KLAIR) Meaning "bright." Among notable people with this name are Red Cross founder Clara Barton and the "It Girl" of silent films, Clara Bow. Variations include *Claire, Clair, Clare, Clarissa,* and *Clayrice.*

Cody (KO-dee) Meaning "pillow." Variations include *Coady, Codee, Codey, Codi, Codie,* and *Kodi.*

Colby (KOLL-bee) Meaning "coal town." This is a region in England famous for the production of a cheese of the same name. Variations include *Cobi, Cobie, Colbi, Colbie,* and *Kolby.*

Corliss (KOR-liss) Signifies "cheerful" and "benevolent." Variations include *Corlisa, Corlise, Corlissa, Corly,* and *Korliss.*

Courtney (KORT-nee) Meaning "from the court." Among notable people with this name are actress Courtney Cox, of TV's *Friends,* and rocker Courtney Love. Variations include *Cortney, Courtena, Courtenay, Courtene, Courtnae, Courtnay, Courtnee, Cortnea, Cortnee, Cortneia, Cortni, Cortnie, Cortny, Corttney,* and *Courteney.*

Cristy (KRIS-tee) A familiar form of Cristina. Variations include *Cristey, Cristi, Cristie, Crysti, Crystie, Crysty,* and *Kristy.*

Dae (DAY) Literally means "day." Variations include *Daelleen, Daellena,* and *Daesha.*

Daisy (DAY-zee) Meaning "eye of the day," it is the name of a white and yellow flower. MTV host Daisy Fuentes. Variations include *Daisee, Daisey, Daisi, Daisie, Dasey, Dasi, Dasie, Dasy, Daysee, Daysie, Daysy,* and *Dacey.*

Dale (DAIL) Meaning "valley." Dale Evans, actress and singer, and wife of Roy Rogers.

Dana (DAY-na) Meaning "from Denmark" or "bright as day." Actress Dana Delaney. Variations include *Daina, Dainna, Danah, Dane, Daniah, Danja, Danna,* and *Dayna.*

Darcie (DAR-see) Meaning "the dark."

Dawn (DAWN) Meaning "sunrise" or "dawn." Olympic gold medalist Dawn Fraser and novelist of New York Dawn Powell. Variations include *Dawna, Dawne, Dawnee, Dawnele, Dawnell,* and *Dawnelle.*

Delicia (DEH-lee-sha) Suggests "delight." Variations include *Dalicia, Dalise, Dalisha, Dalisse,* and *Delise.*

Delsie (DEL-see) A familiar form of Delores, which means "sorrowful."

Devonna (DEH-von-na) Signifies "from Devonshire." Variations include *Davonna*, *Devon*, *Devona*, and *Devonda*.

Domina (DA-min-oh) A short form of Dominica and Dominique, meaning "lady."

Doralynn (DOR-a-lynn) A combination of Dora and Lynn. Variations include *Doralin*, *Doralyn*, and *Doralynne*.

Eartha (UR-tha) Meaning "earthy." Among notable people with this name is singer and actress Eartha Kitt. A variation is *Ertha*.

Easter (EE-stir) Meaning "Easter time." Variations include *Eastan*, *Eastlyn*, and *Easton*.

Eda (ED-da) Meaning "prosperous, happy." A short form of Edana and Edith.

Edeline (ED-ah-leen) Meaning "noble" or "kind." Variations include *Adeline*, *Edelyne*, *Ediline*, and *Edilyne*.

Edie (EE-dee) A familiar form of Edith. Singers Edie Adams and Eydie Gorme. Variations include *Eadie*, *Edi*, *Edy*, *Edye*, *Eyde*, and *Eydie*.

Edith (EE-dith) Meaning "rich gift." Famous persons with this name include actress Dame Edith Evans, former first ladies Edith Roosevelt and Edith Wilson, and writer Edith Wharton, who penned *The Age of Innocence*. Variations include *Eadith*, *Eda*, *Ede*, *Edie*, *Edita*, *Edite*, *Editha*, *Edithe*, *Edyth*, *Edytha*, and *Edythe*.

Edwina (ed-WEEN-a) Meaning "prosperous friend." A feminine form of Edwin. Variations include *Eddy*, *Edina*, *Edweena*, *Edwena*, *Edwine*, and *Edwyna*.

Elberta (ell-BURT-a) A form of Alberta. Variations include *Elbertha*, *Elberthina*, *Elberthine*, *Elbertina*, and *Elbertine*.

Elisa (eh-LEE-sa) A short form of Elizabeth. Actress Elisa Donovan. Variations include *Elecea*, *Eleesa*, *Elesa*, *Elesia*, *Elisia*, Elissa, *Elisya*, *Ellisa*, *Ellisia*, *Ellissa*, *Ellissia*, *Ellissya*, *Ellisya*, Ellyssa, *Elysa*, *Elysia*, *Ilissa*, and *Ilyssa*.

Elise (ell-EES) A short form of Elizabeth. Variations include *Eilis*, *Eilise*, *Elisee*, *Elisse*, *Elizi*, Ellecia, *Ellice*, *Ellise*, *Ellycea*, and *Elyce*.

Elissa (eh-LEE-sa) A form of Elizabeth. Short form of Melissa. Variations include *Elyssa*, *Ellissa*, *Ellyssa*, *Ilissa*, *Ilyssa*.

Ellen (ELL-en) A form of Eleanor or Helen. Among notable people with this name are actress Ellen Corby; former first lady Ellen Arthur, wife of Chester Arthur; comedian Ellen DeGeneres, and novelist Ellen Glasgow. Variations include *Elen*, *Elin*, *Ellan*, *Ellena*, *Ellene*, *Ellin*, *Ellyn*, *Ellynn*, and *Elyn*.

Ellice (EH-leese) An alternate form of Elise, which is the French version of Elizabeth. Variations include *Ellecia*, *Ellyce*, and *Elyce*.

Ellie (ELL-ee) Short form of Eleanor, Ella, and Ellen. Variations include *Ele*, *Elie*, *Elli*, and *Elly*.

Elva (ELL-va) Meaning "elfin." Variations include *Elvenea*, *Elvia*, *Elvina*, *Elvinea*, *Eivinia*, and *Elvinna*.

Emily (EM-ih-lee) Meaning "hardworking." Among notable people with this name are author Emily Brontë, poet Emily Dickinson, and legendary etiquette expert Emily Post. Variations include *Emilee and Emilie*.

Emma (EM-ma) Signifies "universal." Among notable people with this name are poet Emma Lazarus and British actress Emma Thompson.

Eppie (EP-pee) A familiar form of Euphernia. Eppie is advice columnist Ann Landers's real first name. Variations include *Effie*, *Effy*, and *Eppy*.

Ernestine (UR-nes-teen) Meaning "earnest" or "sincere." A feminine form of Ernest. Variations include *Erna*, *Ernesia*, *Ernesta*, *Ernestina*, and *Ernesztina*.

Esme (ES-me) Meaning "gracious guardian."

Essie (ESS-see) A short form of Estelle or Esther. Variations include *Essa*, *Essey*, *Essie*, and *Essy*.

Estee (ES-tee) A short form of Estelle or Esther. Among notable people with this name, fragrance developer Estée Lauder. Variations include *Esta* and *Esti*.

Ethel (ETH-ul)   Meaning "noble." Famous persons so named include actress Ethel Barrymore; singer Ethel Waters; Ethel Kennedy, widow of RFK. Variations include *Ethelin, Etheline, Ethelle, Ethelyn, Ethelynn, Ethelynne,* and *Ethyl*.

Evelyn (EV-eh-lynn)   Meaning "hazelnut." President John F. Kennedy's personal secretary and confidante was Evelyn Lincoln. Variations include *Aveline, Evaleen, Evalene, Evaline, Evalyn, Evalynn,* and *Evalynne*.

Evline (EV-lynn)   An alternate form of Evelyn. Variations include *Evleen, Eviene, Evlin, EvIina, Evlyn, Evlynn,* and *Evlynne*.

Faith (FAYTH)   Meaning "loyalty." Novelist Faith Baldwin singer Faith Hill. Variations include *Fayth* and *Faythe*.

Farah (FAHR-rah)   Meaning "beautiful" or "pleasant." Variations include *Fara, Farra, Farrah,* and *Fayre*.

Faren (FAHR-ren)   Meaning "wanderer." Variations include *Faran, Fare, Farin, Faron, Farrahn, Farran, Farrand,* Farren, *Farrin, Farron, Farryn, Farye, Faryn, Feran,* and *Ferin*.

Felicity (feh-LISS-ih-tee)   A form of Felicia. Variations include *Falicity, Felicita,* and *Felicitas*.

Flair (FLAIR)   Signifies "style" or "verve." Variations include *Flaire* and *Flare*.

Florence (FLA-rence)   Meaning "flowering." Variations include *Florie, Flori, Florri, Florrie, Floris, Florisa, Florise, Floss, Flossi,* and *Flossy*.

Frances (FRAN-sis)   Meaning "free." Frances McDormand won an Academy Award for playing a pregnant police chief Marge Gunderson in *Fargo*. Variations include *Fanny, Fran, Frania, Franney, Franni,* and *Frannie*.

Freddie (FRED-dee)   Familiar form of Frederica and Winifred. Variations include *Fredda, Freddy, Freddie, Fredi,* and *Fredy*.

Frederica (FRED-eh-ree-cah)   Meaning "peaceful ruler." Opera singer Frederica "Flika" Von Stade. Variations include *Freeda, Freddig, Freddie, Freddy, Freddi,* and *Fredy*.

Gardenia (GAR-deen-ya)   Meaning the sweet-smelling flower, named for its discoverer Alexander Garden. Variations include *Deeni, Denia,* and *Gardena*.

Garnet (GAR-nit)   Meaning "dark red gemstone." This is the birthstone for January. Variations include *Garnetta* and *Garnette*.

Garyn (GAH-rin)   Meaning "spear carrier." A feminine form of *Gary*. Variations include *Garan, Garen,* and *Garryn*.

Gayle (GALE)   A form of Gail.

Gayna (GAY-nah)   A familiar form of Guinevere. Variations include *Gaynah, Gayner,* and *Gaynor*.

Genna (JEN-nah)   A form of Jenna. Variations include *Gen, Gennae, Gennay, Genni, Gennie,* and *Genny*.

Georgeanne (jor-JANNE)   A combination of Georgia and Ann. Variations include *Georgann, Georganne, Georgean,* and *Georgeann*.

Georgene (jor-JEEN)   A familar form of Georgia. Variations include *Georgeina, Georgena, Georgienne, Georgina,* and *Georgine*.

Georgia (JOR-jia)   Feminine form of George.

Georgina (jor-JEEN-a)   A form of Georgia. Variations include *Georgena, Georgene,* and *Georgine*.

Gilda (GILL-da)   Meaning "gilded." The late and great comedian Gilda Radner. Variations include *Gilde, Gildi,* and *Gildie*.

Ginette (GIN-et)   A form of Genevieve. Variations include *Gin, Ginetta, Ginnetta,* and *Ginnette*.

Ginny (JIN-nee)   A familiar form of Ginger or Virginia.

Golda (GOLD-a)   Meaning "gold." Notable persons with this name former Israeli prime minister Golda Meir and actor Goldie Hawn. Variations include *Golden, Goldi, Goldie, Goldina,* and *Goldy*.

Graceanne (GRAYS-ann)   A combination of Grace and Ann. Variations include *Graceann, Graceanna, Graciana,* and *Gratiana*.

Gypsy (JIP-see) A name given to the Romany people which has come to mean "wanderer." The life of burlesque queen Gypsy Rose Lee became the basis for the musical *Gypsy*. Variations include *Gipsy* and *Gypsie*.

Hadley (HAD-lee) Meaning "heather field." Variations include *Hadlea*, *Hadlee*, and *Hadleigh*.

Happy (HAH-pee) Signifying "cheerful." A famous Happy was Happy Rockefeller, the wife of former vice president Nelson Rockefeller.

Harley (HAR-lee) Meaning "long field." Variations include *Harlee*, *Harleen*, *Harleigh*, *Harli*, *Harlie*, *Harlina*, *Harline*, and *Harly*.

Harleyann (HAR-lee-ann) A combination of Harley and Ann. Variations include *Harlann*, *Harlanna*, *Harlanne*, *Harleyanna*, and *Harleyanne*.

Hattie (HAT-tee) A familiar form of Harriet. Hattie McDaniel of *Gone with the Wind* fame, and former U.S. senator Hattie Caraway. Variations include *Hatti*, *Hatty*, *Hetti*, *Hettie*, and *Hetty*.

Hayley (HAY-lee) Meaning "hay meadow." Hayley Mills is a well-known actress with this name. Variations include *Hailey*, *Hailea*, *Hailee*, *Hailley*, *Hailly*, *Haylee*, *Haylie*, and *Hayly*.

Hazel (HAY-zell) Meaning "hazelnut tree." Among notable people with this name is former U.S. senator Hazel Abel and jazz pianist Hazel Scott. Variations include *Hazal*, *Hazell*, *Hazelle*, and *Hazyl*.

Heather (HEH-thur) Signifies a flower associated with Scotland. Among well-known women with this name are Melrose Place's Heather Locklear and model Heather Stewart-Whyte. Variations include *Heath*, *Heatherlee*, and *Heatherly*.

Heaven (HEV-en) Signifying "paradise." Variations include *Heavenly*, *Heavin*, *Heavyn*, and *Heven*.

Henrietta (HEN-ree-etta) Meaning "ruler of the household." It is the feminine form of *Henry*. Among notable people with this name are Zionist Henrietta Szold and astronomer

Henrietta Leavitt. Variations include *Harriet*, *Hattie*, *Hatty*, *Hendrika*, *Heneretta*, *Henna*, *Henrietta*, *Hennriette*, and *Henny*.

Hertha (HUR-tha) Meaning "child of the earth." Variations include *Heartha* and *Hirtha*.

Hollis (HOLL-iss) Meaning "near the holly bushes." Variations include *Hollise*, *Hollyce*, and *Holyce*.

Holly (HOLL-lee) As in the shrub. Actress Holly Hunter. Variations include *Hollee*, *Holley*, *Holli*, and *Hollie*.

Hope (HOPE) Signifying the quality of hope. Actress Hope Lange.

Ivy (EYE-vee) Signifting the climbing plant. Variations include *Ivey* and *Ivie*.

Jami (JAY-mee) A feminine for James, meaning "the supplanter." Variations include *Jayme*, *Jaymi*, *Jamia*, *Jaymie*, and *Jaymine*.

Jamilynn (JAM-ih-lynn) A combination of Jami and Lynn. Variations include *Jamielin*, *Jamieline*, *Jamielyn*, *Jamielyne*, *Jamielynn*, and *Jamielynne*.

Jan (JAN) A short form of Jane, Janet, and Janice, meaning "God's gracious gift." Notable people with this name include Congresswoman Jan Schakowsky. Variations include *Jani*, *Jania*, *Jandy*, *Jannie*, *Janney*, and *Janny*.

Jane (JANE) A femininie form of John, meaning "God's gracious gift."

Janet (JAN-it) A form of Jane. Famous persons with this name include actresses Janet Gaynor and Janet Leigh, and singer Janet Jackson. Variations include *Janeta*, *Janete*, *Janett*, *Janetta*, *Janette*, *Janita*, *Jannet*, *Janneta*, *Jannetta*, and *Jannette*.

Janie (JAY-nee) A familiar form of Jane. Variations include *Janey* and *Jani*.

Janis (JAN-iss) A form of Jane, meaning "God's gracious gift." Legendary rock singer Janis Joplin. Variations include *Janees*, *Janeesa*, *Janesa*, *Janese*, *Janessa*, *Janesse*, *Janice*, and *Janise*.

Jennifer (JEN-ih-fur) Meaning "white wave." Popular actresses who share this name include Jennifer Love Hewitt, Jennifer Grey,

Jennifer Beals, and Jennifer Jason-Leigh. Variations include *Jenny* and *Jinny*.

Jeraldine (JER-all-deen)   A form of Geraldine. Variations include *Jeraideen, Jeraldene, Jeraidina,* and *Jeraldyne*.

Jetta (JET-ta)   Suggesting a jet-black gemstone.

Jill (JILL)   A short form of Jillian. Notable actresses with this name include Jill Clayburgh, Jill Eikenberry, and Jill Saint John. Variations include *Jil, Jillie, Jillisa, Jillissa, Jilly,* and *Jillyn*.

Joanna (jo-AN-na)   A form of Joan. Actress Joanna Kerns. Variations include *Janka, Jo, Joana, Jo-Ana, Joandra, Joanka, Joananna,* and *Joananne*.

Joanne (JO-ann)   A form of Joan. Comedian Joanne Worley of *Laugh-In*. Variations include *Joanann, Joananne, Joann, Jo-Ann, Jo-Anne, Joeann,* and *Joeanne*.

Jobeth (JO-beth)   A combination of Jo and Beth. Actress Jobeth Williams.

Joline (JO-leen)   Alternate forms of Jolene. A variation is *Joleen*.

Jonquil (JON-quill)   A kind of narcissus flower.

Joy (JOY)   Meaning "jewel" or "delight." Joy Philbin, wife of Regis.

Juliann (JUL-ee-ann)   A form of Julia, meaning "youthful." Variations include *Juliane, Julianne, Julieann, Julie-Ann, Julieanne,* and *Julie-Anne*.

Julie (JU-lee)   A form of Julia, meaning "youthful." Among notable people with this name are actresses Julie Andrews and Julie Newmar. Variations include *Jule, Julee, Juli, Julien, Juliene, Julienne, Jullie,* and *July*.

Kady (KAY-dee)   A combination of the initials K. and D.

Kaltha (KAL-tha)   Meaning "marigold."

Karalynn (KAR-ah-lynn)   An alternate form of Carolyn, which means "little and womanly." Variations include *Karalin, Karaline, Karalyn, Karalyne,* and *Karalynne*.

Kathy (KATH-ee)   Familiar forms of Katherine and Kathleen. Variations include *Kaethe, Kathe, Kathey, Kathi, Kathie, Katka,* and *Katia*.

Kathryn (KATH-rin)   A form of Katherine, meaning "pure." Variations include *Kathren, Kathrine,* and *Kathryne*.

Katie (KAY-tee)   A familiar form of Katherine. Actress Katie Holmes, from the TV series *Dawson's Creek*. Variations include *Kati, Katy, Kayte,* and *Kaytie*.

Kelly (KELL-lee)   Signifies "pasture by the spring."

Kenda (KEN-da)   Meaning "water baby." Variations include *Kendra, Kenndra, Kentra, Kentrae, Kindra,* and *Kyndra*.

Kendall (KEN-dall)   Meaning "valley of Kent." Variations include *Kendahl, Kendal, Kendalle, Kendel, Kendele, Kendell, Kendelle, Kendyl, Kendyle, Kendyll, Kindal, Kindall, Kyndal,* and *Kyndall*.

Kenenza (KEN-en-za)   A form of Kennice.

Kennice (KEN-niss)   Meaning "beautiful." A feminine form of Kenneth. Variations include *Kanice, Kenese,* and *Kennise*.

Kerrie (KERR-ee)   Meaning a king's name. A variation is *Kerry*.

Kimberly (KIM-bur-lee)   Signifies "meadow of the royal fort." Among notable people with this name are actresses Kim Basinger, Kimberly McCullough, and Kimberly Williams. Variations include *Cymbre, Kim, Kimba, Kimbely, Kimber, Kimbereley, Kimberely, Kimberlee, Kimbalee, Kimberlea, Kimberleigh, Kymberlee, Kymberley, Kymberlie, Kymberly,* and *Kymberlyn*.

Kinsey (KIN-see)   Meaning "offspring" or "relative." A variation is *Kinsee*.

Kortney (KORT-nee)   An alternate form of Courtney. Variations include *Kortnay, Kortnee, Kortni, Kortnie,* and *Kortny*.

Lallie (LALL-ee)   Meaning "babbler." Variations include *Lalli* and *Lally*.

Lane (LAIN)   Meaning "narrow road." Variations include *Laina, Laney, Lanie, Lanni, Lanny, Lany*, and *Layne*.

Lark (LARK)   Meaning "skylark."

Laura (LAW-ra)   Meaning "crowned with laurel."

Lauren (LAW-ren)   A form of Laura, meaning "crowned with laurel." Actress Lauren Bacall. Variations include *Laureen, Laurena, Laurene, Laurin, Lauryn, Laurynn, Loren, Lorena, Loreena, Lorenia, Lorenna, Lorina*, and *Lordne*.

Laurie (LAW-ree)   A familiar form of *Laura*, meaning "crowned with laurel." Performance artist Laurie Anderson. Variations include *Lari, Larilia, Laure, Lauri, Lauri, Lawrie*, and *Lori*.

Leeann (LEE-ann)   A combination of Lee and Ann. A form of Lian. A notable person with this name is country singer Lee Ann Rimes. Variations include *Lean, Leana, Leane, Leann, Leanna, Leanne, Leean, Leeanna, Leeanne, Leian, Leiann, Leianna*, and *Leianne*.

Leigh (LEE)   A form of Lee. Variations include *Leigha, Leighann, Leighanna*, and *Leighanne*.

Letty (LET-ee)   A familiar form of Leticia. Variations include *Letta, Letti*, and *Lettie*.

Lilibeth (LIL-ah-beth)   A combination of Lilly and Beth. Variations include *Lillbet* and *Lilybet*.

Lindsey (LIND-zee)   Meaning "linden tree island" or "camp near the stream." Lindsey Wagner played *The Bionic Woman*. Variations include *Lin, Linsey, Linsi, Linsle, Linzee, Linzi, Linzy, Lyndsey, Lynsey, Unsy*, and *Unzey*.

Lizabeth (LIHZ-ah-beth)   A short form of Elizabeth. Variations include *Liza, Lizabetta, Lizantan, Lizannen, Lizbeth, Lizina, Usabet, Usabeth*, and *Usabette*.

Lolly (LOLL-ee)   A familiar form of Laura.

Loretta (law-RET-ta)   A familiar form of Laura. Screen star Loretta Young. Variations include *Larrietta, Lauretta, Laurette, Loretah, Lorette, Lorita*, and *Lorrette*.

Louisa (LOU-eez-a)   A familiar form of Louise. A well-known Louisa is *Little Women* novelist Louisa May Alcott. Variations include *Eloisa, Lousian, Louisane, Louis-Ann, Louiza*, and *Lovisa*.

Love (LOVE)   Literally signifying "love," "kindness," or "charity."

Lucetta (lou-SET-ta)   A familiar form of Lucille. Variations include *Lucette*.

Lucille (LOU-seal)   Meaning "shine." Comedian Lucille Ball shares this name with B.B. King's favorite guitar. Variations include *Lucila, Lucile, Lucilla*, and *Lucy*.

Luvena (lou-VEEN-ah)   Meaning "little" or "beloved."

Lynn (LINN)   Meaning "waterfall." Among notable people with this name are actress Lynn Redgrave, as well as former congresswoman Lynn Schenk. Variations include *Lin, Lina, Linn, Lyn, Lynette, Lynlee, Lynna*, and *Lynnell*.

Lynnell (lynn-ELL)   An alternate form of Lynn. Variations include *Linell, Linnell, Lynell, Lynella, Lynelle*, and *Lynnelle*.

Mada (MAID-a)   A short form of Madeline and Magdalen, meaning "woman of Maydala." Variations include *Madda* and *Mahda*.

Maddie (MADD-eee)   A familiar form of Madeline. Variations include *Maddi, Maddy*, and *Mady*.

Mae (MAY)   An alternate form of May. Among notables with this name are Mae Jemison, the first African-American woman in space, and the unforgettable Mae West. Variations include *Maellea, Maelleah, Maellen*, and *Maelle*.

Malva (MAL-vah)   A form of Melba. Variations include *Malvi* and *Malvy*.

Marabel (MAR-ah-bell)   A form of Mirabel, meaning "a great beauty." Variations include *Marabella* and *Marabelle*.

Marcellen (mar-SELL-en)   A form of Marcella, which means "warlike." Variations include *Marcelen, Marcelin, Marcelina, Marceline*, and *Marcellin*.

Marcy (MAR-see) A familiar form of Marcella and Marcia, which means "warlike." Congresswoman Marcy Kaptur. Variations include *Marcee, Marci, Marcie, Marcita,* and *Marcy.*

Maretta (MAR-et-ta) A familiar form of Margaret, which means "pearl." Variations include *Maret* and *Marette.*

Marge (MARJ) A short form of Margaret and Marjorie. A variation is *Margie.*

Marian (MAR-ee-ann) A form of Maryann. Among celebrated women with this name is jazz pianist Marian McPartland and opera singer Marian Anderson. Variations include *Mariana, Mariane, Mariann, Marianne, Marion, Marrian, Marrianne, Maryann,* and *Maryanne.*

Maridel (MAR-ih-dell) A form of Marabel.

Marigold (MAR-ee-gold) Meaning the golden yellow flower, which combines Mary and "gold." Variations include *Maragold* and *Marrigold.*

Markeisia (mar-KEE-sha) A combination of Mary and Keisha. Variations include *Markesha, Markesia,* and *Markiesha.*

Marla (MAR-la) A short form of Marlena and Marlene, which means "high tower." Notable people with this name include actress Marla Gibbs and Marla Maples. Variations include *Marlah* and *Marlea.*

Marlee (MAR-lee) A form of Marlene, which means "high tower." One famous Marlee is actress Marlee Matlin, who can be convincing even when not speaking. Variations include *Marlea, Marleah, Marli, Marlie, Marle,* and *Marley.*

Marley (MAR-lee) A familiar form of Marlene. Variations include *Marlee, Marli, Marlie,* and *Marly.*

Marlis (MAR-liss) A combination of Maria and Lisa. Variations include *Marles, Marlisa, Marlise, Marlys, Marlyse,* and *Marlyssa.*

Marsha (MAR-sha) A form of Marcia, meaning "warlike." Actor Marsha Mason. Variations include *Marsia* and *Martia.*

Marta (MAR-ta) A short form of Martha and Martina, meaning "lady." Variations include *Martá, Martä,* and *Marte.*

Maryann (MAR-e-ann) Combinations of Mary and Ann. Among notable people with this name: film critic MaryAnn Johanson. Variations include *Mariann, Marianne, Maryanna,* and *Maryanne.*

Mattie (MAT-ee) Familiar forms of Martha and Matilda. Variations include *Matte, Mattey, Matti,* and *Matty.*

Maud (MAWD) Short forms of Madeline and Matilda. Maude Abbott was a pioneer in cardiology, Irish actor Maud Gonne. Variations include *Maudie, Maude, Maudine,* and *Maudlin.*

Megan (MEG) A familiar form of Margaret. Variations include *Meg, Meggi, Meggie,* and *Meggy.*

Mercia (mur-SEE-a) A form of Marcia, meaning "warlike."

Mercy (MUR-see) "Compassion; mercy." Variations include *Mercey, Merci, Mercie, Mersey.*

Merilyn (MER-ih-lynn) A combination of Merry and Lynn. Variations include *Merelyn, Merralyn* and *Merrilyn.*

Merry (MER-ree) Meaning "cheerful" or "happy." Variations include *Merie, Merri, Merrie,* and *Merrilyn.*

Mildred (MILL-dred) Meaning "gentle counselor." Variations include *Mil, Mila, Mildrid, Millie,* and *Milly.*

Millie (MILL-ee) Familiar forms of Camille, Emily, Melissa, Mildred, Millicent. Millie Criswell is a romance novelist. Variations include *Mill, Milla,* and *Milley.*

Missy (MISS-ee) A familiar form of Melissa and Millicent. Rap singer Missy Elliot, and mountain bike extraordinaire Missy "The Missile" Giove. Variations include *Missi* and *Missie.*

Misty (MISS-tee) Meaning "enveloped by mist." Variations include *Missty, Mistee, Mistey, Misti,* and *Mistie.*

Myla (MY-la)   Meaning "merciful."

Nancy (NAN-see)   A form of Ann, meaning "gracious." Among notable people with this name is former first lady Nancy Reagan. Variations include *Nanci*, *Nancie*, and *Nancey*.

Nedda (NED-da)   "Wealthy guardian." A feminine form of Edward. The tragic heroine of Leoncavallo's opera *I Pagliacci*. Variations include *Neddi*, *Neddie*, *Neddy*.

Nellie (NELL-ee)   A familiar form of Eleanor, Helen, and Cornelia. Opera singer Nellie Melba is the person who lent her name to Melba Toast. Nellie Bly was a pioneer in investigative journalism. Variations include *Neli*, *Nell*, *Nella*, *Nelley*, and *Nelly*.

Nollie (NOLL-ee)   A familiar form of Magnolia. Variations include *Nolley*, *Nolli*, and *Nolly*.

Odella (ODE-el-la)   Meaning "wood hill." Variations include *Odele*, *Odelle*, and *Odelyn*.

Osma (OZ-ma)   Meaning "divine protector." A feminine form of Osmond. Also *Ozma*.

Paige (PAYJ)   Meaning "young child."

Patia (PAT-ee-a)   A familiar form of Patience or Patricia.

Patience (PAY-shence)   Signifying the virtuous quality. Variations include *Paciencia*, *Patia*, and *Patty*.

Patricia (PAT-rih-sha)   Actress Patricia Arquette, congresswoman Patty Murray, and singing diva Patti Labelle. Variations include *Patte*, *Pattee*, *Patti*, and *Patty*.

Peace (PEES)   Literally signfying "peaceful" or "at peace with oneself."

Piper (PIE-pur)   "Pipe player." Actress Piper Laurie.

Pippa (PIP-ah)   A short form of Phillipa. A well-known children's book heroine is Pippi Longstocking. Variations include *Pippi* and *Pippy*.

Pollyanna (pol-ee-ANN-ah)   A combination of Polly and Anna.

Primrose (PRIM-rose)   Meaning "first rose." Variations include *Primarosa* and *Primula*.

Princess (PRIN-cess)   Suggesting "daughter of royalty." Variations include *Princcess*, *Princella*, *Princetta*, *Princie*, and *Princilla*.

Purity (PUR-ih-tee)   Signifying the quality of pureness. Variations include *Pura*, *Pureza*, and *Purisima*.

Queenie (QUEEN-ee)   Meaning "queen." Variations include *Queen*, *Queena*, *Queenette*, *Queeny*, and *Quenna*.

Quinn (QUINN)   Signifies "queen." Variations include *Quin* and *Quinna*.

Randall (RAN-dall)   Meaning "protected." Variations include *Randa*, *Randah*, *Randal*, *Randel*, *Randell*, and *Randelle*.

Randi (RAN-dee)   Familiar forms of Miranda and Randall. Variations include *Rande*, *Randee*, *Randey*, *Randie*, and *Randii*.

Raven (RAY-vin)   Meaning "blackbird." Variations include *Ravena*, *Ravennah*, *Ravi*, *Ravin*, *Ravyn*, *Rayven*, and *Rayvin*.

Reanna (RAY-nah)   An alternate form of Raine, meaning "queen."

Rennie (REN-nee)   A familiar form of Renata. Variations include *Reni*, *Renie*, and *Renni*.

Rina (REE-nah)   A short form of names ending in -rina, for example, Katarina. Variations include *Reena* and *Rena*.

Roberta (rah-BUR-tah)   Meaning "bright fame." A feminine form of Robert. Singer Roberta Flack. Variations include *Bobbi*, *Robin*, *Robbi*, *Robbie*, and *Robby*.

Robin (RAHB-in)   Meaning a type of bird. An alternate form of Roberta. Actresses Robin Wright-Penn and Robin Givens. Variations include *Robbi*, *Robbie*, *Robbin*, *Robby*, *Robena*, and *Robyn*.

Robinette (RAHB-in-ett)   A familiar form of Robin. Variations include *Robernetta*, *Robinet*, *Robinett*, and *Robinita*.

Rodnae (ROD-nay)   Meaning "island clearing." Variations include *Rodna*, *Rodnetta*, and *Rodnicka*.

Roz (ROZ)   Short form of Rosalind and Rosalyn. Author Roz Denny Fox, TV news anchor Roz Abrams. A variation is *Ros*.

Rosalie (ROSE-ah-lee)   A form of Rosalind. Variations include *Rosalea, Rosalee, Rosalene, Rosalia, Roselia,* and *Rosilee*.

Roseanne (rose-ANN)   A combination of Rose and Ann. Roseanne Barr got her start in stand up comedy. Variations include *Rosan, Rosann, Roseann, Rozann,* and *Rozanne*.

Rosemary (ROSE-mare-ee)   A combination of Rose and Mary. Singer Rosemary Clooney, aunt of George. Variations include *Romi* and *Romy*.

Rosie (ROSE-ee)   A familiar form of Rosalind, Rosanna, and Rose. Talk show host and actress Rosie O'Donnell. Variations include *Rosey, Rosi, Rosy, Rozsi,* and *Rozy*.

Rosina (ROSE-een-ah)   A familiar form of Rose. Rosina Lhévinne was a legendary piano teacher. Variations include *Rosena, Rosenah, Rosene, Rozena,* and *Rozina*.

Rowina (ROW-an)   Meaning "tree with red berries."

Royale (ROY-al)   Meaning "royal." Variations include *Royal, Royalle, Ryal,* and *Ryale*.

Royanna (roy-AN-nah)   Meaning "queenly" or "royal." A feminine form of Roy, meaning "king." Variations include *Roya, Royalene, Roylee,* and *Roylene*.

Rula (ROOL-ah)   Meaning "ruler." Among notable people with this name is actor Rula Lenska.

Rusti (RUS-tee)   Meaning "redhead."

Sable (SAY-bull)   Literally "sable" or "sleek." Wrestling star Sable. Variations include *Sabel, Sabela,* and *Sabella*.

Saffron (SAF-ron)   Suggesting the dried stamens of the saffron flower which are used as a spice or a dye.

Sage (SAYJ)   Meaning "wise." Variations include *Sagia* and *Saige*.

Salliann (SAL-lee-ANN)   A combination of Sally and Anne. Variations include *Sallian, Sallianne, Sallyann,* and *Sally-Ann*.

Sally (SAL-lee)   A familiar form of Sarah, which means "princess." Among notable people with this name are the first American woman in space, Sally Ride, and actress Sally Kellerman. Variations include *Sal, Sallee, Salletta, Sallette, Salley, Salli, Salliann,* and *Sallie*.

Saundra (SAWN-dra)   A form of Sandra and Sondra. Actresses Saundra Santiago and Saundra Quarterman. Variations include *Saundee, Saundi, Saundie,* and *Saundy*.

Scarlett (SCAR-let)   Signifying "bright red." *Gone with the Wind's* Scarlett O'Hara, the southern belle heroine of Margaret Mitchell's classic novel. Variations include *Scarlet, Scarlette,* and *Skarlette*.

Seelia (SEE-lee-ah)   A form of Sheila.

Sella (SELL-lah)   A short form of Selena. Variations include *Seeley* and *Selah*.

Sharee (SHAR-ee)   A form of Cheri, meaning "dear." Variations include *Shareen, Sheri,* and *Sharine*.

Shelby (SHELL-bee)   "Estate on the ledge." Variations include *Shel, Shelbe, Shelbee, Shelbey, Shelbie,* and *Shellby*.

Shelley (SHELL-lee)   Meaning "meadow on the ledge." Actresses Shelley Winters, Shelley Duvall, and Shelley Long; Congresswoman Shelley Berkley; country singer Shelley Streeter. Variations include *Shelee, Sheley, Sheli, Shelia, Shelica, Shelicia,* and *Shelly*.

Sherry (SHER-ree)   Meaning "white meadow." Country singer Sherrie Austin. Variations include *Sheri, Sherrey,* and *Sherrie*.

Shirlene (SHIR-leen)   An alternate form of Shirley. Variations include *Shirleen, Shirline,* and *Shirlynn*.

Shirley (SHIR-lee)   "Bright meadow." Among notable people with this name are former congresswoman and presidential candidate Shirley Chisholm and actress Shirley McLaine.

Variations include *Sherlee, Sherleen, Sherley,* and *Sherli.*

Shyla (SHY-lah)   An alternate form of Sheila.

Sidonie (SIH-don-ee)   "A follower of Saint Denis." A variation is *Sydney.*

Sigourney (si-GORE-nee)   Meaning "victorious conquerer." Among notable people with this name is actress Sigourney Weaver. Variations include *Signe* and *Sigourny.*

Spring (SPRING)   Signifying the season. Actress Spring Byington.

Stacia (STAY-see-yah)   A short form of Anastasia. Variations include *Stasia* and *Staysha.*

Starling (STAR-ling)   Signifying the name of a bird. Television reporter and lawyer Starr Jones. Variations include *Starr, Starleen, Atarleena, Starlena, Starlene,* and *Starlynn.*

Stockard (STOCK-ard)   English place name. Stockard Channing played Rizzo in the movie *Grease* and has since excelled on Broadway.

Stormy (STOR-mee)   Meaning "tempestuous." Variations include *Storm, Storme, Stormi,* and *Stormie.*

Summer (SUM-mer)   Signifying the season. Olympic champion swimmer Summer Sanders. Variations include *Sommer, Sumer,* and *Summar.*

Sunny (SUN-nee)   Meaning "bright" or "cheerful." Variations include *Sunni* and *Sunnie.*

Suzanne (sue-ZANN)   A form of Susan. Among notable people with this name are dancer Suzanne Farrell, folk singer Suzanne Vega, and actress Suzanne Sommers. Variations include *Susanne, Suszanne, Suzane,* and *Suzann.*

Sybella (sib-ELL-ah)   A form of Sybil. Variations include *Sibel, Sibell, Sibella, Sibelle, Sybel,* and *Sybelle.*

Tallis (TAL-liss)   Meaning "forest." A variation is *Tallys.*

Tammy (TAM-mee)   Variations include *Tamia, Tamiah, Tamie,* and *Tamiya.*

Tandy (TAN-dee)   Meaning "team." Variations include *Tanda, Tandee, Tandi, Tandie,* and *Thandie.*

Tatum (TAYT-um)   Meaning "light-hearted." Actress Tatum O'Neal. Variations include *Tate* and *Tatumn.*

Taye (TAY)   A short form of Taylor. Variations include *Tay, Taya, Tayah, Tayana,* and *Tayiah.*

Taylor (TAY-lor)   Literally means "tailor." Singer Taylor Dane. Variations include *Tailor, Taiylor, Talor, Talora, Taye, Tayla, Taylar, Tayler, Tayllor,* and *Taylore.*

Teal (TEEL)   Signifying a blue green color. Variations include *Teala, Teale, Tealia,* and *Teill.*

Tetty (TET-tee)   A familiar form of Elizabeth.

Timothea (tim-oh-THEE-ah)   Meaning "honoring God." A feminine form of Timothy. Among notable people with this name is jazz singer Timothea. Variations include *Thea, Timmi, Timmie,* and *Timotheya.*

Toriana (TOR-ee-AN-ah)   A familiar form of Victoria, meaning "victorious." A combination of Tory and Anna. Variations include *Tori, Torian, Toriann, Torianna,* and *Torianne.*

Torillyn (TOR-il-lin)   A combination of Tory and Lynn. Variations include *Tory, Torilynn,* and *Torrilyn.*

Trilby (TRILL-bee)   The name of a soft hat. Variations include *Trilbi, Trilbie,* and *Trillby.*

Tuesday (TOOZ-day)   Signifying the day of the week. Among notable people with this name is actress Tuesday Weld.

Twyla (TWHY-lah)   Meaning "woven of double thread." Choreographer Twyla Tharp has been a dance innovator most of her career. Variations include *Twila* and *Twilla.*

Tyler (TIE-ler)   Meaning "tailor." Variations include *Tyller* and *Tylor.*

Tyne (TYN) Signifying an English river. Among notable people with this name is actress Tyne Daly.

Unice (YOU-niss) A form of Eunice, meaning "gloriously victorious."

Unity (YOU-nit-ee) Meaning "unity." Variations include *Unita* and *Unitee*.

Vanetta (va-NET-tah) A form of Vanessa. Variations include *Vaneta*, *Vanneta*, *Vannetta*, and *Venetta*.

Vanity (VAN-nit-ee) Meaning "vain." Variations include *Vanita* and *Vanitty*.

Velvet (VELL-vet) Meaning "velvety." Variations include *Velvetta* and *Velvina*.

Victoria (VIC-TOR-ee-ah) Meaning "victorious."

Walker (WALL-kur) Meaning "cloth-walker." Also *Wallker*.

Wallis (WALL-iss) Meaning "from Wales." A feminine form of Wallace. The Dutchess of Windsor, Wallis Simpson. Variations include *Wallie*, *Walliss*, and *Wallys*.

Wanett (wan-NET) Meaning "pale complexioned." Variations include *Wanette*, *Wannetta*, and *Wannette*.

Waynette (WAYN-ett) Meaning "wagon maker." A feminine form of Wayne. Variations include *Waynel* and *Waynelle*.

Wenda (WEN-dah) Signifies "fair."

Wendelle (WEN-dell) Meaning "wanderer." Variations include *Wendall*, *Wendalyn*, *Wendeline*, and *Wendella*.

Weslee (WES-lee) Meaning "western meadow." A feminine form of Wesley. Variations include *Weslea*, *Wesley*, and *Weslie*.

Whitley (WHIT-lee) Meaning "white field." A variation is *Whitely*.

Whitney (WHIT-nee) Meaning "white island." Singer Whitney Houston is a pop diva of today. Variations include *Whiteney*, *Whitne*, *Whitni*, *Whitnee*, *Whitnie*, *Whitny*, *Whitteny*, *Whitnei*, *Whitni*, *Whittnie*, and *Whytnie*.

Wileen (will-EEN) A short form of Wilhelmina, meaning "protectress." Variations include *Wilene*, *Willeen*, and *Willene*.

Willette (will-ETT) A familiar form of Wilhelmina, meaning "protectress," and Willa.

Willie (WILL-lee) A familiar form of Wilhelmina, meaning "protectress." Variations include *Willina*, *Willisha*, and *Willishia*.

Willow (WILL-oh) As in "willow tree." Among notable people with this name, fashion model Willow Bay.

Wilona (WILL-ona) Meaning "desired." Variations include *Willona*, *Willone*, and *Wilone*.

Winnie (WIN-nee) A familiar form of Edwina, Gwyneth, and Winnifred. The name of A. A. Milne's mischievous and adorable Pooh bear as well as South African rebel leader Winnie Mandela. Variations include *Wina*, *Winne*, *Winney*, *Winni*, *Winny*, amd *Wynnie*.

Yetta (YET-tah) A short form of Henrietta. Variations include *Yette* and *Yitta*.

Yudelle (you-DELL) An alternate form of Udele.

Zelene (zell-EEN) Meaning "sunshine."

Zeta (ZAY-tah) Meaning "rose." Also the last letter of the Greek alphabet. Film star Catherine Zeta Jones has this as a middle name. Variations include *Zetana* and *Zetta*.

France

France is the most phonetically evolved of the Romance languages. Its soft, nasal, yet elegant sounds are the result of Frankish and Celtic influences on Latin. While the vast majority of French children have names that are traditional in nature, with either a historic or religious origin, the French have often borrowed names from English, German, Italian, and Spanish sources. French children often have composite names like Jean-Pierre or Marie-Claire.

FRANCE: BOYS

Adrien (ah-dree-EN) Meaning "dark" or "from Adria." A variation is *Adriene.*

Aimon (eh-MOH) Meaning "house."

Alain (ah-LANH) Meaning "handsome" or "harmony." A form of Alan. Among the famous people with this name is French actor Alain Delon. Variations include *Alaen, Alainn, Alayn,* and *Allain.*

Alaire (ah-LAIR) Meaning "joyous."

Albert (ahl-BEAR) Meaning "noble and bright." Variations include *Adelbert, Ailbert, Al, Albertik, Alberto, Alberts, Albie, Albrecht, Alvertos, Aubert, Elbert,* and *Ulbrecht.*

Alexandre (ahl-ex-AHND-re) A form of Alexander, which is Greek for "protector of men." Author Alexandre Dumas gave the world *The Three Musketeers* and *The Man in the Iron Mask.*

Amando (ah-mahn-DOH) A form of Amadeus, which means "he who loves God." Variations include *Amand, Amandio, Amaniel,* and *Amato.*

Amato (ah-mah-TOH) Meaning "loved."

Ames (AHM) Signifies "friend."

André (ahn-DRAY) A form of Andrew, which is Greek for "manly." Notable people with this name include tennis star Andre Agassi and conductor Andre Previn. Variations include *Andra, Andrae, Andre, Andrecito, Andree, Andrei,* and *Aundri.*

Ansel (ahn-SELL) Meaning "follower of a nobleman." Photographer Ansel Adams cap-tured beautiful western landscapes. Variations include *Ancell, Ansa,* and *Ansell.*

Antoine (ahn-TWAN) A form of Anthony, which is Latin for "of inestimable worth." Variations include *Antoin, Antionne, Antoini,* and *Atoine.*

Aramis (ah-ram-EE) One of the Three Musketeers. Variations include Airamis, Aramith, Aramys, and Aran.

Arnaud (ar-NO) Meaning "strong as an eagle." Variations include *Arnauld, Arnault,* and *Arnoll.*

Audon (oh-DONH) Meaning "old" or "wealthy." A variation is *Audelon.*

Avent (av-ONH) Meaning "born during Advent." Variations include *Aventin* and *Aventino.*

Averill (ah-VREEL) Meaning "born in April." Governor and ambassador Averill Harriman.

Aymon (ay-MONH) Meaning "mighty" or "wise protection."

Bailey (bay-LEE) Meaning "bailiff" or "warden." Variations include *Bail, Bailie, Baily, Bayley,* and *Bayly.*

Beau (BO) Meaning "handsome." The actor Beau Bridges, as well as his brother Jeff, is following in his father Lloyd's Hollywood footsteps. Variations include *Beale* and *Bo.*

Beaufort (bo-FOR) Meaning "beautiful fort."

Beaumont (bo-MONH) Meaning "beautiful mountain."

Beauregard (bo-ray-GAHR) Meaning "handsome."

Belden (bel-DONH) Meaning "beautiful glen." Variations include *Beldin, Beldon, Bellden,* and *Belldon.*

Bellamy (bell-ah-MEE) Signifies "beautiful friend." Variations include *Belamy, Bell, Bellamey,* and *Bellamie.*

Benoit (ben-WAH) A form of Benedict, meaning "blessed."

Berger (ber-ZHER) Meaning "shepherd."

Blaise (BLEHZ) A form of Blaze, from Latin for "stammerer." The philosopher Blaise Pascal is equally renowned for his contributions to mathematics. Variations include *Blayse, Blaisot, Blas, Blase, Blasi, Blasien,* and *Blasius.*

Boone (BOON) Meaning "good." Variations include *Bon, Bone,* and *Bonne.*

Borden (bor-DONH) Meaning "cottage."

Bourne (BOORNH) Meaning "border."

Boyce (BWAHC) Meaning "woods" or "forest." Variations include *Boice, Boise, Boy, Boycey,* and *Boycle.*

Burke (BOORK) Meaning "fortress" or "castle." Variations include *Berk, Berke, Birk, Bourke, Burk,* and *Burkley.*

Cable (KABL) Meaning "rope."

Cannon (ka-NONH) Meaning "church official" or "large gun." Variations include *Cannan, Canning,* and *Canon.*

Carvell (kar-VELL) Meaning "village on the marsh." A variation is *Carvel.*

Cassius (ka-SHUH) Signifies "hollow." The boxer Muhammad Ali was born Cassius Clay. Variations include *Cassia, Cassio,* and *Cazzie.*

Chaney (sha-NEE) Meaning "oak." Variations include *Chayne, Cheney, Cheyn, Cheyne,* and *Cheyney.*

Chante (shan-TAY) Meaning "singer." Variations include *Chantha, Chanthar, Chantra, Chantry,* and *Shantae.*

Chase (SHAS) Signifies "hunter."

Chevalier (sh-val-YAY) Meaning "cavalier" or "knight." Variations include *Chev* and *Chevy.*

Christophe (kris-TOFF) A form of Christopher, meaning "Christ bearer." A variation is *Christoph.*

Clark (KLAHRK) Meaning "clergyman" or "scholar." Legendary screen star Clark Gable. Variations include *Clarke, Clerc,* and *Clerk.*

Claude (KLOHD) Meaning "lame." The Impressionist painter Claude Monet and composer Claude Debussy were both French. Variations include *Claud, Claudan, Claudel, Claudell, Claudian, Claudien, Claudin, Claudio,* and *Claudius.*

Coco (ko-KO) A familiar form of Jacques, which is the French form of Jack. Variations include *Coko* and *Koko.*

Collar (ko-LAHR) A form of Nicholas, meaning "victory of the people."

Cordell (kor-DELL) Meaning "rope maker." Variations include *Cord, Cordale, Corday, Cordel, Cordelle, Cordie, Cordy,* and *Kordell.*

Crépin (kray-PAHN) A form of Crispin, meaning "curly-haired."

Dandri (dand-REE) A combination of the prefix De and André. Variations include *D'andre, D'Andri, Dandrae, D'andrea, Dandras, Dandray, Dandre, Deandri, Deandra, Deaundre, De Aundre,* and *Dondrea.*

Darrell (dah-RELL) Meaning "darling," "beloved," or "copse of oak trees." Variations include *Dare, Darel, Darell, Darral, Darrel, Darrill, Darrol, Darryl, Derrell, Dahrll, Darryle, Darryll, Daryl, Daryle, Daryll,* and *Derryl.* A famous Darryl is baseball player Darryl Strawberry.

Dax (DAKS) Meaning "water."

Delano (deh-la-NOH) Signifies "nut tree." President Franklin Roosevelt's middle name was Delano.

Delroy (del-RWAH) Meaning "belonging to the king." Actor Delroy Lindo. Variations include *Delray, Delree, Delroi, Elroy,* and *Leroy.*

Demont (deh-MONH) Meaning "mountain."

Destin (des-TIN) Meaning "destiny" or "fate." Variations include *Destine*, *Deston*, and *Destry*.

Didier (did-ee-AY) Meaning "desired" or "yearned for." A masculine form of Desiree.

Dominique (do-min-EEK) A form of Dominic, which is Latin for "the Lord's." On the masculine side is Dominique Wilkins, who played professional basketball. Variations include *Domeniqu*, *Domenque*, *Dominiqu*, *Domnenique*, *Domnique*, *Domoniqu*, and *Domonique*.

Donatien (do-na-tee-YEN) Signifies "gift."

Drury (dru-REE) Meaning "loving."

Duk (DOOK) Meaning "leader" or "duke." Variations include *Dukey*, *Dukie*, and *Duky*.

Duval (doo-VALL) A combination of the prefix Du and Val. Variations include *Duvall* and *Duveuil*.

Edouard (eh-DWARD) A form of Edward, which is of Anglo-Saxon origin and means "prosperous guardian." Famous Edouards include the Impressionist painter Edouard Manet. A variation is *Edoard*.

Elroy (el-RWAH) Latin for "royal." An alternate form of Delroy and Leroy. A variation is *Elroi*.

Emille (eh-MEEL) A form of Emil, which means "industriously winning." Variations include *Emiel*, *Emile*, and *Emilie*.

Etienne (eh-tee-YEN) A form of Stephen, Greek for "crown" or "garland." Designer Etienne Aigner's. Variations include *Etian* and *Étienn*.

Fabron (fah-BRONH) Meaning "little blacksmith" or "apprentice." Variations include *Fabre* and *Fabroni*.

Fermin (fair-MIHN) Meaning "firm" or "strong." Variations include *Ferman*, *Firmin*, and *Furman*.

Ferrand (feh-RAND) Signifying "iron gray hair." Variations include *Farand*, *Farrand*, *Farrant*, and *Ferrant*.

Firman (feer-MOHN) Meaning "firm" or "strong." A variation is *Ferman*.

Florent (floh-ROHN) Meaning "blossoming." Variations include *Florenci*, *Florencio*, *Florentin*, *Florentino*, *Florentyn*, *Florentz*, *Florinio*, and *Florino*.

Fontaine (fon-TENN) Meaning "fountain."

Fortuné (for-TUNE-ay) Meaning "fortunate" or "lucky." Variations include *Fortun*, *Fortunato*, and *Fortunio*.

Franchot (fran-SHO) A form of Francis, meaning "from France." One famous Franchot was actor Franchot Tone.

François (fran-SWAH) A form of Francis, meaning "from France." Poet Francois Villon and the New Wave film director Francois Truffaut.

Fraser (fra-SEHR) Meaning "strawberry."

Frayne (FREHN) Signifies "dweller at the ash tree."

Gage (GAGZH) Meaning "pledge." A variation is *Gager*.

Garland (gar-LANH) Meaning "wreath of flowers" or "prize."

Garner (gar-NEHR) Signifies "army guard" or "sentry." A variation is *Garnier*.

Garrison (gah-ree-SONH) Meaning "protection" or "stronghold." A variation is *Garris*.

Gaspar (gas-PAHR) A form of Casper, which is a variation on the Slavic name Casimir meaning "proclamation of peace." Variations include *Gáspár*, *Gaspard*, *Gaspare*, *Gasparo*, *Gasper*, and *Gazsi*.

Gaston (gas-TONH) A name that signifies Gascony, France. A variation is *Gascon*.

Gautier (gau-tee-YAY) A form of Walter, which means "powerful" or "mighty warrior." Variations include *Galtero*, *Gaultier*, *Gaultiero*, and *Gauthier*.

Gaylord (guy-LOHR) Meaning "lively" or "high-spirited." Famous American Gaylords include the Wisconsin politician Gaylord Nelson. Variations include *Gaillard*, *Gallard*, *Gayelord*, *Gayler*, and *Gaylor*.

Gédéon (ge-de-ONH) A form of Gideon, from the Hebrew for "brave warrior" or "indomitable spirit."

Georges (JOHRJ) A form of George, from the Greek for "farmer" or "tiller of the soil." Georges Pompidou served as both prime minister and president of France. A variation is *Geórges*.

Géraud (gzher-OH) A form of Gerard, which means "spearman."

Germain (gzher-MANH) Meaning "German."

Gervaise (gzher-VEHZ) Meaning "virtuous." Variations include *Jervis*, *Garvais*, *Garvaise*, *Garvey*, *Gervais*, *Gervasio*, *Gervaso*, *Gervayse*, *Gervis*, and *Gerwazy*.

Gillett (gzhee-YAY) Meaning "young Gilbert." Variations include *Gelett*, *Gelette*, and *Gillette*.

Granger (granh-GZHAY) Meaning "farmer." Variations include *Grainger* and *Grange*.

Granville (gran-VEEL) Meaning "big town." Variations include *Gran*, *Granvel*, *Granvil*, *Granvile*, *Granvill*, *Grenville*, and *Greville*.

Griswold (greez-WOLD) Meaning "gray forest." Variations include *Gris* and *Griz*.

Grosvener (groh-ve-NAY) Signifies "big hunter."

Guillaume (gee-OAM) A form of William, which means "determined protector." A variation is *Guillaums*.

Hamlet (am-LAY) Meaning "little village" or "home." The most famous Hamlet is Shakespeare's tragic hero.

Hamlin (am-LANH) Meaning "loves his home." Variations include *Hamblin*, *Hamelen*, *Hamelin*, *Hamlen*, *Hamlyn*, and *Lin*.

Harbin (ar-BANH) Meaning "little bright warrior." Variations include *Harben*, and *Harbyn*.

Harcourt (ar-COUR) Meaning "fortified farm." Variations include *Court* and *Harcort*.

Henri (en-REE) A form of Henry, which means "ruler of the home." A variation is *Henrico*.

Hervi (er-VEE) A form of Harvey.

Hewitt (yew-EET) Meaning "little smart one." Variations include *Hewe*, *Hewet*, *Hewett*, *Hewle*, *Hewit*, *Hewlett*, and *Hewlitt*.

Hyacinthe (ya-SAHNT) Meaning "hyacinth."

Jacques (JZHOCK) A form of Jacob, James, which is Hebrew for "the supplanter." For decades, Jacques Cousteau was a leader in marine biology.

Jasper (jzhass-PERH) Meaning "green ornamental stone."

Jay (JZHAY) Meaning "blue jay." A famous American Jay was the financier and railroad magnate Jay Gould.

Jean (JZHONH) A form of John, from the Hebrew for "gracious is God." Variations include *Jian*, *Jeannah*, *Jeannie*, *Jeannot*, *Jeanot*, and *Jene*.

Jehan (yay-ANH) A form of John, which is Hebrew for "gracious is God." A variation is *Jehann*.

Jemond (jzheh-MONH) Suggests "worldly." Variations include *Jemon*, *Jimond*, *Jemonde*, and *Jemone*.

Jermaine (jzher-MEN) An alternate form of Germain, which is Latin for "German."

Jerard (jzhehr-AHR) A form of Gerard, which is a variation of Teutonic name Gerald, meaning "spearman." Variations include *Jarard*, *Jarrard*, *Jerardo*, *Jeraude*, and *Jerrard*.

Jules (JZHOOL) A form of Julius, from the Latin for "youthful." Science fiction author Jules Verne. Variations include *Jole* and *Jule*.

Justis (jzhou-STEE) Meaning "just." Variations include *Justs* and *Justus*.

Kristophe (kris-TOFF) A form of Cristopher, which is Greek for "Christian."

Kurt (KOUR) A short form of Kurtis and alternate form of Curt, which means "courteous." Variations include Kort and Kuno.

Kurtis (kour-TEE) An alternate form of Curtis, based on French for "which is courteous" or "courteous." Variations include *Kurt, Kurtice,* and *Kurtiss.*

Lafayette (la-fai-ETT) Originally a surname. The marquis de Lafayette fought with the patriots in the American Revolution. Variations include *Lafalete* and *Lafayett.*

Lamond (la-MONH) Meaning "world." Variations include *Lammond, Lamondre, Lamund,* and *Lemond.*

Lancelot (lans-LO) Meaning "attendant." The legendary Sir Lancelot du Lac was a knight of King Arthur's round table. Variations include *Lance, Lancelott, Launcelet,* and *Launcelot.*

Landry (lan-DREE) Meaning "ruler." Variations include *Landre, Landré,* and *Landrue.*

Laramie (la-ra-MEE) Signifying "tears of love."

Laron (la-RONH) Signifying "thief." Variations include *Laran, La'ron, La Ron, Laronn,* and *La Ruan.*

Larrimore (lah-ree-MOHR) Signifying "armorer." Variations include *Larlmore, Larmer,* and *Larmor.*

LaSalle (la-SAL) Meaning "hall." Variations include *Lasalle, Lascell,* and *Lascelles.*

Laurent (law-RONH) A form of Laurence. A variation is *Laurente.*

LaValle (la-VAL) Meaning "valley." Variations include *Lavail, Laval, Lavalei,* and *Lavalle.*

Leggett (le-GETT) Meaning "one who is sent" or "delegate." Variations include *Legate, Leggitt,* and *Liggett.*

Lemar (le-MARH) An alternate form of Lamar, which is Old German for "land famous." Variations include *Lemario* and *Lemarr.*

Leron (le-RONH) Which means "round" or "circle."

Leroy (le-RWAH) Meaning "the king." Variations include *Delroy, Elroy, Lee, Leeroy, LeeRoy, Leigh, Leral, Lerol, LeRol, LeRoy,* and *Roy.*

Leverett (lev-RETT) Meaning "young hare." Variations include *Lev, Leveret, Leverit,* and *Leveritt.*

Lionel (lee-onh-EL) Meaning "lion cub." Actors Lionel Barrymore and Lionel Stander. Variations include *Leonel, Lional, Lionell, Lionello, Lynel, Lynell,* and *Lyonel.*

Luc (LUKE) A form of Luke, meaning "light." The director Luc Besson gained international fame with his film *La Femme Nikita.* A variation is *Luce.*

Lucien (lou-SHEN) A form of Lucius, meaning "light." Artist Lucien Freud.

Lyle (LEEL) Meaning "island." Football defensive lineman Lyle Alzado of the Denver Broncos. Variations include *Lisle, Ly,* and *Lysle.*

Mace (MAHS) Meaning "club."

Macy (mah-SEE) Meaning "Matthew's estate." Variations include *Mace* and *Macey.*

Manger (monh-GZHAY) Meaning "stable."

Manville (man-VEEL) Meaning "great town."

Marc (MAHRK) A form of Mark, from the Latin for "warrior." The 20th-century artist Marc Chagall.

Marcel (mar-SAHL) A form of the Italian name Marcellus and Latin name Mark. Novelist Marcel Proust wrote *Remembrance of Things Past* from his bed; the mime Marcel Marceau performed wordlessly everywhere. Variations include *Marcell, Marsale,* and *Marsel.*

Marin (mahr-ANH) Meaning "sailor." Variations include *Marine, Mariner, Marino, Marius,* and *Marriner.*

Marion (mah-ree-ONH) A masculine form of Mary, from the Hebrew for "bitter" or "sea of bitterness." The given first name of screen actor John Wayne was Marion. A variation is *Mariano.*

Markese (mahr-KEHZ) An alternate form of Marquis. Variations include *Markease, Mar-*

keece, Markees, Markeese, Markel, Markeice, Markeis, and *Markice.*

Marlon (mahr-LONH) A form of Anglo-Saxon name Merlin, meaning "falcon." Actor Marlon Brando revolutionized American acting in *A Streetcar Named Desire.*

Marmion (mahr-mee-YONH) "Small."

Marquis (mar-KEYS) Meaning "nobleman." Among the famous people with this name is the pro basketball player Marquis Haynes. Variations include *Marcquis, Marcuis, Markis, Markuis, Marquee, Marqui, Marquie,* and *Marquist.*

Marshall (mahr-SHALL) A military title. Culture commentator Marshall McLuhan wrote *The Medium Is the Message.* Variations include *Marschal, Marsh, Marshal, Marshel,* and *Marshell.*

Mason (mah-SONH) Meaning "stone worker." Variations include *Mace* and *Malson.*

Mathieu (ma-TIEU) A form of Matthew, from the Hebrew for "God's gift." Variations include *Mathie, Mathieux, Mathiew, Matthieu, Matthiew, Mattieu,* and *Mattieux.*

Maxime (maks-EEM) Meaning "most excellent." A variation is *Maxim.*

Melville (mel-VEEL) Meaning "mill town." A variation is *Milville.*

Merle (MEHRL) Short form of Merlin, Merrill. Country musician Merle Haggard. A variation is *Meryl.*

Merville (mer-VEEL) Meaning "sea village."

Michel (me-SHELL) A form of Michael, from the Hebrew for "Who is like God." Composer Michel Legrand; actor Michel Piccoli. Variations include *Michaud, Miche, Michee,* and *Michon.*

Montague (monh-ta-GEEU) Meaning "pointed mountain." Variations include *Montagu* and *Monte.*

Montre (MONHTR) Meaning "show." Variations include *Montray, Montres,* and *Montrez.*

Montréal (monh-tree-ALL) Meaning "royal mountain." A city in Quebec. Variations include *Montrall* and *Montrale.*

Moore (MOOR) Meaning "dark-skinned." Variations include *Maurice, Moor, Mooro,* and *More.*

Morell (mor-ELL) Signifying "dark" or "from Morocco." Variations include *Moor, Moore, Morill, Morrell, Morrill, Murrel,* and *Murrell.*

Mort (MOHR) A short form of Morten, Mortimer, Morton. Variations include *Mortey, Mortie,* and *Morty.*

Mortimer (mohr-tee-MAY) Meaning "still water." Variations include *Mort* and *Mortymer.*

Narcisse (nar-SEES) A form of Narcissus, from the Greek for "daffodil." In Greek mythology, Narcissus was the young man who fell in love with his own reflection. Variations include *Narkis* and *Narkissos.*

Neville (neh-VEEL) Meaning "new town."

Noé (no-AY) A form of Noah, from the Hebrew for "rest."

Noël (no-EL) Signifying "day of Christ's birth." Variations include *Natal, Noel, Noil, Nole, Noll, Nowel,* and *Nowell.*

Norman (nor-MANH) Meaning "norseman." A name for the Scandinavians who conquered England in 1066. Award winning author Norman Mailer. Variations include *Norm, Normand, Normen, Normle,* and *Normy.*

Norrois (nor-WAH) Signifying "northerner."

Norville (nor-VEEL) Meaning "northern town." Variations include *Norval, Norvel, Norvell, Norvil, Norvill,* and *Norvylle.*

Olivier (oh-lee-VYAY) A form of Oliver, from the Latin for "olive" or "olive tree."

Orville (or-VEEL) Meaning "golden village." Orville Wright and his brother Wilbur were the first to fly an airplane. Variations include *Ory, Orval, Orvell, Orvie,* and *Orvil.*

Page (PAZH) Meaning "youthful assistant." Variations include *Padget, Paggio, Paige,* and *Payge.*

Parnell (pahr-NELL)   Signifies "little Peter."

Pascal (pa-SKAL)   Meaning "born on Easter or Passover." Variations include *Pace, Pascale, Pascalle, Paschal, Paschalls, Pascoe, Pascow, Pascual,* and *Pasquale.*

Patrice (pa-TREES)   A form of Patrick, from the Latin for "noble; patrician."

Percival (per-see-VALL)   Meaning "pierce the valley" or "pierce the veil of religious mystery." In Chrétien de Troyes's epic, the knight-hero who sees the Holy Grail. Wagner's Parsifal is about this story. Variations include *Parsafal, Parsefal, Parsifal, Parzival, Perc, Perce, Perceval, Percevall, Percivall, Percy, Peredur,* and *Purcell.*

Peverell (pev-RELL)   Meaning "piper." Variations include *Peverall, Peverel,* and *Peveril.*

Philippe (phil-EEP)   A form of Philip, from the Greek for "lover of horses." Variations include *Phillipe* and *Phillepe.*

Pierre (pee-YAIR)   A form of Peter, Greek for "rock." Fashion designer Pierre Cardin and Pierre Clementi. Variations include *Peirre, Piere,* and *Pierrot.*

Pierre-Luc (pee-YAIR-LUKE)   A combination of Pierre and Luc.

Platt (PLAH)   Signifying "flat land." A variation is *Platte.*

Pomeroy (pomh-eh-RWAH)   Meaning "apple orchard." Variations include *Pommeray* and *Pommeroy.*

Prewitt (pre-WEE)   Meaning "brave little one." Variations include *Preuet, Prewet, Prewett, Prewit, Pruit,* and *Pruitt.*

Purvis (puhr-VEE)   Meaning "providing food." Variations include *Pervis, Purves,* and *Purviss.*

Quennell (keh-NELL)   Signifies "small oak." Variations include *Quenell,* and *Quennel.*

Quincy (kaahn-SEE)   Meaning "fifth son's estate." Music producer Quincy Jones of Motown fame. Variations include *Quincey, Quinn, Quinnsy,* and *Quinsey.*

Ranger (ran-GZHAY)   Meaning "forest keeper." Variations include *Rainger* and *Range.*

Raoul (rah-OOHL)   A form of Ralph, from the Anglo-Saxon for "wolf counselor" and Rudolph, which means "famed wolf." Variations include *Raol, Raul, Raúl,* and *Reuel.*

Rapier (rap-ee-YAY)   Meaning "blade-sharp."

Raul (rah-OOHL)   A form of Ralph, from the Anglo-Saxon for "wolf counselor."

Rawlins (wah-LANH)   A form of Roland, meaning "fame of the land." Variations include *Rawlinson* and *Rawson.*

Ray (RAY)   Meaning "kingly" or "royal." Singer Ray Charles; TV series star Ray Romano.

Raynard (ray-NAHR)   An alternate form of Renard and Reynard, which in Old German means "mighty," and in French means "fox." Variations include *Raynard, Reinhard, Reinhardt, Renard, Renardo, Renaud, Rennard, Rey,* and *Reynardo.*

Rémy (raah-ME)   Meaning "from Rheims, France." Variations include *Ramey, Remee, Remi, Rémi,* and *Remmy.*

Renaud (ray-NAOU)   A form of Reynard and Reynold. Variations include *Renauld* and *Renauldo.*

René (ruh-NAY)   Meaning "reborn." Variations include *Renat, Renato, Renatus, Renault, Renee,* and *Renny.*

Reynard (ray-NAHR)   Meaning "wise; bold; courageous" or "fox." Variations include *Raynard, Reinhard, Reinhardt, Renard, Renardo, Renaud, Rennard, Rey,* and *Reynardo.*

Romain (roh-MAANH)   A form of Roman, meaning "of Rome." A variation is *Romane.*

Rondel (rohn-DELL)   Meaning "short poem." Variations include *Rondale, Rondall, Rondeal, Rondell, Rondie, Rondy,* and *Ronel.*

Roy (RWAH)   Meaning "king." A short form of Royal and Royce. Variations include *Conroy, Delroy, Fitzroy, Leroy, Rey, Rol,* and *Ruy.*

Royal (rwah-YAHL)   Meaning "kingly" or "royal." Variations include *Roy, Royale,* and *Royall.*

Ruskin (rou-SKAANH) This name signifies "redhead." Variations include *Rush* and *Russ*.

Russell (rous-SELL) Meaning "redhead" or "fox colored." Famous people with this name include the physicist Russell Varian Lukela and actor Russell Crowe. Variations include *Roussell, Rush, Russ, Russel, Russelle,* and *Rusty.*

Saber (SABR) Meaning "sword." Variations include *Sabir* and *Sabre.*

Salaun (SALOH) A form of Solomon, meaning "peaceable."

Sargent (sahr-GZHAN) Meaning "army officer." Sargent Shriver was the first director of the Peace Corps. Variations include *Sargant, Sarge, Sergeant,* and *Sergent.*

Saville (sa-VEEL) Meaning "willow town." Variations include *Savil, Savile, Savill, Savylle, Seville,* and *Siville.*

Scoville (sko-VEEL) Meaning "Scott's town."

Searlas (SHARL) A form of Charles. Variations include *Skarlas* and *Searius.*

Sebastien (se-bas-TYANH) Form of Sebastian. A variation is *Sebasten.*

Senior (sen-WAH) Meaning "lord."

Sennett (sen-NAY) Meaning "elderly." A variation is *Sennet.*

Séverin (say-VRAANH) Meaning "severe." Variations include *Seve, Séve Severan, Severian, Severiano, Severo, Sevien,* and *Sevrin.*

Seymour (say-MOURH) Meaning "prayer," and honors Saint Maur. Variations include *Maurice, Seamor, Seamore,* and *Seamour.*

Sidney (seed-NEE) Signifying "from Saint Denis, France." Actor Sidney Poitier came to fame in *The Blackboard Jungle.* Variations include *Cydney, Sid, Sidnee, Sidon, Sidonio, Sydney,* and *Sydny.*

Simeon (sim-ay-YONH) A form of Simon, which is Hebrew for "Who hears?" A variation is *Simone.*

Sinclair (sanh-KLAYR) Meaning "from Saint Clair." Author Sinclair Lewis was the first American to win the Nobel Prize for literature. Variations include *Sinclare* and *Synclair.*

Sorrel (sor-RELL) Meaning "reddish brown." Variations include *Sorel* and *Sorrell.*

Stéphane (stay-fanh-EE) A form of Stephen, from the Greek for "crown." Variations include *Stefáne* and *Stephine.*

Sylvain (syl-VANH) A form of Silvan and Sylvester.

Talon (tah-LONH) Meaning "claw" or "nail." Variations include *Tallin* and *Tallon.*

Tanguy (tan-GHEE) Meaning "warrior."

Telford (tel-FOHR) Meaning "iron cutter." Variations include *Tellek, Telfer, Telfor,* and *Telfour.*

Teppo (teh-PO) A familiar form of Stephen, from the Greek for "crown" or "garland."

Thayer (tie-YEHR) Meaning "nation's army." A variation is *Thay.*

Thilbault (tee-BO) A form of Theobald and Tybalt, which means "bold for the people." Variations include *Thibaud* and *Thlbaut.*

Thiérry (tier-REE) A form of Theodoric, which means "the people's ruler." Variations include *Theirry* and *Theory.*

Tiennot (tian-NO) A form of Stephen, from the Greek for "crown." A variation is *Tien.*

Travers (twra-VER) Signifies "crossroads." Variations include *Travaress, Travaris, Travarius, Travarus, Traver, Traverez, Travis,* and *Travorus.*

Tyson (tee-SONH) Meaning "son of the German." Supermodel Tyson, famed for his provocative underwear ads. Variations include *Tison, Tiszon, Tyce, Tyesn, Tyeson, Tysen, Tysne,* and *Tysone.*

Urson (oor-SONH) A form of Orson, from the Latin for "bear" or "bear-like." Variations include *Ursan* and *Ursus.*

Vachel (va-SHELL) Meaning "small cow." Poet Vachel Lindsay. Variations include *Vache* and *Vachell.*

Vallis (val-LEE) Signifying "from Wales, England."

Vardon (var-DONH) Meaning "green hillock." Variations include *Varden, Verdan, Verdon,* and *Verdun.*

Vere (VER) Meaning "true."

Vernon (ver-NONH) Meaning "springlike" or "youthful." Former U.S. congressman Vernon Walters. Variations include *Vern, Vernen,* and *Verney.*

Vemey (ver-NAY) Meaning "alder grove." A variation is *Vernie.*

Victoir (vic-TWAHR) A form of Victor, from the Latin for "the conqueror."

Wyatt (we-YAT) Meaning "little warrior." Lawman Wyatt Earp of the old west; Andrew Wyeth, American painter. Variations include *Wiatt, Wyat, Wye,* and *Wyeth.*

Yves (EEV) A form of Ives, meaning "archer." Among notables with this name are actor Yves Montand and designer Yves Saint Laurent. Variations include *Yvens* and *Yvon.*

Yvon (ee-VONH) An alternate form of Ivan, a Russian form of John, from the Hebrew for "God's gracious gift," and Yves, from the Scandinavian for "an archer." A variation is *Ivon.*

FRANCE: GIRLS

Alair (ah-LAIR) A form of Hilary, from the Latin for "cheerful." Variations include *Ali* and *Allaire.*

Abrial (ah-bree-ALL) Meaning "open." Variations include *Abreal, Abreale,* and *Abriale.*

Amber (ahm-BEHR) Signifies the color. Among notable people with this name are supermodel Amber Valletta and actress Amber Barretto.

Angélique (an-ge-LEEK) A form of Angela, meaning "angelic," "angel," or "heaven's messenger."

Annette (an-NET) A form of Ann, from the Hebrew for "full of grace." Actresses Annette Funicello and Annette Bening. Variations include *Anet, Aneta, Anetra, Anett, Anetta, Anette, Annett,* and *Annetta.*

Antoinette (an-twan-NET) A form of Antonia, from the Latin for "priceless." Antoinette Perry, for whom the Tony Awards are named. Variations include *Anta, Antanette, Antoinella, Antoinet, Antonella, Antonetta,* and *Antonette.*

Ariane (ah-ree-AN) Forms of Ariadne, from the Greek for "holy one." Variations include *Aeriann, Airiann, Ari, Arianie, Ariann,* and *Arianne.*

Arielle (ah-ree-EL) A form of Ariel, meaning "lion of God." Variations include *Aeriell* and *Ariella.*

Auberte (oh-BEHRT) A form of Alberta, meaning "noble" or brightening." Variations include *Auberta, Aubertha, Auberthe,* and *Aubine.*

Aubrie (oh-BRIE) An alternate form of Aubrey, which means "elf ruler." A variation is *Aubri.*

Babette (ba-BETT) A familiar form of Barbara, which is Greek for "the stranger." *Babette's Feast* was a sumptuous movie about a woman who loved to cook. Variations include *Babita* and *Barbette.*

Belle (BELL) A short form of Arabella, which means "beautiful." Variations include *Belinda, Belita, Belli, Bellina,* and *Isabel.*

Bernadette (ber-nah-DETT) Meaning "brave like a bear." Broadway musical star Bernadette Peters. Variations include *Bera, Beradette, Berna, Bernadet, Bernadett, Bernadetta, Bernarda,* and *Bernardette.*

Berneta (ber-net-TA) A short form of Bernadette.

Bertille (behr-TEEL) An alternate form of name Bertha, which means "shining."

Bette (BET) An alternative to Betty, a short form of the Hebrew name Elizabeth, meaning "pledged to God." Among the famous people are Bette Midler and Bette Davis. Variations include *Beta, Beti, Betka, Bett, Betta, Betti,* and *Bettie.*

Billie (bih-LEE)   A familiar form of Belle, which means "beautiful," and Wilhelmina, which means "the protectress" or "the guardian." Among notable people with this name are jazz singer Billie Holiday and actress Billie Burke.

Blaise (BLEZ)   Meaning "one who stutters." Variations include *Blasha, Blasia, Blaza, Blaze,* and *Blazena.*

Blanche (BLONSH)   Meaning "white." Famous Blanches include Blanche DuBois, tragic heroine of *A Streetcar Named Desire;* Blanche Castile, medieval queen of France; senator Blanche Bruce; and congresswoman Blanche Lincoln. Variations include *Blanca, Blanch, Blancha,* and *Blinney.*

Blondelle (blon-DELL)   Meaning "blond" or "fair-haired." Variations include *Blondell* and *Blondie.*

Briar (bree-YAR)   Meaning "heather." Variations include *Brear, Brier, Briet, Brieta, Brietta, Brya,* and *Bryar.*

Brigitte (bri-GZHEET)   A form of Bridget, meaning "mighty" or "strong." Among notable people with this name are actresses Brigitte Bardot and Brigitte Nielsen. Variations include *Brigette, Briggitte, Brigit,* and *Brigita.*

Cachet (ka-SHAY)   Meaning "prestigious" or "desirous." Variations include *Cache* and *Cachea.*

Camille (ka-MEEL)   Signifies "young ceremonial attendant." One well-known Camille is writer Camille Paglia. Variations include *Cam, Camey, Cami, Camie, Camill, Camilla, Cammi, Cammie, Cammille,* and *Cammy.*

Cantrelle (kan-TRELL)   Meaning "song." A variation is *Cantrella.*

Caressa (kar-eh-SAH)   Variation of Caresse, which means "endearing" or "beloved one." Variations include *Caresa, Carese, Caresse, Carissa,* and *Karessa.*

Caroline (kah-ro-LEEN)   Signifies "little and womanly." Among notable people with this name are former first lady Caroline Harrison, wife of Benjamin Harrison, and Princess Caro-

line of Monaco. Variations include *Caralin, Caraline, Carileen, Carilene, Carilin,* and *Cariline.*

Cerise (ser-EEC)   Meaning "cherry" or "cherry red." Variations include *Cera, Cerea, Cerese, Ceri,* and *Ceria.*

Chadee (sha-DEE)   Signifies "from Chad," the country in Africa. Variations include *Chaday, Chadday, Chade, Chadea,* and *Sade.*

Chantal (shan-TALL)   Meaning "song." Among notable people with this name is writer Chantal Chawaf. Variations include *Chandal, Chanta, Chantaal,* and *Chantae.*

Charlotte (shar-LOTT)   "Little and womanly." See Caroline. Famous Charlottes include novelists Charlotte Brontë and Charlotte Lennox. Variations include *Carla, Carlotta, Carly, Char, Chara, Charil, Charl, Charla, Charle, Charlene, Charlet, Charlett,* and *Charletta.*

Charmaine (shehr-MEHN)   From Carmen, in Latin meaning "song" and in Spanish meaning "from Mount Carmel." Variations include *Charamy, Charma,* and *Charmain.*

Cher (SHARE)   Meaning "beloved" or "dearest." Multi-media pop star Cher chose this as her only name.

Chéri (she-REE)   A familiar form of Cher. Variations include *Cherie* and *Chirie.*

Cherise (sher-EEC)   Meaning "dear one." Variations include *Charisa, Charise, Cherece, Chereese, Cheresa, Cherese, Cheresse,* and *Cherice.*

Cheryl (she-REEL)   Meaning "beloved." Actress Cheryl Tiegs, a well-known model in the 1970s, and Cheryl Ladd, famous as one of Charlie's Angels. Variations include *Charel, Charil, Charyl, Cherelle, Cherilyn, Cherrelle, Cheryl-Ann, Cheryl-Anne, Cheryle,* and *Cherylee.*

Christabel (kreest-ah-BELL)   Meaning "fair Christian." Variations include *Christabella, Christable, Cristabel,* and *Kristabel.*

Christine (kreest-TEEN)   A form of the Greek name Christina, meaning "Christ bearer." Among notable people with this name is medieval author Christine de Pizan. Variations include *Chrisa, Christeen, Christen, Christene, Christi, Christie, Christin,* and *Christy.*

Cinderella (sin-deh-reh-LA) Meaning "little cinder girl." The fairy tale heroine who escaped a life by the hearth to marry a prince.

Claire (KLAIR) Meaning "famous one" or "bright." Actresses Claire Bloom and Claire Trevor. Variations include *Clair, Clairette, Klaire,* and *Klarye.*

Claudette (kloh-DET) From the Latin name Claudia, meaning "the lame." Actress Claudette Colbert. A variation is *Clauddetta.*

Colette (ko-LET) A familiar form of Nicole, from the Greek for "victory of the people." Colette was a French feminist writer. Variations include *Coe, Coetta, Coletta, Collet, Collete, Collett, Colletta,* and *Collette.*

Cosette (ko-SET) A familiar form of Nicole, from the Greek for "victory of the people." Variations include *Cosetta, Cossetta, Cossette,* and *Cozette.*

Damica (da-MEE-ka) Meaning "friendly." Variations include *Damee, Dameeka, Dameka, Damekah, Damicah, Damie, Damika,* and *Damikah.*

Danielle (dahn-YELL) Meaning "God is my judge." A feminine form of Daniel. Among notable people with this name is romance writer Danielle Steele. Variations include *Danae, Daneen, Daneil, Daneille, Danelle, Dani, Danial,* and *Danialle.*

Darcelle (dar-SELL) A form of Darci, which means "the dark one." Variations include *Darcel, Darcell, Darcella, Darsel, Darsell, Darsella,* and *Darselle.*

Darielle (dar-ee-YELL) An alternate form of Daryl, from the Anglo-Saxon name *Darlene* meaning "dear" or "little darling." Variations include *Dariel, Darriel,* and *Darrielle.*

Darlene (dar-LEEN) Meaning "little darling." Congresswoman Darlene Hooley is among the notable people with this name. Variations include *Darilynn, Darla, Darlean,* and *Daryl.*

Daryl (dah-REEL) A short form of Darlene. Among notable people with this name: actress Daryl Hannah, who starred as a mermaid in the movie *Splash.*

Denise (deh-NEES) A feminine form of Dennis, which means "follower of Dionysus," the mythological god of wine. Actresses Denise Nicholas and Denise Richards. Variations include *Danice, Danise, Denese, Deney, Deni, Denica, Denice, Denie, Deniece, Denisha,* and *Denisse.*

Desirée (day-zee-RAY) Meaning "desired" or "longed for." Variations include *Desara, Desarae, Desarai,* and *Desi.*

Dessa (des-SAH) A form of Desiree.

Destiny (deh-stee-NEE) As in "fate." Variations include *Desnine, Desta, Destanee, Destanie, Desteni, Destin, Destinee, Destinie,* and *Destiney.*

Dija (dee-ZHA) Meaning "before." Variations include *Daija, Daisia, Daja, Dasha, Deejay, Dejanelle,* and *Dejon.*

Dior (dee-OHR) Meaning "golden." Variations include *Diora, Diore, Diorra,* and *Diorre.*

Dixie (dee-SEE) Meaning "tenth." Among the noteworthy people with this name are TV actress Dixie Carter and former congresswoman Dixie Graves.

Dominique (doh-me-NEEK) A form of Dominica and Dominika, meaning "born on the Lord's day." The world's famous Dominiques include two Olympic gymnasts, Dominique Moceanu and Dominique Dawes. Variations include *Domanique, Domeneque, Domenique, Domineque, Dominiqua,* and *Domonique.*

Elaine (ay-LEN) A form of Helen, meaning "light." Among notable people with this name, the writer and comedian Elaine May. Variations include *Elain, Elaina, Elainia, Elainna, Elana, Elane, Elania,* and *Elanie.*

Elise (ay-LEEZ) A short form of Elizabeth, from the Hebrew for "pledged to God." Also *Elysia, Eilis, Eilise, Elese, Elisee, Elisie, Elisse, Elizi, Ellice, Ellise, Ellyce, Ellyse,* and *Ilise.*

Elita (ay-lee-TA)   Signifies "chosen." Variations include *Elida, Elitia, Elitie, Ellita, Ellitia, Ellitie, Ilida, Ilita,* and *Litia.*

Eloise (el-WAHZ)   French version of the Latin name Louise, meaning "battle maiden." Variations include *Elois, Eloisa,* and *Eloisia.*

Emmaline (eh-ma-LEEN)   A variation on Emily, which means "industrious." Variations include *Emalina, Emaline, Emelina, Emeline, Emilina, Emiline,* and *Emmalina.*

Esmi (ez-ME)   A familiar form of Esmeralda, meaning "emerald." Variations include *Esma* and *Esme.*

Estelle (es-TELL)   Signifies "star." Among notable people with this name are actresses Estelle Getty of *The Golden Girls* and Estelle Parsons of *Bonnie and Clyde.* Variations include *Essie, Estee, Estel, Estela, Estele, Estelina, Estelita, Estell, Estella, Estrella,* and *Estrellita.*

Etoile (eh-TWAHL)   Meaning "star."

Evaline (ehv-ah-LEEN)   A form of Evelyn, from the Hebrew for Eve meaning "life" or "living." Variations include *Evalin, Evalina, Evalyn, Eveleen, Evelene, Evelina,* and *Eveline.*

Evette (ee-VET)   An alternate form of Yvette, which is related to Yvonne, meaning "the archer." Variations include *Evett* and *Ivette.*

Evonne (ee-VON)   An alternate form of Yvonne, meaning "the archer." Australian tennis star Evonne Goolagong. Variations include *Evanne, Eve, Evenie, Evenne, Eveny, Evette,* and *Evon.*

Fancy (fahn-SEE)   Signifies "betrothed."

Faye (FAY)   Meaning "fairy" or "elf." Actress Faye Dunaway starred in *Network* and *Bonnie and Clyde.*

Femi (feh-ME)   Meaning "woman."

Fifi (fee-FEE)   A familiar form of Josephine, from the Hebrew for "she shall add." Variations include *Feef, Feefee,* and *Fifine.*

Fleur (FLERH)   Meaning "flower." A variation is *Fleure.*

Fontanna (fon-TAN-NA)   Meaning "fountain." Variations include *Fontaine, Fontana, Fontane, Fontanne,* and *Fontayne.*

Francine (fron-SEEN)   Meaning "from France." Variations include *Franceen, Franceine, Franceline,* and *Francene.*

Françoise (fron-SWAZ)   Meaning "from France." Notable French women with this name include writers Françoise Sagan of *Bonjour Tristesse* and Françoise-Therese Aumerle de Saint-Phalier Dalibard.

Frédérique (fre-der-EEK)   Originates from Frederica, which means "peaceful." Supermodel Frederique van der Wal is known for her heavy-lidded look. Variations include *Frédérike, Frédérique, Friederike,* and *Rike.*

Gabrielle (gab-ree-YELL)   A feminine form of Gabriel, meaning "heroine of God." Volleyball star Gabrielle Reece, film actress Gabrielle Anwar. Variations include *Gabbey, Gabbi, Gabbie, Gabey, Gabi, Gabie, Gabielle, Gabreil, Gabrial, Gabriela, Gabrielle, Gabriell, Gabriella, Gaby,* and *Gavriella.*

Garland (gahr-LANH)   Meaning "wreath."

Gay (GUY)   Meaning "merry." Variations include *Gae, Gai, Gaye, Gayla, Gaylaine, Gayle, Gayleen, Gaylen, Gaylene,* and *Gaylyn.*

Gena (zheh-NA)   A short form of Geneva, Genevieve, and Iphigenia. Film actress Gena Rowlands. Variations include *Geanna, Geena, Geenah, Gen,* and *Genah.*

Geneva (zhen-EE-va)   A short form of Genevieve, meaning "juniper tree." Variations include *Geena, Gen, Gena, Geneive,* and *Geneve.*

Geneviève (zhen-eh-vee-YEV)   See *Guinevere.* Famous people with this name include Poet Genevieve Taggard. Variations include *Gen, Gena, Genaveve, Genavieve, Genavive, Geneva, Geneveve, Genoveva, Genoveve, Genovieve,* and *Genovive.*

Genevra (zheh-NAY-vrah)   See *Guinevere.* Variations include *Gen* and *Ginevra.*

Georgette (zhor-JETT)   A form of Georgia, from the Greek for "farmer." Among notable people with this name is romance author Georgette Heyer. Variations include *Georgeta, Georgett, Georgetta,* and *Georjetta.*

Germaine (zher-MENH) Signifies "from Germany." Variations include *Germain, Germana, Germanie, Germaya, Germine,* and *Jermaine.*

Gervaise (zher-VEZ) Meaning "skilled with a spear." A feminine form of Jarvis.

Gigi (zhee-ZHEE) A familiar form of Georgina and Eugenia. Variations include *Geegee* and *G.G.*

Guinevere (gueh-nuh-VAIR) Meaning "white and smooth." Guinevere was the legendary wife of King Arthur. Variations include *Gayna, Generva, Genn, Ginetta,* and *Guenevere.*

Hélène (eh-LENH) From the Greek name Helen, meaning "light." Variations include *Helaine, Helayne, Heleen, Hiline, Helenor,* and *Heline.*

Heloise (el-WOZ) From the Latin-based name Louise, meaning "battle maiden." Famous people with this name include the author of "Heloise's Helpful Hints," a syndicated household advice column and medieval philosopher Heloise, fabled lover and wife to philosopher Abelard. Variations include *Hélöise, Heise, Helsey, Helsie,* and *Helsy.*

Isabeau (eez-ah-BO) See Isabel in Spanish names.

Ivette (ee-VETT) A form of Yvette. Variations include *Ivete, Iveth, Ivetha,* and *Ivetta.*

Ivonne (ee-VON) A form of Yvonne. Variations include *Evonne, Ivon, Ivona, Ivone, Ivonna,* and *Iwona.*

Jacqueline (zha-KLEAN) Meaning "the supplanter." A feminine form of Jacques. Notable people with this name include first lady Jacqueline Kennedy Onassis and actress Jacqueline Bisset. Variations include *Jacalyn, Jackalyn, Jackie, Jacklyn, Jaclyn, Jacqualin, Jacqualine, Jacqualyn, Jacquelyn, Jacquelynn,* and *Jacquelyne.*

Jacqui (zha-KEE) A short form of Jacqueline. Variations include *Jacquay, Jacqui, Jacquee, Jacqueta, Jacquete,* and *Jacquetta.*

Jaime (ZHEM) Meaning "I love." Variations include *Jaima, Jaimee, Jaimey,* and *Jaimi.*

Jaimee (zhe-MAY) A form of Jaime.

Janelle (zha-NELL) A form of the Hebrew name Jane, which means "gracious is God." Variations include *Janel, Janell, Jannel, Jaynel,* and *Jaynell.*

Janine (zha-NEEN) A form of the Hebrew name Jane, which means "gracious is God." Variations include *Janeen, Janenan, Janene, Janina, Jannina,* and *Jannine.*

Jeanette (zhuh-NETT) See also Janelle. Among notable people with this name, operetta star Jeanette MacDonald. Variations include *Jeanete, Jeanett, Jeanetta,* and *Jeanita.*

Jermaine (zhair-MEN) An alternate form of Germaine, meaning "a German." Variations include *Jermain, Jerman, Jermane,* and *Jermayne.*

Jessamine (zhess-ah-MEEN) From Persian name Jasmine, meaning "fragrant flower." Author Jessamyn West. Variations include *Jessamin, Jessamon, Jessamy,* and *Jessamyn.*

Jewel (zhu-ELL) Meaning "precious gem." Pop singer Jewel has chosen this as her only name. Variations include *Jewell, Jewelle, Jewellee, Jewellie,* and *Jule.*

Jolie (zho-LEE) Meaning "pretty." Among notables with this name is Jolie Gabor, mother of Zsa Zsa and Eva. Variations include *Jolea, Jolee, Joleigh, Joley, Joli, Jollee, Jollie, Jolly, Joly,* and *Jolye.*

Joséphine (zho-se-FEEN) Signifies "God will add," or "God will increase." A feminine form of Joseph. International star Joesphine Baker and the Empress Josephine, wife of Napoleon. Variations include *Fina, Jo, Joey, Josee, Josie, Josefa, Josefena, Josefina, Josefine,* and *Josepha.*

Josette (zho-ZETT) A familiar form of Josephine. A variation is *Josetta.*

Juliet (zhu-lee-AY, zhu-lee-ET) Forms of Julia. Among notable people with this name, Romeo's lover, dancer Juliet Prowse, and Girl Scouts founder Juliette Low. Variations include *Julet, Julieta, Julietta, Juliet, Julliet, Jullietta,* and *Juliette.*

Karessa (kar-SAH)   A form of Caressa. Variations include *Karese*, *Karess*, and *Karesse*.

Laine (LEN)   Meaning "wool." A short form of Elaine. Variations include *Laina*, *Lainee*, *Lainey*, and *Layney*.

Leala (lay-AL-ah)   Meaning "loyal." Variations include *Lealia*, *Lealie*, and *Leial*.

Lisette (lee-ZETT)   Form of Lisa, which is short for the Hebrew name Elizabeth, meaning "pledged to God."

Lorraine (loh-RENH)   Signifying "from Lorraine." Playwright Lorraine Hansberry wrote *A Raisin in the Sun*, and actress Lorraine Bracco starred in *Goodfellas*.

Lucie (lou-SEE)   A familiar form of Lucy, meaning "shining."

Lyla (lee-LAH)   Meaning "island."

Madeleine (mahd-LENH)   Signifies "woman of Magdala." Famous Madeleines include Secretary of State Madeleine Albright, actress Madeleine Stowe, and author Madeleine de Souvre. Variations include *Madellaine* and *Madelayne*.

Mallorie (ma-lo-REE)   A form of Mallory.

Manette (ma-NETT)   A form of Mary, which is Hebrew for "bitter."

Manon (mah-NONH)   A familiar form of Marie, which is Hebrew for "bitter."

Mardi (MAR-dee)   Meaning "born on Tuesday."

Margaux (mar-GO)   A form of Margaret, from the Greek for "pearl." Among notable people with this name is the actress Margaux Hemingway, granddaughter of Ernest Hemingway. Variation include *Margeaux*, *Margo*, *Margot*, *Mago*, and *Margaro*.

Marguerite (mar-gur-EET)   See also Margaux. Among notable people with this name are French authors Marguerite Duras, who wrote *The Lover*, and Nobel Prize-winning Marguerite Yourcenar. Variations include *Margarete*, *Margaretha*, *Margarethe*, *Margarite*, *Margerite*, *Marguaretta*, and *Marguarette*.

Maribel (mar-ee-BELL)   Meaning "beautiful Mary."

Marie (mar-EE)   A variation on the Hebrew name Mary, meaning "bitter." Chemist Marie Curie discovered radiation. Variations include *Maree* and *Marietta*.

Marion (mar-ee-ONH)   From the Hebrew Mary, meaning "bitter." Among notable Marions are actress Marion Ross of *Happy Days* and former Health Education, and Welfare Secretary Marion Folsom. Variations include *Marrian*, *Marrion*, *Maryon*, and *Maryonn*.

Marjolaine (mar-zho-LEEN)   Signifies "marjoram."

Marquise (mar-KEYS)   Meaning "noblewoman." Variations include *Markese*, *Marquees*, *Marquese*, *Marquice*, *Marquies*, and *Marquiese*.

Marvella (mar-VAY-ya)   Meaning "marvelous." Variations include *Marva*, *Marvel*, *Marvela*, *Marvele*, *Marvelle*, *Marvely*, *Marvetta*, and *Marvette*.

Maurelle (mo-RELL)   Meaning "dark" or "elfin." Variations include *Mauriel*, *Mauriell*, and *Maurielle*.

Maurise (mo-REESE)   A feminine form of Maurice, which means "dark-skinned" or "Moorish." Variations include *Maurisa*, *Maurissa*, *Maurita*, and *Maurizia*.

Mauve (MOHV)   Signifies "violet-colored." A variation is *Malva*.

Mavis (ma-VEESE)   Meaning "thrush." Among notable people with this name are singers Mavis Fan and Mavis Staples. Variations include *Mavies*, *Mavin*, *Mavine*, *Mavon*, and *Mavra*.

Mélisande (meh-lee-SAHND)   A from of Melissa, meaning "honeyed." Variations include *Lisandra*, *Malisande*, *Malissande*, *Malyssandre*, *Mélésande*, *Melisandra*, and *Mélisandre*.

Merle (MEHRL)   Meaning "blackbird." Merle Oberon starred in the films *Wuthering Heights* and *The Scarlet Pimpernel*. Variations include *Merl*, *Merla*, *Merlina*, and *Merline*.

Michelle (me-SHELL)   A feminine form of Michael, which means "Who is like God."

Among notable people with this name are Michelle Phillips of The Mamas and the Papas and film actresses Michelle Pfeiffer and Michelle Yeoh. Variations include *Mechelle, Mia, Michel, Michele, Michile, Michell, Michella, Mischel, Mischelle, Misha,* and *Shelly.*

Miette (me-ETT) Signifies "small" or "sweet."

Mignon (meen-YON) Meaning "cute" or "graceful." Variations include *Mignonette, Minnionette, Minnonette, Minyonette,* and *Minonne.*

Mimi (me-ME) A familiar form of Miriam, which means "bitter." Also a common nickname for Emily. Famous Mimis include the comsumptive heroine of the opera *La Bohème* and actress Mimi Rogers.

Minette (mee-NETT) Meaning "faithful defender." Variations include *Minnette* and *Minnita.*

Mirane (mee-RAN) See Mary in Hebrew names. Variations include *Meraine* and *Merrane.*

Monique (mo-NEEK) A form of the Latin name Monica, meaning "advisor." Writer Monique Wittig. Variations include *Moniqua, Moniquea,* and *Moniquie.*

Musetta (moo-SET-ta) Meaning "little bagpipe." A variation is *Musette.*

Nadette (nah-DETT) A short form of Bernadette.

Nadine (nah-DEEN) From Nadia, the Russian form of the name Hope. Among notable people with this name is Nobel Prize-winning author Nadine Gordimer of South Africa. Variations include *Nadean, Nadeen,* and *Nadene.*

Naeva (neh-VA) A form of the Latin-based name Eve, meaning "life" or "living." A variation is *Nahvon.*

Nanette (na-NETT) A form of Nancy, which is a form of Ann, meaning "full of grace, mercy, and prayer" in Hebrew. Among notable people with this name are the actress Nanette Fabray, Nanette, the eponymous heroine of the musical *No, No, Nanette.* Variations include *Nan, Nanete,* and *Nannette.*

Nettie (ne-TEE) A familiar form of Annette, Nanette, and Antoinette. Variations include *Neti, Netie, Netta, Netti,* and *Netty.*

Nicolette (nee-ko-LETT) A form of the Greek name Nicole, meaning "victory of the people." Variations include *Nettei, Nicholette, Nicoletta, Nikkolette,* and *Nikolette.*

Nicoline (nee-ko-LEEN) A familiar form of the Greek name Nicole, meaning "victory of the people." Variations include *Nicholine, Nicholyn, Nicoleen, Nicolene,* and *Nicolyn.*

Ninon (nee-NONH) A form of *Nina,* meaning "girl."

Noelle (no-ELL) Feminized form of Noel, which means "Christmas." Variations include *Noell, Noella, Noelleen,* and *Noellyn.*

Odetta (oh-DETT-ah) A form of Odelia, meaning "prosperous." Among notable people with this name is folk singing great Odetta. Variations include *Oddetta* and *Odette.*

Oralia (oh-ral-YA) A form of the Latin Aurelia, meaning "golden." Variations include *Oralis, Orelie, Oriel, Orielda,* and *Orielle.*

Orva (or-VA) Meaning "golden" or "worthy."

Page (PAGZH) "Young assistant." Variations include *Padget, Padgett, Paget, Pagett, Pagi,* and *Payge.*

Pascale (pa-SKAL) A feminine form of Pascal meaning "Easter child." Variations include *Pascalette, Pascaline, Pascalle,* and *Paskel.*

Patrice (pa-TREES) An alternative form of Patricia, meaning "well-born" or "of noble family" in Latin. Opera singer Patrice Munsel. Variations include *Patrease, Patrece, Patresa, Patriece, Patryce,* and *Pattrice.*

Pier (pee-YAY) A form of the Greek name Petra, meaning "rock." Among notable people with this name is Pier Angeli, who starred in *Somebody Up There Likes Me.*

Pleasance (plez-AHNS) Meaning "pleasant."

Questa (kes-TA) Meaning "one who seeks."

Quiterie (kee-teh-REE) Meaning "tranquil." A variation is *Quita.*

Raula (rauw-LAH) A feminine form of Raoul, which means "wolf counselor." Variations include *Raoula, Raulla,* and *Raulle.*

Rémi (ray-MEE) Signifies "from Rheims." Variations include *Rémée, Rémie,* and *Rémy.*

Renee (ren-AY) Meaning "reborn." Among notable people with this name are the writer Renee Vivien and the actress Renee Zell weger. A variation is *Renae.*

Renie (ray-NEE) Meaning "reborn." Variations include *Renae, Renata, Renay, Rene,* and *Renell.*

Renita (ray-nee-TA) A form of Renata, which is Latin for "reborn." Variations include *Reneeta, Renetta,* and *Renitza.*

Richelle (ree-SHELL) An alternative to Ricarda, a feminized version of the name Richard, meaning "the ruler." Variations include *Richel, Richela, Richele,* and *Richell.*

River (ree-VAY) Meaning "stream" or "water." Variations include *Rivana, Rivers,* and *Riviane.*

Romaine (ro-MENH) Signifies "from Rome." Variations include *Romana, Romanda, Romanelle, Romanique,* and *Romayne.*

Romy (ro-MEE) A familiar form of Romaine. Actress Romy Schneider.

Rosabel (ro-sa-BELL) Meaning "beautiful rose." Variations include *Rosabella* and *Rosabelle.*

Russhell (rou-SHELL) Meaning "redhead" or "fox-colored." A feminine form of Russell. Variations include *Rushell, Rushelle,* and *Russhelle.*

Salina (sa-lee-NA) Meaning "solemn" or "dignified." Variations include *Salena, Saleena,* and *Salinda.*

Sarotte (sar-OHTT) A form of Sarah, from the Hebrew for "a princess."

Satin (sah-TANH) Meaning "smooth" or "shiny." A variation is *Satinder.*

Shanta (shan-TA) A form of Chantal, meaning "song." Variations include *Shantae, Shantai, Shantay, Shantaya, Shantaye,* and *Shantea.*

Shari (sha-REE) A form of Cheri, meaning "beloved" or "dearest." Children's entertainer Shari Lewis was known for her work with the sock puppet Lambchop. Variations include *Scherie, Sheeree, Shere, Sheree, Sherie,* and *Sharise.*

Sharice (sha-REESE) An alternate form of Cherise. Variations include *Shareese, Sharese, Sharica, Sharicka, Shariece, Sharis,* and *Sharise.*

Sharla (shar-LA) A short form of Sharlene and Sharlotte.

Sharlene (shar-LEEN) An alternate form of Charlene, which means "little and womanly." Variations include *Scharlene, Sharlaine, Sharlane, Sharlee, Sharleen,* and *Sharleine.*

Sherice (sheh-REESE) An alternate form of Sherry. Variations include *Scherise, Sherece, Shereece, Sherees, Shereese,* and *Sherese.*

Sherita (sheh-ree-TA) A form of Sherry. Variations include *Shereta, Sheretta, Sherette,* and *Sherrita.*

Sherleen (shehr-LEEN) A form of Sheryl. Variations include *Sherileen, Sherlene,* and *Sherline.*

Sherry (sheh-REE) A familiar form of Sheryl, which means "beloved" or "dearest." Variations include *Sherey, Sheri, Sherissa, Sherrey,* and *Sherri.*

Sheryl (sheh-REEL) Meaning "beloved" or "dearest." An alternate form of Cheryl. Singer, songwriter Sheryl Crow. Variations include *Sheral, Sherell, Sheriel, Sheril,* and *Sherill.*

Sidonie (see-donh-EE) Signifies "from Sidonia," an ancient Phoenician city. Among notable people with this name is writer Sidonie Gabrielle Colette. Variations include *Sidanni, Sidoine, Sidona, Sidonia, Sidony,* and *Sydney.*

Solange (so-LANGZH) Meaning "with dignity." A variation is *Soledad.*

Solenne (so-LEN) Meaning "solemn" or "dignified." Variations include *Solaine, Solène, Solenna, Solina, Soline,* and *Souline.*

Sorrel (so-RELL) Signifies "reddish brown." The name of a wild herb.

Susammi (su-sa-ME) A combination of Susan, from the Hebrew for "a lily," and Aimee, meaning "friend." Variations include *Suzami*, *Suzamie*, and *Suzamy*.

Susette (su-ZETT) A familiar form of Susan, from the Hebrew for "a lily." Well-known people with this name include Susette La Flesche, Native American rights advocate, writer, and artist. Variations include *Susetta*, *Suzetta*, *Suzette*, and *Suzzette*.

Sydney (seed-NEE) A feminine form of Sidney, which means "from St. Denis, France." Variations include *Sy*, *Syd*, *Sydania*, *Sydel*, *Sydelle*, and *Sydnee*.

Tallis (tahl-LEE) Meaning "forest." A variation is *Tallys*.

Toinette (twahn-ETT) A short form of Antoinette, meaning "priceless." Variations include *Toinetta*, *Tola*, *Tonetta*, *Tonette*, and *Toni*.

Turquoise (tur-KWAZ) A blue-green, semiprecious stone.

Véronique (ver-onh-EEK) A form of Veronica, from the Latin for "true image." A variation is *Vironique*.

Vi (VEE) A short form of Viola and Violet. Variations include *Violet* and *Vye*.

Villette (veel-ETT) Meaning "small town." A variation is *Vietta*.

Violet (vee-oh-LAY) A purplish blue flower. Among notable people with this name are authors Violet Paget and Violette Leduc. Variations include *Vi*, *Violetta*, *Violette*, *Vyolet*, *Vyoletta*, and *Vyolette*.

Vonna (vo-NA) An alternate form of Yvonne.

Yvette (ee-VET) A familiar form of Yvonne. Among notable people with this name is actress Yvette Mimieux. Variations include *Yavette*, *Yevett*, and *Yevette*.

Yvonne (ee-VON) Meaning "young archer." Among notable people with this name are the actress Yvonne De Carlo and the dancer and actress Yvonne Craig.

Germany

German given names reveal a rich and mixed heritage that is on the one hand highly conservative, having shown little change since the Middle Ages, and on the other hand extremely inventive and adaptive to outside influences, be they French, Italian, Spanish, or English. More traditional names were drawn from ancient Latin, Germanic, and even Slavic sources. Early Germanic names such as Wolfram, Bernhard, Michael, or Bertram have remained unaltered since the 12th and 13th centuries. Some famous Germans of the 20th century include Bertolt Brecht, Rainer Maria Rilke, Günter Grass, Heinrich Böll, Thomas Mann, Kurt Schwitters, Kurt Weill, Rainer Fassbinder, and Martin Heidegger.

Some of the names that follow are surnames or unconventional names in Germany; for instance, few Germans would name their child "Albern," "Schön," or "Schmidt." However, this does not preclude their usage in the United States and elsewhere, where different rules apply.

Pronunciation:

a = "ah" as in "tall" (sharply articulated)
a = "ai" as in "ache" or "e" as in "deck"
aa = "ah" as in "tall"
ä = "ah" as in "hat"
e = "eh" as in "fate" or "e" as in "deck"
i, ie = "ee" as in "beep" or "i" as in "fig"
o = "oh" as in "rope" or "eh" as in "fate" (both sharply articulated)
ö = "ur" as in "ghurka"
ü = "ew" as in "crew"
ei, ai = "i" as in "ride"
au = "ow" as in "now"
au, eu = "oy" as in "boy"
ch = "kh" (a harsh throaty sound)
d = "t" as in "mat" if at the end of a word, "d" as in "dark" elsewhere
j = "y" as in "yet"
s = "z" as in "zebra" if before a vowel, "ss" as in "dress" if at the end of a word
sch = "sh" as in "ship"
st = "sht" if at the beginning of a word, "st" elsewhere
th = "t" as in "table"
v = "f" as in "fate" or "v" as in "vain"
w = "v" as in "vote"
z = "ts" as in "hats"

GERMANY: BOYS

Abelard (AH-BEH-lard) This name means "highborn and steadfast." Variations include *Ab, Abalard, Abelhard, Abi, Abilard,* and *Adelard.*

Adelard (AH-DE-lard) Meaning "noble eagle." Variations include *Adal, Adalar, Adalard, Addy, Adel,* and *Adelar.*

Adler (AD-ler) Meaning "eagle." Variations include *Ad, Addler,* and *Adlar.*

Aimery (EH-mer-y) An alternate form of Emery, which means "home rule." Also *Aime, Aimerey, Aimeric,* and *Amerey.*

Alaric (AL-er-ick) A name that means "ruler of all." Also *Alarick, Alarik, Aleric, Allaric, Allarick, Alric, Alrick,* and *Ulrich.*

Albert (AL-bert) Meaning "highborn and bright." Famous Alberts include the brilliant physicist Albert Einstein, South African freedom fighter Albert Luthuli, and existentialist author Albert Camus. Also *Adelbert, Ailbert, Al, Albertik, Alberto, Albrecht, Alvertos, Aubert Elbert,* and *Ulbrecht.*

Alder (OL-der) This name signifies "alder tree."

Aldous (AL-dus) Meaning "old friends." See Alden, also under English names. *Brave New World* author Aldous Huxley is one noteworthy person with this name. Variations include A*ldis, Aldo, Aldon,* and *Aldus.*

Alger (AL-jur) Meaning "noble spearman."

Algis (AL-jis) This name means "spear."

Aloysius (Al-uh-WISH-iss) An alternate form of Louis, which means "famous warrior." Also *Alaols, Alois, Aloisius, Aloisio,* and *Aloys.*

Alphonse (AL-fonce) Meaning "eager for battle." Among famous people with this name is Alphonse D'Amato (aka "the Fonz") former U.S. senator from New York. Variations include *Alf, Alfonso, Alonzo, Alphons, Alphonsa, Alphonso, Alphonsus, Alphonza,* and *Alphonzus.*

Altman (ALT-min) Meaning "old man." Filmmaker Robert Altman did the film version of *M*A*S*H.* Variations include *Altmann* and *Atman.*

Alvan (AL-vin) An alternate form of Alvin. A variation is *Alvand.*

Alwin (AL-win) An alternate form of Alvin. Variations include *Ailwyn, Alwyn, Alwynn,* and *Aylwin.*

Amory (AM-ery) Form of Emory, which means "home ruler." Variations include *Amery* and *Amor.*

Anno (ON-no) A familiar form of Johann, derived from the Hebrew John, meaning "God's gracious gift."

Anselm (AN-selm) Meaning "divine helmet." Among notable people with this name is Anselm von Canterbury. Variations include *Anse, Anselme, Anselmi, Anselmo,* and *Elmo.*

Anson (AN-sin) A name that signifies "divine."

Archibald (AR-chi-bald) Meaning "bold and valorous." Poet Archibald MacLeish is one well-known person with this name. Variations include *Arch, Archaimbaud, Archambault, Archibaldo, Archie,* and *Arkady.*

Archie (AR-chie) A familiar form of Archer, Archibald. A variation is *Archy.*

Aric (AR-ick) An alternate form of Richard, which means "powerful ruler."

Arlo (AR-low) An alternate form of Charles, which means "farmer." Folk singer Arlo Guthrie is one famous Arlo.

Arno (AR-no) This names signifies "eagle-wolf."

Arnold (AR-neld) Meaning "eagle strength." Well-known Arnolds include historian Arnold Toynbee, golfer Arnold Palmer, and actor Arnold Schwarzenegger. Variations include *Arnald, Arnaldo, Arnaud, Arne, Arnel, Arnell, Anrey, Anri,* and *Arnie.*

Arvin (AR-vin) Meaning "friend of the people." Variations include *Arvie, Arvind, Arvinder, Arvon,* and *Arvy.*

Auberon (AW-ber-on) An alternate form of Oberon. Variations include *Auberron* and *Aubrey.*

Aubrey (AW-bree) A name that means "noble" or "bearlike." Artist Aubrey Beardsley is one well-known Aubrey.

Audie (AW-dee) Meaning "noble" or "strong." Notable men with this name include World War II hero Audie Murphy who portrayed himself on screen.

Aurick (AW-rick) This name means "protecting ruler."

Baden (BÄ-den) Meaning "bather." A variation is *Bayden.*

Baldemar (BALL-deh-mar) Meaning "bold" or "famous." Variations include *Baldemer, Baldomero, Baumar,* and *Baumer.*

Baldric (BALL-drick) Meaning "brave ruler." Variations include *Baldrick* and *Baudric.*

Baldwin (BALL-dwin) This name means "bold friend." Variations include *Bald, Baldovino, Balduin, Baldwinn, Baldwyn, Baldwynn,* and *Baudoin.*

Ballard (BÄL-lerd) Meaning "brave" or "strong." A variation is *Balard.*

Bardolf (BAR-dolf)   Meaning "ax wolf."

Barnum (BAR-nuhm)   Meaning "barn" or "storage place." One famous Barnum was showman Phineas T. Barnum, an important figure of the 19th century.

Baron (BÄR-ren)   Meaning "nobleman" or "baron." Variations include *Baaron, Baronle, Barrion, Barron,* and *Baryn.*

Barrett (BÄR-et)   This name signifies "strong as a bear." Variations include *Bar, Baret, Barret, Barrette,* and *Barry.*

Bastien (BÄS-chin)   A short form of Sebastian, meaning "respectful." Variations include *Baste* and *Bastiaan.*

Benedikt (BEN-eh-dikt)   A form of Benedict, meaning "blessed." Variations include *Bendek, Bendik, Benedek,* and *Benedik.*

Berg (BURG)   Meaning "mountain." Variations include *Berdj, Bergh,* and *Berje.*

Bergen (BER-gen)   Meaning "hill dweller." Variations include *Bergin* and *Birgin.*

Bernal (BER-nul)   A name that means "strong as a bear." Variations include *Bernald, Bernaldo, Bernel, Bernhold,* and *Bernold.*

Bernard (Ber-NARD)   Meaning "brave as a bear." Celebrated Bernards include author Bernard Malamud and philanthropist Bernard Baruch. Variations include *Bear, Bearnard, Benek, Ber, Bern, Bernabé, Bernadas, Bernal, Bernardel, Bernardin, Bernardo, Bernhardt, Bernie,* and *Bjorn.*

Berthold (BER-told)   This name means "bright," "illustrious," or "brilliant ruler." Among notable people with this name is German poet Bertold Brecht who wrote *Mother Courage and Her Children.* Variations include *Bert, Berthoud, Bertold,* and *Bertolde.*

Bertram (BER-trum)   Meaning "bright raven." One famous Bertram is architect Bertram Goodhue. A variation is *Bert.*

Bertrand (BER-trand)   Meaning "bright shield." Philosopher Bertrand Russell. Also *Bert, Bertran, Bertrando,* and *Bertranno.*

Bing (BING)   This name means a "pot-shaped hollow." One popular Bing was singer and actor Bing Crosby.

Bogart (BOW-gart)   Signifying "strong as a bow." A notable person with this name was screen legend Humphrey Bogart.

Bruno (BROO-no)   Meaning "brown haired" or "brown skinned." Among noteworthy people with this name is conductor Bruno Walter. Variations include *Brunon* and *Bruns.*

Bryon (BRY-in)   A name that means "cottage."

Buck (BUCK)   Meaning "male deer." One well-known person with this name is Hollywood screnwriter and actor Buck Henry. Variations include *Buckie, Buckley, Buckner, Bucko,* and *Bucky.*

Buell (BYOOL)   This name has the meaning "hill."

Burke (BURK)   Meaning "from the fortified settlement." Variations include *Berk, Berke, Birk, Burk,* and *Burkley.*

Burl (BURL)   A short form of Berlin, meaning "light face." One well-known Burl is folk singer Burl Ives. A variation is *Berl.*

Carl (KARL)   Meaning "man." Among notable people with this name are poet Carl Sandburg, astronomer Carl Sagan, and composer Carl Orff. A variation is *Carroll.*

Chadrick (CHAD-rick)   A name that means "mighty warrior." Variations include *Chaderick* and *Chadric.*

Charles (CHAR-uls)   Meaning "farmer." Among well-known people with this name are naturalist Charles Darwin and author Charles Dickens, who both hail from 19th-century England. Variations include *Charley, Charlie,* and *Charly.*

Claus (CLAWS)   A short form of Nicholas. One famous Claus is Claus Schenk Graf von Stauffenberg, German military officer who in 1944 was executed for his failed attempt to assassinate Hitler. Variations include *Claas, Claes, Clause,* and *Klaus.*

Clovis (KLO-vis)   This name means "renowned soldier." A variation is *Louis.*

Conrad (Kon-rad) Meaning "brave advisor." Among noteworthy people with this name are hotelier Conrad Hilton, as well as German physicist Wilhelm Conrad Röntgen who discovered X rays in 1895 and won the Nobel Prize in 1901. Variations include *Connie, Conrade, Conrado, Corrado,* and *Konrad.*

Darick (DÄR-ick) An alternate form of Derek. A variation is *Daric, Darico, Darek, Darik, Darrec, Darrick, Darick,* and *Danyk.*

Dedrick (DED-rick) Meaning "the people's ruler." Variations include *Dederick, Dedric, Dedrix, Detrek, Diedrich, Diedrick,* and *Dietrich.*

Derek (DERR-ick) A short form of Theodoric, meaning "light face," which signifies "ruler of the people." One of today's most popular Derks is actor Derek Jacobi, the star of I, Claudius. Variations include *Dereck, Derecke, Deric, Derick, Dericka, Derrek, Derico, Derik, Derrick, Derique, Derrec, Derreek, Deryck, Deryek,* and *Deryk.*

Detrick (DET-rick) An alternate form of Dedrick. Variations include *Detrek* and *Detric.*

Dick (DIK) A short form of Frederick and Richard. Among famous people with this name are actor Dick Van Dyke and ageless rock and roll promoter Dick Clark. Variations include *Dicken, Dickens, Dickenson, Dickerson, Dickie, Dickson,* and *Dikerson.*

Dietbald (DEET-bald) An alternate form of Theobald. Variations include *Dietbalt* and *Dietbolt.*

Dieter (DEE-ter) A name that means "army of the people." A variation is *Deiter.*

Dietrich (DEE-trick) An alternate form of Dedrick. Notable people with this name include Dietrich Bonhoeffer, a theologian, pastor, and active resistor of Nazism who helped Jews escape from Germany and actively worked toward overthrowing Hitler; and great baritone Dietrich Fischer-Dieskau. Variations include *Deitrick, Diedrich, Dieter, Dieterich, Dieterick,* and *Dietz.*

Dirk (DURK) A short form of Derek and Theodoric. One well-known Dirk is actor Dirk Bogarde. Also *Derk, Dirck, Dirke, Durc, Durk,* and *Dyrk.*

Dolph (DOLF) A familiar form of Adolph and Rudolph. Actor Dolph Lundgren. Variations include *Dolfe, Dolphe,* and *Dolphus.*

Dustin (DUS-tin) A name that signifies "valiant warrior." One of today's popular actors with this name is Dustin Hoffman.

Eberhard (EBBER-hard) Meaning "courage of a boar." One famous person with this name is Eberhard Diepgen is the governing mayor of Germany's capital Berlin. Variations include *Eberhardt, Eberhart, Evard, Everard, Everardo, Everhardt,* and *Everhart.*

Edel (AY-dl) Which means "noble." Variations include *Adel, Edelmar,* and *Edelweiss.*

Eginhard (EGG-in-hard) Meaning "sword power." Variations include *Eginhardt, Einhard, Einhardt,* and *Enno.*

Egon (EE-gon) Meaning "formidable." Among noteworthy people who share this name is sociologist Egon Bittner.

Ehren (EH-rin) A name that means "honorable."

Eiger (AY-gur) An alternate form of Alger. Variations include *Eiger, Eligar,* and *Ellger.*

Ellard (ELL-erd) Meaning "noble" or "brave." Variations include *Allard* and *Ellerd.*

Elman (ELL-min) This name means "noble man." A variation is *Elmen.*

Emerson (EM-er-sin) Meaning "son of Emery." One well-known person with this name is Indy 500 winner Emerson Fittipaldi. Variations include *Emmerson* and *Emreson.*

Emery (EM-ery) Signifying "home ruler." Varaitions include *Emari, Emeri, Emerich, Emmerich, Emmery, Emmo, Emmory, Emory, Inre,* and *lmrich.*

Emmett (EM-mit) This name signifies "industrious" or "powerful." A popular Emmett is circus clown Emmett Kelly.

Emrick (EM-rick) An alternate form of Emery. Variations include *Emerich, Emmerich, Emryk,* and *Imrich.*

Engelbert (ENG-el-burt) Meaning "bright as an angel." One popular entertainer with this name is singer Engelbert Humperdinck. Variations include *Bert, Englebert,* and *Inglebert.*

Erbert (UR-burt) A form of Herbert. Variations include *Ebert* and *Erberto.*

Erhard (AIR-hard) A name that means "strong" or "resolute." Variations include *Erhardt* and *Erhart.*

Eric (ERR-ick) A short form of Frederick. A well-known person with this name is psychologist Erich Fromm. A variation is *Erich.*

Ernst (URNST) A form which means "earnest" or "sincere." A notable person with this name is philosopher Ernst Bloch. A variation is *Erns.*

Eugen (YOU-jin) A form of Eugene, meaning "well born."

Ewald (AY-wald) A name that means "law powerful."

Faber (FAY-ber) A form of Fabian.

Faxon (FAX-in) This name signifies "long haired."

Ferdinand (FER-din-and) Meaning "adventurous voyager." Ferdinand Sauerbruch was a famous surgeon. Variations include *Feranado, Ferdle, Ferdinind, Ferdynand, Fernando, Hernando,* and *Nando.*

Finn (FIN) A name that signifies "from Finland."

Folke (FOAL-kee) An alternate form of Volker, which means "people guard." A variation is *Folker.*

Fonso (FON-zo) A short form of Alphonso. A variation is *Fonzo.*

Fonzie (FON-zee) A familiar form of Alphonse. Variations include *Fons, Fonsie,* and *Fonz.*

Franz (FRONTZ) A form of Francis, meaning "from France." Notable people with this name include Austrian downhill skier Franz Klammer. Variations include *Frantz, Franzen, Franzin, Franzi,* and *Franzy.*

Frederick (FRED-er-rick) This name means "peaceful ruler." One famous Frederick is composer Frederick Lowe of Lerner and Lowe. Variations include *Dick, Eric, Federico, Fico, Fred, Fredd, Freddi, Freddie, Freddy, Fredi, Fredo, Fredic, Fredrich, Fredy, Fredek, Frederic, Frederich. Frederik, Frederric, Friderick, Fridirck, Fridrick,* and *Rick.*

Fremont (FREE-mont) A name that means "noble protector."

Friedrich (FREED-rick) A form of Frederick. Notable people with thi name include German philosopher Friedrich Nietzsche, composer George Frideric Handel. Variations include *Friedel, Friedrick, Frideric, Fridrich, Fridrick, Friedrike,* and *Fryderyk.*

Fritz (FRITZ) A familiar form of Frederick. One popular Fritz is violinist Fritz Kreisler. Variations include *Fritson, Fritts, Friftchen,* and *Fritzi.*

Fulbright (FUL-brite) A name that means "very bright." A variation is *Fulbert.*

Gary (GÄ-ree) Meaning "spearman." Notable people with this name are actor Gary Cooper and golfer Gary Player.

Gerald (JER-eld) Meaning "mighty spearman." Former president Gerald Ford. Variations include *Fitzgerald, Garold, Gary, Gearalt, Gellert, Geralde, Geraldo, Geraud, Jarell, Jarrell, Jerald, Jerry, Kharald,* and *Urald.*

Gerhard (GAIR-hard) A form of Gerard, meaning "mighty spearman." A variation is *Garhard.*

Gert (GURT) This name means "fighter."

Gilen (GILL-in) A name meaning "illustrious pledge."

Goddard (GOD-erd) Meaning "god-hard." Variations include *Godard, Godart, Goddart, Godhardt, Godhart, Gotthard, Gotthardt,* and *Gotthart.*

Godfrey (GOD-free) A form of Geoffrey.

Gottfried (GOD-freed) A form of Geoffrey, meaning "peace of the land." Variations include *Gotfrid, Gotfrids,* and *Gottfrid.*

Gotzon (GOT-sin)   Meaning "God's son" or "angel."

Griswold (GRIZ-wald)   Meaning "gray woods." Variations include *Gris* and *Griz*.

Guthrie (GUTH-ree)   Meaning "war hero." Notable folk with this name include folk singer Woody Guthrie, who sang "This land is your land, this land is my land."

Hackett (HACK-et)   A name that means "little woodcutter." Variations include *Hacket*, *Hackit*, and *Hackitt*.

Hackman (HACK-min)   Meaning "wood-cutter." Actor Gene Hackman.

Hagan (HAG-in)   This name signifies "strong defense." A variation is *Haggan*.

Hamlet (HÄM-lit)   Meaning "little village" or "home." Hamlet is the name of the title hero in Shakespeare's tragic play.

Hamlin (HÄM-lin)   Which means "home lover." Variations include *Hamblin, Hamelin, Hamlen, Hamlyn,* and *Lin*.

Handel (HAND-ul)   A form of John, meaning "God's gracious gift."

Hanno (HAHN-no)   A short form of Johann.

Harbin (HAR-bin)   This name signifies "little bright warrior." Variations include *Harben* and *Harbyn*.

Hardy (HAR-dee)   Meaning "bold" or "daring." Actor Hardy Kruger is one well-known Hardy.

Hartman (HART-min)   Meaning "hard" or "strong."

Hartwig (HART-wig)   A name that means "strong advisor."

Harvey (HAR-vee)   Meaning "army warrior." Variations include *Harv, Hervi, Hervey,* and *Hervy*.

Heinrich (HINE-rick)   An alternate form of Henry, which means "estate ruler." Among celebrated people with this name is German poet Heinrich Heine. Variations include *Heindrick, Heiner, Heinrick, Heinrik,* and *Hinrich*.

Heinz (HI-nz)   A familiar form of Henry.

Helmer (HEL-mer)   This name means "warrior's wrath."

Helmut (HEL-mit)   Meaning "courageous protector." Famous Helmuts include fashion designer Helmut Lang who has done things with rubber, and Helmut Kohl, German chancellor from 1982–98. A variation is *Helmuth*.

Henning (HEN-ning)   An alternate form of Hendrick and Henry, meaning "estate ruler."

Henry (HEN-ree)   Meaning "estate ruler." Among popular people with this name are former secretary of state Henry Kissinger, as well as late actor Henry Fonda. Variations include *Arrigo, Enric, Enrico, Enrikos. Hagan, Hank, Harry, Heinrich, Heinz, Hendrick, Henning, Henri,* and *Henrique*.

Herbert (HURB-ert)   Meaning "glorious soldier." Well-known Herberts include former U.S. president Herbert Hoover and philosopher Herbert Spencer. Variations include *Bert, Erbert, Harbert, Hebert, Hibert, Heberto, Herb, Herbie, Heriberto, Herby,* and *Hurbert*.

Herrick (HERR-ick)   Which means "war ruler." Variations include *Herrik* and *Herryck*.

Hewitt (HYOO-it)   Meaning "little smart one." Variations include *Hewe, Hewet, Hewett, Hewle, Hewit, Hewlett,* and *Hewlitt*.

Hildebrand (HIL-de-brand)   A name that has the name meaning "battle sword." A variation is *Hildo*.

Hilliard (HIL-yard)   Meaning "brave warrior." Variations include *Hillard, Hiller, Hillier, Hillyard,* and *Hillyer*.

Hobart (HO-bart)   This name means "Bart's hill." Variations include *Hobard, Hobby, Hobie,* and *Hoebart*.

Hobert (HO-burt)   This name means "Bert's hill." A variation is *Hobey*.

Horst (HORST)   Meaning "dense grove" or "thicket." Actor Horst Buchholz. A variation is *Hurst*.

Howe (HOW) A name that means "high." One popular Howe is hockey legend Gordie Howe who played into his fifties. Variations include *Howey* and *Howie*.

Hubbard (HUB-berd) An alternate form of Hubert.

Hubert (HYOO-burt) Meaning "bright mind." Among noteworthy people with this name was vice president and statesman Hubert Humphrey. Variations include *Beredei, Bert, Hobart, Hubbard, Huber, Huberto, Huey, Hugh, Hugibert, Humberto,* and *Uberto*.

Hulbert (HUL-burt) A name with the significance "brilliant grace." Variations include *Bert, Hulbard, Hulburd, Hulburt,* and *Hull*.

Humbert (HUM-burt) Meaning "famous hun." Variations include *Hum, Humberto,* and *Umberto*.

Humphrey (HUM-free) Meaning "peaceful strength." One famous Humphrey is Hollywood actor Humphrey Bogart. Variations include *Humfredo, Humfrey, Humfrid, Humfried, Humfry, Humphery, Humphry, Humphrys, Hunfredo, Onofrio,* and *Onufry*.

Ingellbert (ING-ul-burt) An alternate form of Engelbert, meaning "bright as an angel." A variation is *Inglebert*.

Ivo (EEVO) A name signifying "yew wood" or "bow wood." Famous people with this name include Nobel Prize winner for literature Ivo Andric. Variations include *Ibon, Ivar, Ives, Ivon, Ivor,* and *Yvo*.

Jaegar (YAY-ger) Meaning "hunter." Variations include *Jaager* and *Jagur*.

Jarman (JAR-min) "From Germany." A variation is *Jerman*.

Jarvis (JAR-vis) "Skilled with a spear." Variations include *Jaravis, Jarvas, Jarvaska, Jarvoris, Javaris, Jervey,* and *Jervis*.

Jerry (JER-ee) "Mighty spearman." Comedians Jerry Lewis and Jerry Seinfeld.

Johann (YO-han) A form of John, meaning "God's gracious gift." Composer Johann Sebastian Bach, poet Johann Wolfgang von Goethe.

Variations include *Anno, Hanno, Joahan, Johan, Johanan, Johane, Johannas, Johannes, Johansen, Johanson, Johanthan, Johatan, Johathan,* and *Johathon*.

Jorg (YORG) A form of the name George, meaning "farmer." Variations include *Jörg, Jeorg, Juergen, Jungen, Jürgen.* Austrian politician Jörg Haider is among those who have this name.

Josef (Jo-sef) A form of Joseph, meaning "he shall add." Virtuoso pianist Josef Hoffman is one popular Josef.

Jupp (JUP) A form of Joseph, meaning "he shall add."

Kaiser (KAI-zer) A form of Caesar, which means "emperor." A variation is *Kaisar*.

Kass (KASS) This name means "blackbird." Variations include *Kaese, Kasch,* and *Kase*.

Keane (KEEN) A name that has the significance of "sharp." A variation is *Keene*.

Keifer (KEE-fer) A variation of Cooper, meaning "barrel-maker." Actor Keifer Sutherland is one celebrity with this name. Variations include *Keefer, Keiffer, Kiefer,* and *Kieffer*.

Kelby (KEL-bee) Meaning "farm by the spring. "Variations include *Keelby, Kelbee, Kelbey,* and *Kellby*.

Klaus (KLAUS) A short form of Nicholas. Notable people named Klaus include actor Klaus Maria Brandauer. An alternate form of Claus. Variations include *Klaas, Klaes, Klas,* and *Klause*.

Konrad (KON-rad) A form of Conrad, meaning "brave council." Animal behaviorist Konrad Lorenz is one well-known Konrad. Variations include *Khonrad, Koen, Koenraad, Kon, Konn, Konnid, Konrade, Konrado, Kord,* and *Kort*.

Konstantin (KON-stin-teen) A form of Constantine, meaning "unwavering." Variations include *Dinos, Konstancli, Konstandinos, Konstantinas, Konstantine, Konstantinos,* and *Konstantlo*.

Korb (KORB) This name means "basket."

Kort (KORT)   An alternate form of Cort and Kurt, meaning "short."

Krischan (KRISH-in)   A form of Christian, meaning "Christ-bearer."

Kurt (KURT)   A short form of Kurtis, meaning "courteous." Notable people with this name include author Kurt Vonnegut and late rocker Kurt Cobain. Variations include *Kort* and *Kuno*.

Lambert (LAM-burt)   Meaning "bright land." Variations include *Bert, Lambard, Lamberto, Lampard*, and *Landbert*.

Lance (LANCE)   Meaning "spear." One of today's popular Lances is 1999 Tour de France winner Lance Armstrong. Variations include *Lancy, Lantz, Lanz*, and *Launce*.

Leon (LEE-on)   A short form of Leonard and Napoleon. One well-known author is Leon Uris. Variations include *Leo, Léon, Leonas, Léonce, Leoncio, Leondris, Leonek, Leonetti, Leoni, Leonid*, and *Leonidas*.

Leonard (LEN-erd)   This name has the meaning "brave as a lion." One very successful Leonard is composer and conductor Leonard Bernstein. Variations include *Leanard, Lee, Len, Lenard, Lennard, Lennart, Lenny, Leno, Leon, Leonaldo, Léonard, Leonardis*, and *Leonardo*.

Leopold (LEE-uh-pold)   Meaning "brave people." Notable people with Wolfgang's father, Leopold Mozart, also a composer. Variations include *Leo, Leopoldo, Leorad, Lipót, Lopolda, Luepold, Luitpold, Poldi*, and *Poldo*.

Lindberg (LIN-burg)   This name signifies "linden tree mountain."

Linfred (LIN-frid)   A name that means "peaceful" or "calm."

Lonnie (LON-ee)   A familiar form of Alphonse, meaning "prepared for battle." Variations include *Lonnell, Lonniel*, and *Lonny*.

Lonzo (LON-zo)   A short form of Alphonse, meaning "prepared for battle."

Loring (LAUR-ing)   This name signifies "son of the renowned warrior." Variations include *Lorrie, Lorring*, and *Lorry*.

Lothar (LO-thar)   An alternate form of Luther, which means "famous warrior." German soccer player Lothar Matthäus is one popular Lothar. A "ladies man" is sometimes called a lotario. Variations include *Lotaire, Lotarrio, Lothair, Lothaire*, and *Lothario*.

Loudon (LAU-din)   This name means "low valley." Variations include *Loudan, Louden, Loudin*, and *Lowden*.

Louis (LOO-iss)   Meaning "famous battler." Celebrated men with this name include jazz giant Louis Armstrong and innovative chemist Louis Pasteur. Variations include *Aloisio, Aloysius, Clovis, Luigi. Lash, Lewis, Lou, Loudovicus, Louie*, and *Lucho*.

Lucas (LOO-kus)   A form of Lucius, meaning "light." Painter Lucas Cranach. Variations include *Lucassie, Luckas*, and *Lucus*.

Ludwig (LUD-wig)   An alternate form of Louis. Great 19th-century German composer Ludwig van Beethoven. Variations include *Ludovic, Ludovico, Ludvig, Ludvik, Ludwik*, and *Lutz*.

Luther (LOO-thur)   Meaning "famous warrior." Famous Luthers in history include Protestant reformer Martin Luther, civil rights leader Martin Luther King, Jr., and horticulturalist Luther Burbank.

Mandel (MAN-dell)   A name that means "almond." Variations include *Mandeil*.

Manheim (MAN-hime)   This name means "servant's home."

Mann (MAN)   Signifying "man." Among renowned people with such a name is author Thomas Mann. A variation is *Manin*.

Mathe (MATH)   A short form of Matthew, meaning "God's gift."

Matheu (MATH-oo)   A form of Matthew, meaning "God's gift." Variations include *Matheau, Matheus*, and *Mathu*.

Mathias (MA-thy-iss)   A form of Matthew, meaning "God's gift." Variations include *Maitias, Mathi, Mathia, Mathis, Matias, Matthia, Matthias, Mattla, Mattlas*, and *Matus*.

Mauritz (MOR-itz) A form of Maurice, meaning "dark" or "moonsh."

Medgar (MED-gur) A form of Edgar, meaning "lucky spear." Civil rights leader Medgar Evers is one well-known person with this name.

Medwin (MED-win) This name signifies "strong friend."

Meinhard (MINE-hard) Meaning "firm strength." Variations include *Maynard*, *Meinhardt*, *Meinke*, and *Mendar*.

Meinrad (MINE-rod) This name means "strong counsel."

Menz (MENZ) A short form of Clement, meaning "merciful."

Milo (MY-low) Form of the Latin name Miles, meaning "solider." A famous Milo is legendary rock critic Milo Miles. A variation is *Mylo*.

Moritz (MOR-itz) A form of Maurice and Morris. A varition is *Morisz*.

Nando (NON-doh) A familiar form of Ferdinand, meaning "bold alternative." Also *Nandor*.

Nardo (NAR-doh) This name means "strong" or "hardy."

Nedrich (NED-rich) An alternate form of Dedrick and Dietrich. Variations include *Didrich*, *Didrick*, *Didrik*, and *Diederick*.

Oberon (OH-ber-on) Meaning "noble" or "bearlike." The name of the king of the fairies in Shakespeare's *A Midsummer Night's Dream*. Variations include *Auberon*, *Aubrey*, *Oberron*, and *Oeberon*.

Obert (OH-burt) A name that means "wealthy" or "bright."

Odolf (OH-dolf) Meaning "prosperous wolf." A variation is *Odolff*.

Onofrio (Uh-NO-free-oh) An alternate form of Humphrey. Variations include *Oinfre*, *Onfre*, *Onfrio*, and *Onofredo*.

Orlando (Or-LAN-doh) Meaning "famous land." Baseball player Orlando Cepeda is one famous person with this name.

Orman (OR-min) This name means "mariner" or "seaman."

Othman (OTH-min) A name that means "wealthy."

Otto (OD-doh) Meaning "rich." Renowned men with this name include filmmaker Otto Preminger and Otto von Bismarck, Prussian-German statesman in the 19th century. Variations include *Odo*, *Otek*, and *Otello*.

Ottokar (OD-doh-kar) "Happy warrior." Variations include *Otokars* and *Ottocar*.

Paulin (PAW-lin) A form of Paul, meaning "little."

Pepin (PEP-in) Meaning "determined" or "petitioner." One historically known person with this name was Pepin the short, an eighth-century Frankish king and the father of Charlemagne. Variations include *Pepi*, *Peppie*, and *Peppy*.

Pippin (PIP-in) This name has the meaning "father."

Pollard (PAHL-erd) "Close-cropped head." Variations include *Poll*, *Pollerd*, and *Pollyrd*.

Raimund (RAY-mund) A form of Raymond, which means "wise protector." A variation is *Ralmund*.

Rainer (RAY-ner) Meaning "counselor." Among celebrated people with this name is poet Rainer Maria Rilke. Variations include *Rainar*, *Rainey*, and *Rainor*.

Redmond (RED-mund) This name signifies "protecting counselor."

Reinhart (RINE-hart) A form of Reynard, which means "wise" or "courageous." Variations include *Rainart*, *Rainhard*, *Rainhardt*, *Rainhart*, *Reinart*, *Reinhard*, *Reinhardt*, and *Renke*.

Richart (RICH-ert) Meaning "powerful ruler." The original form of Richard.

Richmond (RICH-mund) Meaning "powerful protector." Variations include *Richmon* and *Richmound*.

Ritter (RIT-er) "Knight" or "chivalrous." Actor John Ritter is one well-known person with this name. A variation is *Rittner*.

Roderick (ROD-ur-ick) Meaning "famous ruler." Variations include *Broderick, Rhoderick, Rod, Rodderick, Roddrick, Roddy, Roderic, Roderich, Roderigo, Roderik, Roderyck,* and *Rodgrick.*

Rodman (ROD-min) A name that means "famous man." A variation is *Rodmond.*

Rodrik (ROD-rick) This name means "famous ruler."

Roger (RAJ-ur) Meaning "renowned spearman." Among famous people who have this name are baseball player Roger Maris, actor Roger Moore, and rock-and-roller Roger Daltrey. Variations include *Rodger, Rog, Rogelio, Rogerick, Rogerio, Rogers, Rogiero, Rojelio, Rudiger, Ruggerio,* and *Rutger.*

Roland (ROH-lind) Meaning "renowned land." One well-known person with this name is critic Roland Barthes. Variations include *Orlando, Rawlins, Rolan, Rolanda, Rolando, Rolek, Rolland, Rolle, Rollie, Rollin, Rollo, Rowe, Rowland,* and *Ruland.*

Rolf (ROLF) A short form of Rudolph. See also Ralph, under English names. Variations include *Rolfe, Rolle, Rolli,* and *Rolly.*

Rory (ROHR-ee) A familiar form of Roderick. Actor Rory Calhoun is one renowned Rory.

Roth (ROTH) This name means "red."

Rowland (RAU-lind) An alternate form of Roland.

Rudolf (ROO-dolf) An alternate form of Rudolph. Composer Rudolf Friml. Variations include *Rodolf, Rodolfo, Rudolfo.*

Rudolph (ROO-dolf) Meaning "famous wolf." One popular Rudolph was silent film lothario Rudolph Valentino. Variations include *Dolf, Raoul, Rezsó, Rodolfo, Rodolph, Rodolphe, Rolf, Ruda, Rudek, Rudi, Rudolf, Rudolpho, Rudolphus,* and *Rudy.*

Rune (ROON) This name means "secret."

Rupert (ROO-pert) Signifying "bright fame." See also Robert under English names. Poet Rupert Brooke is one notable person with this name. Variations include *Ruperth, Ruperto,* and *Ruprecht.*

Schafer (SHAY-fer) Meaning "shepherd." Variations include *Schaefer, Shaffar,* and *Shaffer.*

Schmidt (SHMIDT) Meaning "blacksmith." Renowned men with this common last name include former chancellor Helmut Schmidt and author Arno Schmidt.

Schneider (SHNEI-der) This name means "tailor."

Schön (SHURN) A name that means "handsome." Variations include *Schönn* and *Shon.*

Seifert (SY-fert) An alternate form of Siegfried.

Sepp (SEP) See Josef. A variation is *Seppi.*

Siegfried (SIG-freed) Meaning "victorious peace." Among famous men who have this name is author Siegfried Sassoon. Variations include *Seifert, Seifried, Siegfred, Siffre, Sig, Zigfrid,* and *Ziggy.*

Spangler (SPANG-ler) "Tinsmith." A variation is *Spengler.*

Stark (STARK) Meaning "strong" or "vigorous." Variations include *Stärke* and *Starkie.*

Steen (STEEN) "Stone." Variations include *Stein, Steine,* and *Steiner.*

Stefan (STEF-in) A form of Stephen. Notable people with this name include tennis champion Stefan Edberg. Variations include *Staffan, Staffon, SteafeAn, Stefanson, Stefaun, Stefawn, Steffan,* and *Steffon.*

Stern (STERN) This name means "star."

Stoffel (STOF-il) A short form of Christopher, which means "Christ-bearer."

Tab (TAB) Meaning "shining" or "brilliant." Notable people with this name include movie actor Tab Hunter.

Talbert (TAL-burt) A name that means "bright valley."

Tarell (TÄR-il) An alternate form of Terrell. Variations include *Tarelle, Tarrel, Tarrell,* and *Taryl.*

Terrell (TER-el or ter-REL) "Thunder ruler." Variations include *Tarell, Terrail, Terral,*

Terrale, Terrall, Terreal, Terrelle, Terrill, Terryal, Terryel, Tirel, Tirrell, and *Tyrel.*

Terrill (TER-el or ter-REL)   An alternate form of Terrell. Variations include *Terril, Terryl, Terryll,* and *Tyrill.*

Tewdor (TOO-der)   A form of Theodore, which means "divine gift."

Theobald (THEO-bald)   Meaning "people's prince." Variations include *Dietbald, Teoballdo, Thebault, Thebbault, Thibault, Tibalt, Tibold, Tiebold, Tiebout, Toibold, Tybald, Tybalt,* and *Tybault.*

Theodoric (THEO-dor-ick)   Meaning "people's ruler." Variations include *Derek, Dietrich,* and *Dirk.*

Till (TIL)   A short form of Theodoric. Variations include *Thilo, Til, Tillman, Tilman, Tillmann,* and *Tilson.*

Tomas (TOM-is)   A form of the Hebrew Thomas, meaning "twin." Variations include *Thoma, Tom, Tornalsin, Tomaz, Tomdo, Tome, Tomek, Tomelis, Tomico, Tomik, Tornislaw, Tomo,* and *Tornson.*

Toni (TOH-nee)   A form of Anthony, meaning "of inestimable worth." Variations include *Tonie, Tonio, Tonis,* and *Tonnie.*

Traugott (TRAU-git)   Meaning "faith in God."

Ulbrecht (ULL-brekt)   An alternate form of Albert, meaning "noble" or "bright."

Ulf (ULF)   A name that means "wolf."

Ulfred (ULL-fred)   Meaning "peaceful wolf."

Ulger (ULL-ger)   Meaning "warring wolf."

Ullock (ULL-ick)   Meaning "sporting wolf."

Ulmo (ULL-moh)   A name that signifies "from Ulm, Germany."

Ulrich (ULL-rick)   Meaning "wolf power." Among renowned figures with this name is Ulrich von Hutten was a German humanitarian of the 15th century. Variations include *Alaric, Uli, Ull, Ullric, Ulrick, Ulrik, Ulrike, Ulu, Ulz,* and *Uwe.*

Uwe (OO-veh)   A familiar form of Ulrich. One popular person with this name is German soccer star of the 1970s Uwe Seeler.

Varick (VAR-ick)   This name means "protecting ruler." A variation is *Warrick.*

Vasyl (VÄZ-el)   A form of William, meaning "resolute protector." Variations include *Vasos, Vassily, Vassos, Vasya, Vasyuta, Vayaska,* and *Wassily.*

Vemados (VEM-a-dose)   This name means "courage of the bear."

Vemer (VEE-mer)   A name signifying "defending army." A variation is *Varner.*

Verrill (VER-il)   A name that means "masculine."

Viktor (VICK-ter)   A form of Victor, which means "conqueror." Chemist Viktor Meyer. Austrian politician Viktor Klima. Variations include *Viktoras* and *Viktors.*

Vilhelm (VIL-helm)   A form of Wilhelm, which means "determined guardian." Variations include *Vilhelms, Vilho, Vilis, Viljo,* and *Villern.*

Volker (VOHL-ker)   This name means "people's guard." Notable people with this name include filmmaker Volker Schlöndorf. A variation is *Folke.*

Volney (VOHL-nee)   This name means "national spirit."

Wagner (WAG-ner)   Meaning "wagoner" or "wagon maker." A variation is Waggoner.

Waldemar (WAL-duh-mar)   Meaning "powerful" or "famous." Variations include *Vladimir, Valdernar, Waldermar,* and *Waldo.*

Waldo (WAL-doh)   A familiar form of Oswald, which means "God's power," and Waldemar. Famous men with this name include essayist Ralph Waldo Emerson. Variations include *Wald* and *Waldy.*

Walfred (WAL-fred)   A name that means "peaceful ruler."

Wallach (WAL-ick)   A form of Wallace, meaning "from Wales." Also *Wallache.*

Waller (WAL-er)   This name signifies "powerful one."

Walmond (WAL-mund)   A name that has the meaning "mighty ruler."

Walter (WAL-ter)   Meaning "army of power." Renowned men with this name include poet Walt Whitman, animator Walt Disney, and actor Walter Brennan. Variations include *Gualberto, Gualtiero, Ladislav, Vladimir, Valter, Vanda, Vova, Walder, Wally, Walt,* and *Walther.*

Warner (WAR-ner)   Meaning "armed defender." Silent film star Warner Baxter and Senator John Warner are among those who share this name.

Warren (WAR-en)   Meaning "general" or "warden." Actor Warren Beatty and Chief Justice Warren Burger. Variations include *Ware, Waring, Warrenson, Warrin, Warriner,* and *Worrin.*

Weber (WEB-er)   This name means "weaver."

Welby (WEL-bee)   Meaning "farm near the well." Variations include *Welbey, Welbie, Wellbey,* and *Wellby.*

Wendell (WEN-dl or Wen-DELL)   Meaning "wanderer." Politician Wendell Wilkie is one notable person named Wendell.

Wies (WEES)   A name that signifies "renowned warrior."

Wilbert (WIL-burt)   Signifying "brilliant" or "resolute." Variations include *Wilberto* and *Wilburt.*

Wilfred (WIL-fred)   Meaning "determined peacemaker." Varations include *Wilferd, Wilfredo, Wilfrid, Wilfride, Wilfried, Wilfryd, Will, Willfred, Willfried, Willie,* and *Willy.*

Wilhelm (WIL-helm)   Meaning "determined guardian." Renowned Wilhelms include Wilhelm II the last German emperor, who was forced to abdicate in 1918; Wilhelm von Humboldt, a German statesman, philosopher, and linguist of the 18th century whose brother was natural scientist Alexander von Humboldt; and Robert Wilhelm Bunsen, inventor of the Bunsen burner. Also *Willem.*

Willard (WIL-erd)   This name means "bold will."

William (WIL-yums)   Meaning "determined protector." A variation is *Williamson.*

Willie (WIL-ee)   A familiar form of Wilhem. Former German chancellor and winner of the Nobel Prize for peace in 1971 Willy Brandt is among those with this name. Variations include *Wile, Wille, Willey, Willi, Willia, Willy,* and *Wily.*

Willis (WIL-iss)   Meaning "son of Willie." Air-conditioning inventor Willis Carrier and basketball player Willis Reed. Variations include *Willice, Wills,* and *Willus.*

Winfried (WIN-freed)   Meaning "friend of peace."

Wolfgang (WULF-gang)   Meaning "wolf gait." One very well-known Wolfgang is Wolfgang Amadeus Mozart, 18th-century Austrian composer. Variations include *Wolf, Wolff, Wolfgans, Woffie,* and *Woffy.*

Wouter (WOO-ter)   This name has the meaning "powerful warrior."

Yale (YAYL)   A name that signifies "fertile."

Yohann (YO-han)   A form of Johann. Variations include *Yohane, Yohannes,* and *Yohn.*

Zacharias (ZA-kär-ee-us)   A form of the Hebrew Zachariah, meaning "rememberance of God." One notable Zacharia is the inventor of the telescope and microscope Zacharias Janssen. Variations include *Zacarias, Zakarias,* and *Zekarias.*

Zamiel (ZA-meel)   A form of Samuel, meaning "God has heard." Variations include *Zamal* and *Zamuel.*

GERMANY: GIRLS

Ada (AY-dah)   A short form of Adelaide. Among notable people with this name is actress Ada Rehan.

Adalia (a-DAHL-ee-ah)   Meaning "noble." Variations include *Adal, Adala, Adalee, Adali, Adalle, Adalin, Adaly, Adalyn, Addal,* and *Addala.*

Addie (ADD-ee) A familiar form of Adelaide and Adrienne. Variations include Adde, Addey, Addi, Addia, Addy, Adey, Adi, Adie, and Ady.

Adelaide (ADD-el-ade) Meaning "noble" or "serene." Variations include *Ada, Adeela, Adelade, Adelaid, Adelaida, Adeline,* and *Adelle.*

Adelle (AH-del) A short form of Adelaide. Notable women with this name include dancer Adele Astaire (sister and early dance partner of Fred Astaire). Variations include *Adel, Adela, Adele, Adelia,* and *Adell.*

Alberta (al-BURT-ah) Meaning "noble" or "bright." A feminine form of Albert, which means "noble" or "bright." Singer Alberta Hunter is one popular Alberta. Variations include *Albertina, Albertine, Albertyna, Albertyne,* and *Alverta.*

Alda (OL-dah) Meaning "old; elder." A feminine form of Aldo. Variations include *Aldina, Aldine, Aldona,* and *Aidyna.*

Aloisa (AH-low-ee-sah) Meaning "famous warrior." Variations include *Aloisia* and *Aloysia.*

Amalia (uh-MAL-ee-ya) An alternate form of Amelia, which means "hard-working." Aviator Amelia Earhart is one famous Amelia. Variations include *Amalea, Amalee, Amaleta, Amali, Amalie,* and *Amalija.*

Anna (Ä-nah) A form of the Hebrew name Hannah, which means "gracious." Among renowned people with this name are great Russian ballerina Anna Pavlova; psychologist Anna Freud; actress Anna Magnani; *Black Beauty* author Anna Sewall; former first lady Anna Harrison; botanist Anna Atkins; chemist Anna J. Harrison; model Anna Nicole Smith; as well as poet Anna Akhmatova. Variations include *Ana, Anah, Ania, Anica, Anita, Anja, Anka, Annina,* and *Anya.*

Aria (Ä-ree-ah) From the Latin *aer,* this name signifies "melody," especially a melody in an opera.

Aubrey (AW-bree) This name means "noble" or "bearlike."

Audris (AW-dris) Meaning "lucky." A variation is *Audrys.*

Babette (Bä-bet) A familiar form of Barbara, which signifies "strange" or "foreign." Variations include *Babita* and *Barbette.*

Bathilda (buh-TIL-da) A name that means "woman warrior."

Berit (BERIT) Meaning "splendid."

Bernadine (Bur-nuh-DEEN) This name means "brave as a bear."

Bertha (BUR-tha) Meaning "bright" or "illustrious" or "brilliant ruler." A short form of Alberta.

Berti (BUR-tee) A familiar form of Gillberte, which means "shining pledge." Variations include *Berte, Bertie,* and *Berty.*

Billie (BIL-ee) A familiar form of Belle, which means "beautiful," and Wilhelmina. Among renowned people with this name are jazz singing great Billie Holliday and actress Billie Burke.

Birdie (BUR-dee) A familiar form of Bertha.

Bruna (BROO-nah) A short form of Brunhilda. Among notable people with this name is opera singer Bruna Castagna.

Brunhilda (BROON-hil-da) or (BRUN-hil-da) Meaning "armored fighting maid." Variations inclde *Brinhilda, Brinhilde, Bruna, Brunhilde, Brannhilde, Brynhild,* and *Hilda.*

Carol (KÄ-rel) Meaning "farmer." Well-known actors with this name are Carol Channing, famous for *Hello, Dolly!,* and comedienne Carol Burnett who transformed into many characters on her television variety show.

Charlie (CHAR-lee) Meaning "strong" or "womanly." A feminine form of Charles. Short for Charlotte. Variations include *Charla, Charle, Charlea, Charlee, Charleigh, Charley,* and *Charli.*

Christa (KRIS-tah) A short form of Christina, which means "Christian." Among notable people with this name is author Christa Brueck. Variations include *Chrysta, Crista,* and *Crysta.*

Clotilda (KLO-til-da) This name has the meaning "heroine."

Cora (KORAH)   Meaning "maiden." Notable people with this name is civil rights activist Coretta Scott King. A variation is *Coretta*.

Dagmar (DAG-mar)   A name that means "glorious." A variation is *Dagmara*.

Dellana (DEL-ah-na)   Meaning "noble protector." Variations include *Dalanna, Dalayna, Daleena,* and *Dalena*.

Derika (DER-i-ka)   Meaning "ruler of the people." A feminine form of Derek. Variations include *Dereka, Derekia, Derica, Dericka,* and *Derrica*.

Dustine (DUS-teen)   Meaning "valiant fighter." A feminine form of Dustin.

Edda (EDDA)   An alternate form of Hedda, which means "battler." A variation is *Etta*.

Edeline (ED-el-ein) or (ED-el-een)   This name means "noble." A variation is *Edda*.

Elfrida (el-FREE-da)   A name that means "peaceful." Variations include *Elfrea, Elfreda, Elfredda, Elfreeda,* and *Freda*.

Elga (ELGA)   An alternate form of Helga, which means "pious."

Elke (EL-kuh or EL-kee)   Forms of Adelaide and Alice, which means "of noble birth." Among famous people with this name is actor Elke Sommer. Variations include *Elki* and *Iiki*.

Elsbeth (ELS-beth)   A form of Elizabeth, meaning "consecrated to God." Variations include *Elsbet, Elspet, Elspeth, Elspie, Elzbet,* and *Elzbieta*.

Elsie (EL-see)   A familiar form of Elsa, a diminutive form of Elizabeth. Variations include *Elsi* and *Elsy*.

Emelie (EM-eh-lee)   A form of Amelia, which means "hard-working."

Emma (EM-mah)   A short form of Emily, which means "industrious." Flaubert's title heroine Emma Bovary, as well as poet Emma Lazarus are famous Emmas. Variations include *Em, Ema, Emi,* and *Emly*.

Erna (Ur-nah)   Meaning "earnest." A variation is *Ernestine*.

Etta (ET-tah)   A name that signifies "little."

Fernanda (Fur-NAN-dah)   Meaning "daring" or "adventurous." A feminine form of Ferdinand. Variations include *Ferdie, Ferdinanda, Ferdinande, Fern,* and *Fernande*.

Frieda (FREE-dah)   A name that means "peace." Variations include *Frayda, Freda, Fredda, Fredella, Fredia, Freeda,* and *Freida*.

Frederica (FRED-ur-ee-kah)   Signifying "peaceful ruler." A feminine form of Frederick. Among notable people with this name is opera singer Frederica von Stade. Variations include *Federica, Freda, Freddi, Freddie, Fredericka, Frederickina,* and *Frederika*.

Fritzi (FRITZ-ee)   A familiar form of Frederica. Variations include *Friezi, Fritze, Fritzie,* and *Fritzy*.

Galiena (GUH-lee-na)   This name has the meaning "lofty."

Genevieve (JEN-uh-veev)   An alternate form of Guinevere, which means "white wave." Notable people with this name include actress Genevieve Bujold. Variations include *Gen, Gena, Genaveve, Genavieve, Genavive, Geneva,* and *Geneveve*.

Geraldine (JER-uld-een)   Meaning "mighty with a spear." A feminine form of Gerald. Renowned people with this name are politician Geraldine Ferarro; actor Geraldine Page; as well as opera singer Geraldine Farrar, a contemporary of Caruso. Variations include *Geraida, Geraldina, Geraldyna,* and *Geraldyne*.

Gertraud (GER-trowd)   A name that means "fighter." Variations include *Gertrude, Gerta, Trude,* and *Trudy*.

Gertrude (GER-trood)   Meaning "strength of a spear." Among notable people with this name: English Channel swimmer Gertrude Ederle, 'dada' writer Gertrude Stein. Variations include *Gerda, Gert, Gerta, Gertey, Gerti,* and *Gertie*.

Gillberte (GIL-burt-ah)   Meaning "shining pledge." A feminine form of Gilbert. Variations include *Gigi, Gilberta, Gilbertina, Gilbertine,* and *Gill*.

Giselle (GIZ-el or JIZ-el or GHEE-sel-ah) Meaning "pledge" or "hostage." Giselle is the name of an opera by Théophile Gautier. Variations include *Gisel, Gisela, Gisele, Gisile, Gisell, Gisella,* and *Gissell.*

Greta (GRET-ah) A short form of Gretchen and Margaret, which means "pearl." Famous people with this name include classic film star Greta Garbo and marathon champion Greta Waitz. Variations include *Greatal, Greatel, Greeta, Gretal, Grete, Gretel,* and *Grethe.*

Gretchen (GRETCH-in) A form of Margaret, meaning "pearl." Actor Gretchen Mol and singer Gretchen Peters are among those with this name. Variations include *Greta* and *Gretchin.*

Griselda (GRIZ-el-dah) Meaning "gray warrior maid." Variations include *Grisel, Griseldis, Griseldys, Griselys, Grishilda,* and *Grishilde.*

Gudrun (GUH-drun) or (GOOD-roon) This name means "divine guidance."

Hedda (HED-ah) Meaning "battler." Among notable people with this name are the title character of Ibsen's *Hedda Gabler,* and Hollywood gossip columnist Hedda Hopper. Variations include *Heda, Hedaya, Hede, Hedia, Hedvick, Hedvig, Hedvika,* and *Hedwig.*

Hedwig (HED-wig) Meaning "warfare" or "struggle." Notable women with this name include actress Hedy Lamarr and author Hedwig Courths-Mahler. Variations include *Hadwig, Hedda,* and *Hedy.*

Heidi (HI-dee) A short form of Adelaide, which means "noble" or "serene." Heidi is the title character the popular children's story by Johanna Spyri. Variations include *Heida, Heide, Heidie, Hidee, Hidi,* and *Hiede.*

Helga (HEL-gah) This name means "pious."

Helma (HEL-mah) A short form of Wilhelmina, which means "determined guardian." Variations include *Halma, Helme, Helmi,* and *Helmine.*

Hilda (HIL-dah) A short form of Brunhilda and Hildegarde. Among renowned people with this name is poet Hilda Doolittle. Variations include *Helle, Hilde, Hildey,* and *Hildie.*

Hildegarde (HIL-duh-gard) Meaning "fortress." A historical Hildegarde is Hildegard von Bingen, medieval visionary, theologian, and composer. Variations include *Hilda, Hildagard, Hildagarde,* and *Hildegard.*

Ida (EYE-duh) Which means "hard-working." Among notable people with this name are actress Ida Lupino, former first lady Ida McKinley, and physicist Ida Tacke. Variations include *Idette.*

Ilise (IL-eece) A form of Elise. Variations include *Illeshia, Illicia, Ilissa, Illytse, Illycia, Ilyse,* and *Ilyssa.*

Ilse (IL-sah) A form of Elsa, a diminutive of Elizabeth. Variations include *Illsa, Illsey, Ilsie,* and *Illsy.*

Ima (EYE-mah) A familiar form of Amelia.

Imelda (IM-el-dah) Meaning "warrior." Notable persons named Imelda include shoe fancier Imelda Marcos, former first llady of the Philippines. Variations include *Imaida, Irmhilde,* and *Melda.*

Itta (IDDA) A name that signifies "labor."

Johanna (YO-hanna or JO-hanna) From the Hebrew, meaning "God is gracious." Well-known people with this name include romance novelist Johanna Lindsey, and Heidi author Johanna Spyri. Variations include *Janna, Johana, Johanah, Johani, Johanie, Johanka, Johannah,* and *Johanne.*

Karla (KAR-lah) An alternate form of Carla, the feminine form of Carl, signifying "strong."

Karoline (KÄR-o-line) Feminine for Karl. Variations include *Lina* and *Line.*

Katrina (Kuh-TREE-nah) A form of Katherine, which means "pure." Among notable people with this name is Katrina van Tassel, a character in Irving's *The Legend of Sleepy Hollow.* Variations include *Katia, Katreen, Katreena, Katrene, Katri, Katrien,* and *Katrin.*

Klarissa (Kluh-RISS-ah) This name means "clear" or "bright." A variation is *Clarissa.*

Lamia (LAH-mee-ya) Meaning "bright land." A feminine form of Lambert. A variation is *Lama*.

Landra (LAN-drah) This name means "counselor." A variations is *Landrea*.

Lene (LEEN) A form of Helen. German film director Leni Riefenstahl is one renowned person with this name. Variations include *Leni* and *Line*.

Lenia (LEE-nee-yah or LEN-ee-yah) An alternate form of Leona. Variations include *Lenda, Leneen, Lenette, Lenna,* and *Lennah*.

Leona (LEE-oh-nah) Meaning "brave as a lioness." A feminine form of Leon. Hotelier Leona Helmsley. Variations include *Leoine, Leoia, Leollah, Leone, Leonefle, Leonia,* and *Leonice*.

Liese (LEE-see) A familiar form of Elise or Elizabeth, meaning "consecrated to God."

Liesel (LEE-zel) A familiar form of Elizabeth. Among notable people with this name are actress Liesel Matthews and author Lisel Mueller.

Lieselotte (LEE-suh-lot-ah) A combination of Elizabeth and Charlotte. Variations include *Liselotte* and *Lilo*.

Lise (LEESE) A form of Elizabeth. Austrian nuclear physicist Lise Meitner is one notable Lise.

Lois (LO-iss) An alternate form of Louise, which means "famous in battle." Well-known figures with this name include Superman's inamorata, reporter Lois Lane and congresswoman Lois Capps.

Lorelei (LOR-uh-lye) Meaning "alluring." In German folklore, the Lorelei were sirens of the Rhine River who lured sailors to their death. Variations include Lurleen and Lurlene.

Lotte (LOT-ee or LOT-uh) A short form of Charlotte, meaning "strong." Among notable people with this name are singer Lotte Lenya and opera singer Lotte Lehmann. Variations include *Lotie, Lotta, Lottchen,* and *Lottey*.

Louise (LOO-eez) Meaning "renowned warrior." A feminine form of Louis. Famous Louises include silent film sensation Louise Brooks and author Louise Aston. Variations include *Alison, Eloise, Heloise, Lois, Lola,* and *Luella*.

Lovisa (LOW-veesa) An alternate form of Louise.

Luann (LOO-an) This name signifies "graceful woman warrior."

Luella (LOO-el-lah) A familiar form of Louise.

Mallory (MAL-er-ee) A name meaning "army counselor."

Marelda (Muh-REL-dah) This name means "renowned warrior." Variations include *Marella* and *Marilda*.

Margret (MAR-gret) Meaning "pearl." Variations include *Margreta, Margrete, Margreth, Margrett,* and *Margretta*.

Mariel (MÄR-ee-el or mar-ee-EL) A form of Mary, meaning "sea of bitterness" or "sorrow." One popular Mariel is actor Mariel Hemmingway. Variations include *Marial, Marieke, Mariela, Mariele, Madeline, Mariella, Marielle,* and *Mariellen*.

Marila (Muh-RIL-ah) A form of the Hebrew name Mary. Variations include *Marella* and *Marelle*.

Marlena (mar-LAY-nah) A form of Marlene, which means "high tower." Actor Marlene Dietrich. Variations include *Marla, Marlaina, Marleena, Marlina,* and *Marlinda*.

Marlis (MAR-liss) A combination of Maria and Elizabeth.

Matilda (Muh-TIL-duh) Meaning "mighty battler." Variations include *Mahaut, Maitilde, Malkin, Mat, Matelda, Mathilda, Mathilde,* and *Matilde*.

Maude (MAWD) This name means "heroine."

Melia (muh-LEE-ya or MEL-ee-ya) A short form of Amelia. Variations include *Melcia, Melea, Meleah, Meleia, Meleisha, Meli, Meliah, Melida,* and *Melika*.

Meryl (MER-il)   A name that signifies "famous." Among notable people with this name is actress Meryl Streep. Variations include *Merril* and *Merrill*.

Meta (MEDDA)   A short form of Margret. Variations include *Metta*, *Mette*, and *Metti*.

Mileta (MIL-edda)   Meaning "generous" or "merciful." A feminine form of Milo. Variations include *Mila*, *Milessa*, and *Mylie*.

Milia (MIL-ya or mil-EE-ya)   Meaning "industrious." A short form of Amelia and Emily. Variations include *Mila*, *Mili*, *Milla*, and *Milya*.

Mina (MEE-nah)   Meaning "love." Celebrated people with this name include mathematician Mina Rees.

Minna (MIN-nah)   A short form of Wilhelmina. Variations include *Mina*, *Minka*, *Minnie*, and *Minta*.

Mitzi (MIT-zee)   A familiar form of Mary. Among well-known Mitzis is actor Mitzi Gaynor. Variations include *Mieze*, *Mitzee*, and *Mitzie*.

Monika (MON-i-kuh)   A form of Monica, which means "noble." Variations include *Moneeke*, *Moneik*, *Moneka*, *Monieka*, *Monike*, and *Monnika*.

Nan (NÄN)   A short form of Fernanda. Among noteworthy people with this name are photographer Nan Goldin and former congresswoman Nan Honeyman.

Nixie (NIX-ee)   This name means "water sprite."

Odetta (OH-deh-tah or oh-DET-ah)   A form of Odelia, which means "an ode" or "a melody." Among notable people with this name is folk singer Odetta. Variations include *Oddetta* and *Odette*.

Odile (OH-deel)   A name signifying "rich." Variations include *Odila* and *Oda*.

Orlanda (or-LAN-duh)   Meaning "famous land." A feminine form of Orlando. A variation is *Orlantha*.

Otthild (OH-tild or OT-ild)   Meaning "lucky heroine." A variation is *Ottila*.

Porsche (PORSH or PORSH-ah)   A form of Portia. Variations include *Porcha*, *Porchai*, *Porcsha*, *Porcshe*, *Porscha*, *Porschia*, and *Pourche*.

Quinn (KWIN)   A name that means "queen." Variations include *Quin* and *Quinna*.

Ragnild (RAG-nild)   A name that means "all-wise power." Variations include *Reinheld*, *Renilde*, and *Renilda*.

Raymonde (ray-MOND-uh)   Meaning "wise protector." A feminine form of Raymond. Variations include *Rayma*, *Raymae*, and *Raymie*.

Reanna (ree-AN-ah)   An alternate form of Raina, which means "light."

Resi (REES-ee)   A familiar form of Theresa, which means "to reap." Variations include *Resel*, *Ressie*, *Reza*, *Rezka*, and *Rezi*.

Reynalda (Ray-NAL-duh)   Meaning "king's advisor." A feminine form of Reynold.

Richelle (RI-shel)   A form of Ricarda. Variations include *Richel*, *Richela*, *Richele*, *Richell*, and *Richella*.

Rilla (RI-lah)   This name signifes a "small brook."

Roderica (rod-er-EE-kah)   Meaning "renowned ruler." A feminine form of Roderick. Variations include *Rica*, *Rika*, *Rodericka*, *Roderika*, *Rodricka*, and *Rodrika*.

Rolanda (ro-LON-duh)   A name that means "famous land." A feminine form of Roland. Variations include *Ralna*, *Rolaine*, *Rolande*, *Rolene*, and *Rollande*.

Rosamond (ROZ-uh-mund)   Meaning "famous protector." Among notable people with this name is author Rosamond Bernier. Variations include *Rosamund*, *Rosamunda*, *Rosemonde*, and *Rozamond*.

Rudee (ROO-dee)   Meaning "famous wolf." A feminine form of Rudolph. Variations include *Rudeline*, *Rudell*, *Rudella*, *Rudi*, *Rudie*, and *Rudy*.

Rue (ROO)   Meaning "famous." One well-known actress with this name is Rue McLanahan.

Selda (SEL-dah)   A short form of Griselda, which means "gray warrior maid."

Selma (Sel-mah) Meaning "godly helmet." Among notable people with this name is Nobel Prize–winning author Selma Lagerlöf.

Senta (SEN-tah) This name has the meaning "assistant."

Sigfreda (sig-FREE-dah) Meaning "peaceful victory." Variations include *Sigfreida, Sigfrida,* and *Sigfrieda.*

Sigmunda (sig-MUN-dah) Meaning "victorious protector." A variation is *Sigmonda.*

Stina (STEE-nah) A short form of Christina. Variations include *Steena, Stena, Stine,* and *Stinna.*

Sunhild (SUN-hild or SOON-hild) A name that means "swan girl."

Tilda (TIL-dah) A short form of Matilda, which means "might battler." Variations include *Tilde, Tildie, Tildy,* and *Tylda.*

Tillie (TIL-ee) A familiar form of Matilda. Noteworthy people with this name include former congresswoman Tillie Fowler. Variations include *Tilli, Tilly,* and *Tillye.*

Trudy (TROO-dee) A familiar form of Gertrude. Variations include *Truda, Trude, Trudessa, Trudey,* and *Trudi.*

Ulla (UH-lah) This name means "will."

Ulrica (UHL-ri-kah) Meaning "wolf ruler" or "ruler of all." A feminine form of Ulric. A variation is *Rica.*

Ulva (UHL-vah) A name that means "wolf."

Unna (UHN-ah) This name means "woman."

Uta (OO-tah) Meaning "rich." Renowned people with this name include actress Uta Hagen.

Vala (VAH-lah) Meaning "singled out." A variation is *Valia.*

Valda (VAH-duh) Meaning "renowned ruler." A feminine form of Valdemar. Variations include *Valida* and *Velda.*

Vanda (VON-duh or VAN-duh) An alternate form of Wanda. Variations include *Vandana, Vandelia, Vandetta,* and *Vandi.*

Velma (VEL-mah) A familiar form of Vilhelmina.

Verena (ver-EE-nah) A name that means "protective friend." A variation is *Verina.*

Vilhelmina (vil-HELM-in-ah or vil-helm-EE-nah) An alternate form of Wilhelmina, which means "determined guardian." Variations include *Velma, Vilhelmine,* and *Vilma.*

Vilma (VIL-mah) A short form of Vilhemina. Among famous people with this name is actress Vilma Banky.

Walda (WAL-duh) Meaning "ruler." A feminine form of Waldo. Variations include *Waldina, Waldine, Walida,* and *Walida.*

Wanda (WAN-duh) This name means "wanderer." Notable people with this name include harpsichordist Wanda Landowska. Variations include *Vanda, Wahnda, Wandah, Wandely, Wandi, Wandie, Wandis,* and *Wandy.*

Warda (WAR-duh) This name means "guardian." A feminine form of Ward. Variations include *Wardia* and *Wardine.*

Wiebke (WEEB-kee) or (WEEB-kuh) Meaning "the young woman."

Wilda (WIL-duh) This name has the meaning "untamed."

Wilhelmina (wil-hel-MEE-nah) Meaning "determined guardian." A feminine form of Wilhelm. Noteworthy people with this name include Wilhelmina Cole Holladay, founder of the National Museum of Women in the Arts. Variations include *Vilhelmina, Wilhelmine, Willa, Willamina, Willamine,* and *Willemina.*

Willa (WIL-ah) A short form of Wilhelmina. Among notable people with this name are author Willa Cather and former congresswoman Willa Eslick.

Wilma (WIL-mah) A short form of Wilhelmina. Renounced Wilmas are track running star Wilma Rudolph and Wilma Mankiller, the first woman elected chief of the Cherokee Nation. Variations include *Williemae, Wilmetta, Wilmette, Wilmina,* and *Wylma.*

Winifred (WIN-i-fred)   Meaning "friend of peace." Among celebrated people with this name is former congresswoman Winnifred Huck. Variations include *Winifrid*, *Winifryd*, and *Winnifred*.

Winola (win-OH-lah)   This name has the significance "charming friend." A variation is *Wynola*.

Yseult (EE-soolt)   Meaning "ice rule." Variations include *Isolde*, *Yseulte*, and *Ysolt*.

Zelda (ZEL-duh)   A short form of Griselda. One popular Zelda in her day was Zelda Fitzgerald, who lived it up with her husband F. Scott.

Zelma (ZEL-muh)   An alternate form of Selma.

Ireland

Traditionally, Irish parents have chosen names for their babies based on the names of the saints and of figures from Celtic legend. Anglicized versions of Gaelic names have also been used; there has been an interest recently among some Irish people in returning to the Gaelic names themselves. It should be noted that many of these names are not used in Ireland. In addition to popular Irish names, the following list suggests quite a few last names for use as first names.

IRELAND: BOYS

Aidan (AY-dan)   Meaning "fiery." A famous person named Aidan is actor Aidan Quinn. Variations are *Aden, Adin, Aiden, Aydan, Ayden,* and *Aydin.*

Alan (AL-an)   Meaning "handsome" or "peaceful." Blessed Alan de la Roche was one of the Dominican Fathers from the monastery at Dinan, in Brittany. He was an eminent theologian and was famous for his sermons. Alan J. Lerner, wordsmith of Lerner and Lowe musicals and actor Alan Alda are two famous Alans. Variations are *Allan Allen, Ailin, Alani, Alain, Alair, Aland, Alani, Alano, Alanson, Alao, Allan, Allen, Alon, Alun,* and the nickname *Al.*

Ardal (AR-dal)   A form of the Old German name Arnold, which means "strong like an eagle."

Arlen (AR-len)   Meaning "pledge." One famous Arlen is Broadway songwriter Harold Arlen. Other versions are *Arlan, Arland, Arlend, Arlin, Arlyn,* and *Arlynn.*

Arthur (AR-thur)   Of English origin, it means "noble" or "bear." Famous Arthurs include King Arthur of the legendary Round Table, Sir Arthur Sullivan, composer of Gilbert and Sullivan operettas, playwright Arthur Miller, and Sherlock Holmes creator Arthur Conan Doyle.

Baird (BAYRD)   Meaning "bard; traveling minstrel; poet." Variations are *Bairde, Bard, Barde, Bardia,* and *Barr.*

Blaine (BLAYN)   A name that means "thin" or "lean." David Blaine is a famous magician. Another version is *Blayne.*

Blair (BLAIR)   Meaning "field" or "plain." Blair Moody is a United States senator.

Brendan (BREN-din)   Meaning "little raven." Well-known Brendans are author Brendan Behan and journalist Brendan Gill. Alternate forms are *Brenden, Bren, Breendene,* and *Brendin.*

Brian (BRY-an)   A name that means "strong and honorable." Brian Boru was a great 11th-century Irish king. Other famous Brians are actor Brian Donlevy and director Brian DePalma. Alternate forms are *Briano, Briant, Briante, Brien, Brience, Brient, Brin, Briny, Brion, Bryan, Bryant, Bryen,* and *Bryent.*

Brody (BRO-dee)   Meaning "ditch." Other versions are *Brodee, Broden, Brodey, Brodie,* and *Broedy.*

Carney (KAR-nee)   Meaning "the victor." One famous Carney is comedian Art Carney.

Carrick (KAHR-ick)   Meaning "rock." Also seen as *Carooq* and *Carricko.*

Casey (KAY-see)   Meaning "brave." A name made famous by former New York Mets general manager Casey Stengel and disk jockey Casey Kasem. Also *Case, Casie, Casy, Cayse, Caysey,* and *Kacey.*

Cassidy (KAS-sid-ee)   A name that means "clever." Cass Gilbert is a celebrated architect. Also seen as *Cass, Cassady, Cassie, Kass,* and *Kassidy.*

Cavan (KEV-an)   Meaning "handsome." See also Kevin. Variations include *Caven* and *Cavin.*

Cedric (SED-rick)   A name of English origin that means "chief." An example is well-known actor Sir Cedric Hardwicke.

Clancy (KLAN-see)   Meaning "red-headed fighter's child." Made famous by military novelist Tom Clancy. Other versions are *Clancey* and *Claney*.

Conan (KO-nan)   Meaning "praised; exalted." Famous people with this name are Sherlock Holmes creator Sir Arthur Conan Doyle and talk show host Conan O'Brien. Alternate forms are *Conary* and *Conaire*.

Conlan (KON-lin)   Meaning "hero." Most often seen in its familiar form *Connie*, as in baseball general manager Connie Mack. Connie is also a nickname for Conan, Conrad, Constantine, and Conway. Variations of Conlan are *Conlen*, *Conley*, *Conlin*, and *Conlyn*.

Conor (KON-or)   A name that means "strong will; desire." Famous Conors include author and diplomat Conor Cruise O'Brien and award-winning playwright Conor McPherson. Also *Connor*, *Konor*, and *Konnor*.

Conroy (KON-roy)   Meaning "wise man." Variations are *Conry* and *Roy*.

Conway (KON-way)   Meaning "hound of the plain." Country musician Conway Twitty made this name famous. Other versions are *Connie* and *Conwy*.

Corey (KOR-ee)   Meaning "the hollow." Two well-known actors have this name, Corey Haim and Corey Feldman. Variations include *Core*, *Coreaa*, *Cori*, *Corian*, *Corie*, *Corio*, *Correy*, *Corria*, *Corrie*, *Corry*, *Corrye*, *Cory*, and *Kory*.

Cormac (KOR-mac)   Meaning "raven's son." Cormac was a third-century king of Ireland who founded schools. The name is more currently made famous by writer Cormac McCarthy. Other versions are *Cormack* and *Cormick*.

Craig (KRAYG)   Meaning "crag; steep rock." Chef Craig Claiborne brought this name to prominence. Variations are *Crag*, *Craige*, *Craigen*, *Craigery*, *Craigon*, *Creag*, *Cregg*, *Creig*, *Criag*, and *Kraig*.

Cullen (KULL-en)   Meaning "handsome." Also seen as *Cull*, *Cullan*, *Cullie*, and *Cullin*.

Daley (DAY-lee)   Meaning "assembly." One famous Daley is Olympic decathlon gold medalist Daley Thompson.

Darby (DAHR-bee)   A name that means "free."

Darcy (DAHR-see)   A name meaning "dark."

Darren (DAR-in)   A name that means "great one." A famous person with this name is actor Darren McGavin. There are numerous alternate forms including *Daran*, *Darann*, *Darawn*, *Daren*, *Darian*, *Darien*, *Darion*, *Darran*, *Darrian*, *Darrien*, *Darrion*, *Dayran*, *Deran*, *Deren*, *Derran*, *Derren*, *Derrian*, *Derrien*, *Derrin*, *Derrion*, and *Derryn*.

Declan (DECK-lan)   Meaning "man of prayer." Saint Declan was a fifth-century bishop.

Desmond (DEZ-mund)   A name that means "from South Munster," part of an ancient kingdom in Ireland. Bishop Desmond Tutu, South African freedom fighter, is a celebrated carrier of this name. Also seen as *Demond*, *Demonde*, *Demonds*, *Demone*, *Des*, *Desi*, *Desmon*, *Desmund*, *Dezmon*, *Dezmond*, and *Dumonde*.

Devin (DEV-in)   A name that means "poet." Variations are *Deavin*, *Deivin*, *Dev*, *Devan*, *Deven*, *Devon*, *Devlyn*, and *Dyvon*.

Devlin (DEV-lin)   A name that means "brave; fierce." Usually a surname, variations include *Dev*, *Devland*, *Devien*, and *Devlyn*.

Dillon (DIL-lon)   A name that means "loyal." This is both a first name as in Dylan Thomas, famous poet, and as a last name such as actor Matt Dillon. Also *Dilan*, *Dill*, *Dillan*, *Dillen*, *Dillin*, *Dillion*, *Dilly*, *Dillyn*, *Dilon*, *Dilyn*, and *Dylan*.

Donal (DON-el)   Meaning "strong warrior," this name is the equivalent of Dennis.

Donnell (don-EL)   A name that means "brave" or "dark." Also common as a last name.

Donovan (DON-a-vin)   Meaning "dark." British pop star Donovan, born Donovan Leitch, and Philadelphia Eagles quarterback Donovan McNabb are two famous people bearing this name. Variations include *Dohnovan*, *Donavan*,

Donavin, Donavon, Donavyn, Donevon, Donoven, Donovin, Donovon, and *Donvan.*

Dooley (DEW-lee) A name that means "dark hero." A well-known person with this name is actor Dooley Wilson. Another version is *Dooly.*

Duane (DWAYN) Meaning "dark." Also *Deune, Duain, Duaine,* and *Duana.* Duane Hansen, a modern sculptor, brings fame to this name. Variations include *Dawayne, Dawyne, Deune, Duain, Duaine, Duwain, Duwan, Duwane, Duwayn, Duwayne, Dwain, Dwaine, Dwan, Dwane, Dwayne, Dwyane,* and *Dywane.*

Dugan (DEW-gin) Meaning "swarthy." Variations include *Doogan, Dougan, Douggan,* and *Duggan.*

Eamon (AY-min) A name that means "blessed protection." Made famous by Eamon de Valera, first Irish prime minister. Also seen as *Eammon* and *Eamonn.*

Earl (ERL) Meaning "pledge." Former Chief Justice Earl Warren brought honor to this name.

Egan (EE-gin) Meaning "ardent; fiery." This is usually a surname. Variations are *Egann, Egen,* and *Egon.*

Erin (EHR-in) Meaning "peaceful." It is another name for Ireland and is generally used as a girl's name. Also *Erine, Erinn, Eryn,* and *Erynn.*

Evan (EH-vin) Meaning "young warrior." Two famous people with this name are the American novelist Evan Hunter and jazz musician Evan Parker.

Fagan (FAY-gin) Meaning "little fiery one." Garth Fagan is a famous modern dance choreographer. Not generally used as a first name.

Farrell (FAHR-rel) Meaning "heroic." Usually a surname, other versions are *Farrel, Farrill, Farryll,* and *Ferrell.*

Fergus (FUR-gis) A name that means "highest decision." Variations are *Fearghas, Fearghus, Feargus, Fergie, Ferguson,* and *Fergusson.*

Ferris (FEHR-ris) Meaning "rock," this name was made famous by the engineer George

Ferris, who invented the ferris wheel. Also seen as *Fares, Faris, Fariz, Farris, Feris,* and *Ferriss.*

Finian (FIN-ee-in) Meaning "light-skinned; white." St. Finian was an Irish clergyman and is now the patron saint of Ulster. Variations are *Finnian, Fionan, Fionn, Phinean,* and *Phinnian.*

Finlay (FIN-lee) Meaning "light-haired soldier." Variations include *Findlay, Findley, Finlea, Finlee, Finley, Finn, Finnlea,* and *Finnley.*

Finnegan (FIN-eh-gin) Meaning "light skinned." Made famous by the James Joyce novel *Finnegan's Wake.* Another spelling is *Finegan.*

Fitzroy (FITZ-roy) Meaning "son of the king."

Flynn (FLIN) A name that means "son of the red-haired man." Erroll Flynn became famous for his swashbuckling films in the 1940s. Other versions are *Flin, Flinn,* and *Flyn.*

Galbraith (GAIL-brayth) Meaning "Scotsman in Ireland." Economist John Kenneth Galbraith brought this name to prominence. Also seen as *Galbrait* and *Galbreath.*

Galvin (GAL-vin) Meaning "sparrow." Other versions are *Gal, Gail, Gallven, Gallvin, Gaivan, Gavin,* and *Gaiven.*

Gannon (GAN-non) Meaning "light-skinned." Other spellings are *Gannie, Ganny.*

Garrett (GAR-rit) A name that means "brave spearman." Garth Brooks, country singer, has made a version of this name known far and wide. Variations include *Gar, Gared, Garet, Gareth, Garett, Garrad, Garret, Garrette, Garth, Gerald, Gerard,* and *Jarrett.*

Garvey (GAR-vee) Meaning "rough peace." This is usually a last name. Other versions are *Garbhán, Garrvey, Garrvie, Garv, Garvan, Garvie,* and *Garvy.*

Ghilchrist (GIL-chryst) Meaning "servant of Christ." Variations include *Gilchrist, Gilcrist, Gil, Gill, Gilley,* and *Gilly.*

Gillean (GIL-ee-in) Meaning "servant of Saint John." It is more often used as a girl's name. Variations include *Gillan, Gillen,* and *Gillian.*

Gillespie (gil-ES-pee) Meaning "son of the bishop's servant." Usually a surname, it was made famous by jazz great Dizzy Gillespie. One alternate form is *Gillis*.

Gilmore (GIL-mor) Meaning "servant of the Virgin Mary." Also seen as *Gillmore*, *Gillmour*, and *Gilmour*.

Gilroy (GIL-roy) Meaning "servant to the king." Variations are *Gilderoy*, *Gildray*, *Gildroy*, *Gillroy*, and *Roy*.

Girvin (GUR-vin) Meaning "small and tough."

Glenn (GLEN) A short form of Glendon. The actor Glenn Ford is a famous person bearing this name. A variant of this name was also made famous by Big Band leader Glen Miller. Variations include *Gleann*, *Glen*, *Glennie*, *Glennis*, *Glennon*, *Glenny*, and *Glynn*.

Gorman (GOR-min) Meaning "small and blue eyed."

Grady (GRAY-dee) Meaning "noble; eminent." Other versions are *Gradea*, *Gradee*, *Gradey*, *Gradleigh*, *Graidey*, and *Graidy*.

Hagen (HAY-gin) Meaning "youthful."

Haley (HAY-lee) Meaning "ingenious." The actor Haley Joel Osment is a famous person with this name. Also seen as *Halley*, *Haily*, *Hale*, *Haleigh*, *Hayleigh*, and *Hayley*.

Hogan (HOE-gin) Meaning "youth." Championship golfer Paul Hogan and wrestling superstar "Hulk" Hogan have made this name famous.

Hoyt (HOYT) Meaning "mind" or "spirit."

Ian (EE-an) Meaning "God's gracious gift." Ian Fleming, creator of the character James Bond, made this name renowned. Other versions are *Eann*, *Ein*, *Eion*, and *Eann*.

Innis (IN-nis) Meaning "island." Variations are *Innes*, *Inness*, *Inniss*.

Kearny (KURN-ee) Traditionally a surname. Also *Kearn* and *Kearne*.

Keeley (KEE-lee) Meaning "handsome."

Kellan (KEL-lin) This is usually a surname. It is gaining popularity as a boy's first name. Variations include *Kael*, *Kaelen*, *Kaellan*, *Kaelin*, *Kaelyn*, *Kailen*, *Kalley*, *Kaylen*, and *Kaylon*.

Kelly (KEL-lee) Meaning "warrior." Variations are *Kelle*, *Kellen*, *Kelley*, *Kelli*, and *Kely*.

Kelvin (KEL-vin) Meaning "narrow river." It is in fact a river in Scotland. NFL lineman Kelvin Pritchett is a famous person bearing this name. Other versions are *Kelvan*, *Kelven*, *Kelwin*, and *Kelwyn*.

Kendrick (KEN-drik) Meaning "son of Henry."

Kennard (KEN-nahrd) Meaning "brave chieftain." Also seen as *Kenner*.

Kenneth (KEN-eth) Meaning "handsome." It is a name made famous by drama critic Kenneth Tynan and actor Kenneth Branagh.

Kenyon (KEN-yin) Meaning "white haired; blond." Also *Kenyan* and *Kenynn*.

Kermit (KUR-mit) A form of *Dermot*. Variations include *Kermey*, *Kermle*, and *Kermy*.

Kerry (KEHR-ree) Meaning "dark" or "dark haired." It is the name of a county in Ireland. Other versions are *Keary*, *Keri*, *Kerrey*, *Kerri*, and *Kerrie*.

Kerwin (KUR-win) Meaning "little and dark."

Kevin (KEV-in) Meaning "handsome." Famous Kevins include the actors Kevin Costner, Kevin Kline, and Kevin Spacey. Other versions are *Cavan*, *Kavan*, *Keevin*, *Keevon*, *Kevan*, *Keve*, *Keven*, *Keveon*, *Keverne*, *Kivin*, *Kevinn*, *Kevins*, *Kevion*, *Kevis*, *Kevn*, *Kevon*, *Kevron*, *Kevvy*, *Kevyn*, and *Key*.

Kieran (KEER-in) Meaning "dark." More often a girl's name in the United States. Also seen as *Kearn*, *Keiran*, *Keiren*, *Keiron*, *Kern*, *Kernan*, *Kiernan*, *Kieron*, and *Kyran*.

Killian (KIL-ee-in) Meaning "little Kelly." Generally a surname. Other versions are *Kilian*, *Killie*, and *Killy*.

Kinnard (kin-NAHRD) Meaning "tall hill-side."

Kory (KOR-ee) An alternate form of Corey. Variations include *Korey, Kore, Kori, Korle, Korlo, Korrey, Korrie, Korria, Korry,* and *Korrye*.

Kyle (KYL) Which means "narrow piece of land." This name has been made famous by film star Kyle MacLachlan, as well as the actor Kyle Secor. Also spelled *Kyele*.

Larkin Meaning "rough; fierce." One variation is *Larklin*.

Laughlin (LOK-lin) Meaning "land of lakes." Also seen as *Lochlann* and *Lochlain*.

Liam (LEE-im) Meaning "protection," it is another version of William. Rock star Liam Gallagher and actor Liam Neeson have made this name famous.

Logan (LOW-gin) Meaning "valley."

Lomán (lo-MAHN) Meaning "bare."

Lorcan (LOR-kin) Meaning "little and fierce."

Lucas (LEW-kis) Meaning "light." Other versions are *Lucassie, Luckas, Lucus,* and *Lucius*.

Lunn (LUHN) Meaning "warlike." Variations are *Lon* and *Lonn*.

Lynch (LINCH) Meaning "mariner." Also spelled *Linch*.

Magee (ma-GEE) Meaning "son of Hugh." Usually a surname, variations include *MacGee, MacGhee,* and *McGee*.

Maguire (ma-GWYRE) Meaning "son of the beige one." Also spelled *MacGuire, McGuire,* and *McGwire*.

Mahon (MAY-in) Meaning "bear."

Mairtin (MAHR-tin) A form of Martin, which means "warlike." Variations include *Martain* and *Martainn*.

Maitias (ma-TYE-us) A form of Mathias. A variation is *Makhias*.

Maitiú (MATH-ew) A form of Matthew, from the Hebrew for "God is a gift."

Maloney (ma-LOW-nee) Meaning "church-goer." Variations are *Malone and Malony*.

Melrone (MEHL-rown) Meaning "servant of Saint Ruadhan." Also spelled *Maolruadhand*.

Melvin (MEHL-vin) Meaning "armored chief." Actor Melvin Douglas, former defense secretary Melvin Laird, former baseball star Mel Ott. Other forms are *Mal, Mallvin, Malvinn, Malvyn, Malvynn,* and *Mel*.

Merrill (MEHR-ril) Meaning "bright sea." Country singer Merle Haggard made a variation of this name famous.

Mervin (MURV-in) A form of Marvin, meaning "lover of the sea." The short form is Merv, a name made famous by talk show host and producer Merv Griffin. Also *Merv, Mervyn, Mervynn, Merwin, Merwinn, Merwyn, Murvin, Murvyn, Myrvyn, Myrvynn,* and *Myrwyn*.

Michael (MYK-al) From the Hebrew, meaning "Who is like God." This has become a popular British and Irish name. Also *Micheal*.

Mickey (MIK-ee) A familiar form of Michael. Actor Mickey Rooney and baseball star Mickey Mantle come to mind. Other versions are *Mick, Mickie, Micky, Miki,* and *Mikeal*.

Moss (MAWCE) A short form of Maurice or Morris. Playwright Moss Hart brought the name to fame.

Neil (NEEL) Meaning "champion." Playwright Neil Simon, and Neil Armstrong, first human on the moon, lived up to this meaning.

Nevan (NEHV-in) Meaning "holy." Also seen as *Nevin*.

Niall (NEEL) An alternate form of Neil. Niall of the Nine Hostages was a famous Irish ruler who founded the clan O'Neill. Also seen as *Nial* and *Nyle*.

Nolan (NO-lin) Meaning "famous; noble." This name was made famous by record-setting pitcher Nolan Ryan. Other versions are *Noland, Nolen, Nolin, Nollan,* and *Nolyn*.

Odran (O-drin) Meaning "pale green one." Derived possibly from Saint Odran. Also seen as *Odhran, Odrian, Oran, Oren, Orin, Orran, Orren,* and *Orrin.*

Oscar (OS-car) An authentic Irish name that means "deer lover." A most noteworthy Oscar is writer Oscar Wilde.

Owen (O-win) Meaning "born to nobility, young warrior." Famous Owens include rising actor Owen Wilson and the professional wrestler Owen Hart. Variations are *Ioan* and *Eion.*

Owney (OWN-ee) Meaning "elderly." Also spelled *Oney.*

Patrick (PA-trik) Meaning "noble one." St. Patrick is the patron saint of Ireland. Other familiar versions are *Padraic, Padraig,* and *Paddy.*

Peadar (PE-der) Meaning "rock." An Irish form of Peter.

Phelan (FAY-lin) Meaning "wolf." Generally a surname. Thom Phelan is an Irish novelist.

Pierce (PEERCE) Meaning "rock." It is another way of saying Peter. The name has been made famous by the Irish-born actor Pierce Brosnan. Another spelling is *Pearse.*

Piran (PEER-in) Meaning "prayer." He is the patron saint of miners. Also spelled *Peran* and *Pieran.*

Quincy (KWIN-cee) Meaning "fifth." Quincy Jones is a celebrated musician and producer. Variations include *Quincie* and *Quind.*

Quinn (KWIN) A short form of Quincy, Quinlan, and Quinton.

Rafer (RAY-fur) Meaning "one who brings riches," it is a short form of *Rafferty.* Variations include *Raferty, Rafe, Raff,* and *Raffer.*

Reagan (RAY-gin) Meaning "little king." Often a surname.

Reilly (RY-lee) Meaning "valiant." Riley (B.B.) King is a famous musician. Other versions are *Reilley, Rielly, Riley, Rylee,* and *Ryley.*

Renny (REN-nee) Meaning "small and strong." Director Renny Harlin.

Riddock (RID-dok) Meaning "smooth field."

Riddock (RID-dok) Meaning "smooth field."

Riordan (REER-din) Meaning "bard; royal poet." Generally used as a surname. Also seen as *Rearden, Reardin,* and *Reardon.*

Rogan (RO-gin) Meaning "redhead."

Ronan (RO-nin) Meaning "seal." Ronan Keating is an American pop star.

Rooney (ROO-nee) Meaning "red-haired." This is usually a last name.

Rory (RO-ree) Meaning "red king." This was the name of the last king of Irelend, Rory O'Connor.

Ryan (RY-in) Meaning "little king." Actor Ryan O'Neal made this name prominent. Other versions are *Rhyan, Rhyne, Rian, Ryane, Ryann, Ryen, Ryin, Ryne, Ryon, Ryuan,* and *Ryun.*

Scully (SCUL-lee) Meaning "town crier."

Seamus (SHAY-mus) Meaning "conqueror," it is the Irish for James. Seamus Heaney is a Nobel-laureate poet. Other versions are *Seamas, Seumas,* and *Shaymus.*

Sean (SHAWN) The Irish version of John. Sean O'Casey is a famous Irish writer. Actor Sean Connery is a celebrated bearer of this name, as are American actors Sean Penn and Sean Astin. Variations include *Shane, Shaine, Shaughn, Shaun, Shayne, John, Ioan,* and *Owen.*

Sedric (SEHD-rik) A form of Cedric. Variations include *Seddrick, Sederick,* and *Sedrick.*

Shannon (SHAN-un) Meaning "old." The Shannon is the longest river in Ireland. It is more often a girl's name and can also be seen as *Shanan, Shannan, Shannen,* and *Shanon.*

Shea (SHAY) Meaning "courteous." Is also spelled *Shae, Shai, Shayan, Shaye,* and *Shey.*

Sloan (SLOWN) Means "warrior" and is sometimes spelled *Sloane.*

Sweeney (SWEE-nee) Meaning "small hero." One variation is *Sweeny.*

Tady (TAY-dee) Means "poet" and is the Irish version of Timothy.

Thomas (to-MAS)   A Greek name meaning "twin." St. Thomas was one of the Apostles. Actors Tom Selleck and Tom Cruise have brought fame and fortune to this name. Short forms are *Tom* and *Tommy*. Other variations are *Tomas*, *Tomasz*, *Tome*, *Tomie*, and *Tomy*.

Tiernan (Teer-nan)   Meaning "lord."

Torin (TOR-in)   Meaning "chief." Variations include *Thorfin* and *Thorstein*.

Tormey (TORM-ee)   Meaning "thunder spirit."

Troy (TROY)   Meaning "foot soldier." The name was made popular by actor Troy Donahue.

Tynan (TY-nin)   Meaning "dark." A popular nickname is *Ty*.

Tyrone (TIE-rone)   Meaning "from Tyrone," a county in Northern Ireland.

Uaine (OO-ahn)   See Owen.

Uilliam (OOL-yam)   Variant of William. Also *Uileog*, *Uilleam*, and *Ulick*.

Uinseann (OON-shan)   Meaning "conquering" and is another version of Vincent.

Uistean (OO-stayn)   Meaning "intelligent." It is also spelled *Uisdean*.

William (WILL-yam)   A name of German origin meaning "determined defense." William Butler Yeats is probably Ireland's most highly regarded poet.

IRELAND: GIRLS

Adelaide (AH-del-ayd)   Of English origin, means "noble" or "kind."

Ailis (AY-lis)   See Adelaide.

Aine (EN-ya)   Meaning "brightness." Although once used as a boys name, in mythology Aine was the goddess of love and fertility. A variation is *Enya*.

Aisling (AY-sling)   Meaning "vision," is not common as a name, but would be appropriate for a girl who will grow to be a beautiful woman.

Alana (ah-LAHN-ah)   A name that means "attractive; peaceful." Among notable people with this name is women's professional basketball player Aileen Pippin. Alternate forms are *Ali* and *Allena*.

Arlene (ar-LEEN)   Meaning "pledge." This is a feminine form of Arlen. Actresses Arlene Dahl and Arlene Francis have brought fame to this name. Variations include *Aria*, *Arlana*, *Arleen*, *Arleigh*, *Arlen*, *Arlena*, *Arlenis*, *Arlette*, and *Arleyne*.

Artis (AR-tis)   A name that means "noble" or "towering hill."

Barrie (BAR-ree)   Meaning "lance; markswoman." It is a feminine form of Barry. Also seen as *Bari* and *Barri*.

Bedelia (beh-DEEL-ya)   An alternate form of Bridget. Variations include *Bedeelia*, *Biddie*, *Biddy*, and *Bidelia*.

Berget (BUR-jet)   An alternate form of Bridget. Variations include *Bergette*, *Bergit*, *Birgit*, *Birgita*, and *Birgitta*.

Blaine (BLAYN)   Meaning "thin." Socialite Blaine Trump lives up to this name. Other forms are *Blane* and *Blayne*.

Breck (BREHK)   Meaning "freckled."

Breena (BREE-nah)   Meaning "fairy palace." Also *Breina*, *Brena*, and *Brina*.

Brenda (BREHN-dah)   Meaning "little raven." This name was made famous by singer Brenda Lee. Alternate forms include *Breanda*, *Bre-Anna*, *Breauna*, *Breawna*, *Breeana*, *Breeanna*, *Breiana*, *Breiann*, and *Brenna*.

Briana (bree-ANN-ah)   A name that means "strong, virtuous, and honorable" and is a feminine form of Brian. Also *Brianna*, *Brana*, *Breana*, *Breann*, *Bria*, *Briah*, *Briahna*, *Brianne*, *Breanda*, *Bre-Anna*, *Breaun*, *Breawna*, *Breeana*, *Breeanna*, *Breiana*, *Breiann*, *Bryanne*, *Bryn*, *Brynn*, *Breona*, *Brione*, *Brionna*, and *Brionne*.

Bridget (BRID-jet) or **Brigid** (BRI-jed)   A name that means "strong." A very popular name in Ireland due in part to the Irish saint by this name. Recently made famous by actress Bridget

Fonda. Also *Beret, Berget, Biddy, Birgitte, Bride, Bridey, Bridgete, Bridgett, Bridgitte, Briggitte,* and *Brigitt.*

Caitlin (KAYT-lin) An alternate form of Cathleen, which means "pure." Actress Caitlin Mowrey has brought this name to prominence, as has modern dancer Caitlyn Corbettt and country singer Caitlin Hanford. This name is also seen as *Caitlyn, Caeley, Calley, Katelin, Caitlynn, Caitlynne, Catlyn, Catlynne, Kaitlyn, Kaitlan, Kaitland, Kaitleen, Kaitlen, Kaitlinn,* and *Kalyn.*

Cara (KAH-rah) Meaning "friend" and "beloved" in Latin, has been made famous by Olympic medalist Cara Dunne. Alternate forms are *Caralea, Caralee, Caralisa, Carita, Kara,* and *Karry.*

Cassidy (KAS-i-dee) A name which means "clever." Also *Casadee, Casadi, Casadie, Casie, Cass, Cassadi, Cassadie, Cassadina,* and *Cassady.*

Catherine (KA-thur-inn) Meaning "without tarnish" in Latin and Greek. Variations include *Catharin, Cathrene, Cathrine, Carhryn, Katherine, Kathie, Kathy,* and *Kathryn; Catriona* in Gaelic; *Catarina* in Italian and Portuguese; *Caterina* in Spanish; *Trina* and *Trinette* in French; *Trinchen* in German; *Katushka, Kotinka,* and *Kitti* in Russian.

Cathleen (kath-LEEN) A variant of Kathleen. See Catherine. Actress Cathleen O'Donnell brings distinction to this name.

Ciana (KE-an-a) Meaning "stormy," or "roughness," it is the female version of Cain.

Ciara, Cierra (KEER-ah) Meaning "black." This name has been made famous by actress Ciara Hunter. Also *Ceara, Cearra, Ciaara, Ciarra, Ciarrah, Cieara, Ciearra, Ciera, Cierrah,* and *Sierra.*

Cinnie (KIN-nee) Meaning "beauty."

Clare (KLAIR) A name that means "clear" and brings to mind U.S. congresswoman and author Clare Booth Luce.

Clodagh (KLA-dah) The name of a river in county Tipperary. Clodagh Rodgers is a famous singer from Ballymena, Northern Ireland.

Colleen (kahl-EEN) Meaning "girl" or "unmarried woman." Colleen Pinter, star of the TV drama *Another World* brings fame to this name. Also *Coe, Coel, Cole, Coleen, Colene, Coley, Coline, Colleene, Collen, Collene, Collie, Colline,* and *Colly.*

Cordelia (cor-DEEL-yah) Meaning "jewel of the sea," it is the name of the only loyal and loving daughter of Shakespeare's *King Lear.*

Corrie (KOR-ee) Meaning "the hollow." Among the notable people with this name: Corrie ten Boom, a World War II heroine who saved several Jewish people by hiding them. Alternate forms are *Corey, Cori, Coriann, Cori-Ann, Corianne, Corri, CorrieAnn,* and *Corrie-Anne.*

Cristen, Cristin (KRIS-tin) Meaning "Christian." Other forms are *Christen, Christin Cristan, Cristyn, Crystan, Crysten, Crystin, Crystyn,* and *Kristin.*

Dallas (DAL-lis) A name that means "wise." Also seen as *Dalishya, Dalisia, Dalissia, Dallys, Dalyce,* and *Dalys.*

Darby (DAR-bee) Meaning "free."

Darci, Darcy (DAR-cee) Meaning "dark."

Daron (DAHR-un) Meaning "great," it is a feminine form of Darren. Variations include *Daronica, Daronice,* and *Daryn.*

Deirdre (DEER-drah) A name that means "sorrowful" or "wanderer." Deirdre is the heroine of an old Irish folk tale. Alternate forms are *Dedra, Deerdra, Deidra, Deidre, Deirdree, Didi,* and *Dierdre.*

Delaney (deh-LAYN-ee) Meaning "descendant of the challenger," it is most often a surname.

Derry (DEHR-ree) Meaning "redhead." Other versions are *Deri* and *Derie.*

Devin (DEH-vun) Meaning "poet." Variations include *Devon, Devan, Devane, Devanie, Devany,* and *Deven.*

Duana (DWAH-nah) Meaning "song."

Earlene (ur-LEEN) A name that means "pledge."

Eda (EE-dah) Meaning "rich." A short form of Edana and Edith.

Edana (eh-DAN-nah) Meaning "ardent" or "flame." Other forms include *Eda, Edan, Edanna*, and *Aydanna*.

Eileen (i-LEEN) Variant of Helen. This name means "sunlight" and is made famous by actresses Eileen Brennan, Eileen Heckart, and author Eileen Shanahan. Variations are *Aileen, Eilean, Eilena, Eiley, Eilidh, Eilleen, Eillen, Eilyn, Ellene, Illeane, Ileen, Illine*, and *Illyne*.

Eilis (I-lis) The Irish equivalent of *Elizabeth*, meaning "God is satisfied." Also, *Isabel* in Spanish.

Eithne (ITH-nah) Meaning "kernel." Also spelled *Ethna* or *Etney*.

Emer (EE-mer) In Celtic folklore, Emer possessed the six gifts of womanhood: beauty, voice, sweet speech, needlework, wisdom, and chastity.

Ena (EE-nah) A form of the name Helen.

Erin (EH-rin) Meaning "peace," it is another name for Ireland. It's been made famous by figure skater Erin Pearl. Other versions are *Arin, Eran, Eren, Erena, Ereni, Eri, Erian, Erina, Erine, Erinn, Erinna, Erinne, Eryn*, and *Erynn*.

Etain (eh-TAYN) Which means "shining." In Celtic mythology, the name of "the most beautiful, fairest, and gentlest woman in Ireland."

Ethne (ETH-nah) A name that means "little fire." Variations include *Enea* and *Ethnee*.

Fallon (FAL-lun) Meaning "grandchild of the ruler," it is usually seen as a last name. Variations include *Falan, Falen, Falin, Fallan, Fallonne, Fallyn, Falyn*, and *Falynn*.

Feenat (FEE-nat) Meaning "deer."

Finola (fee-NO-la) Derived from *Fionnuala* in Gaelic, meaning "fair-shouldered," this name was very popular in the medieval period. Variations include *Finvola, Nuala*, and also the Scottish *Fenella*.

Fiona (fee-O-nah) Meaning "fair; pale," it is now famous thanks to singer/songwriter Fiona Apple. The name is also found as *Fionna*.

Glenna (GLEN-nah) Meaning "valley; glen." A feminine form of Glenn. Also *Glenda, Glenetta, Glenina, Glenine*, and *Glenn*.

Glynis (GLIN-nis) Meaning "valley." Among the notable people with this name is actress Glynis Johns.

Ide (IDE) Meaning "thirst" and is also spelled *Ida* or *Ita*.

Ina (I-nah) A form of the name Agnes. A few variations are *Ena, Ianna*, and *Inanne*.

Jilleen (jil-LEEN) Variant of Jillian meaning "pure babe." Also *Jileen, Jilene, Jillene*, and *Jillenne*.

Juliane (JUL-ee-in) Meaning "youthful." Celebrities with this name include actresses Gillian Anderson and Julianne Moore. Other versions are *Jill, Jillian, Gill*, and *Gillian*.

Kathleen (kath-LEEN) Meaning "chaste" in Greek. Among the notable people with this name: author Kathleen O'Meara, actress Kathleen Turner. Often shortened to *Kate* or *Kathy*. Variations include *Katheleen, Kathelene, Kathileen*, and *Kathlyn*. Also *Cait, Cateline*, and *Catherine* in French; *Katia* in Russian.

Keara (KEER-ah) Meaning "dark, black." An alternate form is *Kieran*.

Keena (KEE-nah) A name that means "brave." It is also spelled *Keenya* and *Kina*.

Kelly (KEHL-lee) Meaning "brave warrior." Variations include *Kealee, Kealey, Keali, Kealle, Keallie, Keally, Kealyn, Keela, Keeleigh, Keeleigh, Keeley, Keeli, Keelie, Keely, Keli, Kelia, Kelley, Kelli, Kellia, Kelliann, Kellianne*, and *Kellie*.

Kellyn (KEHL-lin) is a combination of Kelly and Lyn. Other versions are *Kelleen, Kellen, Kellene, Kellina, Kelline, Kellynn*, and *Kellynne*.

Kerry (KEHR-ree) Meaning "dark-haired." It is the name of one of the most beautiful counties in Ireland. Variations include the Irish, *Ciarrai*, as well as *Keree, Kerey, Keri, Keriann, Kerianne, Kerri, Kerriann, Kerrianne, Kerrie*, and *Kierra*.

Kevyn (KEV-un)   A name that means "beautiful," it is a feminine form of Kevin. Also *Keva, Kevan, Kevone, Kevonna,* and *Kevynn.*

Kiara (KEER-ah)   Meaning "little and dark," it is a feminine form of Kieran. Also spelled *Kera.*

Kiley (KY-lee)   Meaning "attractive" or "from the straits." Also spelled *Kilee, Kilie, Kyla, Kylea, Kyleah, Kylee, Kyleigh, Kylen, Kylene, Kyli, Kylie,* and *Kylyn.*

Lara (LAH-rah)   Meaning "laurel," it is the Irish version of the Latin name Laura. One variation is *Loretta,* which is also popular in Ireland.

Lasairiona (lah-sa-REE-nah)   Meaning "flame wine." Another version is *Lassarina.*

Mackenzie (ma-KEN-zee)   Meaning "daughter of the wise leader." Generally a surname. Actress Mackenzie Phillips is the daughter of Michelle and John Phillips of The Mamas and the Papas. Variations are *Macenzie, Mackensi, Mackensie, Mackenzee, Mackenzi, Mackenzy,* and *McKenzie.*

Maeve (MAYV)   Meaning "joyous." Among the notable people with this name are a first-century queen of Ireland and author Maeve Binchy. Other versions are *Maevi, Maevy, Maive, Mave,* and *Mayve.*

Maire (MAI-ree)   Meaning "bitterness" or "sorrow," Maire or *Muire,* the form used in early Ireland, was a name so holy that it was not given as a child's name until the end of the fifth century. Today, the name refers to the mother of Jesus and variations are commonly used, such as *Mair, Mairi, Mairia, Mairiam, Maisie, Maisre, Mamie, Mara, Mari, Mariam, Marie, Mary, Marya, Maryam, Maura, Maureen, May, Melle, Moira, Molly, Moya,* and *Moyenna.* Also, *Maria* in Latin and *Miriam* in Hebrew.

Mairead (MA-raad)   A name meaning "pearl," it is the Irish version of Margaret. Mairead Corrigan was a Nobel Peace Prize laureate for her work in the Northern Ireland peace process. Variations include *Maggie, Maighread, Margaret, Meg,* and *Muiread.* Also *Marguerite* in French and *Margaron* in Greek.

Mare (MARE)   An alternate form of Mary, meaning "sorrow." Actress Mare Winningham is also a folk singer of some reknown. Also *Mair, Maira, Maire, Mairi,* and *Mairim.*

Maura (MAWR-ah)   Another alternate form of Mary, meaning "bitterness; sorrow." It's been made famous by actress Maura Tiern. Variations include *Maure* and *Maurette* in French; *Mauricette* and *Maurita* in Spanish; and *Maurigia* in Italian.

Maureen (MAWR-een)   From the Gaelic *Moirin,* which means "little Mary." Variations include *Maurene, Maurine,* and *Moirin.*

Mavelle (MAY-vel)   Means "songbird" and has the nickname *Mavie.*

Mavis (MA-vis)   Meaning "my little darling." Variations include *Mavourna* and *Mavoureen.* Also, *Mavis* in French.

Meagan (MEHG-un)   Meaning "pearl." This name has been brought to prominence by Meagan Ward of the television series *Melrose Place.* It is a very popular girl's name in the United States. Variations are *Maegan, Maeghan, Meagain, Meagann, Meagen, Meagin, Maegan,* and *Meaghan.* Often shortened to *Meg.* Also *Margaron* in Greek.

Meara (MEER-ah)   Meaning "jolly." Generally a surname, as in Anne Meara but may also be a variation of Mary or of Mara, meaning "sea."

Melvina (mehl-VEEN-ah)   "Armored chief." A feminine form of Melvin. A few variations are *Melevine, Melva, Melveen, Melvena,* and *Melvene.*

Meriel (MEHR-ee-el)   Meaning "shining sea."

Moira (MOYR-ah)   Meaning "great." Two women who lived up to their name are author Moira O'Neill and talented dancer and actress Moira Shearer. Variations of the name are *Maura, Moirae, Moirah, Moire, Moya, Moyra,* and *Moyrah.*

Molly (MAHL-lee)   A familiar form of Mary, meaning "bitterness; sorrow." Famous people with this name include the legendary subject of the traditional song "Molly Malone," Molly Bloom of James Joyce's *Ulysses*, actress Molly Ringwald, and writer Molly Ivins. Also written *Moll, Mollee, Molley, Molli,* and *Mollie.*

Mona (MONA)   Meaning "noble." Also, *Maimona* in Arabic, *Mona* in Italian, *Monica* in Latin and Greek, and *Monique* in French.

Myrna (MUR-nah)   Meaning "beloved," it brings to mind actress Myrna Loy. Variations are *Merna, Mirna, Morna,* and *Muirna.*

Neila (NEEL-ah)   Meaning "champion," it is a feminine form of Neil and Niall. Also *Nayela, Naylea, Naylia, Neala, Nealee, Nealie, Nealy, Neela, Neeli, Neelie, Neely, Neile, Neilla, Neille,* and *Nilda.*

Nevina (ne-VEEN-ah)   Meaning "worshiper of the saint" or "holy." It is a feminine form of Nevin. Also written *Nevena* and *Nivena.*

Nia (NEE-ah)   A familiar form of Neila, meaning "female champion." One famous person with this name is singer/actress Nia Peeples. The name might also be spelled *Niah, Nya,* and *Nyah.*

Noni (NO-nee)   A pet name for Nora, meaning "honorable." Also spelled *Nonie.*

Nora (NOR-ah)   Meaning "honor." Variations include *Eleanor, Norah,* and *Noreen.* Also *Honorah* in Latin and *Sarah* in Hebrew.

Nuala (noo-WAL-ah)   A short form of Fionnula, which means "fair shoulder" and is also written *Nola* and *Nula.* Nuala Ní Dhomhnaill and Nuala O'Faolain are two famous Irish writers.

Oibhe (EE-vah)   Meaning "olive."

Oona (OU-nah)   An ancient Irish name meaning "unity." Famous women with this name are Oona O'Neil, daughter of Eugene O'Neil, and Oona Chaplin wife of Charlie Chaplin. Other versions are *Ona, Onna, Onnie, Oonagh, Oonie,* or *Una.*

Orla (OR-lah)   Meaning "golden lady." It may also be spelled *Orfhlaith* or *Orlaith.*

Patricia (pah-TRISH-ah)   A name that means "noble." Among the celebrated people

with this name are actresses Patricia Neal and Patricia Arquette as well as mystery writer Patricia Cornwell. Variations include *Padraign, Padrigin* (PAW-drig-een), and *Payton.* Familiar forms include *Paddy, Paiti, Pat, Patsy, Pattie, Patty,* and *Trish.*

Pegeen (peh-GEEN)   Meaning "a pearl," it is a familiar form of Margaret. Also spelled *Paigin.* Radio broadcaster Pegeen Fitzgerald has brought this name to prominence. *Maggy, Peggy,* and *Peg* are other familiar forms of either name.

Piala (PEE-a-la)   Meaning "prudence."

Ranait (rah-NAYT)   Meaning "graceful" or "prosperous." Variations include *Ronit* and *Renny.*

Reganne (RAY-gin)   A name that means "little ruler," it is a feminine form of Reagan. Other versions are *Reagan, Regan,* and *Regin.*

Riana (ri-AN-nah)   A short form of Briana. Also seen as *Reana, Reanna,* and *Rianna.*

Riley (RY-lee)   Meaning "valiant." Variations are *Rileigh* and *Rilie.*

Riona (ri-O-nah)   A name that means "like a queen." Also spelled *Rionach.*

Rori (RO-ree)   Meaning "red-headed ruler" is the feminine form of Rory. A variation is *Ruari* (ROO-ir-ee).

Rowena (ro-WEE-nah)   Meaning "white mane."

Ryanne (RY-an)   A name that means "little ruler," it is a feminine form of Ryan. Variations include *Raiann, Rhyann, Riana, Riane, Ryana, Ryann,* and *Ryanna.*

Sass (SAS)   Meaning "saxon." Also spelled *Sassie, Sassoon, Sassy.*

Seana (SHAW-nah)   Meaning "wise," it is a form of Jane. Among the notable people with this name is actress Seana McKenna. Other versions are *Seandra, Seane, Seanette, Seann,* and *Seanna.*

Shanley (SHAN-lee)   An uncommon but traditional name meaning "hero's daughter." Also seen as *Shanlee, Shanleigh, Shanlie,* and *Shanly.*

Shanna (SHA-nah)   An alternate form of *Shana* or *Shannon* (meaning "wise; old one") made famous by television journalist Shana Alexander. Other versions are *Shanea, Shannagh, Shannah, Shannan,* and *Shannea.*

Shannon (SHA-nun)   Meaning "small and wise" or "the old one," it is a form of Joan. Among the notable people with this name are gymnast Shannon Miller, astronaut Shannon Lucid, and actress Shannon Dougherty. Also *Shanan, Shann, Shanna, Shannan, Shannen, Shannie, Shannin, Shannon,* and *Shannyn. Shona* in Scottish.

Shea (SHAY)   Meaning "fairy palace." Most often a surname, it is seen in many other versions including *Shae, Shaela, Shaelee, Shaeleen, Shaeline, Shay, Shaylie, Shealy, Shealyn, Sheana, Sheann, Sheanna,* and *Sheannon.*

Sheena (SHEE-nah)   A feminine form of John, meaning "God's gracious gift," and an anglicised form of the Gaelic name Sine, a version of Jane or Jeanne. Sheena was made famous by rock singer Sheena Easton. Other versions are *Shena, Shenada, Shenae, Shenay, Shenda, Shene, Shenea, Sheneda,* and *Shenee.*

Sheila (SHEE-lah)   Meaning "girl" or "young woman," it is derived from the Latin Cecilia, the patron saint of music. Variations include *Sheela, Sheelagh,* and *Sile.* Also *Shelah* in Hebrew.

Shona (SHO-nah)   A form of Jane, meaning "God's gracious gift." Alternate forms include *Shana, Shauna, Shawna, Shonagh, Shonah, Shonalee, Shonda, Shone, Shonee,* and *Shonelle.*

Sinead (shi-NAY-ad)   The Irish form of Jane or Janet, meaning "God's gracious gift," it has been made famous by singer Sinead O'Connor and actress Sinead Cusack. Variations are *Sine, Sinéad,* and *Shaynee,* a nickname. *Seonaid* in Scotland.

Siobhan (shi-VAWN)   An Irish form of Joan, meaning "God's gracious gift," or Susan, meaning "lily," it is one of the most popular of Gaelic names. Among the notable people with this name are actresses Siobhan McKenna and Siobhan Fahey. Other versions are *Shibahn, Shibani, Shibhan, Shioban, Shobana, Shobha, Shobhana, Siobahn,* and *Siobhana.*

Sloane (SLOWN)   Meaning "fighter" is also spelled *Sloan.*

Sorcha (SOR-ha)   A traditional Gaelic name meaning "radiant" or "bright" it is the equivalent of the Hebrew *Sarah,* meaning "princess."

Tara (TAR-rah)   The name of the ancient seat of the High King of Ireland. There are many variations including *Taran, Tareen, Tareena, Taren, Tarene, Tari, Taria, Tarila, Tarilyn, Tarin, Tarina, Taris, Tarisa, Tarise, Tarra, Tarrah,* and *Tarren.* Also *Tarika* in Africa and *Tara* in Sanskrit, meaning "star."

Tipper (TIP-pur)   Meaning "water pourer," this name has been made famous by Tipper Gore, the wife of the U.S. vice president Al Gore.

Treasa (TREE-sah) or (TRAS-ah)   A name meaning "strength" and an Irish form of *Teresa.* It is sometimes seen as *Treise* and shortened to *Trea* (TREE-a), *Teezy, Teri, Terry,* and *Tre.*

Trevina (tri-VEEN-ah)   Meaning "prudent."

Troya (TROY-ah)   Meaning "foot soldier." Variations are *Troi, Troia,* and *Troiana.*

Tullia (TOOL-yah)   A name that means "peaceful; quiet." Other versions are *Tulia* and *Tulliah.*

Ula (OO-la)   A Celtic name meaning "altar." Variations of this name include *Yula,* and in French, *Ulla.*

Una (OO-na)   An Irish name meaning "lamb." Variations of this name include *Orsa, Orsola, Ursa, Ursala, Ursel, Ursina, Ursine, Ursola, Ursule, Ursulina, Ursuline,* and *Ursy.*

Welsh names, many of them taken from Arthurian legend, represent a longstanding pride in the battle of that legendary native Briton, and thousands of real ones, against the invading Angles and Saxons. Some names are also taken from place names in Wales.

WALES: BOYS

Aneurin (an-YUR-in) Meaning "honorable" or "gold." Famous people with this name include the fourth-century Welsh poet. Variations include *Aneirin* and *Nye*.

Arvel (AR-vel) This name means "wept over." A variation is *Arfel*.

Bevan (BEV-an) A name that means "son of Evan." A variations is *Befan*.

Bowen (BOW-en) Meaning "son of Owen." Variations include *Bow*, *Bowe*, and *Bowie*.

Brice (BRICE) Meaning "alert" or "ambitious."

Bryce (BRICE) An alternate form of Brice. Variations include *Brycen*, *Bryceton*, *Bryson*, and *Bryston*.

Caddock (KAD-ok) Meaning "eager for war." A variation is *Cadoc*.

Cai (KAI) A form of the Latin Gaius, meaning "to rejoice." Variations include *Caio*, *Caius*, and *Caw*.

Calder (KAL-dur) This name means "book" or "stream."

Cerdic (KER-dik) Meaning "beloved." Variations include *Caradoc*, *Caradog*, *Ceredig*, and *Ceretic*.

Colwyn (KOHL-win) The name of a river in Wales. Variations include *Colwin* and *Colwinn*.

Cynan (KAI-nan) Meaning "chief." Notable people with this name include the 20th-century author Cynan.

Dafydd (DAV-ith [the "th" has the sound of the "th" in "then"]) From the Hebrew David, which means "beloved." Historical people with this name include the late medieval poet Dafydd ap Gwilym.

Davis (DAY-vis) A name that means "son of David."

Dewi (DEOO-wee) Meaning "prized." Notable people with this name include Dewi Sant (St. David), patron saint of Wales. Variations include *Dew*, *Dewey*, and *Dewie*.

Dilwyn (DILL-win) Meaning "shady place." A variation is *Dillwyn*.

Dylan (DILL-ann) Meaning "the sea." Among famous people with this name include the poet Dylan Thomas. Variations include *Dillon*, *Dyllan*, *Dyllon*, and *Dylon*.

Emlyn (EMM-lin) See Emery under German names. Variations include *Emelen*, *Emlen*, and *Emlin*.

Evan (EV-an) A form of John, meaning "God's gracious gift." Variations include *Ifan*, *Iwan*, *Ioan*, and *Ieuan*.

Gareth (GAR-eth) Meaning "gentle." Notable people with this name include the eponymous knight in Tennyson's poem *Gareth and Lynette*. Variations include *Gar*, *Garith*, *Garreth*, *Garth*, and *Garyth*.

Garnock (GAR-nok) This name means "dweller by the alder river."

Gavin (GAV-inn) Meaning "white hawk." Notable people with this name include the novelist Gavin Maxwell. Variations include *Gav*, *Gavan*, *Gaven*, *Gavinn*, *Gavyn*, *Gavynn*, and *Gawain*.

Gawain (GA-wayne) A form of Gavin. Variations include *Gawaine*, *Gawayn*, *Gawayne*, *Gawen*, and *Gwayne*.

Gerwin (GERR-win) A name the means "fair love."

Gethin (GEH-thin) Meaning "dusky." Variations include *Geth* and *Gethyn*.

Glendower (glen-DOW-er) Meaning "water valley" Notable people with this name include Owen Glendower (Owain Glyndwr), Prince of Wales and English patriot.

Glyn (GLIN) A form of Glendower. A variation is *Glin*.

Gower (GOW-ur) Meaning "pure." Among well-known people with this name is the choreographer Gower Champion.

Griffith (GRIFF-ith) Meaning "fierce chief." Variations include *Gruffudd*, *Griff*, *Griffie*, *Griffy*, and *Gryphon*.

Gwilym (GWIL-im) See Wilhelm under German names. A variation is *Gwillym*.

Howell (HOW-el) A name that means "remarkable." Variations include *Howel* and *Hywel*.

Idris (ID-riss) Meaning "eager lord." Variations include *Idriss* and *Iddys*.

Iolo (YO-low) This name means "the Lord is worthy." Among renowned people with this name is Iolo Morgannwg, an 18th-century Welsh poet. A variation is *Iorwerth*.

Ithel (ITH-el) A name that signifies "generous lord."

Kai (KAI) Meaning "keeper of the keys." A variation is *Cai*.

Kane (KAYN) This name means "beautiful."

Kent (KENT) A name that means "white" or "bright." Notable people with this name include Medieval Welsh poet Sion Cent. A variation is *Cent*.

Llewellyn (luh-WELL-in) Meaning "lion-like." Variations include *Lewis*, *Llewelin*, *Llewellen*, *Llewelleyn*, *Llewellin*, *Llywellyn*, and *Llywelyn*.

Lloyd (LOID) A name that means "gray haired" or "holy." Famous Lloyds include actors Lloyd Bridges and Lloyd Nolan. Variations include *Loy*, *Loyd*, *Loyde*, and *Loydie*.

Maddock (MAD-ok) Meaning "generous." Notable people with this name include Madoc ap Gruffudd, legendary medieval explorer of America. Variations include *Madoc*, *Madock*, and *Madog*.

Malvern (MAL-vern) Which means "bare hill." A variation is *Malverne*.

Meredith (me-RED-ith) This name means "guardian of the sea." Among renowned people with this name is *Music Man* composer Meredith Wilson. Variations include *Meredyth*, *Merideth*, *Meridith*, and *Meredydd*.

Merion (MEH-ree-on) A name signifying "from Merioneth, Wales." Variations include *Meirion* and *Merrion*.

Meurig (MYUR-ig) A form of Maurice which means "moor" or "dark-skinned."

Newlyn (NEW-lin) Meaning "new lake." A variation is *Newlin*.

Parry (PEAR-ee) A name that means "son of Harry." Variations include *Parrey*, *Parrie*, and *Pary*.

Price (PRYS) Meaning "son of the ardent one." A variation is *Prys*.

Reece (REES) Meaning "zealous." Variations include *Reese*, *Reice*, and *Rice*.

Rhys (REES) Welsh form of Reece. Among well-known people with this name is the actor Rhys Williams. Variations include *Rhett* and *Rice*.

Romney (ROHM-nee) This name means "winding river." A variation is *Romoney*.

Taliesin (tal-YES-in) Meaning "radiant brow." Notable people with this name include Taliesin, the fourth-century Welsh poet. Variations include *Tallas* and *Tallis*.

Tarrant (TEAR-ahnt) Meaning "thunder." A variation is *Terrant*.

Trahern (TRA-hern) This name has the meaning "strong as iron."

Tristan (TRIST-ann) Which means "bold." This is the name of a legendary knight whose story of love for Isolde, his uncle's wife, has been told in poetry by Tennyson and in an opera of Wagner. Variations include *Trestan, Treston, Tris, Trisan, Tristano, Tristen, Tristian, Tristin,* and *Trystan.*

Tudor (TIW-door) A form of Theodore, which means "gift of God." This is the name of an English dynasty from Wales. Variations include *Todo* and *Tiwdor.*

Vaughn (VOHN) This name signifies "small." Among those who share this name are composer Ralph Vaughn Williams and bandleader Vaughn Monroe. Variations include *Vaughan, Vaughen, Vaun, Von,* and *Voughn.*

Wyn (WIN) Meaning "fair" or "white."

Yestin (YES-tin) A name that means "just."

WALES: GIRLS

Angharad (ahng-HAR-ahd) Meaning "greatly beloved." One well-known person with this name is Angharad Tomos, author of Welsh children's books.

Blodwyn (BLOD-win) This name has the meaning "flower." Variations include *Blodwen, Blodwynne, Blodyn,* and *Wynne.*

Bronwyn (BRON-win) Meaning "white breasted." Variations include *Bron, Bronia, Bronney, Bronnie, Bronny, Bronwen, Bronwin,* and *Bronwynn.*

Cari (KER-ee) Alternate forms of Carolyn, meaning "little and womanly."

Caron (KAR-on) Meaning "loving," "kind-hearted," or "charitable." Variations include *Carron* and *Carrone.*

Carys (KER-iss) A name that means "love." Variations include *Caris, Caryse, Ceris,* and *Cerys.*

Deryn (DER-inn) Meaning "bird." Variations include *Derren, Derrin, Derrine,* and *Deryne.*

Dilys (DILL-iss) This name means "perfect" or "true."

Enid (ENN-id) Meaning "soul." Notable people with this name include the novelist Enid Bagnold and the former congresswoman Enid Waldholtz.

Glenda (GLEN-da) Meaning "of the glen." Among celebrities with this name is the actor Glenda Jackson. Variations include *Glanda, Glennda,* and *Glynda.*

Glynis (GLIN-iss) Which has the meaning "glen." Notable people with this name include the actress Glynis Johns. Variations include *Glenice, Glenis, Glenise, Glenyse, Glennis,* and *Glennys.*

Guinevere (gwen-EH-veer) This name means "white" or "soft." Guinevere was the wife of King Arthur of the legendary Round Table. Variations include *Gayna, Generva, Genevieve, Genevra, Genn, Ginetta, Guenevere, Gwen, Jennifer, Winifred,* and *Wynne.*

Gwendolyn (gwen-DOH-lin) Meaning "fair ring." In the Aurthurian legend, Gwendolyn is the wife of Merlin the magician. A variation is *Gwyn.*

Gwyneth (GWIN-eth) An alternate form of Gwendolyn. A popular Gwyneth today is actor Gwyneth Paltrow. Variations include *Gweneth, Gwennyth, Gwenyth, Gwyn, Winnie,* and *Wynne.*

Isolde (ih-SOUL-deh) A name that signifies "fair lady." This is the name of the heroine in the medieval romance Tristan and Isolde. Variations include *Isolda, Isolt,* and *Yseult.*

Jennifer (JEN-i-fer) An alternate form of Guinevere, which means "white wave" or "white phantom." Famous actresses who share this name include Jennifer Jones, Jennifer Love Hewitt, Jennifer Aniston. Variations include *Gennifer, Ginnifer, Jen, Jenefer, Jenifer, Jeniffer, Jenipher,* and *Jenna.*

Lowri (LOW-ree) This name has the meaning "crown of laurels."

Megan (MEG-ann) The Welsh form of Margaret, which means "pearl." Variations include *Meeghan, Meehan, Megha, Meghana, Meghann, Meghean, Meghen, Mehgan,* and *Mehgen.*

Meredith (meh-RED-ith) Meaning "protector of the sea." Notable people with this name include the singer/songwriter Meredith Brooks. Variations include *Meredithe, Meredy, Meredyth, Meredythe, Merideth, Meridith, Merridith,* and *Merry.*

Morgan (MORE-gan) Meaning "great" or "bright." In Welsh folklore, Morgan Le Fay was the evil half-sister of King Arthur. Variations include *Morgana, Morgane, Morganette, Morganica,* and *Morgann.*

Myfanwy (muh-VAHN-wee) This name means "my fine one." "Myfanwy" is a popular romantic Welsh song.

Olwen (OHL-wen) Meaning "white footprint." Variations include *Olwenn, Olwin, Olwyn,* and *Olwyne.*

Rhiannon (rhee-ANN-on) A name that signifies "pure," a good sorceress in *The Mabinogion,* a Welsh legend.

Rhianwen (rhee-ANN-wen) This name means "fair maiden."

Rowena (roh-WAY-na) Meaning "fair-haired and slender."

Siân (SHAHN) A female form of John (Sion). Notable people with this name include Siân Lloyd, British television personality.

Sulwen (SILL-wen) A name that signifies "fair as the sun."

Wendy (WHEN-dee) A familiar form of Gwendolyn and Wanda. Suggesting "white" or "light skinned." Among notable people with this name is Pulitzer Prize–winning playwright Wendy Wasserstein. Variations include *Wenda, Wende, Wendee,* and *Wendi.*

Wynne (WIN) A short form of Blodwyn, Guinivere, and Gwyneth. Variations include *Winnie, Wyn,* and *Wynn.*

Finland

Long ruled by foreign powers, including Sweden and the pre-revolutionary Russian Empire, Finland finally declared independence in 1917. During World War II, Finland fought the USSR twice and then the Germans toward the end of the war. In the following half-century, the Finns made a remarkable transformation from a farm/forest economy to a diversified modern industrial economy. Finnish, like Estonian and Hungarian, is an Asiatic-derived language completely unrelated to the other Scandinavian tongues. Many names in Finland are borrowed from Scandinavian, Germanic, and even English sources, such as Johan, Ole, Claes, and Eugen; others are uniquely Finnish in nature, such as with Paavo, Pekka, Esko, or Risto. Famous Finns include the design innovators Alvar Aalto and Eero Saarinen, the film director Renny Harlin, and the composer Jean Sibelius.

FINLAND: BOYS

Antti (ON-tee) This name signifies "virile."

Arto (Arrr-toh) From the Irish for "noble" or "bear."

Frans (FRANS) A form of the Latin Francis, which means "a free man."

Hannes (HAN-nes) A form of John, which means "God is gracious."

Janne (YAN-nay) A form of John, meaning "God is gracious." Variations include *Jann* and *Jannes*.

Joosef (YO-sef) A form of Joseph, which means "he will increase."

Juhana (YOU-hanna) A form of John, which means "God is gracious." Variations include *Juha* and *Juho*.

Juho (YOU-ho) A form of John. Notable men with this name include Finnish statesman, Juho Paasikivi.

Jussi (YOU-see) A form of John, meaning "God is gracious." The operatic tenor Jussi Björling is one noteworthy person with this name.

Kalevi (KA-levi) This name means "hero."

Kosti (KOS-tee) From the Norwegian Gustav, which means "staff of the Goths."

Lasse (LA-say) From the Greek Nikolaus, which means "victory of the people." Film director Lasse Hallström is one famous person with this name.

Mikko (ME-ko) From the Hebrew Mikha'el, which means "Who is like God." Variations include *Mikk*, *Mikka*, *Mikkohl*, *Mikkol*, *Miko*, and *Mikol*.

Niilo (NEE-lo) From the Irish Neil, which means "champion."

Paavo (PA-vo) A form of Paul, which means "small." A variation is *Paaveli*.

Riiku (RREE-ku) A form of Richard, which means "rich and powerful."

Risto (REES-to) A short form of Christopher, which means "Christ-bearer."

Taavetti (TAA-ve-tee) From the Hebrew David, which means "beloved." Variations include *Taavi* and *Taavo*.

Taneli (TA-nel-lee) This name means "God is my judge." Also *Tanella*.

Tapani (TA-Pa-nee) A form of Stephen, which means "a crown." Variations include *Tapamn* and *Teppo*.

Tauno (TAU-no) A form of Donald, from the Celtic for "proud ruler."

Timo (TEE-mo) From the Greek Timothy, meaning "to honor God." A variation is *Timlo*.

Yrjo (UUR-ree-o) From the Greek George, which means " a farmer."

FINLAND: GIRLS

Aila (AI-la) From the Greek Helene, which means "a torch."

Ansa (AN-sa) This name has the significance "constant."

Annikki (AN-ni-kee) A form of the Hebrew name Hannah, which means "grace."

Eeva (AY-va) This name signifies "life." Among notable people with this name are authors Eeva Joenpelto and Eeva-Liisa Manner.

Hanna (HAN-na) A form of Hannah, meaning "grace."

Kalle (KA-le) From the Gaelic Carol, meaning "melody" or "song." Variations include *Kaille* and *Kaylle*.

Kyllikki (KUUL-li-kee) A name that signifies "strong woman."

Lilja (LEEL-ya) This name means "lily."

Liisa (LEE-sa) A form of Elizabeth, which means "consecrated to God."

Maija (MAI-ya) From the Hebrew name Mary, meaning "sea of bitterness." Variations include *Maili* and *Maikki*.

Maria (MA-ree-ah) A form of Mary, which means "bitter." Variations include *Mariae*, *Marjatta*, and *Marjie*.

Marjatta (MA-ya-ta) A form of Margaret, which means "pearl."

Mirjam (MEER-yam) A form of the Hebrew Miriam, which means "sea of bitterness."

Meri (MEH-ree) This name signifies "the sea."

Mielikki (MEE-le-kee) Meaning "pleasing."

Valma (VAL-ma) Meaning "loyal defender."

Norway The practice of naming children in Norway is based on a variety of factors. Often parents will use Old Norse names such as Tor or Thor, Kjell (meaning "stone"), or Frøya (the name of a Norse goddess); or they may resort to Norwegian and Germanic versions of biblical names, such as Jan (John), Mari or Maria (Mary), or Ester (Esther). Since the 1960s, many Norwegians have opted for more "modern" or "multicultural" names. For boys, Tommy, Frank, and Kenneth have gained great popularity. Norway has the Navneloven, a "name law" adopted in 1964 that forbids the use of certain names that might be in some way disadvantageous to the child. Famous Norwegians include writers Knut Hamsun, Henrik Ibsen, Sigrid Undset, and Bjornsterne Bjornson; explorer and anthropologist Thor Heyerdahl; painter Edvard Munch; and composer Edvard Grieg.

NORWAY: BOYS

Aksel (AHK-sell) Meaning "father of peace." Author Axel Munthe. A variation is *Absalom*.

Arve (AHR-vah) Meaning "heir" or "inheritor." Popular Norwegians are violinist Arve Tellefsen and the comic actor Arve Oppsahl.

Audun (OW-doon) This name means "deserted" or "desolate."

Balder (BAWL-dehr) This is the name of the Norse god of light, summer, and innocence.

Bjørn (BYOO-rhn) A form of the German Bernard, which means "brave as a bear." Tennis champion Björn Borg is one famous person with this name. A variation is *Bjarne*.

Birger (BEER-gerr) Meaning "rescue." Among renowned people with this name is Birger Ruud, a great ski jumper who represented Norway abroad in many international contests.

Bodil (BOO-dill) This name has the significance "commanding."

Brage (BRAH-guh) Meaning "poet." The name of the god of poetry and music.

Brede (BREH-duh) Meaning "iceberg" or "glacier."

Dag (DAWG) Meaning "day" or "bright." Former U.N. secretary general Dag Hammarskjöld is among notable figures with this name.

Dyre (DEE-ruh) This name means "dear heart." Dyre Vaa was a Norwegian sculptor active in the 20th century who worked in a classical idiom, and used many mythological motifs.

Einar (AY-nahr) A name that means "battle leader."

Erik (EH-ric) An alternate form of Eric, meaning "honorable ruler." Among historical people with this name is explorer Erik the Red. A variation is *Erikson* as a surname.

Eskil (ESS-kyll) Meaning "divine cauldron."

Frode (FROO-duh) Meaning "wise." A popular Norwegian with this name is soccer player Frode Grodås.

Gaute (GOW-tuh) This name means "great."

Georg (GEH-org) A form of George, from the Greek for "farmer." Composer Georg Telemann and conductor Sir Georg Solti are among renowned Georgs.

Gunnar (GUHN-nahr) A name that means "warrior." An alternate form of Gunther. One well-known Gunnar is musician Gunnar Nelson, grandson of Ozzie and Harriet. A variation is *Gunner*.

Gustav (GOOS-tahf) Meaning "staff of the Goths." Among renowned people with this name are Gustavus Adolphus, a king of

Sweden, Austrian composer Gustav Mahler, and French writer Gustave Flaubert.

Håvard (HOEW-ar) Meaning "rock" or "protector." A popular Norwegian with this name is soccer player Håvard Flo. A variation is *Halvard*.

Håkon (HAWK-uhn) Meaning "of Nordic ancestry." Variations include *Haaken* and *Haakon*.

Harald (HAHR-ahl) Meaning "army chief." An alternate form of Harold. Novelist Harald Kidde. Playwright Harold Pinter, Harold Ross, originator of *The New Yorker* magazine, presidential advisor Harold Ickes. Variations include *Harald* and *Harry*.

Hauk (HOWK) This name means "hawk."

Inge (EEN-guh) A short form of Ingmar and Ingvar, which means "Ing's soldier." A variation is *Igor*.

Ivar (EE-vahr) An alternate form of Ivor, from the Latin for "ivory."

Jan (YAHN) Meaning "son of Jan." Variations include surnames *Jansen, Janssen, Janten, Jantzen, Janzen, Jensen,* and *Jenson*.

Jarl (YAHRL) Meaning "earl" or "nobleman."

Josef (YOO-sehf) A form of Joseph, which means "he will increase."

Kjell (CHEHLL) A name that signifies "spring."

Kleng (CLENG) Meaning "claw." Among notable people with this name is Kleng Peerson, who is considered the very first Norwegian immigrant in America.

Knut (KNOOT) An alternate form of Canute, from the Latin for "white-haired." Variations include *Knud* and *Knut*.

Lars (LAHRS) A form of Lawrence, which means "a crown." Variations include *Larsen, Larson, Larsson, Lasse, Lavrans, Laurits,* and *Lorens*.

Leif (LAYF) This name means "beloved."

Matteus (ma-TEH-oos) From the Hebrew Matthew, meaning "God is a gift."

Magnar (MAHG-nahr) Meaning "strength" or "warrior." Variations include *Magne* and *Agnar*. Agnar Mykle was a 20th-century Norwegian author whose work was published internationally; an obscenity trial over his explicit erotic literature only added to his fame.

Mikkel (MYKK-ehl) A form of Michael, which means "Who is like God." *Mikkel Rev*, "Michael the Fox," is the very first children's song most Norwegian kids learn. In Norwegian folk tales, *Mikkel* is a euphemism for the fox. A variation is *Mikkael*.

Morten (MOH-tehn) A form of Martin, which means "warlike." Popular Mortens include Morten Harket the vocalist in the pop group Aha, which achieved international fame in the eighties. A variation is *Mort*.

Nicolai (NICK-oo-lay) A form of Nicholas, which means "victory of the people."

Nils (NEELS) A form of Neil ("champion") and Nelson ("Neil's son").

Odd (AWDD) Meaning "point." Among renowned people with this name are Odd Nerdrum, a Norwegian figurative painter with great international success and Oddvar Norli, socialist prime minister of Norway in the 1970s. A variation is *Oddvar*.

Odin (OO-dynn) Meaning "ruler." The name of the chief Norse god.

Olaf (OO-lahf) Meaning "ancestor." A patron saint and king of Norway. Variations include *Olav, Ole,* and *Olof*.

Olav (OO-lahv) An alternate form of Olaf. Variations include *Ola, Olavus,* and *Ole*.

Oskar (AWS-kahr) Meaning "divine spearman." Notable people with this name include actor Oskar Werner.

Ottar (OOTT-ahr) This name signifies "point warrior" or "fright warrior."

Otto (OOTT-oo) The name of Saint Odo of Cluny.

Øystein (OY-stayn) Meaning "rock of happiness." Øystein Sunde is a popular singer-songwriter who is known in Norway for his funny tunes.

Petter (PEHT-tehr)   A form of Peter, meaning "a rock." Petter Dass, 18th-century churchman and poet, is among historical figures with this name.

Ragnar (RAHG-nahr)   Meaning "powerful army." Among notable people named Ragna is Ragnar Frisch, Nobel prize–winning economist.

Reidar (RAY-dahr)   This name has the significance "nest warrior."

Rikard (REE-kahr)   A form of Richard, which means "rich and powerful ruler."

Roald (ROO-ull)   Meaning "famous ruler." Explorer Roald Amundsen and author Roald Dahl are notable Roalds.

Roar (ROO-ahr)   A name that means "praised warrior."

Stefan (STEH-fahn)   A form of Stephen, which means "a crown." A variation is *Steffen*.

Steinar (STAY-nahr)   Meaning "rock warrior." A popular Steinar is Steinar Albrigtsen Norwegian rock star.

Stian (STEE-ahn)   A name that means "quick on his feet."

Thor (TOOR)   Meaning "thunder." This is the name of the Norse god of thunder and war. Among notable people with this name is Thor Heyerdahl, a world-famous Norwegian explorer and archeologist. Variations include *Thorin, Tor,* and *Tyrus.*

Thorald (TOOR-ahl)   Meaning "Thor's follower." A variation is *Torald.*

Thorbjørn (TOOR-byoorn)   Meaning "Thor's bear."

Thorleif (TOOR-layf)   Meaning "Thor's beloved."

Thorvald (TOOR-vahl)   Meaning "Thor's forest."

Trygve (TREEG-vuh)   This name signifies "brave victor." Renowned men with this name include Trygve Bratteli, prime minister of Norway during the 1970s and Trygve Lie, the first U.N. secretary general.

Vegard (VEH-gahr)   Meaning "sanctuary" or "protection." Among famous Vegards is Vegard Ulvang Norwegian World Cup champion in cross country skiing.

Vidar (VEE-dahr)   Meaning "tree warrior." One popular Vidar was Vidar Theisen, a long-time weather-announcer on Norwegian television who developed his own fan base.

NORWAY: GIRLS

Astrid (AHS-tree)   Meaning "lovely" or "divine strength." Among notable people with this name is author Astrid Lindgren. A variation is *Astri.*

Bodil (BOO-dill)   Meaning "fighting woman."

Borgny (BORGH-nee)   This name means "help."

Dagny (DAGH-nee)   Meaning "brightness" or "day."

Eldrid (EHLD-ree)   A name that means "fire."

Frøya (FROY-uh)   This name means "noblewoman." The name of the Norse goddess of love. A variation is *Freya.*

Gudrun (GOOD-ruhn)   Meaning "battler." A variation is *Runa.*

Gunda (GUHN-dah)   Meaning "female warrior."

Haldis (HAHL-diss)   A name that means "stone-help."

Hege (HEH-guh)   This name signifies "holy."

Inga (EEN-gah)   A short form of Ingrid. A variation is *Ingebor.*

Ingrid (EENGH-ree)   Meaning "hero's daughter" or "beautiful daughter." Famous Ingrids include actress Ingrid Bergman, the beauty in *Casablanca.* Variations include *Inga* and *Inger.*

Jorunn (YUU-roonn)   A name that means "chief" or "love."

Karen (KAA-earn)   A name that means "pure."

Karin (KAA-reen)   A form of Karen. Novelist Karin Michaelis is one famous Karin. Variations include *Karina* and *Karine*.

Kjersti (CHURR-stee)   An alternate form of Kirsten, which means "stone church."

Kirsti (CHEER-stee)   A familiar form of Kirsten, meaning "Christian." Among notable people with this name is actress Kirstie Alley who played a bar owner on *Cheers*. A variation is *Kirstie*.

Kristin (KREES-tinn)   An alternate form of Kristen. Among celebrated Kristins is film actress Kristin Scott Thomas who came to the attention of Hollywood in *Four Weddings and a Funeral*.

Kristine (KREES-tinn-uh)   A form of Christine, meaning "Christian." Soccer player Kristine Lilly. Variations include *Kristi* and *Kristiane*.

Linnea (lynn-EH-ah)   Meaning "lime tree." Also the name of the national flower of Sweden. A variation is *Linn*.

Liv (LEEV)   This name means "life." One famous person with this name is actress and director Liv Ullmann.

Magnhild (MAGH-nill)   Meaning "strength."

Olaug (OOL-owgh)   Meaning "ancestors."

Olga (OHL-guh)   Meaning "holy." Among renowned women with this name is math theorist Olga Taussky-Todd.

Ragna (RAHNG-nah)   This name signifies "mighty."

Runa (ROO-nah)   A name that means "secret" or "flowing." A variation is *Runna*.

Sigrid (CIG-ree)   Meaning "fair victory." Nobel Prize–winning novelist Sigrid Undset is one famous person with this name.

Silje (SILL-yuh)   A form of Cecilia, meaning "musical."

Siv (SEEV)   This name means "Thor's wife."

Sonja (SAWN-ya)   A form of Sonya, which means "wisdom." Well-known people with this name include skater and film actress Sonja Henie.

Thora (TOO-rah)   Meaning "thunder." A feminine form of Thor. A variation is *Thordis*.

Trude (TROO-deh)   A name that signifies "strength."

Unn (OOHN)   Meaning "she who is loved."

Sweden

Some of the most popular names in Sweden are, to this day, Old Norse names that have a deep connection to Scandinavian history and culture. Åsa, one of the most common names for girls, is an Old Swedish name meaning "goddess," and Bo, a favorite for boys, means "the domiciled." Names derived from Latin, such as Johan, Thomas, Karl, and their corresponding feminine forms, were first introduced during the 1300s when conversion to Christianity began to occur on a larger scale. Swedish names made famous by film and sports celebrities are Ingmar (Bergman), meaning "the god Ing's famous soldier," and Björn (as in the tennis star Borg), which literally means "bear." By law, parents must give their children one or more first names and report these to the Office of Taxation within three months. Names that may be offensive or cause the child discomfort are not approved. Other famous Swedes include the writers Pär Lagerkvist, Nelly Sachs, Harry Edmund Martinson, and Eyvind Johnson.

SWEDEN: BOYS

Alvar (AA-lvar) This is the name of a small shrub native to Sweden.

Anders (AAND-ers) A form of the English name Andrew, meaning "strong." Notable persons with this name include astronomer and inventor of the centigrade thermometer Anders Celsius, as well as physicist Anders Angström.

Frans (FRAANS) From the Latin name Francis, meaning "free man." A famous person with this name is master portrait painter Frans Hals. A variation is *Frants*.

Gustaf (gust-AAV) A form of the Scandinavian name Gustave, meaning "staff of the Goths." A variation is *Gustaaf*.

Hilmar (HEE-LMAAR) Meaning "famous noble."

Kjell (CH-ell) A form of Carl, which means "man."

Krister (KRI-ster) A form of Christian, meaning "a Christian." Variations include *Krist* and *Kristar*.

Kristofer (KRI-stoffer) A form of Christopher, meaning "Christ-bearer." Artist Kristoffer Eckersberg. Variations include *Kristef, Kristoffer, Kristofor*, and *Kristus*.

Lauris (LAU-ris) A form of Laurence, meaning a "laurel" or "crown."

Lennart (LENN-art) A form of Leonard, which means "strong as a lion." A variation is *Lennerd*.

Lukas (LU-kas) A form of Luke, from the Latin meaning "light." Variations include *Loukas, Lukash, Lukasha, Lukass*, and *Lukasz*.

Mathias (MAA-tias) A form of the Hebrew Matthew, which means "light of God." Variations include *Maitias, Mathia, Mathis, Matias, Matthia, Matthias, Mattlas*, and *Matus*.

Mats (MAA-ts) A familiar form of Matthew. One popular Mats is Wimbledon champion Mats Wilander, Sweden's leading tennis player for almost a decade. Variations include *Matts* and *Matz*.

Mikael (Mi-ka-el) A form of Michael, which means "Who is like God." Variations include *Mikaeel* and *Mikaele*.

Niklas (nick-LAAS) A form of Nicholas, meaning "victory of the people." A variation is *Niklaas*.

Nils (Ni-ls) A short form of Nicholas. Among notable people with this name are chemist Nils Sefström and musician Nils Lofgren.

Pål (PAWL) A form of Paul, meaning "small."

Paulo (PAU-lo)   A form of Paul.

Per (PEHR)   A form of Peter, which means "a rock." Per Atterbom is a renowned poet and philosopher with this name.

Reinhold (RAIN-hold)   A form of Ragnar, which means "powerful army." Theologian Reinhold Niebuhr. A variations is *Reinold*.

Rickard (RIK-ard)   A form of Richard, which means "rich and powerful ruler."

Rune (RU-ne)   Meaning "secret."

Stefan (STE-fan)   A form of Stephen, which means "a crown." Variations include *Staffan, Staffon, Steafeán, Stefanson, Stefaun, Steffan,* and *Steffon.*

Stig (STIG)   This name means "mount."

Torkel (TOOR-kel)   Meaning "Thor's cauldron."

Valdemar (VAL-de-MAR)   Meaning "famous power. One famous poet with this name is Valdemar Rördam.

Valter (VAAL-tear)   A form of Walter, which means "army of power." *Valters, Valther, Valtr,* and *Vanda.*

SWEDEN: GIRLS

Anna (AH-na)   A form of Hannah, which means "gracious." Famous persons with this name include the well-known Russian ballerina Anna Pavlova. Variations include *Aneesa, Anissa, Anika, Ana, Anah, Ania, Anica, Anita, Anja, Nana, Nina,* and *Nisa.*

Annalina (AA-na-LEE-na)   A combination of Anna and Lina.

Birgitte (BIRG-it)   A form of Bridget, Celtic for "strong" or "lofty." Among notable people with this name is opera singer Birgit Nilsson. Variations include *Birgit* and *Birgita.*

Britta (BRIT-ta)   Meaning "power."

Charlotta (char-OT-ta)   Meaning "petite and feminine."

Eva (E-va)   A name signifying "life." One popular Eva is supermodel Eva Herzigova.

Evelina (E-va-LEE-na)   A name that means "star."

Freya (FREJ-a)   This name is inspired by a mythological love goddess.

Gudrun (GUUD-run)   Meaning "divine wisdom." A variation is *Gudruna.*

Gunilla (GUN-il-la)   Meaning "battle maiden."

Hulda (HUL-da)   This name means "hidden."

Ingalill (IN-ga-LIL)   A combination of Inge and Lillian.

Johanna (JO-HAN-NA)   From the Hebrew meaning "God is gracious." Among renowned people with this name is the "Swedish Nightingale," soprano Johanna.

Karolina (KAR-uh-LEE-na)   A feminine form of Karl.

Linnea (LIN-ee-ah)   This name signifies "lime tree."

Maj (MY)   From Margaret, meaning "a pearl." Variations include *Mai* and *Maja.*

Malena (MA-lee-na)   A familiar form of Magdalene, which means "high tower."

Sonya (SON-ya)   A name that signifies "wisdom." A famous person with this name is writer Sonja Akeson. Variations include *Sonja* and *Sonia.*

Tora (TOUR-a)   A familiar form of Victoria, from the Latin for "victorious."

Ulla (OO-la)   From the Latin name Ursula, which means "she-bear."

Greece

Greek names tend to come from personages in history, mythology, and religion. Names may also be abstract nouns, such as "happiness." Many Greek names have both male and female versions, as in the case of the Greek name Georgos, or George, and its female counterpart, Georgia. Among the most common names are Yiannis and Georgos for males and Maria for females, all derived from religious tradition.

GREECE: BOYS

Achilleas (a-chee-LE-as)   In Greek mythology, the Trojan hero who slew Hector. His mother, Thetis, bathed him in the river Styx in an effort to make him immortal, but the heel by which she held him remained vulnerable.

Adam (a-THAM)   From the Hebrew, meaning "earth." According to the Old Testament, the first man that God created.

Adonis (A-tho-nees)   In Greek mythology a god known for his beauty. He was said to have been beloved of Apollo and Bacchus.

Aetios (a-E-tee-os)   A Roman general who defeated Attila (A.D. 451); the name of a second-century Greek philosopher.

Agamemnonas (a-ga-ME-mno-nas)   The king of the Mycenae and Argos, general in the Trojan War, and brother of Menelaus whose wife, Helen, was abducted by Paris, and thereby became the cause of the Trojan War. A variation is *Agamemnon.*

Agesilaos (a-gee-SEE-la-os)   The name of the king of Sparta. During his reign, Lycurgus instituted his famous laws which made Sparta a militaristic society.

Aggeles (an-ge-LEES)   This name derives from the word *angelos,* meaning "angel."

Agis (A-gees)   The king of Sparta who waged wars against Athens and liberated many Greek cities. He attempted in vain to restore the Lycurgan laws in Sparta.

Agrippas (a-GREE-pas)   A Roman general, 63 B.C.–A.D. 12. Considered the greatest military organizer and builder in Roman history; the creator of the first permanent Roman fleet and the commander who waged and won the victories under Octavian.

Aias (E-as)   The name of two Homeric heroes.

Aietes (e-ee-tees)   An ancient king of Aia (Kolchida); the son of the Helios; the father of Medea.

Aigisthos (E-gis-thos)   The son of King Thyestes of the Mycenaeans.

Aimonas (E-mo-nas)   The son of Creon.

Aineias (e-nee-as)   The mythic Trojan hero and founder of Rome.

Aischines (e-SHEE-nees)   The rhetorical speaker in the ancient world, 390–314 B.C.

Aischylos (e-SHEE-los)   The ancient Greek tragedian, 526–456 B.C.; father of Greek tragedy.

Aisonas (E-so-nas)   The father and son of Iasona (Jason).

Aisopos (E-so-pos)   The sixth-century B.C. writer of fables, such as "The Fox and the Grapes" and "The Tortoise and the Hare." A variation is *Aseop.*

Akademos (a-KA-thee-mos)   The ancient Attican hero.

Akritas (a-KREE-tas)   The central figure in the Akritic songs of the Byzantine period.

Alexandros (a-LE-xan-dros)   A name that means "protector of men." King of Macedonia, 356–323 B.C. A variation is *Alexis*.

Alexios (a-LE-xi-os)   The name of several Byzantine emperors.

Alkaios (al-KE-os)   The name of a poet from seventh-century B.C. Lesbos.

Alkinoos (al-KI-no-os)   King of the Phaiakians.

Alkmeonas (al-KME-on-as)   The grandchild of Nestor, king of Pylus; head of the family of Alkmeonids.

Amphiaraos (am-phee-A-ra-os)   A hero of the Argonauts.

Anakreondas (a-na-KRE-on-das)   An ancient lyric poet of the sixth century B.C.

Anaxagoras (a-na-KSA-yo-ras)   The king of Argos. Also the name of a philosopher, mathematician, and astronomer from Klazomenes, 500–428 B.C.

Anaximandros (a-na-KSEE-man-thros)   The name of a philosopher from Miletos, 610–547 B.C.

Anaximenes (a-na-ks-ME-nees)   A philosopher from Miletos, 585–528 B.C.

Andreas (an-THRE-as)   Meaning "manly." The biblical Andrew is one of the Twelve Apostles.

Androkles (an-thro-KLEES)   A Christian slave under Tiberius. Androcles is the fabled Roman slave who is spared in the arena by a lion from whose foot he had years before extracted a thorn.

Andronikos (an-THRO-nee-kos)   This name derives from the words *andros*, which means "man," and *neke*, meaning "victory."

Anestes (a-NE-stees)   This name literally means "the one who is risen."

Annibas (a-NI-vas)   A Karchedonian general, 247–183 B.C.

Antalkidas (a-dal-KEE-thas)   A Spartan ruler known for the "Antalkidian Peace" with the Persians, 387 B.C.

Antiochos (a-DI-o-chos)   The name of thirteen kings of Syria during the Hellenistic period.

Antiphontas (an-ti-fon-tas)   One of the ten rhetors of Attica, 481–411 B.C.

Antisthenes (a-di-STHE-nees)   Philosopher of ancient Athens, 444–370 B.C.

Antonios (a-DO-ni-os)   The name of a Christian ascetic. Also the name of the Roman general Marc Antony, lover of Cleopatra, 83–30 B.C.

Apollonas (a-PO-lo-nas)   One of twelve gods of Olympus.

Aristeides (a-ree-STEE-dees)   A politician and general of ancient Athens, 540–460 B.C.

Aristophanes (a-ree-sto-PHA-nees)   The comic playwright in ancient Greece, 452–389 B.C.

Aristoteles (a-ri-sto-TE-lees)   The ancient Greek philosopher from Stagira; who was a teacher of Alexander the Great. A variation is *Aristotle*.

Asklepios (a-SKLEE-pee-os)   God of medicine in ancient Greece; son of Apollo and Koronida.

Athanasios (a-tha-NA-see-os)   A saint in the Greek Orthodox tradition, patriarch of Alexandria, A.D. 293–373.

Athenagoras (a-th-na-GO-ras)   The name of a rhetorical speaker from Syracuse in the ancient world; a patriarch of the ecumenical patriarchate, 1949–1972.

Athmetos (a-THMEE-tos)   The king of the Molossians. Also the name of the king of the Pherae in Thessaly. He married Theone, daughter of Thestor, and then Alcestis, daughter of Pelias.

Athrianos (a-three-a-NOS)   The Roman Philhellenic Emperor, A.D. 76–136.

Charalampos (ha-RA-la-bos)   Derives from the Greek *chara*, which means "joy," and *lampo*, which means "shine." A variation is *Chares*.

Christophoros (hree-STO-fo-ros)   A form of Christopher, meaning "Christ-bearer." A variation is *Christos*.

Demetrios (thee-MEE-tri-os)   Meaning "love of the earth." In Greek mythology Demeter was the goddess of agriculture and fertility. Variations include *Demetres* and *Metsos*.

Demos (TH-mos)   Derives from Greek words *demos* and *demotiko*, meaning "the people" and "popular."

Diodoros (thee-O-tho-ros)   A historian of first century B.C.

Emmanouel (e-ma-nu-EEL)   The name given to Christ. Variations include *Manolis* and *Manos*.

Eukrates (ef-KRA-tees)   Derives from Greek *eu*, which means "well" or "good," and *kratos*, meaning "power."

Giannes (YIA-nees)   A form of John, which means "God is gracious."

Giorgos (GIOR-gos)   "Tiller of the soil."

Iasonas (ee-A-so-nas)   In Greek mythology, the son of Aeson, a king of ancient Greece. He accepted the near-impossible quest of capturing the Golden Fleece in an attempt to gain his rightful place as king. Also *Jason*.

Kostantinos (ko-sta-DEE-nos)   The first Christian emperor, after whom the city of Constantinople (now Istanbul) was named. Variations include *Kostas* and *Ntinos*.

Maurikos (ma-VREE-kos)   Derives from Greek *mauros*, meaning "black."

Michales (mee-CHA-lees)   A form of Michael, which means "Who is like God."

Neoptolemos (ne-o-PTO-le-mos)   In Greek mythology, the son of Achilles (who had fought in the Trojan War) and the prince of Skyros.

Nikolaos (nee-KO-la-os)   Derived from the Greek *nike*, which means "victory," and *laos*, meaning "the people." A variation is *Nikos*.

Odyseas (o-thee-SE-as)   Greek leader in the Trojan War, and the hero of Homer's *The Odyssey*.

Orpheas (or-PHE-as)   In Greek mythology, a Thracian musician so skilled he charmed the beasts, trees, and rivers. He was the husband of the nymph Eurydice.

Paulos (PAV-los)   Derived from the Greek name Paulos, which means "small."

Pericles (pe-ree-KLEES)   A politician in Athens during its Golden Age in the fifth century B.C.

Phaidon (FE-thon)   A son of the god Zeus. He tried to fly Zeus' chariot, the sun, and was burned.

Philip (FILL-up)   Meaning "lover of horses."

Soteres (so-TEE-rees)   Derives from Greek *soter*, which means "savior."

Themistocles (the-MEE-sto-KLEES)   A statesman of fifth-century B.C. Athens whose naval expertise repelled the Persian invasion of Greece. A variation is *Themis*.

Theocharis (the-o-CHA-rees)   Derives from Greek *theos*, which means "god," and *charis*, meaning "grace."

Theseus (thee-SE-as)   An ancient Greek hero who killed the Minotaur of Krete.

Xenophon (ZEN-no-PHON)   A historian of ancient Greece.

GREECE: GIRLS

Aidos (e-thos)   A goddess in Greek mythology; the mother of Sophrosyne.

Aikaterine (e-ka-te-RI-nee)   A second-century saint in the Greek Orthodox tradition. Also the name of the second empress of Russia (1762–1796). Variations include *Katerina* and *Katina*.

Aithousa (E-thou-sa)   The daughter of the sea god Poseidon and Alkyona.

Alexandra (a-le-XAN-thra)   A feminine form of Alexander, which means "protector of man."

Alkeste (AL-kess-stee) Daughter of Pelia and wife of Admetos.

Alkmene (al-KMEE-nee) Mother of Herakles and wife of Amphitrionas.

Alkyone (al-kee-O-nee) A mythological figure.

Amalia (a-ma-LEE-a) Derives from the Latin *amal*, meaning "work." The name of the first queen of Greece and wife of Othonas.

Amaltheia (a-MAL-thee-a) The name of the sacred goat that suckled the baby Zeus in Krete.

Amphidamas (am-phee-THA-mas) The king of Chalcida.

Amphitrite (am-phee-TREE-tee) One of the fifty Nereids, nymphs of the Mediterannean Sea.

Anastasia (a-na-sta-SEEA) Literally, "the one who is resurrected."

Andromache (an-thro-MA-chee) The wife of Hector, who fought in the Trojan War.

Anna (A-na) Meaning "gracious," it is the Greek form of the Hebrew Hannah, who was the mother of the Virgin Mary.

Antigone (a-di-GO-nee) The heroine of Sophocles' tragedy by the same name, and the daughter of Oedipus.

Antonia (a-do-NEE-a) Meaning "priceless."

Aphrodite (a-phro-DEE-tee) Derived from the Greek word *aphroa*, which means "foam." In mythology, the goddess of love and beauty.

Arethousa (a-re-THOU-sa) Daughter of Nerea and Thoridas, a nymph of the forests.

Artemis (AR-te-mees) In Greek mythology one of the twelve gods of Olympus, the goddess of the hunt, and daughter of Zeus and Leto.

Athanasia (a-tha-na-SEEA) Literally, "the one who is immortal."

Athena (a-thee-NA) The goddess of wisdom in Greek mythology.

Barbara (var-VA-ra) Derives from the Greek word *barbaros*, meaning "barbarian" or "foreigner."

Basilike (va-SIL-ih-KEY) An architectural order of Byzantine churches. Derives from the Greek word *basileas*, meaning "king," and *basilikos*, meaning "royal." A variation is *Basilikoula*.

Biktoria (vik-TO-ree-a) Derives from the Latin word *vincere*, which means "to win" or "to conquer."

Christina (hree-STEE-na) Meaning "Christ-bearer."

Daphne (THA-phnee) Meaning "the laurel" or "bay tree." In Greek mythology, a nymph who turned into a laurel tree to escape Apollo.

Demetra (THEE-mee-tra) One of twelve Olympian gods: the goddess of agriculture.

Ebelina (e-ve-LEE-na) A form of Evelyn, meaning "pleasant."

Eirene (ee-REE-nee) Literally, "peace."

Ele (E-lee) Meaning "light."

Elpida (el-PEE-da) Literally, "hope."

Euaggelia (ev-AN-ge-LEE-ah) Derives from the Greek *eu* which means "good" or "well," and *angelos*, meaning "messenger."

Eurydice (ya-RID-i-see) From the Greek *ercry*, which means "broad," and *dike*, meaning "justice." The name of the wife of Orpheus.

Eutychia (ef-tee-HEE-a) Literally, "happiness."

Helene (e-LE-nee) Meaning "torch" or "light." Known for her great beauty, the wife of Menelaus, who was taken to Troy by Paris. Her abduction was the cause of the Trojan War.

Kalliope (ka-LIO-pee) One of the muses. Variation include *Kalli* and *Pope*.

Kostantina (KON-stan-TI-na) A variation is *Ntina*.

Maria (ma-REE-a) Greek form of Mary, meaning "sea of bitterness."

Marigo (ma-ree-YO) A form of Maria. A variation is *Marigoula*.

Melpomene (mel-PAH-meh-nee) The Greek muse of tragedy.

Paulena (pav-LEE-na) From the Latin *paulus*, meaning "small."

Photene (fo-tee-NEE) Derives from the Greek word *phos*, which means "light."

Stamatena (sta-ma-TEE-na) Derives from Greek *stamatao*, which means "to stop."

Xenekoula (xe-nee-KOU-la) Derives from Greek *xenos*, which means "stranger."

Italy

Perhaps the most inexhaustible storehouse of European cultural heritage, Italy has left an indelible mark on the history of Europe and the modern world. Italy's history as a nation is traced to the beginning of the first millenium B.C. when the Italian peninsula was populated by native tribes, all vying for dominance over the peninsular territory. The rise of the Roman Empire forever changed the world. Geopolitical boundaries were formed in Europe, Roman law was set as the paradigm, and Latin became the lingua franca for more than a millennium, later forming the base for many modern European languages; for instance, 60 percent of English vocabulary is derived from Latin. It was in Italy that the first university was founded in Bologna, the Renaissance first took hold, and the Roman Catholic Church achieved its status as a world spiritual and political power. The country was often dominated by foreign powers until its unification in 1870 under the Piedmontese royal family. A republic was declared in 1946 after the country's defeat in World War II.

Traditionally, naming customs in Italy have been largely determined by Catholic practices, and children are often given at least one name originally derived from the hagiographic calendar. Famous Italians include Dante Alighieri, Giovanni Boccaccio, Niccolò Machiavelli, Fra Angelico, Galileo Galilei, Michelangelo Buonarroti, Leonardo da Vinci, Sandro Botticelli, Antonio Vivaldo, Giuseppe Verdi, Guglielmo Marconi, Enrico Fermi, Vittorio de Sica, Federico Fellini, Michelangelo Antonioni, Lina Wertmuller, Sophia Loren, and Claudia Cardinale.

ITALY: BOYS

Adriano (ah-DRIYAH-no) The name is derived from the Italian city of Adria. Well-known persons with this name are the enlightened and forward-thinking Roman emperor Publius Aelius Hadrianus (A.D. 117–138), a patron of the arts and the devoted lover of the handsome Antinoos, as well as Adriano Celentano, celebrated Italian pop singer of the 1960s and 1970s, famous for his extravagant body language on stage.

Alberto (ahl-BEHR-to) See Albert in French names. The skier Alberto Tomba was the first athlete to gain two gold medals in his specialty. The actor Alberto Sordi (1920–), has become the symbol of the modern genre *commedia all'italiana*.

Aldo (AHL-do) Meaning "old; elder." Name of the former Italian prime minister Aldo Moro (1974–1976), killed in 1978 by the terrorist movement Brigate Rosse.

Alessandro (ah-lehs-SAHN-dro) A form of Alexander, meaning "protector of the people." Name of the composer Alessandro Scarlatti (1659–1725), who was employed as a teacher at the court of the infanta Maria Barbara of Spain until his death.

Alfonso (ahl-PHON-so) Derived from the German name Alphonse, meaning "ready for battle." Name of Alfonso V, King of Aragon, and the first king of Naples (1396–1459), who was praised as one of the greatest humanist rulers of his time for his love of books and fine arts.

Amedeo (ah-meh-DEH-o) Meaning "loves God." Name of the Duke of Aosta and Savoia, Amedeo Ferdinando Maria di Savoia, who accepted the crown of Spain after Isabella II was expelled in 1868.

Amerigo (ah-meh-RIY-go) Amerigo Vespucci (1451–1512) was a famous explorer, merchant, and adventurer. North and South

America, portions of which he discovered, are so called after his name.

Angelo (AHN-jeh-lo) Translated literally, means "angel." This name was shared by two influential Renaissance figures: the humanist Angelo Poliziano (1454–1494), and the great portrait painter Agnolo di Cosimo, known as "Il Bronzino" (1503–1572). Variations include *Angiolo* and *Agnolo*.

Antonio (ahn-TO-nio) Meaning "priceless." Cleopatra's lover, Marcus Antonius (83–30 BCE), forfeited his dreams of becoming single ruler of the Roman Republic after becoming ensnared by the alluring charms of the Egyptian queen.

Arrigo (ahr-RIY-go) A variation of the name Harry, meaning "leader of an army." Name of former coach for the Italian National Football Team, Arrigo Sacchi. Variations include *Alrigo* and *Arrighetto*.

Arturo (ahr-TUW-ro) A variation of the name Arthur, which may come from the Celtic for "strong" or "rock" or may be derived from Thor, the name of the Norse god of war.

Benedetto (beh-neh-DEHT-to) Meaning "blessed." The controversial, intellectual historian and philosopher Benedetto Croce (1866–1952) postulated the relationship between life, reality, and history.

Bruno (BROO-no) Meaning "brown-haired." Notable people with this name are painter Bruno Cassinari (1912–1992) and St. Bruno of Cologne, who was responsible for founding the austere monastic order of the Carthusian monks at la Chartreuse (Grenoble) in 1084.

Carlo (CAHR-lo) Italian form of the English name Charles, meaning "man." Variations include *Carolo* and *Carlone*.

Carmine (CAHR-mine) A very popular Italian name, it is Hebrew for "vineyard."

Cirillo (tchiy-RIYL-lo) A form of Cyril, meaning "Lord." Saints Cyril and Methodius evangelized the Slavonic peoples in the ninth century and invented the Cyrillic alphabet, which is still used in Bulgaria, Serbia, and the former Soviet Union.

Cola (KO-la) A familiar form of Nicola, Nicholas. Imbued with dreams of classical grandeur, Cola di Rienzi (1313–1354) had himself elected Tribune of Rome and attempted to establish democratic ideals.

Cristoforo (kriy-STO-pho-ro) The Italian version of the Greek name Christopher, which means "carries Christ."

Daniele (dah-NIYEH-leh) A variation upon the Hebrew name Daniel, meaning "God is judge."

Dante (DAN-teh) Meaning "lasting." Name of the poet Dante Alighieri, author of *The Divine Comedy*.

Donato (do-NA-to) Meaning "gift." An illustrious bearer of this name was the great Renaissance sculptor Donatello (1386–1466), creator of the celebrated bronze statue of David. A common version of this name is *Donatello*.

Edoardo (eh-do-AHR-do) The Italian version of the English name Edward, meaning "prosperous guardian."

Emiliano (eh-miy-LIYA-no) A form of the German Emil, meaning "hard-working," this name was borne by Emiliano Zapata, famous Mexican revolutionary (1879–1919), and by Emiliano di Cavalcanti (1897–1976), Brazilian painter and author.

Emilio (eh-MIY-lio) This Italian version of the German Emil, meaning "hard-working," became popular with fashion designer Emilio Pucci. Variations include the Venetian *Millio* and *Milio*.

Enrico (ehn-RIY-ko) A popular version of the German name Henry, meaning "ruler of his house." The great physicist Enrico Fermi (1901–1954) received the Nobel Prize in 1938 for his discovery of new radioactive elements. Also *Enzo* or *Rico*.

Ettore (EHT-to-reh) Meaning "steadfast." The name Ettore was popularized by the staid, family-loving, humane character of Homer's *Iliad*. Also spelled *Ettorre*.

Fabrizio (phah-BRIY-tsio) Meaning "artisan." Variations include *Fabrice* and *Fabrizius*.

Fausto (PHAHUW-sto) The Italian version of the Latin name Faust, meaning "lucky." The tale of Johannes Faust, charlatan, magician, and enchanter of the 15th and 16th century inspired by Berlioz, Gounod, Boito, Marlowe, and Goethe. The legendary and tragic Fausto Coppi (1919–1960), who won the Giro d'Italia five times and the Tour de France twice, is considered to be the greatest cyclist Italy has ever seen.

Federico (pheh-deh-RIY-ko) The Italian version of the German name Frederick, meaning "peaceful leader." Italian film director Federico Fellini (1920–1993) won the Oscar for lifetime achievement in 1993.

Filippo (phiy-LIYP-po) Meaning "lover of horses," it is the Italian version of the name Philip. Name of the Renaissance architect Filippo Brunelleschi (1377–1446), who designed the Duomo of the impressive Cathedral S. Maria del Fiore in Florence. Also the name of Renaissance painter Filippo Lippi (1406–1469). Variations include *Pippo* and *Filippino*.

Fiorello (phiyo-REHL-lo) Translated literally, means "little flower." Name of the popular New York City mayor Fiorello LaGuardia, in whose memory LaGuardia airport is named.

Flavio (PHLAH-viyo) Meaning "blond." Flavio Gioia invented the compass at Amalfi (Naples) between the 13th and 14th centuries.

Francesco (phrahn-TCHEH-sko) The Italian version of the Latin Francis, meaning "free man." St. Francesco of Assisi (1182–1226) is the patron saint of Italy. Francesco Petrarca (1304–1374) helped pave the way for the Italian Renaissance, and is one of the greatest lyrical poets the Italian language can boast of.

Gabriele (gah-BRIYEH-leh) From the Hebrew name Gabriel, meaning "God is my might." Gabriel Mirabeau (1749–1791) was a protagonists of the French Revolution; writer, poet, militarist, and intellectual Gabriele D'Annunzio (1863–1938), became famous for his eccentric ways and his affair with actress Eleonora Duse. A variation is *Gabriello*.

Gaetano (gah-eh-TAH-no) Meaning "from Gaeta," a central Italian town. Opera composer Gaetano Donizetti (1795–1848) wrote *Lucia di Lammermoor* and *l'Elisir d'amore*. Also spelled *Caetano*.

Geronimo (jeh-RO-niy-mo) A variation of the Greek name Jerome, meaning "divine name." Chief of Apache Chiricahua, Geronimo, fought against the colonists who settled in the southwest and strongly opposed the movement to segregate Indians into camps. He dictated his biography before dying in 1906.

Giacomo (JAH-ko-mo) The Italian version of Hebrew name Jacob, meaning "the supplanter." Composer Giacomo Puccini (1858–1924), wrote *Madama Butterfly* (1904), and *La Bohème* (1896) among other operas. Variations include *Gaimo, Giacamo, Giaco, Giacobbe,* and *Giacobbo*.

Gian (JAHN) The Italian equivalent of John, meaning "God's gracious gift." Variations include *Gianetto* and *Gianni*.

Giancarlo (jahn-KAHR-lo) A combination of the Hebrew name John and the German Charles. The composer Giancarlo Menotti founded and has directed the Spoleto Festival of the Two Worlds since 1957.

Gianni (JAHN-niy) A variation of the name Gian. Notable Giannis include fashion designer Gianni Versace and Gianni Agnelli (1866–1945), the founder of the largest Italian car company, Fiat, in 1899.

Giordano (jor-DAH-no) The Italian version of Hebrew name Jordan, meaning "flowing from God." Philosopher Giordano Bruno (1548–1600) abandoned the Dominican order and was put to the stake for heresy by the Inquisition.

Giorgio (JIYOR-jiyo) Italian version of the Greek name George, meaning "farmer." This name has become popular with the success of Italian stylist Giorgio Armani.

Giotto (JOT-to) A variation upon the German name Geoffrey, meaning "God's peace." The painter and sculptor Giotto di Bondone (ca. 1267–1337).

Giovanni (jiyo-VAHNN-iy)   A version of the name John, meaning "God's gracious gift." Giovanni Pico della Mirandola (1463–1494) was a philosopher and humanist.

Giulio (JUW-liyo)   Italian version of Hebrew name Julius. Six-time prime minister of Italy Giulio Andreotti. Another common form is *Giuliano*.

Giuseppe (juw-SEHP-peh)   The Italian form of the Hebrew name Joseph, meaning "he shall add." Famous Giuseppes include opera composer Giuseppe Verdi (1813–1901), who wrote *Aida*, *La Traviata*, and *Rigoletto*, and Italian patriot Giuseppe Garibaldi (1807–1882). A common variation is *Giuseppino*.

Giusto (JUW-sto)   From the Latin name Justin, meaning "fair; just," it is the name of the great emperor of the eastern Roman Empire, Justinian I (482–565). Also *Giustino*.

Gregorio (greh-GO-riyo)   A form of the Latin Gregory, meaning "guarding." Notable Gregorios includes San Gregorio Magno (535–604), elected Pope in 590, who codified the Gregorian Chant.

Guglielmo (guw-LLIYEHL-mo)   Italian version of the German name William, meaning "unwavering guard." Name of Guglielmo Marconi (1834–1937), Italian scientist and industrialist. In 1909 he shared the Nobel Prize for physics with C. F. Braun. In 1924, he was the first person to connect Great Britain with Australia. It is still a matter of dispute whether he or Bell should be credited with the invention of the telephone.

Guido (GUWIY-do)   Meaning "life." Guido d'Arezzo (990–1050) perfected a system for notating musical pitch on paper and was the first to name musical notes, based on the first letters of a hymn to St. John.

Ignazio (iy-NAH-tsiyo)   From the Latin for "fire." St. Ignatius of Loyola (1491–1556), fervent upholder of the importance of education, founded the Society of Jesus.

Ilario (iy-LAH-riyo)   Meaning "cheerful." This name is famous after St. Ilare of Poitiers, who championed the Catholic Church against the Arian heresy during the fourth century.

Innocenzo (iyn-no-TCHEHN-tso)   Meaning "innocent." This name was used by 13 popes, including Pope Innocenzo III (ca. 1160–1216), who initiated two Crusades. Variations in spelling include *Innocenzio, Inocencio,* and *Innocente.*

Lorenzo (lo-REHN-zo)   Derived from the Latin name Lawrence, meaning "crowned with laurels." Name of the powerful magnate Lorenzo de' Medici (1449–1492), exquisite patron of the arts, poet, and true Renaissance man. Also *Laurentio, Laurenti, Laurenzo, Renzo,* and *Renzino.*

Luciano (luw-TCHIYAH-no)   Meaning "light." Name of the internationally renowned operatic tenor Luciano Pavarotti and of Luciano Bonaparte, brother of Napoleon Bonaparte. Variations include the French *Lucian, Luca, Lucca,* and *Lucio.*

Luigi (luw-IY-jiy)   The Italian form of the German Louis, meaning "glorious in battle." Name of Luigi Pirandello, winner of the Nobel Prize for literature in 1934, and Luigi Einaudi (1874–1961), president of the Republic of Italy. Also *Lui, Luigino,* and *Luiggi.*

Marcello (mahr-TCHEHL-lo)   An Italian version of the Latin name Mark derived from Greek god of war, Mars. Name of actor Marcello Mastroianni, who has appeared in several celebrated films by director Federico Fellini. A variation is *Marcellus.*

Marco (MAHR-ko)   A variation of Marcus and Mark, meaning "war-like." Marco Polo was the 13th-century Venetian merchant and traveler who explored Asia, befriended the Kublai Kan, and wrote a famous account of his adventures entitled *Il Milione*—allegedly because the phrase "a million of these things" is repeated throughout the account.

Mario (MAH-riyo)   Possibly derived from the Greek god Mars or may also be the male form of the name Mary. Notable Marios include the Roman leader Gaius Marius (A.D. 156–186), who held the consulship continuously seven times and was responsible for reforming the Roman army; the Italo-American author Mario Puzo, who wrote *The Godfather*; and former New York governor Mario Cuomo.

Martino (mahr-TIY-no)   A form of Martin, meaning "warlike." Also *Martinos*.

Masaccio (mah-SAHTCH-tciyo)   Alternative form of Tommaso, which is Italian for Thomas, meaning "twin."

Massimo (mahs-SIY-no)   Meaning "greatest." Massimo Troisi (1953–1994), one of the most famous modern Neapolitan comedic actors was the star of *Il Postino*. A variation of this name is *Massimiliano*.

Maurizio (mauw-RIY-tsio)   The Italian version of the Latin name Maurice, which means "dark." Notable people with this name include the French composer Maurice Ravel (1875–1937) and the Belgian Maurice Maeterlinck (1849–1911), who won a Nobel Prize for literature.

Michelangelo (miy-keh-LAHN-jeh-lo)   A combination of *Michael* and *Angelo*. Michelangelo Buonarroti (1474–1564), one of the greatest Italian Renaissance painters, sculptors, and architects, is known for his sculpture of David, the *Tondo Doni*, and the ceiling of the Sistine Chapel. Also spelled *Michalgnolo*.

Michele (miy-KEH-leh)   Italian for Michael, which means "Who is like God." The Florentine Michele di Lando was the leader of the Ciompi rebels in 1378 in Florence.

Nicola (niy-KO-lah)   The Italian version of the Greek name Nicholas, meaning "people's victory." Notable persons with this name include refined Italian stylist Nicola Trussardi and the 13th-century sculptor and architect Nicola Pisano. Variations include *Nico*, *Nicolao*, *Nicolo*, *Niccolò*, and *Nicolao*.

Paolo (PAH-o-lo)   Italian version of Paul, which is Latin for "little." The geographer Paolo dal Pozzo Toscanelli (1397–1482) upheld the notion that the earth was spherical, which inspired Columbus's enterprise. Famous Paolos include Paulo Uccello (1397–1475), who painted the *Battaglia di San Romano* (1456), and the painter Paolo Veronese (1528–1588), one of the greatest exponents of the Venetian Renaissance.

Pasquale (pah-SKWUWAH-leh)   Related to the French name Pascal, meaning "Easter

baby" or "Easter-born." Pasquino was the name of a lyrical writer of the 16th century who popularized sarcastic jokes against the powerful families of Rome. To this date, the tradition of venting political discontent in the form of popular libels is called "pasquinata." Also spelled *Pascuale*.

Patrizio (pah-TRIY-tsiyo)   Meaning "noble; patrician." The monk St. Patrick, patron of Ireland (ca. 390–461), spread the gospel in that land after 432.

Peppe (PEH-peh)   A familiar form of the Hebrew name Joseph. Also *Peppi*, *Peppo*, and *Pino*.

Pietro (PIYEH-tro)   A variation upon the Greek name Peter, meaning "stone." Name of Renaissance painters Piero Della Francesca and Pietro Vannucci, alias Perugin, and writer Pietro Aretino (1492–1556). Also *Piero* and *Pierino*.

Pino (PIY-no)   This name is related to the Hebrew name Joseph, meaning "he shall add" It is also a diminutive of Giuseppe.

Pio (PIY-o)   Meaning "reverent." Pope Pio (Pius) IX was opposed to the unification of Italy. During his papacy in the mid-19th century, the church was stripped of Umbria, Romagna, Marche, and Rome itself, all of which became Italian territories.

Primo (PRIY-mo)   Meaning "first" or "prime quality," it also means "cousin" in Spanish. Notable persons with this name are Holocaust survivor and chronicler Primo Levi (1919–1987) and world champion boxer Primo Carnera (1906–1967).

Raffaele (rahph-phah-EH-leh)   A familiar form of the Latin name Raphael, meaning "helped by God." Renaissance painter Raffaello Sancio and novelist Rafael Sabatini. Variations include *Rafaello* and *Raffaello*.

Renato (reh-NAH-to)   Meaning "reborn." Renato Dulbecco won the Nobel Prize for medicine in 1975.

Renzo (REHN-zo)   An alternative form of Lorenzo related to the Latin name Lawrence, which alludes to "laurels" or "a crown of laurels." It is also a character in the most famous

Italian romantic novel, *The Betrothed* by Alessandro Manzoni.

Roberto (ro-BEHR-to)   The Italian version of Robert, which means "bright fame" or "glory." *Life is Beautiful* actor and director Roberto Benigni.

Rocco (ROK-ko)   Meaning "rock." Name of the theatrical impresario Rocco Landesman and of St. Rocco, who came from Montpellier and worked in Italy to help relieve the sufferings of plague victims.

Romeo (ro-MEH-o)   Meaning "pilgrimmage to Rome" or "Roman." Title character of the Shakespearean play *Romeo and Juliet*, which was first represented in 1597; internationally renowned stylist Romeo Gigli.

Romano (ro-MAH-no)   Meaning "Roman." Romano Prodi, economist and politician, is the current president of the European Union. Also film director Roman Polanski.

Rodolfo (ro-DOL-pho)   Related to Rudolph, meaning "wolf." Name of the flamboyant actor and character Rodolfo Valentino and Russian dancer Rudolf Nureiev, prince of stages worldwide.

Salvatore (sahl-VAH-to-reh)   Meaning "savior." Nobel Prize winner for literature Salvatore Quasimodo, Baritone Salvatore Marchesi. Variations include *Salvato*, *Salviano*, and *Salvatorico*.

Samuele (sah-muw-EH-leh)   Related to the Hebrew name Samuel, which means "God's word." Name of several literary figures including Dr. Samuel Johnson (1709–1784), Samuel Taylor Coleridge (1772–1834), and Shemuel Agnon (1888–1970), the 1966 Israeli Nobel Prize–winning author of *Tales from Jerusalem*.

Sandro (SAHN-dro)   A short form of Greek name Alexander. Renaissance painter Sandro Botticelli (1447–1510) is famous for his *Primavera* and *Birth of Venus*; Sandro Pertini is a former president of the Italian Republic.

Santo (SAHN-to)   Meaning "holy" or "saint." Also *Santos*.

Saverio (sah-VEH-riyo)   Italian for Xavier, which means "bright" in Arabic. St. Francesco Saverio (1506–1552) was sent by the king of Portugal to evangelize the peoples of India and Japan.

Sergio (SEHR-jo)   The Italian version of the Latin name Serge, which means "attendant" or "helper." Fashion designer Sergio Valente. A variation is *Sergino*.

Severiano (seh-veh-RIYAH-no)   Related to the Latin name Severino, meaning "judicious," it is similar in sound to the Turkish name Sevelin, meaning "very loved." Notable people with this name include philosopher Severinus Boetius (480–524), who wrote *The Consolation of Philosophy*, and contemporary flutist Severino Gazzelloni, who bolstered the prestige of the Italian school against the better known French and English ones.

Silvestro (sil-VEH-stro)   Meaning "wild" or "from the forest." Name of Pope Saint Silvester I, who lived through the persecutions of Diocletian to witness Constantine's legalization of Christianity in the year 313.

Silvio (SIL-vee-o)   Meaning "from the forest." Notable persons with this name include former Italian prime minister Silvio Berlusconi; 1938 world champion football player Silvio Piola; and humanist Enea Silvio Piccolomini (1405–1464), who became Pope Pius II.

Stefano (STEH-fa-no)   An alternative form of Stephen, which means "crowned; royal." Famous persons with this name include Stefano Franceso, a Renaissance painter also known as "Giuochi."

Tazio (TAH-zio)   Name of the ancient Sabine king Titus Tatius and of Tazio Nuvolari, a legendary Italian race car driver.

Teodoro (the-o-DOH-ro)   Italian version of the Greek name Theodore, which means "gift of God."

Tiberio (tye-BEH-ree-o)   Meaning "from the Tiber River region." Tiberius Claudius Nero, second Roman Emperor (42 B.C.–A.D. 37), was a valorous and competent military commander. A variation is *Tiberinus*.

Tito (TEE-to) A form of the Greek name Titus, which means "of the giants." This name is associated mainly with personages from Roman antiquity, such as Sabine leader Titus Tatius, historian Titus Livius (59 B.C.–A.D. 17), and emperor Titus Flavius Vespasianus (A.D. 9–79).

Tamaso (tom-MAH-zo) Related to the Hebrew name Thomas which means "twin." Variations include *Tomaso*, *Tomasso*, and *Tomassino*.

Tullio (TOO-lee-yo) Meaning "vivacious." Name of one of the greatest orators ever, Marcus Tullius Cicero, contemporary of Caius Julius Caesar (106–143 B.C.).

Uberto (uu-BEHR-to) A form of the German name Hubert, which means "bright intelligence" or "shining mind."

Ugo (UU-go) An alternative form of the name Hugh, a form of Hubert, meaning "bright intelligence" or "shining mind." Famous persons with this name include poet Ugo Foscolo (1778–1827), philosopher and mystic Ugo of San Vittore (1094–1141), and the Italian Republican statesman Ugo La Malfa (1903–1979).

Umberto (uum-BEHR-to) Related to the Old German name Humbert, which means "bright home." Umberto Eco is the internationally renowned author of *The Name of the Rose* (1982). Variations include *Uberto* and *Umi*.

Urbano (uur-BAH-no) Related to the Latin name Urban, which means "from the city" or "sophisticated." The name belongs to eight popes.

Valerio (vah-LEH-ree-yo) Meaning "strong" or "valorous." Colonel Valerio murdered Fascist leader Benito Mussolini in 1945.

Valentino (vah-len-TEE-no) Italian version of the Latin name Valentine, which means "brave" or "strong." The well-known political philopher Niccolò Machiavelli admired Duke Valentino (1475–1507), who pressed for a strong, unified Italian state.

Vincenzo (vin-TCHEHN-zo) A form of the Latin name Vincent, meaning "conquering." Composer Vincenzo Tommasini and political thinker Vincenzo Gioberti share this name. Variations include *Vincenzio* and *Vicenzo*.

Vitale (vee-TAH-lee) Meaning "vital" or "living."

Vito (VEE-to) A popular Italian name, meaning "alive." This name is particularly widespread in southern Italy due to the presence of the cult of St. Vito the Martyr, who was tortured under the emperor Diocletian in the fourth century. St. Vito is invoked against epilepsy.

Vittorio (vih-TO-ree-yo) Related to the Latin name Victor, meaning "conqueror." Name of the celebrated filmmaker, director, and actor Vittorio De Sica, famous for his neorealist masterpiece *Bicycle Thieves* (1948). Also the name of Vittorio Emanuele III (1869–1947), the "soldier king," who was involved in World War II during the Fascist rule of Benito Mussolini. Variations include *Vittorico*, *Vittoriano*, *Vittorino*, and *Vittore*.

ITALY: GIRLS

Adriana (ah-DRIYAH-nah) Form of the Latin name Adrienne, meaning "dark" or "rich." Among the notable people with this name is famous 17th-century actress Adriana Lecouvreur. Variations include *Adrea* and *Adria*.

Agnese (ah-GNEH-seh) Meaning "gentle." Name of the third century saint, San Agnese, who was martyrized in Rome at the age of twelve.

Aida (ah-IY-dah) Meaning "happy," it is the name of a Verdi opera set in Egypt, and of its eponymous heroine.

Alessandra (ah-lehs-SAHN-drah) A form of the Greek name Alexandra, which means "defender of humanity."

Anna (AHN-nah) A version of the Hebrew name Hannah, which means "full of grace." Similar sounding to the Japanese name Hana, which means "flower." Notable people with this name are mathematician Anna Reinhardt and chemist Anna Harrison, as well as the talented and accomplished Italian actress Anna Magnani. A variation is *Anita*.

Arianna (ah-RIYAHN-nah) A form of the Greek name Ariadne, meaning "divine." Arianna was the daughter of the mythological king of Crete, Minos, who was able to find his way out of a labyrinth by using a thread which was given to him by Arianna.

Bianca (BIYAHN-kah) Meaning "white." This name is a traditional one in great aristocratic families of the past.

Camilla (kah-MIYL-lah) A variation upon the Latin name Camille, which means "young attendant." In Virgil's *Aeneid*, the character Camilla is a warrior maiden. Among the notable people with this name: Prince Charles's lady friend, Camilla Parker-Bowles.

Carlotta (kahr-LOHT-tah) A variation upon the name Charlotte, meaning "little and womanly." Name of the 19th-century empress of Mexico and of the beautiful and mysterious character in Alfred Hitchcock's classic film *Vertigo*. Also *Carletta*, *Carla*, and *Carlina*.

Carolina (kah-roh-LIY-nah) A variation of the Latin name Caroline, which means "little and womanly." Carolina Bonaparte married Joachim Murat in 1800 and became the queen of Naples.

Chiara (KIYAH-rah) A variation of Clara, which means "clear." The name became popular due to the cult of Santa Chiara of Assisi (1194–1253), founder of the second Francescan order.

Costanza (koh-STAHN-zah) Meaning "faithful." The wife of Wolfgang Amadeus Mozart, Kostanza Weber.

Cristina (criys-TIY-nah) Meaning "Christian." Queen Christine of Sweden (1625–1689) invited to her court the most famous intellectuals of her time, such as Descartes and Grotius, and founded the Royal Academy, which later became the Accademia Clementina. Also *Christa*.

Dorotea (doh-roh-THE-ah) Meaning "gift of God." Among the notable people with this name: Dorotea Bucca, pioneering physician of the Middle Ages; and Santa Dorotea, patron saint of gardeners.

Eleonora (eh-leh-oh-NOH-rah) Meaning "light." Notable people with this name include the incandescent actress Eleonora Duse (1858–1924) and Eleonore d'Aquitaine, an influential patron of artists and poets who was queen of France, then of England.

Elisa (eh-LIY-sah) A short form of Elizabeth, meaning "pledged to God." Elisa Baciocchi (1777–1820), was sister of Napoleon. Also *Erlisa* and *Lisa*.

Eva (EH-vah) Meaning "life." Congresswoman Eva Clayton; first lady of Argentina, Eva Peron.

Filomena (phiy-loh-MEH-nah) An alternate form of Philomena, which means "love of song." St. Filomena the Virgin was martyrized in Rome under Diocletian. A variation is *Filemon* and *Filomela*.

Francesca (frahn-TCHEH-skah) A form of the name Frances, meaning "free man."

Gemma (JEHM-mah) Meaning "jewel; precious stone." Gemma Donati married Dante Alighieri in ca. 1290.

Gianna (JAHN-nah) A short form of Giovanna, meaning "giving God." Also *Giana*, *Gianella*, *Gianetta*, *Gianina*, *Giannella*, and *Giannetta*.

Giovanna (joh-VAHN-nah) A form of the name Joan, meaning "God's gracious gift." Name of legendary female pope, Pope Giovanna, who according to legend reigned between 855 and 857.

Giuditta (juw-DIYT-tah) Meaning "praised." Notable persons by this name are celebrated opera singer Giuditta la Pasta and St. Giudittam, martyrized in Milan under the emperor Maximianus.

Giulia (JUW-liyah) A form of the name Julia, meaning "youth." Variations include *Giuliana*, *Giulianna*, *Guila*, and *Guiliana*.

Giustina (juw-STIY-nah) A variation upon the name Justine, meaning "fair and righteous." St. Giustina was martyrized in Rome in A.D. 165.

Isabella (iy-sah-BEHL-lah) A form of the name Isabel, meaning "pledged to God." Among the notable people with this name are actress Isabella Rossellini and Queen Isabella of Castile, who financed Columbus's voyage to America.

Laura (LAH-uw-rah)   Meaning "crown of laurels." St. Laura of Cordova was martyrized by the Saracens in 864. Also *Laurenza, Lorena,* and *Lorenya.*

Letizia (leh-TIY-tsiyah)   From the Latin *laetitia,* meaning "happiness." Name of Napoleon's mother, Maria Letizia Ramorino Buonaparte. Also *Letty, Lettie,* and the Spanish *Leticia.*

Lucia (luw-TCHIY-ah)   Meaning "light." Notable Lucias include Lucia Chase, longtime director of American Ballet Theater, and the title character of Donizetti's *Lucia di Lammermoor.* Other versions are *Luciana* and *Lucianna.*

Lucrezia (luw-KREH-tsiyah)   A form of the name Lucretia. Opera singer Lucrezia Bori.

Margherita (mahr-gheh-RIY-tah)   A form of the name Margaret, meaning "pearl." Margherita di Savoia (1851–1926) was the first queen to reign over unified Italy.

Maria (mah-RIY-ah)   Meaning "bitterness" or "sorrow." Maria Jose was the last queen of Italy; opera singer Maria Callas (1923–1977) was famous for her remarkable voice range and fine dramatic skills. Variations include *Marica, Marise, Marisse,* and *Marissa.*

Mia (MIY-ah)   Meaning "mine." A familiar form of Michaela, Michelle. Among the notable people with this name are actresses Mia Farrow and Mia Sara.

Oriana (oh-riy-AH-nah)   Meaning "the east; sunrise." Among the notable people with this name are contemporary journalist and novelist Oriana Fallaci and the Teatro alla Scala dancer Oriella Dorella. A variation is *Oria.*

Ortensia (ohr-TEHN-siyah)   Meaning "garden." Ortensia Mancini succeeded in animating Parisian high society at the beginning of the 17th century. Variations include *Hortensia* and *Ortense.*

Paola (PAH-oh-lah)   A feminine form of the name Paul, meaning "small." St. Paola was a Roman maiden who founded a convent in the

fourth century; Paola Turci is an Italian pop singer famous for her highly individual style and powerful voice. A variation is *Paolina.*

Patrizia (pah-TRIY-tsiyah)   Meaning "noble." St. Patrizia the Virgin is one of the patron saints of Naples; Patricia McBride was the prima ballerina at the New York City Ballet in 1961.

Rosa (ROH-sah)   A form of the name Rose. Among the notable people with this name are civil rights heroine Rosa Parks and German socialist revolutionary Rosa Luxemburg. Also spelled *Roza.*

Rosalia (roh-sah-LIY-ah)   A combination of Rose and Lily. The patron saint of Palermo, St. Rosalia, withdrew from courtly life to Mt. Pellegrino to lead a chaste life.

Silvia (SIYL-viyah)   This name is derived from the Latin *silva,* which means "wood." Rea Silvia and Mars gave birth to Romulus and Remus, the mythical founders of the city of Rome.

Teodora (teh-oh-DOH-rah)   Meaning "gift of God." Among the notable people with this name are the gymnast Teodora Alexandrova and Empress Theodora (500–548), wife of the emperor Justinian.

Valentina (vah-lehn-TIY-nah)   Meaning "brave." Valentina Tereskova was the name of the first woman ever to navigate in space. Also *Valentia, Valenzia,* and *Valente.*

Violetta (viyoh-LEHT-tah)   Meaning "violet." Violeta Chamorro, elected president of Nicaragua in 1990 after years of the Sandinista dictatorship, has shown that a determined, strong person can bear a sweet name.

Viviana (viy-VIYAH-nah)   Meaning "lively." This name was made popular by the English actress Vivien Leigh (1913–1967), who played the role of Scarlet O'Hara in the 1939 classic *Gone With the Wind.*

Zoe (ZOH-eh)   Meaning "life." Empress Zoe, and daughter of Constantine VIII, succeeded to the throne of Byzantium and extended her power to her husband, Romanus III.

Portuguese-Speaking Regions

Portuguese culture and history are related to the culture and history of Spain but also bear the influence of the Romans, Visigoths, and Moors. Portuguese naming traditions, however, are especially demonstrative of the influence of the Catholic Church, and native speakers of Portuguese frequently name their children after saints and religious feast days. Portuguese exploration and expansion into the New World in pursuit of intercontinental trade helped shape the modern world. In 1488, Bartholemew Dias sailed the first European ship around the southern tip of Africa, opening a sea route to the Orient and the lucrative spice trade. In 1500, the merchant fleet of Pedro Alvarez Cabral, on the route to India, stumbled upon the South American continent instead. Portugal established trading outposts in its territory of this new land, which they called Brazil after *brasile*, a valuable red dye produced from local wood. Portugal energetically colonized the new land and ruled Brazil until 1822, when Brazil gained its independence.

PORTUGUESE-SPEAKING REGIONS: BOYS

Adriano (ah-dree-AH-noh)   A variation upon the name Adrian, meaning "dark" or "from Adria." Name of a Roman emperor and several popes. Also *Adrianno*, *Adrien*, and *Hadrian*.

Alberto (ow-BEHR-toh)   A variation upon the name Albert, meaning "noble and bright." Here the "e" is pronounced like the "e" in "effort." Also *Albert*, *Albrecht*, and *Elbert*.

Ângelo (AHN-ge-loh)   A variation upon the name Angel, which means "saintly."

Antônio (ahn-TOH-neeoh)   A variation upon the name Anthony, meaning "of inestimable worth." Santo Antônio was the father of Christian monasticism. Also *Antoine*, *Antoni*, *Anton*, and *Antjuan* in Spanish.

Benedito (beh-neh-DEE-toh)   A variation upon the name Benedict, meaning "blessed." Also *Bento*.

Bruno (BROO-noh)   Meaning "brown."

Caio (CAIGH-oh)   A form of Gaius, meaning "to rejoice." Also *Caius*.

Carlos (CAHR-los)   A variation upon the name Charles, meaning "man." Antônio Carlos Jobim was a great Brazilian composer. Also *Carlo*.

Cláudio (CLOW-deeoh)   A variation upon the name Claude, meaning "lame." Also *Claudio*.

Cristiano (crees-tee-AH-no)   Meaning "Christian." Also *Christiano*.

Daniel (dah-nee-EHL)   Meaning "God is judge." Here the "e" is pronounced like the "e" in "effort." Also *Danilo*.

Demetre (deh-MEH-tree)   A variation upon the name Dimitri, meaning "lover of the earth." Here the first and second "e" are pronounced like the "e" in "effort." Also *Demetrio*.

Edson (EHD-sohn)   A variation upon the name Edison, meaning "Edward's son." Edson

Arantes do Nascimento, nickname Pelé, is a famous soccer player.

Erasmo (eh-RAHS-moh)   A form of Erasmus, meaning "kindly."

Eugênio (eh-oo-GEH-nee-oh)   A form of Eugenius, meaning "noble; well born."

Fábio (FAH-beeoh)   A variation upon the name Fabian, possibly from the Latin *faba*, meaning "bean." Fábio was a Roman clan name. Here the "á" is an open acute sound. Romance novel model Fabio. Also *Fabiano*.

Flávio (FLAH-veeoh)   A variation upon the name Flavian, meaning "fair; blond." Here the "á" is an open acute sound. Also *Flaviano*.

Francisco (frahn-CEES-coh)   A variation upon the name Francis, meaning "free man." Francisco Buarque de Holanda is a famous Brazilian composer. Also *Francesco*.

Frederico (freh-deh-REE-coh)   A variation upon the name Frederick, meaning "peaceful leader."

Gabriel (gah-bree-EHL)   A variation upon the name Gabriel, meaning "God is mighty."

Gregório (greh-GAHL-reeoh)   A variation upon the name Gregory, meaning "vigilant." Gregório de Matos was one of the first native Brazilian poets.

Gustavo (goos-TAH-voh)   A variation upon the name Gustav, meaning "honorable staff." Gustavo Kuerten is a famous Brazilian tennis player.

Haroldo (ah-ROL-do)   A variation upon the name Harold, which means "leader of an army." Also *Heraldo*, *Heriado*, and *Hiraldo*.

Heitor (ehee-TOHR)   A variation upon the name Hector, which means "steady; unswerving." Heitor Villa-Lobos was an honored Brazilian classical composer.

Hélio (EH-lee-oh)   A form of Helios, meaning "the sun." Here the "e" is pronounced like the "e" in "effort." Also *Élio*.

Hugo (OO-goh)   Meaning "mind; intelligence." Also *Ugo*.

Inácio (ee-NAH-ceeoh)   A form of Ignatius, meaning "the fiery and ardent." Santo Inácio de Loyola was the founder of the Jesuits. Also *Ignácio*.

Ismael (ees-mah-EHL)   A variation upon the name Ishmael, meaning "God will hear." Here the "e" is pronounced like the "e" in "effort."

Jaime (JAIGH-mee)   A variation upon the name James, meaning "the supplanter." Also *Jayme*.

João (joh-OWN)   A variation upon the name John, which means "God's gracious gift." João Cabral de Mello Neto was a distinguished Brazilian writer. Here the "ã" is a very closed nasal sound, not like in "tall."

Joaquim (joh-ah-KEEM)   A variation upon the name Joachim, which means "the lord will judge."

Jorge (JOHR-gee)   A variation upon the name George, meaning "farmer; tiller of the soil." Jorge Amado is a distinguished Brazilian writer. Also *George*.

Júlio (JOO-leeoh)   Meaning "divinely youthful." Also *Julio* and *Giulio*.

Lauro (LOW-roh)   A variation upon the name Lawrence, meaning "crowned with laurel."

Leonardo (leh-oh-NAHR-doh)   Meaning "brave as a lion," it is a variation upon the name Leonard. Also *Leônidas*.

Leopoldo (leh-oh-POHL-doh)   A variation upon the name Leopold, which means "patriotic."

Lúcio (LOO-ceeoh)   A form of Lucius, meaning "light." Lúcio Costa was the founder of modern architecture in Brazil. Also *Lucio* and *Luca*.

Luís (LOOEESH)   A variation upon the name Louis, which means "renowned in battle."

Márcio (MAHR-seeoh)   A form of Marcus, meaning "belonging to Mars; warrior." Also *Marcio*.

Martinho (mahr-TEEN-oh)   A variation upon the name Martin, meaning "warlike."

Milton (meel-TOHN) Meaning "from the mill town." Milton Nascimento is a great Brazilian composer.

Nestor (nehs-tohr) Meaning "venerable wisdom."

Nicolau (nee-coh-LOW) A variation upon the name Nicholas, meaning "victory of the people." Also *Nicolas*.

Olavo (oh-LAH-voh) A variation upon the name Olaf, meaning "ancestor."

Oscar (ohs-CAHR) Meaning "divine spear." Also *Oschar*.

Otávio (oh-TAH-veeoh) A form of Octavius, meaning "eighth." Also *Octávio*.

Paulo (POW-loh) A variation upon the name Paul, meaning "little." São Paulo, the apostle.

Patrício (pah-TREE-seeoh) A variation upon the name Patrick, which means "noble; patrician."

Pedro (PEH-droh) A variation upon the name Peter, meaning "rock; stone." Pedro was the nickname given by Christ to the apostle Simão.

Régis (REH-geesh) A form of Rex, meaning "king." Also *Reginaldo*.

Ricardo (ree-CAHR-doh) A variation upon the name Richard, meaning "powerful ruler."

Ronaldo (roh-NOW-doh) A variation upon the name Ronald, meaning "mighty ruler." Also *Rinaldo*.

Saulo (SOW-loh) A form of Saul, meaning "longed for; desired."

Sebastião (seh-bahs-tee-OWN) A variation upon the name Sebastian, meaning "respected; reverenced." Here "ã" is a very closed nasal sound, not like in "cow." Sebastião Tapajós is a renowned Brazilian classical guitarist.

Sérgio (SEHR-geeoh) A variation upon the name Serge, meaning "the attendant." Here the "e" is pronounced like the "e" in "effort."

Simão (see-MOWN) A variation upon the name Simon, Peter, meaning "rock" or "stone."

Tomás (toh-MAHS) A variation upon the name Thomas ("the twin"). Tomás was one of the twelve disciples of Jesus. Here "á" is an open acute sound. Also *Tomásio*.

Tito (TEE-toh) A form of Titus, meaning "safe; saved." Also *Titto*.

Urbano (OOR-bah-noh) A variation upon the name Urban, meaning "from the city." Also *Urbanno*.

Valério (vah-LEH-reeoh) A variation upon the name Valery, meaning "strong." Here the "e" is pronounced like the "e" in "effort." Also *Vallerio*.

Vicente (vee-CEHN-tee) A variation upon the name Vincent, which means "the conqueror."

Vítor (VEE-tohr) A variation upon the name Victor, meaning "victorious."

Zacarias (zah-kah-REEAHS) A form of Zachariah, which means "the Lord's remembrance." Also *Zacharias*.

PORTUGUESE-SPEAKING REGIONS: GIRLS

Adriana (ah-dree-AH-nah) A variation upon the name Adriano, meaning "dark" or "from Adria." Also *Adrianna*, *Adriene*, and *Adrienne*.

Alice (ah-LEE-ceh) Meaning "truth." Also *Alícia*.

Ângela (AHN-ge-lah) A variation upon the name Ângelo, meaning "saintly." Here "ân" is a closed nasal sound, not like in "tall."

Antónia (ahn-TOH-neeah) A variation upon the name Antônio, meaning "of inestimable worth." The "an" is a closed nasal sound, not like in "tall." Also *Antonia*.

Beatriz (bee-Ah-TREESH) Meaning "she brings joy." Beatriz Segall is a famous Brazilian actress. Also *Beatrix*.

Benedita (beh-neh-DEE-tah) A variation upon the name Benedito, meaning "blessed."

Benedita da Silva is a respected Brazilian politician. Also *Benta*.

Branca (BRAHN-cah)   A variation upon the name Bianca, meaning "white."

Carla (KAHR-lah)   Meaning "strong."

Carmen (KAHR-mehn)   Meaning "a song." Carmen Miranda was a fantastic Brazilian singer, very popular in the United States.

Cíntia (SEEN-teeah)   A variation upon the name Cynthia, which means "moon." Also *Cinthia*.

Cláudia (KLOW-deeah)   A variation upon the name Cláudio, meaning "lame." Also *Claudia*.

Cristina (crees-TEE-nah)   A variation upon the name Cristiano, meaning "fair Christian." Also *Christina*.

Dália (DAH-leeah)   Meaning "from the valley."

Diana (DEEAH-nah)   Diana was the Roman goddess of the hunt. Also *Diane*.

Diná (dee-NAH)   A form of Dinah, which means "judged; exonerated." Dinah Silveira de Queiroz was a distinguished Brazilian writer. Also *Dinah*.

Edna (EHD-nah)   Meaning "rejuvenation." Here the "e" is pronounced like the "e" in "effort."

Efigênia (eh-fee-GEH-neeah)   Meaning "sacrifice." In Greek mythology, Efigênia was the daughter of Agamemnon.

Elisabete (eh-lee-zah-BEH-teh)   A variation upon the name Elizabeth, meaning "pledge of God." Elisabete was the mother of John the Baptist. Also *Elizabete*.

Eugênia (eh-oo-GEH-neeah)   A variation upon the name Eugênio, meaning "noble; well born."

Fátima (FAH-tee-mah)   A daughter of the prophet Muhammad.

Fernanda (fehr-NAHN-dah)   A variation upon the name Fernando, meaning "adventurer." Fernanda Montenegro is a Brazilian actress, nominated for the Oscar for best actress in 1999.

Flávia (FAH-bee-ah)   A variation upon the name Flávio, meaning "fair; blond." Here the "á" is an open acute sound.

Francisca (frahn-CEES-cah)   A variation upon the name Francisco, meaning "free man."

Gabriela (gah-bree-EH-lah)   A feminine form of Gabriel, which means "woman of God." *Gabriela* is the title of a Brazilian novel by Jorge Amado. Here the "e" is pronounced like the "e" in "effort." Also *Gabriele, Gabrielle*.

Glória (gloh-reeah)   A variation upon the name Gloria, meaning "glory." Here the "o" is an open acute sound.

Graça (GRAH-ssah)   A variation upon the name Grace, meaning "graceful."

Helena (eh-LEH-nah)   A variation upon the name Helen, meaning "a torch." Also *Elena*.

Heloísa (eh-LOH-EE-sah)   A form of Luíza, meaning "honorable fighter."

Hortênsia (ohr-TEHN-seeah)   Meaning "gardener." Hortênsia is a famous Brazilian basketball player.

Iolanda (ee-oh-LAHN-dah)   Meaning "violet flower."

Íris (EE-rees)   Meaning "rainbow." Íris was the Greek goddess of the rainbow.

Jane (JAH-nee)   A variation upon the name João. Also *Janne*.

Jaqueline (jah-keh-LEE-nee)   Meaning "the supplanter."

Júlia (JOO-leeah)   A variation upon the name Júlio, meaning "divinely youthful." Also *Julia* and *Giulia*.

Laura (LOW-rah)   A variation upon the name Lauro, meaning "crowned with laurel."

Letícia (leh-TEE-ceeah)   Meaning "joy; delight."

Lídia (LEE-deeah)   Meaning "woman of Lydia."

Lúcia (LOO-ceeah)   Meaning "light," it is a variation of the name Lucio. Also *Lucia*.

Luiza (loo-EEZAH)   A variation upon the name Lewis, meaning "battle maiden." Also *Luíse* and *Heloísa*.

Márcia (MAHR-seeah)   A variation upon the name Marcos, which means "belonging to Mars; warrior."

Marina (mah-REE-nah)   Meaning "of the sea."

Marta (MAHR-tah)   A variation upon the name Martha, meaning "lady."

Mónica (moh-NEE-kah)   Meaning "adviser," it is a form of the name Monique.

Nádia (NAH-deeah)   Meaning "hope."

Natália (nah-TAH-leeah)   A variation upon the name Nathalia, meaning "child of Christmas."

Norma (NOHR-mah)   Meaning "the model." Here the "o" is an open acute sound.

Odete (oh-DEH-tee)   A variation upon the name Odette, meaning "patriot." Here the "o" is an open acute sound.

Olívia (oh-LEE-veeah)   A variation upon the name Olive "the olive tree." Also *Lívia*.

Patrícia (pah-TREE-seeah)   A variation upon the name Patrício, meaning "noble; patrician."

Paula (POW-lah)   A variation upon the name Paulo, meaning "little."

Regina (reh-GEE-nah)   Meaning "queen."

Rosa (ROH-sah)   A variation upon the name Rose. Here the "o" is an open acute sound.

Sebastiana (She-bahsh-TEEAH-nah)   A variation upon the name Sebastião, which means "respected; reverenced."

Selma (SEHL-mah)   Meaning "the fair." Here the "e" is pronounced like the "e" in "effort."

Sofia (soh-FEEAH)   A form of Sophia, meaning "wisdom." Also *Sônia*.

Tânia (TAH-neeah)   A variation upon the Latin name Tatiana, meaning "unknown." Also *Tania*.

Telma (TEHL-mah)   A variation upon the name Thelma, meaning "nursing."

Teresa (teh-REH-sah)   Meaning "the harvester." Madre Teresa de Calcutá, winner of the Nobel Peace Prize. Also *Tereza*.

Tônia (TOH-neeah)   A short form of Antônia. Tônia Carreiro is a famous Brazilian actress.

Úrsula (OOR-soo-lah)   Meaning "she-bear."

Valéria (vah-LEH-reeah)   A variation upon the name Valério, which means "strong." Here the "e" is pronounced like the "e" in "effort."

Vera (VEH-rah)   Meaning "true."

Viviane (vee-VEEAH-nee)   Meaning "full of life."

Vitória (vee-TOH-reeah)   A variation upon the name Vítor, which means "the conqueror." Here the "o" is an open acute sound.

Zoé (zoh-EH)   Meaning "life." Here the "e" is pronounced like the "e" in "effort."

Spanish-Speaking Regions

A few Germanic names, such as Alfonso and Elvira, have survived from the period when the Visigoths ruled Spain and are in frequent use in Spanish-speaking countries. Yet the vast majority of children's names reflect the fervent devotion of these countries to the Catholic faith. Girls' names offer strong illustrations of this point. The Virgin Mary is honored by a large variety of names, consisting of names including her attributes and names that are metaphors for her attributes. Maria Consuelo (Mary of Consolation) and Maria Luz (Mary of Light) are two of the former, while Mercedes (mercy) and Pilar (pillar of the church) are two of the latter. The names of holy days and other important religious occasions are often given to girls, for example Anunciación (the Annunciation) and Concepción (the Immaculate Conception). Boys are frequently given saints' names, often, as in Italy, to venerate a local patron saint such as St. Ramiro of León. People in Spanish-speaking countries are also very fond of pet names and nicknames. Although girls are often called by the formal names, boys are rarely addressed by them.

SPANISH-SPEAKING REGIONS: BOYS

Alberto (al-bert-o) Meaning "noble and bright." Variations include *Adalberto, Al, Albert, Albertino, Berto,* and *Tico.*

Alejandro (al-lay-HAN-dro) A form of the Greek name Alexander, which means "man's defender and protector." Variations include *Alejindra, Alijo, Alexis,* and *Alexjindro.*

Alfonso (al-fon-so) Derives from the German name Alphonse, which means "prepared for battle." Alfonso Lopez Pumarejo was a two-term president of Colombia. Variations include *Affonso, Alfons, Alfonse, Alfonsus, Alfonza,* and *Alfonzo.*

Alfredo (al-FRAY-do) Derives from the Old English Alfred, which means "wise as an elf." Alfredo Zayas y Alfonso was an early 20th-century president of Cuba. Variations include *Alfeo* and *Alfrido*; also *Alfredo* in Italian.

Alonso (ah-LON-zo) A form of the German name Alphonse, which means "prepared for battle." Pro basketball player Alonzo "Zo"

Mourning turns up the Miami Heat as starting center. Variations include *Alano, Alanzo, Alon, Alonzo, Elonzo, Lon,* and *Lonnie.*

Alvaro (AL-va-roh) Meaning "just; wise." Alvaro Obregón was president of Mexico.

Andrés (AN-dres) From Greek name Andrew, meaning "manly." Guitar virtuoso Andrés Segovia charmed millions with his playing. Variations include *Andras, Andris, Andreo,* and *Andrez*; also *Andriano* in Portuguese.

Antjuan (an-TWAN) From the Latin name Anthony, meaning "of inestimable worth." Variations include *Antajuan, Anthjuan, Antuan,* and *Antuane.*

Aquila (AH-keel-ah) Meaning "eagle." Variations include *Acquilla, Aquill, Aquilas, Aquilla,* and *Aquillino.*

Araldo (ah-RAL-doh) A form of the Anglo-Saxon name Harold, which means "army commander." Variations include *Arallodo, Aralt, Aroldo,* and *Arry.*

Armando (ar-MAN-doh) A form of Armand, which is a variant on the German name Herman, meaning "noble warrior." A variation is *Armondo*.

Arrio (AHRR-ree-oh) Meaning "war-like." Variations include *Ario, Arrow, Arryo,* and *Aryo*.

Barto (BAR-toh) A form of the Hebrew name Bartholomew, meaning "son of the furrows; farmer." Variations include *Bardo, Bartoli, Bartolo,* and *Bartos*.

Bebe (be-be) Means "baby," a term of endearment.

Bernardo (behr-NAR-doh) A variation of the name Bernard, which means "bear." Famous Bernardos include director Bernardo Bertolucci, who disturbed viewers worldwide with his film *Last Tango in Paris*, and painter Bernardo Strozzi. Variations include *Barnardino, Barnardo, Barnhardo, Benardo, Bernave, Bernhardo, Berno,* and *Nardo*.

Blanco (BLAN-koh) Meaning "shining" or "white."

Bonaro (bo-NAR-oh) "Friend." Variations include *Bono* and *Bonar*.

Carlos (CAHR-los) The Spanish form of Charles, which means "man." Writer and mystic Carlos Castañeda gives fame to this name. Variations include *Carlo, Charlie, Charly, Chico,* and *Chacho*.

Cesar (SAY-zar) A form of the Latin name Caesar, meaning "long dark hair." Variations include *Cesare, Cesareo, Cesario, Cesaro, Sarito,* and *Sarit*.

Chago (CHAG-go) A form of Jacob, meaning "the supplanter." Variations include *Chango* and *Chanti*.

Charro (CHA-ro) Meaning "cowboy," it can also be spelled *Charo*.

Che (CHAY) A familiar form of Jose. Ernesto "Che" Guevara was a military revolutionary who fought for dictator Fidel Castro in the late 1950s during the Cuban Revolution. His guerrilla tactics immortalized him in American pop culture. Variations include *Chay*.

Checha (CHAY-chah) A familiar form of Jacob, which means "the supplanter."

Chico (CHEE-ko) Meaning "boy," it is also a nickname for Francisco, meaning "free man." Also *Chiquito*.

Chuminga (chew-MEEN-gah) A familiar form of Dominic, meaning "belonging to God." A variation is *Chumin*.

Chumo (CHEW-mow) A familiar form of Thomas, which means "twin."

Cid (SID) Meaning "Lord" or "commander." The epic poem *The Song of the Cid*, written in 1140 by an author who remains anonymous, was one of the earliest significant works in the canon of Spanish literature. A variation is *Cyd*.

Clemente (klay-MEN-tay) A form of the Latin name Clement, meaning "kind; gentle." Cuban-born baseball great Roberto Clemente (1934–1972) tragically died in a plane crash when delivering relief supplies to Nicaraguan earthquake victims. Variations include *Clemento* and *Clemenza*.

Cordero (kor-DER-oh) Spanish for "baby bee," it is most commonly found as a surname. Variations include *Cordaro, Cordario,* and *Cordeal*.

Cristóbal (Kris-TOE-bal) Derived from the name Christian, meaning "God within." Variations include *Christobal, Chrystal, Cristo, Cristoban, Cristovan,* and *Tobal*.

Cruz (KROOZ) Meaning "cross." Also *Kruz*.

Currito (ku-REE-toh) A variation of the French name Curtis, meaning "courteous." A variation is *Curcio*.

Dario (DAR-ee-o) Meaning "wealthy."

Decarlos (de-KAR-los) Usually found as a surname, a combination of the prefix De, meaning "of," and Carlos, "man." Variations include *Dacarlos, Decarlo,* and *Di'carlos*.

Desiderio (day-see-DARE-ee-oh) Meaning "desired." Television producer, actor, and musician Desi Arnaz was the Cuban band leader and hot-tempered husband of lovable red-head Lucille Ball. Variations include *Desi* and *Desidario*.

Diego (dee-AY-go) A form of the Hebrew name Jacob, meaning "supplanter." Controversial

20th-century artist and activist Diego Rivera (1886–1957) is known for both his paintings and his communist beliefs. Variations include *Iago* and *Diaz*.

Domingo (doh-MEEN-go) Meaning "born on Sunday." Opera star Placido Domingo is one of the Three Tenors. Variations include *Demingo*, *Domings*, and *Mingo* and the surnames *Dominques* and *Dominguez*.

Edmundo (ed-MOON-doh) A form of the Anglo-Saxon name Eadmund, meaning "rich and fortunate." Also *Mundo*.

Eduardo (eh-DWAHR-doh) A form of the name Eadmund, meaning "rich and fortunate." Architect Eduardo Torroja Miret.

Elvio (EL-vee-oh) Meaning "yellow" or "blond."

Emilio (eh-MEEL-lee-oh) From the Latin Emil, meaning "industrious" or "pleasing." Filipino revolutionary Emilio Aguinaldo (1864–1964) continued fighting for Filipino freedom even after serving as the first president of the Phillipines. Other notables include Emiliano Zapata (1879–1919), a Mexican revolutionary, and actor Emilio Estevez.

Enrique (en-REEK-KAY) A form of the name Henry, meaning "ruler of his house." Former Brazilian president Enrique Penaranda Castillo singer Enrique Iglesias, son of Julio Iglesias. Variations include *Enrigui*, *Enriquez*, *Enrrique*, *Rickie*, and *Ricky*.

Ermano (ehr-MAN-oh) A form of the name Herman, meaning "soldier," it is also Spanish for "brother" if spelled with an H, as in Hermano. Variations include *Ermin*, *Hermano*, *Herman*, and *German*.

Ernesto (ehr-NES-toh) A form of the name Ernest, meaning "sincere." Revolutionary Ernesto "Che" Guevara fought for Castro in Cuba. Variations include *Ernester*, *Neto*, *Nesto*, *Ernie*, and *Erny*.

Estiban (es-TEE-bahn) A form of the Greek name Stephen, meaning "crowned; royal." Variations include *Estevao*, *Estiven*, *Estabon*, *Estefan*, *Estefano*, and *Estephan*.

Eugenio (you-HEN-ee-oh) A form of the Greek name Eugene, meaning "born of high rank." Classical scholar and writer Eugenio de Ochoa.

Farruco (fahr-rouk-oh) A form of the name Francis, Francisco, meaning "free man." A variation is *Frascuelo*.

Federico (feh-dehr-EEK-oh) A form of the name Frederick, meaning "peaceful leader." Variations include *Frederico*, *Federic*, and *Federigo* and the nicknames *Freddy*, *Rickie*, *Ricky*, and *Rico*.

Felipe (feh-LEEP-ay) A form of the name Philip. Composer Felipe Pedrell. Variations include *Felipo*, *Filip*, *Filippo*, and *Flip*.

Félix (FE-lix) Latin for "blessed; lucky." Variations include *Feliciano* and *Felice* (fe-LEES), which means "happy" in Spanish.

Fermin (fehr-MEEN) Meaning "firm; strong." Variations include *Ferman* and *Firmin*.

Fernando (fehr-NAN-doh) A form of the name Ferdinand, which means "adventurer; explorer." Fernando Lamas, famously vain actor, was the embodiment of Latin suave. Variations include *Ferdinando*, *Fernand*, and *Fernandez*.

Francisco (frahn-SEES-ko) From the Latin name Franciscus, meaning "free man." A very popular name because of Saint Francis of Assisi. Artist Francisco de Goya painted unforgettable portraits and was forced into exile because of his politics. Variations include *Chico*, *Chilo*, *Cisco*, *Farruco*, *Franco*, *Frank*, *Frankie*, *Franklyn*, *Frisco*, *Paco*, and *Pancho*.

Galeno (gah-LANE-oh) Meaning "bright little child." Other versions are *Galen*, Greek for "calm," and *Galan*, Spanish for "gentleman."

Garcia (gahr-SEE-ah) Meaning "mighty with a spear," it is most often used as a surname. 1982 Nobel Prize–winning author Gabriel García Márquez, a magical realist novelist who wrote *One Hundred Years of Solitude*.

Geraldo (heh-RAL-doh) A form of the Old German name Gerald, meaning "rules with a sword." Television journalist Geraldo Rivera, once Gerry Rivers, was a pioneer in tabloid television. A variation is *Gerardo*.

Gilberto (hil-BEHR-toh) A form of the name Gilbert, which means "bright pledge or oath."

Gitano (he-TAN-oh) Meaning "gypsy." Forms of this name appear throughout romance languages and are usually used to say someone is crafty and magical, hardly the slur it once was.

Gonzalo (gon-SAL-oh) Meaning "wolf." Variations include *Gonsalve*, *Gonzales*, and *Gonzalez*.

Gualberto (gwahl-BEHR-toh) A form of the name Walter, which means "powerful warrior." Variations include *Gualterio* and *Guadalberto*.

Guillermo (gee-YEHR-mo) A form of the name William, which means "great protector." Argentine tennis star Guillermo Vilas.

Gustavo (goo-STAV-oh) Meaning "honorable staff" or "support of the Goths." Former Colombian president Gustavo Rojas Pinilla. Variations include *Gustaves*, *Gusto*, *Tavo*, and *Tabo*.

Gutierre (goo-TEE-yer-ay) Derived from the name Walter, meaning "powerful warrior." Andalucian poet Gutierre de Cetina. *Gutierrez* and *Gutierres* are common Hispanic surnames in Portuguese.

Heraido (ehr-AYE-doh) A form of the name Harold, meaning "leader of an army." Variations include *Herald*, *Heraldo*, and *Hiraldo*.

Heriberto (ehr-ee-BEHR-toh) A form of the name Herbert, meaning "shining soldier."

Hernando (ehr-NAN-doh) A form of the name Ferdinand, meaning "adventurer; explorer." Notable persons with this name ironically include, 15th- and 16th-century explorers Hernando de Soto and Hernando Cortés. Both explored what later became the southern United States. Variations include *Hernandes*, *Hernandez*, and *Hernán*.

Hilario (EE-lar-ee-yo) A form of the Latin name Hilary, which means "joyful; cheery."

Honorato (on-or-RAH-to) Meaning "honorable."

Huberto (ooh-BEHR-toh) A form of the German name Hubert, which means "highy intelligent." Also *Humberto*.

Jacinto (ha-SEEN-toh) Derived from "hyacinth," a violet flower. Variations include *Giacinto*, *Jacindo*, and *Jacinte*.

Jade (HA-day) A precious green stone that is reputed to promote good luck.

Jaguar (HAG-wahr) A wild cat similar to a leopard, but native to the Americas. A variation is *Jagguar*.

Jaime (HI-may) A form of the Hebrew name Jacob, meaning "follower." Composer and conductor Jaime Nunó. Variations include *Jaimey*, *Jaimie*, *Jaimito*, and *Jayme*.

Jairo (HI-roh) Meaning "God enlightens." Variations include *Jairus* and *Jarius*.

Jando (HAN-doh) A form of the name Alexander, meaning "man's defender and protector." A variation is *Jandino*.

Javier (hav-ee-YEHR) Meaning "owner of a new house." Javier Pérez de Cuéllar was the United Nations Secretary General. Variations include *Jabier* and *Xavier*.

Joaquin (hwah-KEEN) A form of the Hebrew name Joachim or Yehoyakem, meaning "God's choice." Ace pitcher Joaquin Andujar came to fame with the Houston Astros. Variations include *Joaquin*, *Jocquin*, *Jocquinn*, and *Juaquin*.

Jorge (HOR-HAY) A form of the name George, meaning "farmer." Novelist Jorge Luis Borges. A variation is *Jorrin*.

Jose (HO-SE) Derived from the Hebrew name Joseph, which means "he will multiply." Variations include *Cepito*, *Che*, *Cheche*, *Chepe*, *Josefe*, *Pepe*, *Pepito*, and *Peppo*.

Juan (WAHN) A form of the name John, meaning "God's gracious gift." King Juan Carlos of Spain. Variations include *Juancho*, *Juanito*, *Juann*, and *Juaun*.

Kiki (KEE-kee) A nickname derived from the name Henrique (Henry) meaning "ruler of his house." Professional basketball star Kiki Vandeweghe.

Leandro (lay-AN-dro) Meaning "brave; lion-like," it is derived from the name Leander. Variations include *Leandra, Leandres, Leandros,* and *Uandre.*

Lobo (LO-bo) Meaning "wolf."

Lorenzo (lo-REN-so) A form of the name Lawrence, meaning "crowned with laurel." Soap opera actor Lorenzo Lamas, son of Fernando Lamas. Variations include *Chencho, Loren, Laurencio, Lauro,* and *Lencho.*

Luis (lou-EEC) Both French and German royal descent, the name Luis derives from the name Louis, which means "glory in war." Painter Luis de Vargas is probably not as well known as Luis, the Latin-American denizen of *Sesame Street.*

Macario (ma-KAR-ee-oh) Meaning "happy" or "blessed."

Manuel (MAH-nuel) Meaning "God within us." Variations include *Emmanuel, Mannie, Manny, Mano, Minel,* and *Mango,* also the name of a tropical fruit.

Marcos (MAHR-kos) Originally derived from the Greek god Mars, a form of the name Mark, meaning "rebellious battler." Variations include *Marco* and *Markos.*

Martin (mar-TEEN) Derived from the Greek god Mars, meaning "rebellious battler." Variations include *Martee, Martez, Martie, Martinez,* and *Martines,* and in Portuguese, *Martis* and *Martise.*

Mateo (ma-TAY-oh) A form of the name Matthew, meaning "God's gift." Sculptor Mateo Alonso. Variations include *Matias, Matteo,* and *Matteos.*

Mauricio (mau-REE-cee-oh) A form of the name Maurice, which is Latin for "dark Moor."

Maximo (MAH-ksmo) Meaning "superior," it is a form of the name Maximilian. Maximo Gomez, Cuban general. Variations include

Massimo, Maxi, Maximiano, Maximiliano, Maximino, and *Miximo.*

Menico (men-EE-ko) A short form of Domenico, meaning "belonging to Sunday."

Miguel (mee-GHEL) A form of the Hebrew name Michael, meaning "Who can compare to God." Miguel Asturias won a Nobel Prize for literature; Spain's greatest-ever cyclist, Miguel Indurain, won the Tour de France five times. Variations include *Migeel, Migel, Miguelly, Migul,* and *Mique* (MEE-ke).

Moises (MOY-ses) A form of the Hebrew name Moses, meaning "taken from the water." Baseball star Moises Alou comes from a baseball-playing Dominican family. Variations include *Moisis, Moisey,* and *Moisis.*

Montana (mon-TAN-ah) Meaning "mountain." Variations include *Montano* and *Montanez.*

Montez (mon-TEZ) Meaning "dweller in the mountains."

Mundo (MOON-doh) A short form of Edmundo. The word *mundo* means "world" in Spanish.

Napier (nahp-ee-YER) Meaning "new city." Variations include *Neper.*

Natal (nah-TAL) The name is Spanish for "birth." Variations include *Natale, Natalino, Natalio,* and *Nataly.*

Natan (nah-TAN) Meaning "God has given." Natan Sharansky was a political activist in Russia. Variations include *Nataneal* and *Nataniel.*

Navarro (nah-VAR-ro) Meaning "plains." A variation is *Navarre.*

Nelo (NAY-lo) A form of the name Daniel, meaning "God is judge." A variation is *Nello.*

Nemesio (nem-ESS-ee-oh) Meaning "just." A variation is *Nemi.*

Nero (neh-RO) Latin for "powerful; stern." Famous persons include the fifth emperor of the Roman Empire. Variations include *Neron, Nerone,* and *Nerron.*

Nevada (ne-VA-da)   Meaning "covered in snow." A variation is *Navada*.

Nicho (NEE-cho)   A form of the name Denis, which evolved from Dionysius, the name of the Greek god of wine.

Nifto (NEEF-toh)   Meaning "young child."

Oro (O-ro)   Meaning "golden."

Osvaldo (os-VAL-doh)   A form of the name Oswald, meaning "forest god." Variations include *Osvald*, *Osvalda*, and *Ozzy*.

Otello (oh-TELL-oh)   A form of the German name Otto, meaning "wealthy." The title character in the 16th-century Shakespearean tragedy *Othello*.

Pablo (PAH-blo)   From the Greek name Paulos, meaning "small." Artist Pablo Picasso forever changed the art world with his modernist visions. Other notable persons include virtuoso cellist Pablo Casals. Variations include *Pable* and *Paublo*, as well as *Pueblo*, which means "town" in Spanish.

Pancho (PAN-cho)   A form of Francisco, meaning "free man." Pancho Villa, Mexican revolutionary. A variation is *Panchito*.

Pascual (pas-KWAL)   A form of the name Pascal, meaning "Easter." Pascual Orozco was a Mexican revolutionary. Variations include *Pasqual* and *Pascal*.

Patricio (pah-TREE-see-oh)   A form of the name Patrick, meaning "patrician; aristocratic."

Paulo (POW-lo)   From the Greek name Paulos, meaning "small." Variations include *Pablo* and *Paulino*.

Perico (PER-ee-ko)   The diminutive of Pedro, it was what affectionate fans called Pedro Delgado, winner of both le Tour de France and la Vuelta de España. Variations include *Pequin* and *Perequin*.

Pedro (PAY-dro)   A form of the name Peter, meaning "rock." Spanish filmmaker Pedro Almodóvar's comedies amuse as much as they outrage. Variations include *Peyo*, *Perico*, *Piti*, and *Pitin*.

Pilar (pee-LAHR)   Meaning "pillar."

Pirro (pee-RRO)   Meaning "flaming hair."

Placido (PLAS-ee-doh)   Meaning "serene." Star tenor Placido Domingo. Variations include *Placidus*, *Placyd*, and *Placydo*.

Ponce (PON-say)   From the Latin Pontius, meaning "fifth son." Spanish explorer Juan Ponce de León searched Florida for the fountain of youth.

Porfirio (por-FEER-ee-oh)   Meaning "purple stone." Porfirio Díaz was a president of Mexico. Variations include *Porphirlos* and *Prophyrios*.

Quico (KEE-ko)   A familiar form of many names. Also *Paco*.

Quiqui (KEE-kee)   A familiar form of Enrique. Variations include *Quinto* and *Quiquin*.

Quito (KEE-toh)   A short form of Quinton, which means "fifth." Quito is the capital of Ecuador.

Rafael (rah-fai-EL)   Meaning "God has healed." Author Rafael Sabatini. Variations include *Rafaelle*, *Rafaello*, *Rafaelo*, *Rafa*, *Raffael*, and *Raffaelo*.

Ramon (rah-MON)   A form of the name Raymond, meaning "wise protector." Actor Ramon Navarro. Also *Romone*.

Raynaldo (ray-NAL-doh)   An alternate form of Renaldo, Reynold. Variations include *Raynal*, *Raynald*, and *Raynold*.

Renaldo (ray-NAL-doh)   A form of the name Reynold, meaning "powerful; full of courage." Variations include *Raynaldo*, *Reinaldo*, *Reynaldo*, *Rinaldo*, *Renaldo*, and *Renardo*.

Rey (RAY)   Meaning "king." A short form of Reynardo, Reynaldo, Reynold. A variation is the surname *Reyes*.

Reymundo (ray-MOON-doh)   A combination of *rey*, meaning "king" and *mundo*, meaning "world." Variations include *Reimundo*, *Raymundo*, and *Reymon*.

Rico (REE-ko)   Meaning "rich" in Spanish, it is also a short form of the names Ricardo, Enrique, or Federico.

Rio (REE-oh) Meaning "river."

Roberto (roh-BEHR-toh) A form of the Anglo-Saxon name Robert, meaning "bright fame." Baseball legend Roberto Clemente.

Rodas (ROAD-as) An alternate form of Rhodes.

Rodolfo (ro-DOLF-oh) A form of the name Rudolph, meaning "bold wolf." Variations include *Rudi*, *Rudolfo*, and *Rodolpho*.

Rodrigo (rod-REE-go) A form of the name Roderick, meaning "distinguished ruler." Rodrigo Díaz de Vivar was the given name of the legendary Spanish leader El Cid.

Rodriguez (rod-REE-guess) Meaning "son of Rodrigo." Variations include *Rodrigues* in Portuguese.

Rogelio (roh-HAY-lee-oh) Means "famous warrior" and is a form of the name Roger. Variations include *Rogerio* and *Rogerios*.

Rojo (RO-ho) Meaning "red."

Rolando (roh-LAHN-do) From the Old German translation, meaning "famous land." Variations include *Lando*, *Olo*, *Orlando*, *Orly*, and *Roly*.

Rollon (roy-ONH) Meaning "famous wolf."

Salamon (SAL-ah-mohn) Derived from the Hebrew word Shalom, meaning "peace." A variation is *Salomon*.

Salvador (SAL-vah-dor) Meaning "savior." Former Chilean president Salvador Allende was popular with his people, but not his military. A variation is *Salvadore*.

Sanson (san-SOHN) A form of the Hebrew name Samson, meaning "of the sun." Variations include *Sansone* and *Sansun*.

Santana (san-TAHN-ah) Meaning "Saint Anna." Antonio Santa Ana, a revolutionary general and president of Mexico, fought to make Texas part of Mexico. Also *Santanna*.

Santiago (san-tee-YA-go) A form of the name James, meaning "supplanter." A variation is *Iago*.

Santo (SAN-toh) Meaning "saint." Variations include *Santos*.

Segundo (say-GOON-doh) Meaning "second."

Sidonio (sih-DON-ee-oh) A form of the name Sidney, derived from "Saint Denis," which in turn is derived from the name of the Greek god of wine, Dionysius.

Taddeo (tah-DE-oh) A form of Thaddeus, meaning "God be praised," the name of one of the twelve apostles. Variations include *Deo* and *Tadeos*.

Teobaldo (tay-oh-BALL-doh) A form of the German name Theobald, meaning "brave leader of the people." Variations include *Teo*, *Theo*, *Tibolt*, *Tibor*, and *Tybol*.

Teodoro (tay-oh-DOHR-oh) Meaning "gift from God."

Terencio (teh-REHN-see-oh) A form of the name Terrence.

Tito (TEE-to) A popular Spanish nickname derived from many names. Popular Puerto Rican salsa band leader Tito Puentes.

Tomas (toh-MAS) A form of the name Thomas, meaning "twin." Variations include *Tomasio* and the Italian name *Tomasino*.

Vicente (vee-SEN-tay) From the Latin word *vincere*, "to conquer." Vicente Alexandre, Nobel Prize–winner for literature. Variations include *Vicente* and *Visente*.

Victorio (veek-TOR-ee-oh) From the Latin for "victorious." Variations include *Victor*, *Victorellio*, and *Victorino*.

Vida (VEE-dah) Spanish for "life." Pitcher Vida Blue was asked by his boss to change his name to True Blue. A variation is *Vidal*.

Virgilio (veer-HEEL-ee-oh) A form of the name Virgil, meaning "virgin; maiden."

Waterio (wah-TEHR-ee-oh) A form of the name Walter, meaning "ruler of the people." Also *Gualtiero*.

Wilfredo (wil-FRAY-doh) Meaning "peace," it is a form of the name Wilfred. Boxer

Wilfredo Benitez. Variations include *Fredo*, *Wifredo*, and *Willfredo*.

Ximenes (hee-MEN-es) A form of the name Simon, meaning "to be heard." Variations include *Ximenez*, *Ximon*, *Ximun*, and *Xymenes*.

Yago (YAH-go) A form of the name Jacob, meaning "the follower." The Spanish version of the name of Othello's duplicitous aide Iago in Shakespeare's play *Othello*.

SPANISH-SPEAKING REGIONS: GIRLS

Adalia (ah-DAHL-ee-ya) Meaning "noble." Variations include *Adal*, *Adala*, *Adalee*, *Adali*, *Adalle*, *Adalin*, and *Adaly*.

Adana (ah-DAHN-ah) A form of the name Adam, meaning "earth" or "man of the earth."

Adonia (ah-DOHN-ee-ya) Meaning "beautiful." A feminine form of Adonis. A variation is *Adonya*.

Alameda (ala-MAY-dah) Meaning "poplar tree."

Alanza (ah-LAN-sa) Meaning "noble and eager." A feminine form of Alphonse.

Alegria (ah-LEG-ree-ah) Meaning "happiness." Variations include *Allegra* and *Allegria*.

Alejandra (ah-lay-HAN-dra) A form of the name Alexandra, meaning "protector of the people." Variations include *Alandra*, *Alejandrina*, and *Alexandra*.

Alita (ah-LEE-tah) Meaning "little wing."

Alma (AHL-mah) Meaning "soul."

Alva (AHL-vah) "White; light skinned." Variations include *Alvana*, *Alvanna*, and *Alvannah*.

Amada (ah-MAH-da) Meaning "beloved." Variations include *Amadea*, *Amadi*, and *Amadia*.

Amaranta (ah-mah-RAN-ta) Meaning "flower that never fades."

Ana (AH-na) A derivative of the name Hannah, meaning "graceful." Variations include *Anita* and *Anna*.

Anunciación (ah-noon-see-ah-see-OHN) A name honoring the angel Gabriel's annunciation to the Virgin Mary that she would give birth to the son of God.

Ascención (ah-sen-see-OHN) A name honoring the ascension of Christ into heaven 40 days after his resurrection.

Asunción (ah-soon-see-OHN) A name honoring the assumption of the Virgin Mary into heaven. It is the name of the capital of Paraguay.

Belicia (beh-LEE-see-ah) Meaning "dedicated to God." Variations include *Beli*, *Belia*, and *Belica*.

Belinda (beh-LEEN-dah) Meaning "beautiful." A name English poet Alexander Pope gave to the shallow heroine of his satiric poem "The Rape of the Lock." Variations include *Bel*, *Belindra*, *Bella*, *Belynda*, *Linda*, and *Lynda*.

Benita (beh-NEE-tah) Latin for "God has blessed her." Variations include surname *Benitez* and nickname *Nita*.

Bonita (bo-NEE-tah) Meaning "pretty." Among the famous people with this name is actress Bonita Granville. Variations include *Bonnie* and *Bonny*.

Brisa (BREE-sa) Meaning "breeze." Variations include *Brissa* and *Bryssa*.

Calida (cah-LEE-dah) Meaning "warm; ardent." Variations include *Calina*, *Calinda*, *Callida*, and *Kalida*, and also *Calidad*, which means "quality."

Catalina (cat-ah-LEEN-ah) A form of the name Catherine, meaning "pure." Variations include *Cataleen*, *Catalena*, and *Catalia*.

Cecilia (se-SEE-lee-ah) Patron saint of music, also a form of Cecil. Variations include *Celia*, *Ceyla*, and *Xylia*.

Chalina (cha-LEEN-ah) A form of the name Rose.

Charo (CHA-ro) A familiar form of the name Rosa. Also the name of popular Latina actress of variety and talk show television.

Chavella (cha VAY-ya) An alternate form of Isabel, which means "dedicated to God." Variations include *Chavelle*, *Chevelle*, and *Chevie*. Also slang for "young girl."

Chiquita (chih-KEE-tah) Meaning "little one." Variations include *Chica*, *Chickie*, *Chicky*, *Chikita*, and *Chiquilla*.

Clara (clah-REE-tah) Meaning "clear" or "sure." Variations include *Clareta*, *Clarabella*, and *Clarissa*.

Coco (KO-ko) Meaning "coconut." Notable persons include fashion giant Coco Chanel.

Concepcion (kohn-sep-see-OHN) A name honoring the immaculate conception of the Virgin Mary. A variation is *Conchita*.

Conchita (kohn-CHEE-tah) A nickname for Concepcion, it also means "little shell." Tennis player Conchita Martinez and actress Maria Conchita Alonso. Variations include *Chita* and *Concha*.

Constanza (kohn-STAN-sa) A form of the name Constantine, meaning "steady and loyal."

Consuelo (kohn-SWAY-lo) Meaning "consolation." Santa Maria del Consuelo is a name for the Virgin Mary. Variations include *Consolata*, *Consuela*, and *Consuella*.

Corazon (kor-ah-SOHN) Meaning "heart." Former Phillipines president Corazon Aquino, who, with the help of her supporters, turned out corrupt president Fernando Marcos.

Damita (da-MEET-ah) Meaning "small noblewoman." Variations include *Damee*, *Damesha*, *Dameshia*, *Damesia*, and *Dametia*.

Daniela (dahn-ee-EL-an) A form of the name Daniel, meaning "God is judge."

Dolores (do-LOHR-ess) Meaning "sorrowful." Among the notable people with this name are Dolores Huerta, co-founder of the United Farm Workers union, and actress Dolores Del Rio. Variations include *Delores*, *Deloria*, *Dolly*, and *Dolorio*.

Dulce (DOOL-se) Meaning "sweet." Don Quixote's damsel in distress in Miguel de Cervantes' 16th-century romance. Variations include *Dulcina* and *Dulcita*.

Eldora (el-DOHR-ah) Meaning "golden" or "gilded." Variations include *Dora*, *Eldoree*, *Eldorey*, *Eldori*, *Eldoria*, and *Eldorie*.

Elisa (ay-LEE-sa) A short form of Elizabeth, meaning "blessed by God." Among the notable people with this name is actress Elisa Donovan. Variations include *Alicia*, *Alycia*, *Eleesa*, *Elesia*, *Elisia*, *Elysa*, and *Ellisa*.

Enrica (en-REEK-ah) Derived from Henry, meaning "ruler of his house." Variations include *Enrieta*, *Enrietta*, *Enriqua*, and *Rica*.

Esmeralda (es-me-RYE-dah) Meaning "emerald." Variations include *Emelda*, *Esmi*, *Esmeraida*, *Esmerilda*, *Esmiralda*, and *Ezmerelda*.

Esperanza (es-peh-RAN-sah) Meaning "hope." Variations include *Esperansa* and *Esperanta*.

Estrella (es-TRE-yah) Meaning "star." Variations include *Estrellita* and *Strella*.

Evita (eh-VEET-ah) A form of the name Eve, meaning "breath of life." Argentinian politician Evita Peron worked as health and labor minister under her husband's presidency.

Florida (floh-REE-dah) Meaning "blooming flower" Variations include *Flor*, *Floridia*, and *Florinda*.

Gitana (jee-TAN-ah) Meaning "gypsy" or "wanderer."

Gracia (gra-SHAH) Meaning "God's grace" or "thanks."

Guillerma (ghee-YER-mah) A form of the name Wilhelmina, meaning "protector of the people." A variation is *Guilla*.

Hermosa (ehr-MO-sah) Meaning "beautiful."

Inez (ee-NES) Meaning "purity," it is a form of the name Agnes. Variations include *Agnesa*, *Ines*, *Inesa*, and *Inessa*.

Isabel (ee-sah-BELL) A form of the name Elizabeth, meaning "pledged to God." Variations include *Isa*, *Isabela*, and *Isabella*.

Jade (HA-day) The name of the precious stone. Variations include *Jada*, *Jadah*, *Jadea*, *Jadee*, and *Jaden*.

Jaira (HYE-rah) Meaning "Jehovah teaches." Variations include *Giajaira* and *Jajaira*.

Javiera (ha-vee-YER-ah) A feminine form of Javier, which means "owner of a new house." Variations include *Javeera*, *Vera*, and *Xaviera*.

Josefina (ho-sah-FEE-nah) Feminine form of Joseph, which means "God will multiply." Among the notable people with this name is author Josefina Estrada.

Juanita (wan-NEE-tah) Feminine form of the name Juan, which means "God's gracious gift." Among the notable people with this name are former secretary of commerce Juanita Kreps and congresswoman Juanita McDonald. Variations include *Juana*, *Juandalyn*, and *Juanetta*.

Juliana (HOO-lee-ahn-ah) Meaning "youthful." Juliana was a queen of the Netherlands. Variations include *Julia*, *Julietta*, and *Jullianna*.

Landra (LAN-dra) Meaning "counselor." Also *Landrea*.

Leya (LAY-ah) Meaning "the law."

Linda (LEEN-dah) Meaning "pretty." Actresses Linda Carter and Linda Evans are icons of the seventies, along with singer Linda Ronstadt and television journalist Linda Ellerbee. Variations include *Lin*, *Lindee*, *Lindy*, and *Lynda*.

Lola (LO-lah) A familiar form of Carlota, Dolores, Louise. A variation is *Lolita*.

Lorena (lo-REN-ah) Derived from the name Laura, which means "laurel." Variations include *Lorenita*, *Lorenza*, and *Loretta*.

Luisa (loo-EEZ-ah) A form of the name Louis, meaning "glory in war." Opera singer Luisa Tetrazzini whose name was attached to the popular dish chicken Tetrazzini.

Luz (LOOS) Meaning "light." Variations include *Lucia*, *Lusita*, *Luciana*, and *Lucianna*.

Lynda (LEEN-dah) Meaning "pretty."

Manuela (man-WAY-lah) A form of the name Emmanuelle, meaning "God within us."

Margarita (mah-garr-REE-tah) A form of the name Margaret, Greek for "pearl." Also the name of a popular cocktail. Variations include *Margareta*, *Margaritis*, *Margaritta*, *Margharita*, *Margo*, and *Rita*.

Mariana (mah-ree-AHN-ah) A form of the name Mary, meaning "bitter." Variations include *Marianna*, *Marriana*, *Marrianna*, and *Maryana*.

Marisol (mah-ree-SOLE) Meaning "sea and sun." Among the notable people with this name, pop artist Marisol (Marisol Escobar). Variations include *Marissa*, *Marizol*, and *Marysol*.

Marta (may-EE-tah) Meaning "warlike," derived from Mars, the Greek god of war. Variations include *Martica* and *Martina*.

Maruca (mah-ROO-kah) A form of the name Mary, meaning "bitterness."

Miel (ME-el) Meaning "honey."

Melosa (may-LOS-ah) Meaning "sweet; tender."

Mercedes (mehr-SAY-des) Meaning "merciful." Among the notable people with this name are actresses Mercedes McCambridge and Mercedes Ruehl.

Miguela (mee-GHEL-ah) A form of the name Michaela, meaning "Who can compare to God." Variations include *Miguelina* and *Miguelita*.

Milagros (mee-LAHG-ros) Meaning "miracle." Variations include *Mila*, *Milagritos*, *Milagro*, *Milagrosa*, and *Milarios*.

Montana (mohn-TA-nah) Meaning "mountain." Also *Montanna*.

Mora (MO-rah) Meaning "blueberry." Variations include *Morea*, *Moria*, and *Morita*.

Nieve (NE-e-veh) Meaning "snow."

Novia (NO-vee-ah) Meaning "sweetheart." Variations include *Nova* and *Nuvia*.

Oleda (oh-LAY-dah) An alternate form of Alida, a ancient Greek city where fine clothes were made and worn. Variations include *Leda*, *Oleta*, *Olida*, and *Olita*.

Orquidea (or-KEE-dee-ah) Meaning "orchid." Also *Orquidia*.

Paloma (pa-LO-mah) "Dove." Fragrance designer Paloma Picasso is a daughter of modern artist Pablo Picasso. Variations include *Palloma*, *Palometa*, and *Palomita*.

Pancha (PAHN-cha) Meaning "free." A feminine form of Pancho. Variations include *Paca* and *Panchita*.

Paquita (pa-KEE-tah) A feminine dimininutive of Francisco, meaning "free man." Variations include *Panchita* and *Paqua*.

Paz (PAAS) Meaning "peace."

Piedad (pie-ay-DOD) Meaning "devoted; pious."

Pilar (PEE-lahr) Meaning "pillar; column." A name that honors the Virgin Mary, the pillar of the Catholic Church. Variations include *Peelar* and *Pillar*.

Primavera (pree-mah-VER-ah) Meaning "spring."

Querida (keh-REE-dah) Meaning "dear; beloved."

Ramona (rah-MOHN-ah) "Wise guardian." Famous people with this name include actress Ramona Milano. Variations include *Ramonda* and *Raymona*.

Reina (RAY-nah) Meaning "queen." Variations include *Reginalda*, *Reine*, *Renalda*, and *Renia*.

Reseda (ray-SAID-ah) Meaning "fragrant mignonette blossom."

Rica (REE-kah) Meaning "rich," it is also a short form of Erica, Frederica, Ricarda. Also *Ricca*.

Ricarda (ree-KAR-dah) A feminine form of Richard, meaning "rich and powerful ruler." A variation is *Rica*.

Rocio (RO-see-oh) Meaning "dewdrops." A variation is *Rodo*.

Rosa (RO-sah) A form of the name Rose. Rosa Parks, who inspired the American civil rights movement by refusing to give up her bus seat to a white man in Montgomery, Alabama. Variations include *Charo*, *Rossi*, and *Rosita*.

Rosalinda (ro-sah-LEEN-dah) Meaning "fair rose." Among the famous people with this name: actress Rosalind Russell. Variations include *Rosalina*, *Rosalinda*, *Rosalinde*, *Rosaly*, *Rosalyn*, and *Rosalynda*.

Rosario (ro-SAAR-ee-oh) Meaning "rosary." Among the notable people with this name: poet Rosario Castellanos.

Rosita (ro-SEE-tah) A familiar form of Rose. Variations include *Roseeta* and *Roseta*.

Salvadora (sal-vah-DOOR-ah) Meaning "savior."

Sancia (SAN-see-ah) Meaning "holy; sacred." Variations include *Sanceska*, *Sancha*, *Sancharia*, *Sanchia*, and *Sancie*.

Savannah (sah-VAAN-ah) Meaning "treeless plain." Variations include *Sahvannah* and *Savana*.

Sevilla (seh-VEE-ah) A name that means "from Seville," a region in Spain. A variation is *Seville*.

Socorro (so-KOR-oh) Meaning "a cry for help."

Tijuana (tee-ah-WAN-ah) Means "Aunt Jane." Tijuana is a Mexican town on the border with the United States. Variations include *TaJuana*, *Tajuanna*, *Thejuana*, and *Tiawanna*.

Tina (TEE-nah) A short form of Augustina, Martina, Christina, Valentina. Singer Tina Turner. Variations include *Teanna*, *Teena*, *Teina*, and *Tena*.

Valencia (vah-LEN-see-ah) Meaning "strong." A region in eastern Spain. Variations include *Valecia*, *Valenica*, *Valenciana*, *Valenciano*, *Valentia*, and *Valenzia*.

Verdad (ver-DAD) Meaning "truth."

Vianca (vee-AHN-kah) A form of the name Bianca, meaning "shining white." Also *Vivianca*.

Vina (vee-NEE-tah) Meaning "vine."

Vitoria (vee-TOR-ee-ah) A form of the name Victoria, meaning "victorious." Variations include *Victoria*, *Vittoria*, and *Vittorina*.

Ynez (ee-NES)   A form of the name Agnes, meaning "pure." Variations include *Inez* and *Ynes*.

Yuana (ee-WAN-ah)   An alternate form of Juana.

Zaneta (sah-NAY-tah)   A form of the name Jane, meaning "God's gracious gift." A feminine form of Zane. Variations include *Zanita* and *Zanna*.

Zarita (sahr-EE-tah)   A form of the name Sarah, which is Hebrew for "princess."

Zaviera (sah-vee-EHR-ah)   A form of the name Xavier, which means "brilliant one." Variations include *Zavera* and *Zavirah*.

Zelia (say-LEE-ah)   Meaning "sunshine." Also *Xylia*.

Zerlina (sehr-LEEN-ah)   Meaning "beautiful dawn." Zerlina is a character in Mozart's opera *Don Giovanni*. Variations include *Zerla* and *Zerlinda*.

Zita (SEE-tah)   Meaning "rose."

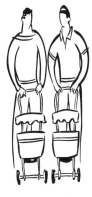

Hawaii

Though Hawaii is a part of the United States, its heritage and naming traditions are distinct from those of continental America. Most Hawaiian names come from objects of beauty, but beyond that tradition, Hawaiian naming customs violate conventional rules. The names typically don't express a child's gender, except for certain flower names that are used mostly for girls; most names can be used for boys or girls. In addition, Hawaiians often add names to names to make illustrative phrases, producing long, polysyllabic baby names. Compared with many existing Hawaiian names, the names selected here are short. Combine at your own inspiration or risk.

Pronunciation:
a = "ah" as in "tall"
e = "eh" as in "fate"
i = "ee" as in "feet"
o = "oh" as in "rope"
u = "oo" as in "soon"
w (when after o or u) = "w" as in wash
w (when after e or i) = "v" as in valley
w (at the beginning of a word or when after a) = "w" or "v"
h, k, l, m, and n are pronounced as in English

HAWAII: BOYS

Aukai (OW-kai)   From *au* meaning "swim" and *kai* meaning "sea," this name means "seafarer."

Ka'eo (KAH-eh-oh)   "The victorious."

Kahale (KAH-hah-leh)   Meaning "home."

Kaholo (KAH-ho-loh)   A name that means "the run."

Kainoa (KAH-e-noah)   Literally means "the name" or "unrestricted sea."

Kaipo (KAH-e-po)   Signifies "sweetheart."

Kalama (KAH-la-ma)   Meaning "the torch." Also *Kalam.*

Kalani (KAH-la-nee)   A name signifying "the heavens" or "chief." Royalty in Hawaii are often referred to as *lani.* Also *Kalan.*

Kamaka (KAH-ma-ka)   Meaning "the eye." A variation is *Namaka.*

Kamakani (KAH-ma-kah-nee)   Meaning "the wind."

Keahi (KEH-ah-hee)   An elemental name that means "flames."

Kealoha (KEH-ah-LO-ha)   Meaning "the love."

Keawe (KEH-ah-veh)   Meaning "strand."

Kekapa (KEH-ka-pa)   Meaning "tapa cloth."

Kekipi (KEH-key-pee)   Meaning "rebel."

Kekoa (KEH-ko-ah)   Signifies "bold and courageous; warrior."

Keli'i (KEH-lee-E)   Meaning "chief." See Kalani.

Keola (KE-oh-la)   Meaning "life."

Kiele (KEE-eh-leh)   Meaning "gardenia," a plant that was introduced to the Hawaiian Islands.

Kona (KO-nah)   A directional name that means "south." Also *Konala.*

Konane (KO-na-neh)   Meaning "bright."

Lani (LA-nee)   "Heaven." See Kalani.

Lono (LOH-noh)   This is the name of the Hawaiian god of peace and farming—the god of the harvest.

Lulani (LOU-la-nee)   "Highest point in heaven." From *lu*, "scattered," and *lani*, "heaven."

Mahi'ai (MA-hee-aee)   Meaning "farmer."

Makani (MA-ka-nee)   Meaning "wind."

Mamo (MA-mo)   A name that means "yellow flower" or "yellow bird."

Mano (MA-no)   Literally meaning "shark," this is the name of the Hawaiian shark god.

Maka (MA-ka)   Meaning "eyes." Also *Namaka*.

Mililani (ME-lee-la-nee)   Meaning "heavenly caress."

Nahele (NA-he-leh)   Meaning "forest."

Nohea (NOH-heh-ah)   A name that signifies "handsome" or "beautiful."

Onaona (OH-na-oh-na)   "Pleasant fragrance."

HAWAII: GIRLS

Alamea (AH-la-me-ah)   Meaning "ripe" or "precious."

Alani (AH-la-nee)   Meaning "orange" or "orange tree."

Aloha (Ah-lo-ha)   "Love." Also *Alohi*.

Amaui (AH-mau-ee)   A native Hawaiian plant.

Anela (AH-ne-la)   This is the Hawaiian form of the English name Angel.

Ani (AH-nee)   A gentle name that means "wave," "beckon," or "blow softly."

Anuhea (Ah-nu-heh-ah)   Meaning "cool mountain breeze."

Aolani (AU-lah-nee)   Meaning "heavenly cloud."

Mele (MEH-le)   Meaning "song" or "poem."

Miliani (ME-lee-ah-nee)   "Caress." Also *Mila* and *Milanni*.

Mililani (ME-lee-lah-nee)   Meaning "to praise; to exalt; to treat as a favorite." Variations include *Mila* and *Milliani*.

Halia (HA-lee-AH)   "A premonition."

Haunani (HAOW-na-nee)   Meaning "beautiful dew."

Ilima (E-lee-ma)   The name of the flower of Oahu. Golden in color, it is delicate and fragile.

Inoa (E-no-ah)   Literally meaning "name."

Iolana (E-oh-la-na)   Meaning "soaring like a hawk."

Iolani (E-oh-la-nee)   Meaning "royal hawk."

Kai (KAEE)   "Sea."

Kalama (KAH-la-ma)   Meaning "torch."

Kalani (KAH-lah-nee)   A name that signifies "chief" or "sky." Also *Kailani, Kalanie,* and *Kaloni.*

Kalei (KAH-lay)   "The garland." Variations include *Kahlei, Kailei,* and *Kaylei.*

Kalena (KAH-leh-nah)   Meaning "stretch." Other versions are *Kalleena* and *Kalina.*

Kanani (KAH-na-nee)   Meaning "beautiful." Also *Kana, Kanae,* and *Kanan.*

Kani (KAH-nee)   Meaning "sound" or "music."

Kanoa (KAH-no-ah)   A name that means "free," as in unrestricted.

Kapua (KAH-pu-ah)   Meaning "blossom."

Kaulana (KAU-la-na)   Meaning "famous." Variations include *Kaula, Kauna,* and *Kahuna.*

Kawena (KAH-ve-nah)   Meaning "the glow."

Ke'ala (KEH-AH-la)   Meaning "fragrant."

Keiki (KAY-kee)   Meaning "child." Also *Keikana* and *Keikanne.*

Keilani (KAY-la-ne)   Meaning "glorious leader" or "glorious heavens." Also *Keflan* and *Keflana.*

Kiele (KEY-eh-le) Meaning "gardenia" or "fragrant blossom." Other versions are *Kiela, Kieley, Kieli,* and *Kielli.*

Kona (KO-nah) Meaning "south."

Konane (KO-na-neh) A name that means "bright as moonlight."

Laka (LA-ka) Meaning "tame." Also the name of the Hawaiian goddess of the hula dance.

Lani (LA-nee) Meaning "sky" or "heaven."

Lea (LEH-ah) The name of the Hawaiian goddess of canoe makers.

Lei (LAY) A familiar form of *Leiiani.*

Leilani (LAY-la-nee) Meaning "heavenly flower" or "heavenly child." Variations include *Lani, Lei, Lelani,* and *Lelania.*

Lokelani (LO-keh-la-nee) Meaning "a heavenly rose."

Mahina (ma-HEE-na) Meaning "moon; moon glow."

Makala (MA-kah-la) Meaning "to forgive, loosen, or undo."

Maʻemaʻe (MA-eh-MA-eh) Meaning "pure."

Makana (MA-ka-na) Meaning "gift; present."

Makani (MA-ka-nee) Meaning "wind."

Malana (MA-la-na) A name that means "to move together."

Malie (MA-lee-eh) Meaning "tranquil; calm."

Mamo (MA-mo) Translated as "safflower" or "yellow bird," this name can also mean "descendant."

Mana (MA-na) "Spiritual or divine power." Also *Manal* and *Manali.*

Moana (MO-ah-na) Meaning "ocean" or "fragrance."

Mohala (MO-ha-la) Meaning "blossoming; shining forth." Also *Moala.*

Nalani (NA-la-nee) "Of the heavens." Variations include *Nalanle* and *Nalany.*

Nana (NA-na) Meaning "look." Among notable people with this name is actress Nana Visitor.

Noelani (NO-eh-la-nee) A name that means "a heavenly mist." A variation is *Noela.*

Okalani (OH-kah-la-nee) Meaning "heaven." Also *Okilani.*

Olina (OH-lee-na) Meaning "joyous."

Pikake (PEE-ka-keh) Meaning "jasmine."

Pua (POO-ah) Meaning "flower."

Pualani (POO-ah-la-nee) Meaning "heavenly flower." Also *Puni.*

Ululani (OO-lou-la-nee) Meaning "heavenly inspiration."

Uluwehi (OO-lou-weh-hee) Meaning "growing in beauty."

Wainani (WAI-na-nee) Signifies "beautiful water."

Wehilani (WEH-hee-la-nee) Meaning "heavenly adornment."

Native American

The scores of Native American tribes and their many subgroups amount to hundreds of cultures. The generalizations that follow about Native American naming practices are therefore quite broad. Many Native American names have traditionally been taken from nature, and from the perspective of being part of nature. Other names come from events or conditions at the time of the child's birth, from tribal symbols or totems, or from a striking characteristic of the newborn.

Pronunciation:

Perhaps 250 original languages and several linguistic families exist north of Mexico. Consequently, a great variety of pronunciation exists. Many of these languages incorporate phonemes (single letter sounds) that are so different from English phonemes that an English speaker must hear and mimic each sound several times to get it right. For instance, Zuñi, Cherokee, Choctaw, Navajo, and Tsimshian have a bilateral voiceless hiss at the tongue's "l" position, like the Welsh double "l," spelled here as "hl" or "lh." Other languages have nasalization like that in French, such as Dakota/Lakota/Nakota and the pueblo Tanoan languages (with Kiowa), Athabascan (Navajo and Apache), and Muskogean (Choctaw). In addition to these complexities, in some language families such as Athabascan and Tanoan, the spoken tone or pitch distinguishes the meanings of otherwise identical words. Leveling such "foreign-sounding" lingual characteristics toward plain English, Latin letters fails to do phonetic justice to these languages but allows us to print representations of their remarkable names.

NATIVE AMERICAN: BOYS

Achachak (ah-chah-CHAHK)   Meaning "spirit." Algonquian language family.

Adoeette (ah-DOH-ay-ET)   Meaning "great tree." The name of a Kiowa chief born in 1845.

Ahanu (ah-HAH-new)   Meaning "he laughs" in Massachusett, an Algonquian language.

Ahiga (ah-hee-GAHN)   Meaning "combat." From the Navajo, which is from the Athabascan family of languages.

Ahmik (AH-mik)   Meaning "beaver." This name comes from an Algonquian language called Ojibwa, Ojibway, Ojibwe, or Chippewa. A variation is *Amik*.

Ahote (ah-HO-teh)   Meaning "restless one" in Hopi, a Uto-Aztecan language.

Ahuli (ah-HOO-lee)   Meaning "drums." This name comes from the Iroquoian language Cherokee.

Akecheta (ah-GHEE-chee-tah)   A name signifying "warrior." From the Dakota or Lakota, which are Siouan languages.

Akule (ah-KOO-leh)   Meaning "he looks up." Source unknown.

Alo (AH-lo)   From the Hopi for "spiritual guide."

Anevay (ah-neh-VAH-ee)   Meaning "superior." Source unknown.

Apiatan (ah-pee-AH-tahn)   Meaning "wooden lance" in Kiowa, a Tanoah language.

Apisi (ah-PEE-see)   The word used for "coyote." From the Blackfoot.

Aranck (ah-RAHNK)   Meaning "star." From the Delaware, an Algonquian language.

Askook (ah-SKOOK)   Meaning "snake." A Massachusett word.

Atihk (uh-TIHK)   A Cree word meaning "caribou" or "reindeer." It is an Ojibwa word when spelled Atik.

Atohi (ah-toe-HEE) Meaning "woods" in Cherokee.

Atsadi (ah-tsah-DEE, ah-jah-DEE) The Cherokee word for "fish."

Atsidi (ah-tsee-DEE) Literally meaning "hammer," this Navajo word signifies "smith."

Avonaco (ah-vo-NAH-ko) Meaning "leaning bear." From Cheyenne, an Algonquian language.

Awi-Equa (ah-wee-ay-KWAH) Literally means "deer-big," this Cherokee word signifies "elk."

Beshkno (BESH-gno) Meaning "bald eagle." From the Algonquian language Potawatomi.

Boisso (BOY-so) Meaning "cat." From the Arapaho.

Chapa (CHAH-pah) Meaning "beaver." From Dakota or Lakota. Also spelled *Shappa*.

Chapowits (CHAH-po-wits) Meaning "many coyotes." From the Nez Percé or Sahaptin, both of which are Penutian languages.

Chatan (CHAY-tahn) From the Dakota or Lakota for "hawk."

Chayton (CHAY-tahn) Meaning "falcon." From the Dakota or Lakota language.

Chesmu (CHESS-moo) Meaning "gritty." Source unknown.

Cheveyo (CHEH-veh-yo) A Hopi name that means "spirit warrior."

Chogan (CHO-gun) Meaning "blackbird," a Narragansett name from the Algonquian family of languages.

Chunta (CHOON-tah) Meaning "cheating" in Hopi.

Chuslum (CHUS-lum) A Nez Percé or Sahaptin word for "bull."

Ciqala (JEE-qhhah-lah) Meaning "little one." From the Dakota or Lakota.

Cochise (ko-CHEESS) The name of a great Apache chief.

Dakota (dah-KHO-tah) Meaning "friend." Also a tribal name.

Danpa (DON-PAY) Meaning "shoulderblade." A Kiowa name.

Degatoga (day-gah-toe-GAH) From a Cherokee phrase meaning "standing together."

Demothi (deh-MO-tee) Signifies "talks while walking." Source unknown.

Denali (deh-NAH-lee) Meaning "the great one" or "the high one," It is another name for Mt. McKinley. From the Athabascan family of languages.

Dichali (dee-CHAH-lee) Meaning "speaks a lot." Source unknown.

Diwali (dee-WAH-hlee) Meaning "bowls." Colonel Bowles, Cherokee chief, first to move his people west of the Mississippi.

Dohasan (doh-HAH-sayn) A name from the Kiowa line of chiefs meaning "little bluff."

Dohate (do-HAH-tee) Meaning "bluff." Another Kiowa name.

Dustu (doos-TOO) A Cherokee name meaning "spring frog."

Dyami (dee-AH-mee) Meaning "soaring eagle." Source unknown.

Ehepikwa (aa-haa-PIK-wuh) Meaning "tarantula." From the Sauk, an Algonquian language.

Elki (EL-kee) Meaning "hanging over the top." A name from the Miwok or Moquelumnan, members of the Penutian family language.

Elsu (EL-soo) Meaning "soaring falcon." Miwok or Moquelumnan in origin.

Enapay (AY-nah-pah-ee) A Dakota or Lakota name that means "goes out bravely," "brave appearance," or "he appears."

Enokid (AY-no-kid) Meaning "one who is working" or "one who works." From the Ojibwa.

Enyeto (en-YEH-toh) Miwok or Moquelumnan in origin, this name means "walks like a bear."

Eyota (ee-YO-tah[n]) A Dakota or Lakota word signifying "great," "greater," or "greatest."

Gad (gahd) Meaning "juniper tree." From the Navajo.

Gawonii (gah-wo-nee-EE) Meaning "he's speaking." From the Cherokee.

Gigabe (GHEE-GAH-beh) The Potawatomi word for "boy."

Gomda (GOHM-da) Meaning "wind." Of Kiowa origin.

Gosheven (go-SHAY-ven) Meaning "great jumper." Source unknown.

Guyapi (goo-YAH-pee) Meaning "honest." Source unknown.

Hahnee (HAH-nee) Used for fooling evil spirits, this name means "begger." Source unknown.

Hakan (HAH-kahn) Meaning "fiery." Source unknown.

Halian (hah-lee-AHN) Meaning "youthful." A Zuñi name derived from the Spanish name Julian.

Hania (HAH-nee-ah) Meaning "spirit warrior." Hopi in origin.

Hanska (HAHN-skah) Meaning "tall." From the Dakota or Lakota.

Hassun (HAH-sun) Meaning "stone." A Massachusett name.

Heinmot (HAYN-moht) A Nez Percé or Sahaptin name meaning "thunder."

Helaku (heh-LAH-koo) Meaning "sunny day." Source unknown.

Hemene (he-me-ne) Meaning "wolf." Of Nez Percé or Sahaptin origin.

Hiamovi (he-uh-MO-vee) The Cheyenne for "high chief."

Hinto (HEEN-toh) Meaning "blue." From the Dakota or Lakota. See also Yahto.

Hinun (hee-NOON) Meaning "spirit of the storm." Source unknown.

Hohots (HO-hohts) Nez Percé or Sahaptin for "bear."

Holata (ho-LAH-tah) Meaning "alligator." From the Seminole, a member of the Muskogean family or languages.

Honani (ho-nah-nee) Meaning "badger." From the Hopi.

Honi (HO-nee) The Arapaho word for "wolf."

Honon (HO-nohn) Meaning "bear." From the Miwok or Moquelumnan.

Hotah (HO-tah) Meaning "gray" or "brown." Dakota or Lakota in origin.

Hototo (ho-TOH-toh) Meaning "whistler." Source unknown.

Howi (HO-wee) Meaning "turtle dove." Miwok or Moquelumnan in origin.

Huritt (HOO-rit) From the Delaware, a name signifying "good" or "it is good."

Huslu (HOOS-loo) Meaning "shaggy bear." Source unknown.

Hute (HOO-teh) The name of a star in the Big Dipper. Source unknown.

Igasho (ee-gah-shoh) Meaning "wanderer" or "seeker." Also spelled *Igashu*. Source unknown.

Iiniwa (eee-NEE-wah) From the Blackfoot, meaning "bison" or "buffalo."

Inteus (een-TAY-oos) Meaning "proud" or "unashamed." Source unknown.

Istaqa (ees-tah-qa) Meaning "coyote man." Hopi in origin.

Istas (EE-stahs) Meaning "snow on the ground." Source unknown.

Istu (EE-stoo) Meaning "sugar-pine sugar." From the Miwok or Moquelumnan.

Ituha (ee-too-hah) Meaning "sturdy oak." Source unknown.

Iye (EE-yeh) Meaning "smoke." Source unknown.

Jassy (DJAH-see) Meaning "moon," it is the name of the creator of all plant life and also of the planet Venus. From the tribe Tupí-Guaraní of South America.

Jolon (ho-LOHN) Meaning "valley of the dead trees." From the Salinan tribe of California. Also *Jolyon*.

Kachada (kah-chah-dah) A Hopi word that means "white man."

Kaga (KAH-gah) Meaning "writer." Source unknown.

Kangee (KAHN-ghee) From the Dakota or Lakota for "crow."

Kangee Tanka (KAHN-ghee-THAN-kah) Meaning "raven" ("crow-big"). Also of Dakota or Lakota origin.

Kanuna (kah-noo-NAH) From the Cherokee, meaning "bullfrog." Also *Kanunu*.

Kele (keh-leh) Meaning "sparrow" or "hawk." From the Hopi.

Ketiwa (KEH-tee-wuh) Meaning "eagle." From the Sauk.

Kijika (kee-JEE-kah) Meaning "silent walker." Source unknown.

Kilchii (keelh-CHEEE) From the Navajo for "red boy."

Kiyiya (ke-YEE-yah, ke-YI-yah) Meaning "howling wolf." From the Yakima tribe in Washington or the Sahaptin, which is a Penutian language. Also *Kiyiyah*.

Klah (thl'ah-EE) From the Navajo for "left-handed." Also spelled *Tlah*.

Kohana (ko-HAH-hah) Meaning "swift." From the Dakota or Lakota.

Koi (KOY) Meaning "panther" in Choctaw, a Muskogean language.

Kono (KO-no) Meaning "squirrel eating a pine nut." Miwok or Moquelumnan in origin.

Kosumi (ko-soo-mee) Meaning "spear fisher." From the Miwok or Moquelumnan.

Kotori (ko-to-ree) Meaning "screech owl spirit" in Hopi.

Kuruk (koo-rook) Meaning "bear." From the Pawnee, a Caddoan language.

Kusinut (koo-see-noot) A Yakima or Sahaptin name that means "horseless."

Kuzih (KOO-zeeh) Signifying "good speaker." From the Carrier, an Athabascan language.

Kwahu (KWAH-hoo) The Hopi word for "eagle."

Kwam (KWAHM) The Zuni form of John, from the Hebrew *Yehohaanaan*, "God is gracious."

Lallo (LAHL-lo) Meaning "little boy." Kiowa in origin.

Langundowi (lahng-oon-DOH-wee) Meaning "peaceful." From the Delaware.

Lanu (LAH-noo) A Miwok or Moquelumnan name that means "running around a pole."

Lena (LEH-nah) Meaning "flute" in Hopi.

Lise (LEE-say) Meaning "salmon's head coming out of the water." Of Miwok or Moquelumnan origin.

Liwanu (lee-wah-noo) Meaning "growling bear." Miwok or Moquelumnan in origin.

Lokni (lohk-nee) Meaning "raining through the roof." From the Miwok or Moquelumnan.

Lonan (LO-nahn) A Zuñi word meaning "cloud."

Lonato (loh-NAH-toh) Meaning "flint stone." Source unknown.

Lootah (LOO-tah) From the Dakota or Lakota, name meaning "red."

Lusio (LOO-seeo) Meaning "light." The Zuni form of Lucius, from the Latin *lux*.

Luyu (loo-yoo) Meaning "head shaker." A Miwok or Moquelumnan name.

Mahkah (MAH-kah) A name that signifies "earth." From the Dakota or Lakota word *maka*, or *makak*.

Mahpeeya (MAHH-pee-yah) Meaning "sky." Also Dakota or Lakota.

Mahwah (MAH-wah)   Meaning "wolf," this name springs from Algonquian languages.

Makya (mah-kee-ah)   Meaning "eagle hunter." Hopi in origin.

Mammedaty (MAHM-meh-DAH-tee)   Meaning "walking above." From the Kiowa.

Manipi (mah-NEE-pee)   Meaning "walking wonder," of Dakota or Lakota origin.

Masou (MAA-sow)   Hopi in origin, this name means "supernatural being." Other versions are *Masauuh* and *Masi*.

Maska (MAH-skah)   Meaning "powerful." Source unknown.

Mato (MAH-toe)   Meaning "bear." From the Dakota or Lakota.

Matoskah (mah-TOE-skah)   Meaning "white bear." From the Siouan languages Dakota and Lakota.

Menewa (me-NEE-wah)   A name signifying "great warrior." From the Creek, a language of the Muskogean family of languages.

Micco (MIH-ko)   Seminole for "chief."

Mika (MEE-kah)   Meaning "raccoon." From the Siouan language Ponca.

Mikanopy (mee-kah-NO-pee)   Means "head chief" in Seminole.

Mikasi (mee-KAH-see)   Meaning "coyote." From the Omaha, a Siouan language.

Milatap (MIL-ah-tahp)   Meaning "given." From the Delaware.

Minco (MING-ko)   The Choctaw word for "chief."

Mingan (MING-ahn)   Meaning "gray wolf." From the Cree, which is an Algonquian language.

Misae (mee-SAH-ay)   Meaning "white, hot sun." From the Siouan language Osage.

Misu (MEE-soo)   Meaning "rippling water." Miwok or Moquelumnan in origin.

Miwok (MEE-wawk)   The name of a tribe, it is also the word for "man."

Moki (MO-kee)   Meaning "deer." From the Hopi.

Molimo (MO-lee-mo)   Meaning "bear going under shade tree." From the Miwok or Moquelumnan.

Momobi (MO-mo-bee)   Meaning "lizard" of Hopi origin.

Motega (mo-TEH-gah)   Meaning "new arrow." Source unknown.

Motsqueh (MOHTS-kweh)   Nez Percé or Sahaptin for "chipmunk."

Muata (mwah-tah)   Meaning "yellow jackets in their nest," a Miwok or Moquelumnan name.

Muracho (MOO-rah-choh)   Meaning "white moon." Source unknown.

Nahmay (nah-MAY)   "Sturgeon." Of Ojibwa orgin.

Nakai (naah-KAH-ee)   The Navajo word for "Mexican." Also *Naakaii*.

Nakos (NAH-kos)   Meaning "sagebrush." From the Arapaho.

Namid (NAH-mid)   Meaning "dancer." This is probably the legendary coyote, who jumped off a mountain because he wanted to dance with the stars. From the Ojibwa.

Nantan (nahn-TAHN)   Meaning "spokesman," "chief," or "captain," it is from the Apache for the Spanish *capitán*.

Napayshni (nah-PAY-shnee)   Meaning "he does not flee" or "courageous." Dakota or Lakota in origin.

Nasheakusk (nuh-SHAY-kusk)   Meaning "loud thunder." From the Sauk.

Nashoba (nah-SHO-bah)   Meaning "wolf," this name is Choctaw in origin.

Nastas (NAH-stah-SEE)   Meaning "curved like foxtail grass." From the Navajo. Also spelled *Nastasi*.

Nawat (NAH-waht)   Meaning "left handed." Source unknown.

Nayati (nah-YAH-tee)   Meaning "wrestler." Source unknown.

Nayavu (nah-yah-voo) Meaning "clay." A Hopi name.

Nenemehkiwa (neh-neh-MEHK-ih-wuh) Meaning "thunder." From the Sauk.

Nepwahkawa (neh-PWAH-KAH-wuh) Meaning "he is intelligent." Sauk in origin.

Netatasit (NAY-tuh-TAH-sit) Meaning "he is wise." From the Algonquian language Mi'kmaq.

Nigan (nee-GAHN) Meaning "ahead" or "first." Ojibwa in origin.

Nikan (nih-KAHN) From the Potawatomi this name means "my friend" or "my brother."

Nindakando (NIN-duh-KAHN-doh) Meaning "I watch and lie in ambush." From the Ojibwa.

Nitis (nih-tiss) Signifying "my-friend" or "my-confidant." From the Delaware. Also *Netis*.

Nodin (NO-din) An Ojibwa name, meaning "wind."

Nokonyu Meaning "katydid's nose." Source unknown. Variations include *Noko* and *Nokoni*.

Nokosi (no-KO-see) Meaning "bear." Seminole in origin.

Notaku (no-TAH-koo) Meaning "growling bear." From the Miwok or Moquelumnan.

Odakotah (oh-dah-KHO-tah) Meaning "friendship." Of Dakota or Lakota origin.

Ogaki (oh-GAH-kee) Meaning "crow." From the Arapaho.

Ogima (O-ghee-muh) The Potawatomi word for "chief."

Ogimus (OH-ghee-muss) Meaning "little chief." From the Oijbwa. Also *Okemos*.

Ogleesha (O-glee-sha) Meaning "red shirt." From the Dakota or Lakota.

Ohanko (o-HAHN-ko) Meaning "incautious." Source unknown.

Ohanzee (o-HAHN-zee) Meaning "shadow." From the Dakota or Lakota.

Ohitekah (o-HEE-tih-kah) Dakota or Lakota for "brave."

Ohiyesa (o-HEE-yeh-sah) Meaning "winner." Dakota or Lakota in origin.

Okomi (oh-KOH-mee) An Arapaho name meaning "coyote."

Olamon (O-luh-mun) A Penobscot word of Maine meaning "red paint."

Olowin (o-LO-win) Meaning "west." From the Miwok or Moquelumnan.

Onacoma (oo-nay-guh-MAH) Meaning "white owl," from the Cherokee.

Osceola (OS-see-OH-luh) From *Asi-yaholo*, Creek for "black-drink crier."

Otadan (o-TAH-dahn) Meaning "abundant." Source unknown.

Otaktay (o-TAHK-tay) Meaning "kills many" or "strikes many," this Dakota or Lakota name denotes a successful hunter.

Otskai (OHTS-ky) Meaning "going out." From the Nez Percé or Sahaptin.

Ourayi (OO-ray) This name can either signify "arrow" or an attempt to pronounce the English name Willie. From the Ute, Uto-Aztecan language.

Pacho (PA-choh) Meaning "eagle." Source unknown.

Pahana (pa-HAH-nah) A Hopi word that means "lost white brother," "Anglo," or "European."

Palliton (PAH-lih-tohn) Meaning "he has spoiled it." From the Delaware.

Patakusu (pah-tah-KOO-soo) Meaning "ant biting a person." Of the Miwok or Moquelumnan.

Pataman (PAH-tuh-mun) Signifies "to pray." From the Delaware.

Patwin (PAAT-win) This name means "man" in the language of the Patwin, a tribe of California.

Pay (PYE or PIE) Meaning "he is coming." Of Algonquian origin.

Payat (PAH-yaht)   Meaning "he who comes" or "he who is coming." From the Delaware.

Peji, **Pezi** (PAY-jee) or (PAY-zee)   Meaning "grass." From the Dakota or Lakota.

Peopeo (peeo-peeo)   A Nez Percé or Sahaptiu name meaning "bird."

Pitalesharo (pee-tah-LAY-sha-ro)   Meaning "chief of men." From the Pawnee. Also *Pitaresharu*.

Powa (PAH-wuh)   An Algonquian name that means "wealthy."

Punokamida (poo-no-KAH-me-dah)   Meaning "horse." From the Blackfoot.

Qaletaqa (qah-leh-tah-qah)   Meaning "guardian of the people." Hopi in origin.

Quanah (KWAY-nah)   Meaning "fragrant." From Comanche, a Uto-Aztecan language. Quanah Parker, Comanche chief.

Raini (RYE-nee)   According to legend the Munduruku god Raini created the world by placing it in the shape of a flat stone on another god's head. From the Tupí-Guaraní.

Sahale (sah-HAH-leh)   Meaning "above." Source unknown. Variations include *Sael*, *Sahel*, and *Sahli*.

Sahkonteic (sah-KOHN-taych)   Meaning "white eagle." From the Nez Percé or Sahaptin.

Sakima (SAH-ghee-muh)   An Ojibwa name that means "chief" or "one who knows medicine well."

Samoset (O-SAH-mo-set)   Meaning "he walks over much," this is Wampanoag name from Massachusetts. Also *Osamoset*.

Sani (SAH-NEE)   Meaning "old." From the Najavo.

Sapa (SAH-pah)   Meaning "black." From the Dakota or Lakota.

Setangya (set-AYNG-yay)   Meaning "sitting bear." From the Kiowa. Also *Satank*.

Satanta (set-TAIN-tay)   Meaning "white bear." From the Kiowa.

Sequoia (seh-KWO-yuh)   From the Cherokee *sikwayi*, the original meaning of which is now lost. Variations include *Sequiah*, *Sequiyah*, and *Sequoya*.

Setimika (set-EE-MEE-kah)   A Kiowa name that means "charging bear."

Sewati (seh-WAH-tee)   Meaning "curved bear claw." From the Miwok or Moquelumnan.

Shakunuta (shah-KOO-noo-tah)   Meaning "coming sun." Of Pawnee origin.

Shappa (SHAH-pah)   *See* Chapa.

Shenandoah (sheh-nun-DOH-uh)   Oneida chief, born about 1716, died 1816. Also found as *Skenandoa* and *Shenandoa*.

Shiye (shee-yeh)   Meaning "my son" or "my nephew," this is the word a Navajo man uses when referring to his male child or nephew.

Sipatu (see-pah-too)   Meaning "pulled out." From the Miwok or Moquelumnan.

Siwili (se-WEE-lee)   Meaning "long fox's tail." Source unknown.

Skah (SKAH)   Meaning "white." From the Dakota or Lakota.

Songan (sahn-GAHN)   Meaning "strong," "firm," or "tight." From the Ojibwa.

Sugmuk (sug-muk)   Meaning "dark earth." From the Potawatomi.

Sugnog (sug-nog)   A Potawatomi name meaning "blackbird."

Tadi (TAH-dee)   Meaning "wind." From the Omaha.

Tadzi (TAH-dzee)   Meaning "loon." From the Carrier.

Taima (tah-EE-muh)   Meaning "thunderbolt." Source unknown.

Tapco (TAYP-ko)   The Kiowa word for "antelope."

Tashunka (TAH-SHOONG-kah)   Meaning "horse," this Dakota or Lakota name derives from *Shunka-wakan*, which literally means "dog-sacred."

Tatonka (TAH-TAHNG-kah) Meaning "large deer" ("ruminant-large"). From the Dakota or Lakota.

Tawa (TAH-wah) Meaning "sun." From the Hopi.

Teetonka (TEE-TAHNG-kah) Meaning "big lodge." Dakota or Lakota in origin.

Teluhci (teh-LOO-chee) Literally means "bear making dust as it runs." From the Miwok or Moquelumnan.

Texas (TAY-shahs) Meaning "friends" or "allies." From the Hasinai or Caddo, a Caddoan language.

Tiktu (TIK-too) From the Miwok or Moquelumnan, it means "bird digging up potatoes."

Tiskyai (TEE-skee-I) Meaning "skunk." From the Yakima or Sahaptin.

Tkhabaha (TKHAH-bohn-hah) A Navajo name meaning "at water's edge."

Tohon (toh-HOHN) Meaning "mountain lion." Source unknown.

Tokala (to-KAH-lah) Meaning "gray fox." From the Dakota or Lakota.

Tsiyi (jee-YEE) From the Cherokee, meaning "copper."

Tsiyv (jee-YUH) From the Cherokee meaning "canoe."

Tskiri (TSKEE-ree) Meaning "wolf." From the Pawnee. Aslo *Skidi*.

Tuari (too-WAH-ree) Meaning "young eagle." This name is from the Hokan family of languages.

Tumu (TOO-moo) Meaning "deer thinking of eating wild onions." Of Miwok or Moquelumnan origin.

Tyee (TYE-ee) Meaning "chief." From the Chinook tribe of Nootka, Vancouver.

Tyonek (tye-YO-nek) Meaning "little chief," this name is linguistically from the Athabascan language family and geographically from Knaiakhotana, Alaska.

Ulzumati (ool-zoo-MAH-tee) Meaning "grizzly bear." From the Miwok or Moquelumnan.

Unaduti (oo-NAH-doo-tee) Meaning "bushy-headed." Dennis W. Bushyhead was a mixed blood Cherokee chief born in Tennessee.

Usti (oos-DEE) Meaning "little." From the Cherokee. Also *Usdi*.

Viho (VEE-ho) A Cheyenne name meaning "chief."

Waban (WAH-bun) Meaning "dawn" or "east wind." From the Algonquian. Also *Wabon*.

Waboyan (WAW-bo-YAHN) Meaning "white hide" or "blanket." From the Potawatomi.

Wadjiw (WAH-jeew) Meaning "mountain." Algonquian in origin.

Wagosh (WAW-gohsh) The Potawatomi word for "fox."

Wahkan (wah-kah[n]) Meaning "sacred" or "holy." From the Dakota or Lakota.

Wahkoowah (wah-KOO-wah) From the Dakota or Lakota, it means "charging."

Wahya (wah-hyah) The Cherokee word for "wolf."

Wakiza (wah-KEE-zah) Meaning "determined warrior." Source unknown.

Wamblee (WAHM-blee) Meaning "eagle." From the Dakota or Lakota.

Waneta (wah-NAY-tah) Meaning "charger," it is the name of notable Yanktonai Sioux.

Wapi (WAH-pee) Meaning "lucky." From the Dakota or Lakota.

Wapiti (WAH-pih-tee). Literally meaning "white rump," this Potawatomi name signifies "elk."

Wattan (WAHT-tahn) The Arapaho word for "black."

W'dellsin (wuh-DELL-sin) Meaning "he is so" or "he does so." Of Delaware origin.

Wesa (way-sah) Meaning "cat." From the Cherokee.

Wichado (wee-CHAH-doh) Meaning "willing." Source unknown.

Wichasha (wee-CHAH-shah) Meaning "sage." From the Dakota or Lakota.

Wichitokapa (we-CHEE-to-kah-pah) Meaning "the eldest-born son." From the Dakota or Lakota.

Wikvaya (wik-vah-yah) A Hopi name meaning "one who brings."

Wilu (WEE-loo) Meaning "chicken hawk squawking." From the Miwok or Moquelumnan.

Wiluye (wee-LOO-yeh) Meaning "eagle singing while flying." Of Miwok or Moquelumnan origin.

Wingi (WEENG-ghee) A Delaware name that means "willing."

Wohali (wo-HAH-lee) The Cherokee word for "eagle."

Wuliton (WOO-lee-tohn) Meaning "to do well." From the Delaware.

Wuyi (WOO-yee) Meaning "flying turkey vulture." From the Miwok or Moquelumnan.

Yabe (YAH-beh) Signifying "male deer." A Potawatomi name.

Yaholo (yah-HO-lo) Meaning "crier." Creek in origin.

Yahto (YAH-toh) Meaning "blue." From the Dakota or Lakota. See also Hinto.

Yakez (YAH-kehz) The Carrier word for "heaven."

Yansa (YAHN-sah) Meaning "buffalo." From the Cherokee.

Yiska (yis-KAHN) A Navajo name that means "the night has passed."

Yiskah (yis-kahh) Meaning "he shot it (with bow and arrow)." From the Navajo.

Yona (yo-NUHN) Meaning "bear." From the Cherokee.

NATIVE AMERICAN: GIRLS

Abequa (AH-be-KWAY) Meaning "stays (at home)-woman." This name comes from an Algonquian language called Ojibwa, Ojibway, Ojibwe, or Chippewa.

Abey (AH-bay) Meaning "leaf." From the Siouan language Omaha.

Abeytu (ah-BAY-too) Meaning "green leaf." From the Omaha.

Adoeette (ah-DOH-ay-ET) Meaning "great tree." The name of a Kiowa chief born in 1845.

Agasga (ah-gahs-GAH) A Cherokee name that means "it is raining."

Ahona (AH-ho-nah) Meaning "red." From the Zuñi, a language isolate that probably belongs to the Penutian family of languages.

Ahwi (AH-HWEE) Meaning "deer." From the Cherokee.

Ahyoka (ah-hyo-kah) Meaning "she brought happiness." Of Cherokee origin.

Alaqua (ah-LAH-kwah) Meaning "sweet gum tree." From the Muskogean language Seminole.

Alawa (uh-luh-way) Meaning "pea," this name is from the Algonquian language known as Micmac or Mi'kmaq.

Algoma (al-GO-muh) The explorer and ethnologist Henry Rowe Schoolcraft coined this word for the wide Canadian area near lakes Superior and Huron, made of al- from "Algonquian," the linguistic name, and *goma*, "lake."

Ama (ah-MAH) The Cherokee word for "water."

Amitolanne (AH-me-toh-lahn-nay) Meaning "rainbow." From the Zuñi.

Anamoha (uh-nuh-MO-huh) Meaning "dog." From the Sauk, an Algonquian language.

Angbetu (ahng-BAY-too) Meaning "day." From the Siouan language Dakota or Lakota.

Anjeni (ahn-JAY-nee) Meaning "spirit." The Algonquian form of the French and English "angel." Also *Angeriwa*.

Ankti (AHNK-tee) Meaning "repeat dance." From the Hopi, a Uto-Aztecan language.

Aponi (ah-po-nee) Meaning "butterfly." Source unknown.

Aquene (uh-KWEE-neh) A name that means "peace." Massachusett or Wampanoag language of the Algonquian family of languages.

Aqwenasa (ah-gway-nuh-suh) Meaning "my home." From the Cherokee.

Asshawequa (ash-shah-WEE-hkway) This name means "singing bird woman." Sauk in origin.

Atepa (ah-teh-pah) Meaning "tent." From the Choctaw, a Muskogean language.

Atsila (ah-tsee-LAH, ah-jee-LAH) Meaning "fire." From the Cherokee, an Iroquian language.

Atsilusgi (ah-ji-LUSS-ghee) Meaning "blossom." From the Cherokee.

Awendela (ah-wen-DAY-lah) Meaning "morning." Source unknown.

Awenita (ah-way-NEE-tah) Meaning "fawn." Source unknown.

Ayita (ah-yee-TAH) A Cherokee name that means "first in dance."

Ayita (ah-YEE-tah) Meaning "the worker." Source unknown.

Ayuhwasi (ah-yoo-HWA-see) Meaning "meadow" or "savannah." From the Cherokee. Variations include *Hiawassee* and *Hiwassee*.

Bena (bee-NAY) The Ojibwa for "partridge."

Byhallia (BY-HULL-ee-yah) Meaning "white oaks standing." Derived from the Chocktaw word *baii*.

Catori (kah-toe-ree) "Seed carrier kachina." From the Hopi.

Chanlyuha (CHAHN-leew-hah) Meaning "generous." Of Dakota or Lakota origin.

Chapa (CHAH-pah) Meaning "beaver." From the Dakota or Lakota.

Chenoa (CHEE-no-uh) Probably means "otter-place," from the Cherokee *tsiya*, "otter."

Cheyenne (shah-YAAN) Tribal name from Siouan Dakota *Sha-hi-ye-na*, meaning "people of alien speech" (literally "red-speak, red-come").

Chilali (chee-LAH-lee) Meaning "snow bird." Source unknown.

Chimalis (chee-MAH-lees) Meaning "bluebird." Source unknown.

Chimayo (chee-MAH-yo) "Good obsidian." From Tewa, a Tanoan language, through Spanish.

Chitsa (CHEET-sah) Meaning "fair in skin color," a name from the Kutchakutchin, known as the "giant-people" of Alaska.

Cholens (CHO-lenss) Meaning "bird." From the Delaware, a Lenape or Algonquian language.

Chumni (choo-mnee) "Dewdrops." From the Dakota or Lakota.

Coahoma (KO-uh-HO-nah) Meaning "red panther." From the Choctaw.

Fala (FUHL-lah) Meaning "crow." Choctaw in origin.

Dakota (dah-KHO-tah) Meaning "friend." Also a tribal name. Another spelling is *Dakotah*.

Dezba (dez-bah) A name that means "going to war." From the Navajo, an Athabascan language.

Doli (DOH-lee) The Navajo word for "bluebird."

Donoma (doe-NO-mah) Meaning "sun is there." From the Omaha *don*, meaning "sun."

Doya (doe-yah) "Beaver." A Cherokee name.

Dyani (d-YAH-nee) Meaning "deer." From the Zia and San Felipe, which are Keresan languages.

Ehawee (ee-HAH-wee[n]) "She laughs." Dakota or Lakota in origin.

Elki (EL-kee) Meaning "hanging over the top." From the Miwok or Moquelumnan, which are Penutian languages.

Enola (ee-NO-luh) Meaning "solitary." It is a purely English word written backwards but often used by Indians; also a place name in Arkansas, Nebraska, and Pennsylvania.

Etania (ay-TAY-nee-uh) Meaning unknown. The name of a Seminole town in Florida. Also *Etenia* and *Etonia*.

Ethete (eh-theh-teh) Meaning "good." From the Algonquian language Arapaho.

Eyota (ee-YO-tah[n]) Meaning "great," "greater," or "greatest." From the Dakota or Lakota.

Gigyago (ghee-gheeyah-go) Meaning "girl." From the Potawatomi, an Algonquian language. Also *Gigangow* and *Kikiyako*.

Gogi (go-ghee) "Summer." From the Cherokee.

Gola (go-lah) "Winter." From the Cherokee.

Hachi (HAH-chee) Meaning "stream." From the Seminole.

Halona (HAAL-o-nah) A Zuñi name meaning "of good fortune."

Hanhepi·wi (hahn-HAY-pee-wee) Meaning "the moon" or "night luminary." From the Dakota or Lakota.

Hateya (hah-TAY-yah) Meaning "footprints in the sand." Of Miwok or Moquelumnan origin.

Hausu (HOUSE-oo) A Miwok or Moquelumnan name meaning "bear yawning upon awakening."

Helaku (heh-LAH-koo) Meaning "sunny day." Source unknown.

Helki (HEL-kee) Meaning "touching." A Miwok or Moqueumnan word said of the jacksnipe as it digs the ground. Also *Helkey*, *Helkie*, and *Helky*.

Heltu (HEL-too) Meaning "bear reaching out." From the Miwok or Moquelumnan.

Hesutu (heh-SOO-too) Meaning "picking up a yellow jackets' nest." From the Miwok or Moquelumnan.

Heta (HAY-tah). A Hopi word that signifies a race to the village after a rabbit hunt, and used by the rabbit clan. Also *Yeta*.

Hialeah (HY-uh-LEE-uh) Probably means "pretty prairie." From the Seminole.

Hola (HO-lah) Meaning "seed-filled club." From the Hopi.

Hongvi (hong-vee) Meaning "strong one." From the Hopi.

Honon (HO-nohn) "Bear." Of Miwok or Moquelumnan origin.

Howi (HO-wee) "Turtle dove." Miwok or Moquelumnan in origin.

Huata (HWAH-tah) "Basket carrier." From the Miwok or Moquelumnan.

Humita (hoo-mee-tah) A Hopi name signifying "shelled corn" or "corn kernels."

Huyana (hoo-YAH-nah) Meaning "falling rain." From the Miwok or Moquelumnan.

Ikeinan (EE-kay-ee-nahn) The Zuñi word for "heart."

Imala (EE-mah-lah) Meaning "disciplinarian." Source unknown.

Inoli (ee-NOH-lee) Meaning "badger." From the Cherokee.

Isi (ee-see) Meaning "deer." From the Choctaw.

Izusa (ee-ZOO-sah) Meaning "whetstone for axes." From the Dakota or Lakota.

K'ohana (K-O-hah-nah) The Zuñi word for "white."

K'ai' (k'ai) A Navajo name meaning "willow."

Kaaka (KAH-kah) Meaning "older sister." See also Qööqa. From the Hopi.

Kachina (KAH-tsee-nah) "Spirit of the invisible forces of life." Hopi, from *ka* meaning "respect" and *china* meaning "spirit."

Kaliska (kah-LISS-kah) Meaning "coyote chasing deer." From the Miwok or Moquelumnan.

Kamama (kah-mah-mah) "Butterfly." From the Cherokee.

Kamata (kah-MAH-tah) "Gambler." Miwok or Moquelumnan in origin.

Kantico (KAAN-tih-ko) Meaning "she dances," it is the name of a dancing festival. From the Virginian, an Algonquian language.

Kasaan (guh-SAHN) "Pretty town." Name of a Haida town in Alaska.

Kaya (KAH-yah) Meaning "wise child." A Hopi name composed of *kaaka*, "older sister" and *hoya*, "little."

Kewanee (kee-WAW-nee) Meaning "prairie hen." From the Potawatomi.

Kiana (kee-AH-nuh) Meaning "concealed one." From the Algonquian language Fox or Sauk.

Kimi (KEE-mee) Meaning "secretly." From the Delaware.

Kimimila (kee-MEE-mee-lah) Meaning "butterfly." From the Dakota or Lakota.

Kinta (KIN-tah) The Choctaw word for "beaver."

Kiona (kah-YO-nuh) Meaning "brown hills." Source unknown.

Kishi (KEE-shee) Meaning "panther." From the Hasinai or Caddo, a Caddoan language.

Kiyuga (kee-yoo-GAH) Meaning "chipmunk." From the Cherokee.

Kono (KO-no) A Miwok or Moquelumnan name meaning "squirrel eating a pine nut."

Kosa (KO-sah) Meaning "sheep." From the Cheyenne, an Algonquian language.

Kosumi (ko-soo-mee) Signifies "spear fisher." From the Miwok or Moquelumnan.

Kwanita (kwah-NEE-tah) The Zuñi form of the Spanish *Juanita*, meaning "God is gracious."

Kwasa (KWA-sah) Meaning "fur robe" or "fur dress." From the Hopi.

Lanu (LAH-noo) Meaning "running around the pole." Miwok or Moquelumnan in origin.

Lenmana (LEN-mah-nah) "Flute girl." A Hopi name.

Leotie (lee-o-TEE-eh) Meaning "prairie flower." Source unknown.

Leyati (lay-yah-tee) Meaning "shaped like an abalone shell." From the Miwok or Moquelumnan.

Litonya (lee-TOE-nyah) The Miwok or Moquelumnan word for "hummingbird."

Lokni (LOHK-nee) Meaning "raining through the roof." From the Miwok or Moquelumnan.

Lolotea (LO-lo-tay-ah) Zuñi form of Spanish *Dorotea* or *Dorothy*, from Greek "gift of gods."

Lomasi (lo-MAH-see) Meaning "pretty flower." Source unknown.

Lusela (loo-SAY-lah) Meaning "bear swinging its foot while licking it." From the Miwok or Moquelumnan.

Luyu (LOO-yoo) "Pecking bird." Of Miwok or Moquelumnan origin.

Magaskaween (mah-GAH-ska-wee[n]) Which means "swan woman." From the Dakota or Lakota.

Magena (mah-GEH-na) Meaning "coming moon." From the Omaha.

Mahala (mah-HAH-lah) "Woman." A Californian name from two possible sources: the Spanish *mujer*, "woman," or the Yokuts *muk'ela*. Also *Mohale*.

Mahkoseseha (MAH-KO-she-SAY-hah) Meaning "fawn" or "little bear cub." From the Sauk.

Wewenethiwa (WAY-weh-NEH-thee-wuh) A Sauk name that means "she is beautiful."

Mai (MAW[N]-ee) Meaning "coyote." From the Navajo.

Makaween (mah-KAH-wee[n]) Meaning "earth woman." From the Dakota or Lakota.

Malia (mah-LEE-ah) The Zuñi form of María or Mary, from the Aramaic *Miryam*, "bitter."

Malila (mah-LEE-lah) Meaning "salmon swimming fast upstream." Miwok or Moquelumnan in origin.

Mansi (MAHN-see) Meaning "Indian paintbrush (flower)." From the Hopi.

Maralah (mah-RAH-lah) Meaning "born during an earthquake." Source unknown.

Mausi (MOUSE-ee) Meaning "plucking flowers." Source unknown.

Meda (mee-DAY) An Ojibwa name that means "shaman" or "medicine." Also *Mite* and *Mide*.

Metikla (meh-TIK-lah) Meaning "reaching a hand under water to catch a fish." From the Miwok or Moquelumnan.

Migina (mee-GHEE-nah) Meaning "returning moon." From the Omaha.

Migisi (mih-ghih-zih) "Eagle." An Ojibwa name.

Mimiss (MEE-miss) Meaning "little dove." From the Potawatomi.

Mina (MEE-nah) Meaning "knife." From the Dakota or Lakota.

Minal (MEEN-ahl) Meaning "fruit." Plural of *miin*, "berry" or "fruit," but in the Delaware language it specifically means "huckleberries." From the Delaware.

Minowa (me-NO-wah) Meaning "moving voice." Source unknown.

Minya (MIN-yah) An Osage name meaning "older sister."

Misae (mee-SAH-ay) Meaning "white, hot sun." From the Siouan language Olsage.

Misu (MEE-soo) Meaning "rippling water." Of Miwok or Moquelumnan in origin.

Mitena (me-TAY-nah) Meaning "born at the new moon." From the Omaha.

Mituna (mee-TOO-nah) Meaning "fish wrapped in leaves." From the Miwok or Moquelumnan.

Momuso (mo-MOO-so) A Miwok or Moquelumnan name that means "yellow jackets crowded in their nests for the winter."

Mona (MO-nah) Meaning "gathering jimsonweed seed." From the Miwok or Moquelumnan.

Muata (MWAH-tah) "Yellow jackets in their nest." Miwok or Moquelumnan in origin.

Muna (MOO-nah) "Overflowing spring." From the Hopi.

Namid (NAH-mid) Meaning "dancer." This is probably the legendary coyote, who jumped off a mountain because he wanted to dance with the stars. From the Ojibwa.

Nanaba (nah-NAH-bah) Meaning "war returned with her." From the Navajo.

Nashja (NASH-jah) The Navajo word for "owl."

Nashota (nah-SHO-tah) Meaning "twin," it is a place name in Wisconsin signifying double rivers. From the Ojibwa.

Natane (nah-TAH-neh) The Arapaho for "my-daughter."

Nejee (NEE-JEE) "My-friend." From the Ojibwa.

Netanesa (neh-TAH-neh-suh) Meaning "my-daughter." From the Fox or Sauk.

Netatasit (NAY-tuh-TAH-sit) Meaning "she is wise." From the Micmac.

Netis (NEE-tiss) A Delaware name meaning "my-friend."

Ngöyva (NGERY-vah) "Chases it." Hopi in origin.

Niabi (nee-AH-bee) The Osage for "fawn."

Nibaw (nee-bah-oo) Meaning "I am standing tall." An Ojibwa name.

Nika (NEE-kah) Meaning "wild goose." From the Ojibwa.

Nina (NEE-nah) Meaning "mighty." Source unknown.

Nita (NEE-tah) Meaning "bear." From the Choctaw.

Nokomis (no-ko-mis) Signifies "my-grand-mother" in Ojibwa.

Noquisi (NO-kwee-see) "Star." From the Cherokee.

Noya (no-yah) "Sand." From the Cherokee.

Nuna (NOO-nah) Meaning "land," it is the name of a Nunatogmiut Eskimo village at Port Hope, Alaska.

Ogin (o-GEEN) Meaning "wild rose." Source unknown.

Ogow (O-go) Meaning "doe." From the Potawatomi.

Olathe (o-LAH-theh) Meaning "beautiful." From a Shawnee's surprise at seeing a place in Kansas. Also *Olathia*.

Onatah (o-nah-TAH) Meaning "daughter of the earth and corn spirit." An Iroquois name.

Onean (OH-nay-ahn) "Yellow." From the Zuñi.

Oneida (o-NIGH-dah) A tribal name that means "standing rock," referring to a large sienite boulder near one of the Oneida villages. Also *Onida* and *Onyda*.

Onssi (OHNN-see) Meaning "eagle." From the Choctaw.

Opa (O-pah) Meaning "large owl." From the Choctaw.

Orenda (o-REN-dah) Meaning "magical power." From the Iroquois.

Otewomin (o-TAY-wo-min) Literally meaning "heart-berry," it signifies "strawberry." From the Potawatomi.

Pakuna (pah-KOO-nah) Meaning "deer bounding while running." A Miwok or Moquelumnan name.

Papina (pah-PEE-nah) A name that means "vine growing on oak tree." Miwok or Moquelumnan in origin.

Pakwa (PAH-kwah) The Hopi word for "frog."

Pamuya (PAH-moo-yah) Meaning "water moon" (*pa-muya*). From the Hopi.

Pana (PAH-nah) Meaning "partridge." From the Blackfoot, an Algonquian language.

Patakusu (pah-tah-KOO-soo) From the Miwok or Moquelumnan, it means "ant biting a person."

Pati (PAH-tee) Meaning "fish baskets." From the Miwok or Moquelumnan.

Pavati (PAH-vah-tee) Meaning "clear water." From the Hopi.

Pazi (PAH-zee) "Yellow bird." From the Siouan language Ponca.

Peni (PAY-nee) Meaning "mind." From the Carrier, an Athabascan language.

Petah (PAY-tah) The Blackfoot word for "golden eagle."

Poloma (po-hlo-mah) Meaning "bow." From the Choctaw.

Ponola (po-NO-lah) Meaning "cotton." From the Choctaw.

Powaqa (po-WAH-qah) Meaning "witch." From the Hopi.

Qööqa (KER-kah) Hopi for "older sister." See also Kaaka.

Quanah (KWAY-nah) Meaning "fragrant." From the Comanche, an Uto-Aztecan language.

Rozene (ro-ZEEN) Meaning "rose blossom." Possibly from Spanish and English. Also *Rosina*.

Sadzi (sah-dzee) A Carrier name signifying "disposition."

Sahpooly (sah-POO-lee) The Kiowa word for "owl."

Saloli (sah-LO-lee) Meaning "squirrel." From the Cherokee.

Sanuye (sah-NOO-yeh) Meaning "red cloud(s) at sunset." A Miwok or Moquelumnan name.

Sapata (sah-PAH-tah) Meaning "dancing bear." From the Miwok or Moquelumnan.

Sasa (SAH-sah) Meaning "goose." Cherokee in origin.

Satinka (sah-TEENK-kah) Meaning "magic dancer." Source unknown.

Sewati (seh-WAH-tee) Meaning "curved bear claw." From the Miwok or Moquelumnan.

Shada (SHAH-dah) Meaning "pelican." From the Salish family of languages. Also *Shadia*.

Sibeta (see-BAY-tah) Meaning "finding a fish under a rock." From the Miwok or Moquelumnan.

Sihu (SEE-hoo) Meaning "flower." A Hopi name.

Sikya (SEE-kee-ah) A Hopi word that can mean "small canyon" or "yellow."

Sinopa (SIN-O-pah) Meaning either "kit foxes" or "Piegans." From the Blackfoot.

Sipatu (see-PAH-too) Miwok or Moquelumnan for "pulled out."

Sisika (SEE-see-kah) Meaning "swallow." From San Felipe, New Mexico.

Slana (slah-nah) The name of an Alaskan Ahtena village at Slana and Copper rivers. Source unknown.

Sonoma (so-NO-mah) "Ground place." A Yukian Wappo place in California in a language similar to Miwok.

Soso (SO-so) Meaning "squirrel biting hole in pine nut." From the Miwok or Moquelumnan.

Soyala (so-yah-lah) Hopi for "time of winter solstice."

Suki (SOO-kee) Meaning "eagle." From the Miwok or Moquelumnan.

Suleta (soo-LAY-tah) Meaning "soaring bird" or "to fly around." Of Miwok or Moquelumnan origin.

Suni (SOO-nyee) Meaning "middle." Of Zuñi origin.

Sunki (soon-kee) Meaning "swift." From the Hopi.

Suwanee (soo-WAH-nee). The name of two towns: one Seminole, one Cherokee. Meaning unknown.

Taa (TAH) Meaning "seed" or "corn." From the Zuñi.

Tadewi (TAH-deh-wee) The Omaha word for "wind."

Taini (TYE-nee) Meaning "new moon." From the Omaha.

Taipa (TYE-pah) Meaning "flying quail." From the Miwok or Moquelumnan.

Takala (tah-kah-lah) Hopi for "corn tassel."

Takenya (tah-KEN-yah) Meaning "falcon." Of Miwok or Moquelumnan origin.

Tala (DAHL-ah) A Yuchi name meaning "wolf."

Talasi (tah-lah-see) A Hopi name that means "pollen." Also *Talasea* and *Talasia*.

Tama (TAY-mah) Meaning "sudden crash (of thunder)." Name of a Fox chief, whose name is preserved in Tama, Iowa. Also *Taima*.

Tashi (TAH-shee) Meaning "washtub." From the Zuñi.

Thliana (THLEE-ah-nah) Meaning "blue." Also of Zuñi origin.

Tiimu (TEE-ee-moo) "Caterpillar coming out of the ground." From the Miwok or Moquelumnan.

Tiiva (TEEE-vah) Meaning "more than one dance; dances." From the Hopi. See *Ankti*.

Tiktu (TIK-too) Meaning "bird digging up potatoes." From the Miwok or Moquelumnan.

Tiponya (tih-POHN-yah) Meaning "great horned owl poking her hatching egg." Miwok or Moquelumnan.

Tiwa (TEE-wah) From the Zuñi, meaning "onions."

Toski (TOHS-kee) Meaning "squash bug." From the Hopi.

Totsi (TOH-tsee) Hopi for "moccasin" or "shoe."

Tsomah (TSOH-mah) Meaning "yellow hair." From the Kiowa.

Tsooro (TSOH-ro) Meaning "bluebird." A Hopi name.

Tsula (DZOO-lah) The Cherokee word for "fox."

Tuketu (too-KAY-too) "Bear making dust as it runs." From the Miwok or Moquelumnan.

Tukuli (too-KOO-lee) "Caterpillar crawling down a tree." Also Miwok or Moquelumnan in origin.

Tupi (TOO-pee) Meaning "pulled up." From the Miwok or Moquelumnan.

Tusa (TOO-sah) From the Zuñi meaning "prairie dog."

Tutskwa (TOOT-skwah) The Hopi word for "earth."

Tuuwa (TOO-wah) Meaning "sand." From the Hopi.

U'una (oo'oo-nah) Meaning "remember." From the Hopi.

Unega (oo-nay-GUH) Cherokee for "white."

Urika (oo-REE-kah) Meaning "useful." Perhaps confused with the English "eureka," from the Greek *heureka*, "I have found it." An Omaha name.

Usdi (OOS-DEE) Cherokee word for "baby." Also *Usti*.

Use (OO-seh) Meaning "salmon's head coming out of the water." From the Miwok or Moquelumnan.

Utana (yu-TAH-nuh) A name with three possible sources and meanings: "woman of my country," from the Timucua *utina*; "big," from the Cherokee *utana*; or *ute* (yoot) possibly meaning "high dwellers" or "pine land." Many Utanas were born in Utah, and many elsewhere have Indian ancestry. Variations include *Uinta*, *Utahan*, and *Utaanah*.

Utina (OO-tee-nah) Meaning "woman of my country." From the Timucua.

Wachiween (WAH-chee-wee[n]) Meaning "dancing girl." From the Dakota or Lakota.

Wakanda, **Wakenda** (wah-KAHN-dah, wah-KEN-dah) A Dakota or Lakota name that signifies "spiritual and mystic power."

Waki (WAH-kee) Meaning "shelter." From the Hopi.

Wanekia (wah-NEH-kee-ah) Meaning "makes life." From the Paiute, a Uto-Aztecan language.

Wapun (WAW-bun) The Potawatomi word for "dawn."

Washta (WAH-shtay) Meaning "good." From the Dakota or Lakota. Also *Washte*.

Wauna (WAH-oo-nah) Meaning "snow geese honking." Of Miwok or Moquelumnan origin.

Wawetseka (wuh-WAY-ji-kuh) A name that means "woman dressed up prettily." From the Potawatomi.

Weeyaya (WE-ee-yah-yah) Meaning "sunset." From the Dakota or Lakota.

Wichahpi (wee-CHAHH-pee) Meaning "star." From the Dakota or Lakota.

Wigmunke (WEEG-moong-keh) Dakota or Lakota for "rainbow."

Wilanu (we-LAH-noo) Meaing "pouring water on flour." From the Miwok or Moquelumnan.

Wilu (WEE-loo) "Chicken hawk squawking." From the Miwok or Moquelumnan.

Winona (weh-NO-nah) Meaning "first-born daughter," this name is an imprecise translation from Santee Sioux *win*, "woman," and an unknown ending. Actress Winona Ryder and country singer Wynona Judd. Variations include *Winnie*, *Winonah*, *Wynnona*, *Wynona*, and *Wenona*.

Wit'e (WEET-ay) Meaning "new moon." From the Dakota or Lakota.

Woya (WO-YAH)   The Cherokee word for "dove." Also *Woyi*.

Wuyi (WOO-yee)   Meaning "turkey vulture flying." From the Miwok or Moquelumnan.

Wyanet (WYE-ah-NEH-tah)   An adaptation of Winnetka, a town in Illinois, whose name is based on the nice, Algonquian-sounding word *winne*, meaning "beautiful."

Yanaba (yah-NAH-bah)   "She meets the enemy." A Navajo name.

Yatokya (YAA-toh-keeah)   Meaning "sun." From the Zuñi.

Yeluchi (yeh-LOO-chee)   Meaning "bear walking silently." From the Miwok or Moquelumnan.

Yenene (yeh-NAY-neh)   This name means "shaman" or "medicine man." From the Miwok or Moquelumnan.

Yepa (yay-PAH)   Meaning "snow." From the Tarahumara, who live in Chihuahua, Mexico.

Yoluta (yo-LOO-tah)   Meaning "goodbye-to-spring flower." Source unknown.

Yona (yo-nuh)   Meaning "bear." From the Cherokee.

Yoki (YO-kee)   Meaning "it rained." From the Hopi. Also *Yooki*.

Yoomee (YOO-mee)   Meaning "star." A name from the Coos, a Penutian language.

Yoskolo (yo-SKO-lo)   Meaning "breaking off pinecones." From the Miwok or Moquelumnan.

Yotimo (yo-TEE-mo)   "Yellow jacket carrying food to its hive." Also from the Miwok or Moquelumnan.

Yutu (YOO-too)   Meaning "coyote out hunting." Of Miwok or Moquelumnan origin.

Zaltana (zahl-TAH-nah)   Meaning "mountain." Also the name of the Knaiakhotana (Athabascan) clan in Cook Inlet, Alaska.

Ziracuny (ZEE-rah-KOO-nee)   Kiowa for "water monster."

Zitkala, Zintkala (zi[n]t-KAH-lah)   A Dakota or Lakota word that signifies "small bird."

Zonta (ZOHN-tah)   Meaning "trusted" or "honest." From the Dakota or Lakota.

United States

The world's broadest blend of nationalities, religions, races, and cultures, the United States draws from an array of name sources and naming traditions. In 1820, the U.S. population already hailed from numerous backgrounds: Native American, Dutch, English, African, French, German, Spanish, and Swedish. Since then an additional 63 million immigrants have expanded that mix. American diversity and inventiveness shine through in this list composed of created names and nicknames.

AMERICA: BOYS

Bubba (BUH-buh) Meaning "brother." Football great Bubba Smith.

Buddy (BUD-dee) A familiar form of Bud. Actor Buddy Ebsen. Variations include *Buddey* and *Buddie*.

Buster (BUS-tur) "Hitter" or "puncher." Early *Tarzan* actor Buster Crabbe and silent film star Buster Keaton.

Cazzie (KAH-zee) A familiar form of Cassius, meaning "hollow." Former New York Knicks basketball player Cazzie Russel. Variations include *Caz* and *Cazz*.

Ceejay (SEE-jay) A combination of the initials C. and J. Variations include *Cejay* and *C.J.*

Chuck (CHUK) A familiar form of Charles, from the Teutonic for "man." Actor Chuck Connors and rapper Chuck D. Variations include *Chuckey*, *Chuckie*, and *Chucky*.

Daquan (da-KWAN) A combination of the prefix Da and Quan. Variations include *Daquain*, *Daquann*, *Daquawn*, *Daqwan*, and *Dequann*.

Dejuan (deh-WAHN) A combination of the prefix De and Juan. Variations include *Dajuan*, *Dejan*, *Dejon*, *Dejun*, *Dewan*, *Dewon*, *Dijaun*, *D'juan*, *Dujuan*, and *D'Won*.

Demarcus (deh-MAR-kus) A combination of the prefix De and Marcus. Variations include *Damarcus*, *Demarkis*, and *D'Marcus*.

Demichael (deh-MIKE-al) A combination of the prefix De and Michael. A variation is *Dumichael*.

Deshawn (deh-SHAWN) A combination of the prefix De and Shawn. Variations include *Dashaun*, *Dashawn*, *Desean*, *Deshaun*, *Deshauwn*, *Deshawan*, *D'Sean*, *D'shaun*, *D'Shaun*, and *D'Shawn*.

Gabby (GAB-bee) or (GAY-bee) A familiar form of Gabriel. Gabby Hayes was an actor who always played a grizzled old westerner and a frequent sidekick of John Wayne's characters. Variations include *Gabbi*, *Gabbie*, *Gabi*, *Gabie*, and *Gaby*.

Hank (HANK) A familiar form of Henry, meaning "estate ruler." Baseball great Hank Aaron.

J (JAY) An initial used as a first name. Dr. J was the sobriquet of basketball legend Julius Erving. A variation is *Jay*.

Jace (JAY-see) A combination of the initials J. and C. Variations include *JC*, *J.C.*, *Jacey*, *Jaice*, *Jayce*, and *Jaycee*.

Jack (JAK) A form of Jacob or John. Actors Jack Oakie and Jack Nicholson, golf champion Jack Nicklaus, and jazz musician Jack Teagarten share this name. Variations include *Jackie*, *Jacko*, *Jackub*, and *Jacque*.

Jackie (JAK-ee) A familiar form of Jack. Comedian Jackie Gleason shared the name with the first player to break the color line in baseball, Jackie Robinson. A variation is *Jacky*.

Jajuan (jew-WHAN) A combination of the prefix Ja and Juan. Variations include *Juwann, Juwaun, Juwon,* and *Juwoan.*

Jayde (JAY-dee) A combination of the initials J. and D. Variations include *JD, J.D.,* and *Jayden.*

Jaylee (JAY-lee) A combination of Jay and Lee. Variations include *Jaylen, Jaylin, Jayion,* and *Jaylun.*

Jazz (JAZ) The name of a musical genre that was created in the United States. Variations include *Jaz, Jazze, Jazzman, Jazzmen, Jazzmin, Jazzmon,* and *Jazzton.*

Jimbo (JIM-bo) A familiar form of James, which means "conqueror." A variation is *Jimboo.*

Jock (JOK) A familiar form of Jacob, John, and Jonathan. Actor Jock Mahoney. Variations include *Jocko, Joco,* and *Jocoby.*

Jorell (JOR-ell) Meaning "he saves." Variations include *Jorel, Jorelle, Jorl, Jorrel,* and *Jorrell.*

Juwan (jew-WAHN) An alternate form of Jajuan. Basketball star Juwan Howard. Variations include *Juwann, Juwaun, Juwon,* and *Juwuan.*

KC (KAY-see) A combination of the initials K. and C. Boston Celtics great K. C. Jones. Variations include *Kacey, Kc, K.C., Kcee,* and *Kcey.*

Keshawn (KEY-shawn) A combination of the prefix Ke and Shawn. Keyshawn Johnson is a wide receiver for the New York Jets. Variations include *Keyshawn, Kesean, Keshaun,* and *Keshon.*

Lanny (LAN-nee) A familiar form of Lawrence or Laurence, both of which mean "crowned with laurel." Former White House counsel Lanny Davis. Variations include *Lannie* and *Lennie.*

Levon (LEE-vawn) Levon Helm was the drummer of the popular rock group The Band. Variations include *Lavon, Leevon, Levone, Levonn,* and *Lyvonne.*

Lucky (LUK-ee) Meaning "fortunate." Variations include *Luckie,* and *Luckson.*

Maverick (MAV-ur-ik) Meaning "independent." A variation is *Mavrick.*

Mychall (MY-call) A form of Michael, which is Hebrew for "Who is like God." Variations include *Mychall, Mychalo, Mycheal,* and *Mykall.*

Okie (OH-kee) "From Oklahoma." Variations include *Ok* and *Oak.*

Philly (PHIL-lee) A familiar form of Phillip. A variation is *Phillie.*

Rangle (RANG-gul) Meaning "cowboy." Variations include *Rangler* and *Wrangle.*

Rebel (REB-ul) Literally a "rebel." A variation is *Reb.*

Red (RED) Meaning "redhead." Boston Celtics manager Red Auerbach, comedians Red Skelton and Red Buttons. A variation is *Redd.*

Reno (REE-no) Meaning "gambler." After the city in Nevada, famous for gaming. Variations include *Renos* and *Rino.*

Rocky (ROCK-ee) Literally meaning "hard as a rock." The name of real-life boxers Rocky Marciano and Rocky Graziano and fictional fighter Rocky Balboa. Variations include *Rocco, Rock, Rockey,* and *Rockie.*

Tex (TEKS) Meaning "from Texas." Actor Tex Ritter and cartoonist Tex Avery are examples. A variation is *Telas.*

Tiger (TIE-gur) Meaning "tiger" or "powerful and energetic." Golf phenomenon Tiger Woods. Variations include *Tige, Tye,* and *Tyger.*

TJ (TEE-jay) A combination of the initials T. and J. Variations include *TeeJay, T.J., T Jae,* and *Tjayda.*

Tyron (TIE-ron) See Tyrone in Irish names. Variations include *Tyronn, Tyronna,* and *Tyronne.*

Woody (WOOD-ee) A familiar form of Woodrow and Heywood. Folk singer Woody Guthrie, filmmaker Woody Allen. Variations include *Wooddy* and *Woodle.*

Ziggy (ZIG-ghee) A familiar form of Siegfried and Sigmund. Ziggy Marley leads the Melody Makers in the reggae world. A variation is *Ziggie.*

AMERICA: GIRLS

Aiyana (EYE-ON-ah)   "Forever flowering." A variation is *Ayana*.

Amberly (AM-bur-lee)   A form of Amber. Variations include *Amberle, Amberlea, Amberlee, Amberlie,* and *Amberlyn*.

Anaba (ANN-ah-ba)   Meaning "she returns from war."

Andy (ANN-dee)   A short form of Andrea, meaning "womanly," and Fernanda, meaning "adventurous voyager." Actress Andy McDowell. Variations include *Ande, Andea, Andee,* and *Andi,*

Anetra (a-NET-tra)   A form of Annette. A variation is *Anitra*.

Angeni (AN-gen-ee)   Meaning "spirit." Variations include *Ange, Angee,* and *Angey*.

Annjanette (ANN-jan-ett)   A blend of Ann and Janette. Variations include *Angen, Angenett, Angenette, Anjane, Anjanetta,* and *Anjani*.

Baby (BAY-bee)   "Baby." Variations include *Babby, Babe,* and *Bebe*.

Barbie (BAR-bee)   A familiar form of Barbara. The doll of the same name is a staple of American girlhood. Variations include *Barbee, Barbey, Barbi,* and *Barby*.

Barbra (BAR-bra)   A form of Barbara, which means "the stranger." Singer/actress/director Barbra Streisand. Variations include *Bab, Babs, Barbee, Barbey, Barbi, Barbie,* and *Barby*.

Bea (BEE)   A short form of Beatrice, from the Latin for "she brings joy." A variation is *Bee*.

Becky (BEK-ee)   A familiar form of Rebecca, which means "servant of God." Variations include *Becki* and *Beckie*.

Betsy (BET-see)   A familiar form of Elizabeth, meaning "pledged to God." Among notable people with this name is the seamstress of the first U.S. flag, Betsy Ross. Variations include *Betsey, Betsi, Betsie,* and *Bitsie*.

Bettina (bet-TEE-na)   A blend of Beth and Tina. TV journalist Bettina Gregory. Variations include *Betina, Betine, Betti,* and *Bettine*.

Billie-Jean (BILLY-jean)   A blend of Billie and Jean. Variations include *Billiejean, Billyjean,* and *Billy-jean*.

Billie-Jo (BILLY-jo)   A blend of Billie and Jo. Variations include *Billiejo, Billyjo,* and *Billy-jo*.

Blondie (BLON-dee)   A familiar form of the French name Blondell. The band Blondie, led by Debbie Harry, had a number of hits in the late seventies and early eighties. Variations include *Blondee, Blondey,* and *Blondy*.

Bobbette (BAHB-ett)   A familiar form of Roberta, which means "bright fame." Variations include *Bobbet* and *Bobbetta*.

Bobbi (BAHB-ee)   A familiar form of Barbara and Roberta. Among the notable people with this name: former congresswoman Bobbi Fiedler. Variations include *Baubie, Bobbie, Bobbisue, Bobby,* and *Bobbye*.

Bobbi-Ann (BAHB-ee-AN)   A blend of Bobbi and Ann. A variation is *Bobbie-Ann*.

Bobbi-Jo (BAHB-ee-JO)   A blend of Bobbi and Jo. Variations include *Bobbiejo, Bobbie-Jo, Bobbijo,* and *Bobby-Jo*.

Bobbi-Lee (BAHB-ee-LEE)   A blend of Bobbi and Lee. Variations include *Bobbie-Lee, Bobbilee, Bobbylee,* and *Bobby-Leigh*.

Bonnie-Bell (BAHN-ee-BELL)   A blend of Bonnie and Belle, signifying "good and beautiful." Variations include *Bonnibell, Bonnibelle, Bonniebell, Bonniebelle, Bonnybell,* and *Bonnybelle*.

Brandy-Lynn (BRAN-dee-LIN)   A blend of Brandy and Lynn. Variations include *Brandalyn, Brandalynn, Brandelyn,* and *Brandelynn*.

Brenda-Lee (BREN-dah-LEE)   A blend of Brenda, meaning "little raven," and Lee, which means "meadow." Variations include *Brendalee, Brendaleigh, Brendalli,* and *Brendaly*.

Brie-Ann (BREE-ann)   A form of the Irish name Briana. Variations include *Brieann, Brieanna, Brieanne,* and *Brie-Anne*.

Brooklyn (BROOK-linn)   A blend of Brooke, which means "stream," and Lynn, meaning "waterfall"; also the name of a borough of New York City. Variations include *Brookellen, Brookelyn, Brooklin, Brooklynn,* and *Brooklynne.*

Buffy (BUF-fee)   Meaning "buffalo" or "from the plains." Among notable people with this name are folksinger Buffy Saint-Marie and television's *Buffy the Vampire Slayer.* Variations include *Buffee, Buffey, Buffie,* and *Buffye.*

Cailey (KAY-lee)   Alternate forms of Kaylee and Kelly. Variations include *Caelee, Caeley, Caelie, Cailie, Callee, Caleigh, Caylee, Cayley,* and *Caylie.*

Cailin (KAY-lin)   A form of Caitlin. Variations include *Caileen, Cailene, Cailine, Cailyn, Cailynn, Cailynne, Cayleen, Caylene, Caylin, Cayline, Caylyn,* and *Caylyne.*

Candi (KAN-dee)   A familiar form of Candace, Candice, and Candida. Variations include *Candee, Candie, Candy, Kanda, Kandhi, Kandi, Kanhdie,* and *Kahdy.*

Capri (kah-PREE)   The name of an Italian island. Variations include *Kapri* and *Kaprice.*

Carlissa (kar-LISS-ah)   A feminine form of Charles, meaning "little and womanly." Variations include *Carleesia, Carleeza, Carlesia, Carlis, Carlise, Carlisha, Carlisia, Carliss, Carlisse,* and *Carlissia.*

Carolann (KAHR-ol-ANN)   A form of Caroline.

Chenoa (chen-OH-ah)   Meaning "white dove."

Cherokee (CHER-oh-key)   A Native American tribal name. Variations include *Cherika, Cherkita,* and *Sherokee.*

Cholena (cho-LANE-ah)   Meaning "bird."

Cissy (SIS-ee)   A familiar form of Cecelia and Cicely, names originating from the Latin for "blind." Variations include *Cissey, Cissi,* and *Cissie.*

Coralee (KOR-ah-lee)   A blend of Cora and Lee. Variations include *Coralea, Cora-Lee, Coralena, Coralie, Corella, Corilee,* and *Koralie.*

Crystalin (KRIS-tah-lin)   A form of Crystal. Variations include *Cristilyn, Crystalina, Crystal-Lee, Crystallyn, Crystal-Lynn,* and *Crystallynn.*

Dafny (DAFF-nee)   A form of Daphne, the name of a maiden who resisted the courtship of Apollo and was transformed into a laurel tree. Variations include *Dafany, Daffany, Daffie, Daffy, Dafne, Dafney,* and *Dafnie.*

Dakota (dah-KOAT-ah)   A Native American tribal name. Variations include *Dakotah, Dakotha, Dekoda, Dekota, Dekotah,* and *Dekotha.*

Danella (dan-EL-lah)   A form of Danielle, meaning "God is my judge." Variations include *Danela, Danelia, Danelle, Donella,* and *Donnella.*

Danessa (dan-ESS-ah)   A blend of Danielle and Vanessa. Variations include *Danesa, Danesha, Danessia, Daniesa, Daniesha, Danisa,* and *Danissa.*

Danessia (dan-ESS-ee-ah)   An alternate form of Danessa. Variations include *Danesia, Danieshia, Danisia,* and *Danissia.*

Danyel (dan-YELL)   A form of Danielle. Variations include *Daniyel, Danya, Danyae, Danyail, Danyaile, Danyal, Danyale, Danyea, Danyele, Danyell, Danyella,* and *Danyelle.*

Darilynn (DAR-ih-lin)   A form of Darlene, which means "dear" or "little darling." Variations include *Daralin, Daralynn, Daralynne, Darilin, Darilyn, Darilynne, Darlin, Darlyn, Darlynn, Darlynne, Darylin, Darylyn, Darylynn,* and *Darylynne.*

Darnesha (dar-NEE-shah)   An alternate form of Darnelle, which means "great." Variations include *Darneshia, Darnesia, Darnisha, Darnishia,* and *Darnisia.*

Dashawna (da-SHAW-na)   A blend of the prefix Da and Shawna. Variations include *Dashawn, Dashawnda, Deshawna* and *Deshawnda.*

Davalinda (day-vah-LIN-dah)   A blend of Davida, which means "beloved," and Linda, meaning "pretty." Variations include *Davalynda, Davelinda, Davilinda, Davylinda* and *Davalynda.*

Deandra (DEE-ann-dra)   A blend of the prefix De and Andrea. Variations include *Deandre, Deandrea, Deandree, Deandria, Deanndra, Diandra, Diandre,* and *Diandrea.*

Debra (DEB-rah)   A form of Deborah, which is Hebrew for "bee." Among notable people with this name are romance author Debra Cowan and actress Debra Winger. Variations include *Debbra*, *Debbrah*, and *Debrah*.

Dedra (DEAD-rah)   A form of Deirdre, meaning "sorrowful wanderer." Variations include *Deeddra*, *Deedra*, and *Deedrea*.

Deena (DEE-nah)   A form of Deana, Dena, and Dinah.

Denisha (de-NEE-shah)   A form of Dennis, which means "follower of Dionisus." Variations include *Deneesha*, *Denesha*, *Deneshia*, *Deniesha*, and *Denishia*.

Dolly (DAH-lee)   A form of Dolores and Dorothy. Country singer Dolly Parton. Variations include *Dol*, *Doll*, *Dollee*, *Dolley*, *Dolli*, and *Dollie*.

Dondi (DOHN-dee)   A familiar form of Donna, which means "lady." Variations include *Dondra*, *Dondrea*, and *Dondria*.

Dory (DOR-ee)   Familiar forms of Dora, Doria, Doris, and Dorothy. Variations include *Dore*, *Dorey*, *Dori*, *Dorie*, *Dorree*, *Dorri*, *Dorrie*, and *Dorry*.

Emilyann (EM-ih-lee-AN)   A blend of Emily, which means "industrious," and Ann, meaning "full of grace, mercy, and prayer." Variations include *Emileane*, *Emileann*, *Emileanna*, *Emileanne*, *Emiliana*, *Emiliann*, *Emilianna*, and *Emilianne*.

Emmalee (EM-ma-lee)   A blend of Emma and Lee. Variations include *Emalea*, *Emalee*, *Emilee*, *Emmaleigh*, *Emmali*, *Emmaliese*, and *Emmalyse*.

Emmylou (EM-mee-LOU)   A blend of Emmy and Lou. Country singer Emmylou Harris. Variations include *Emlou*, *Emmelou*, *Emmilou*, and *Emylou*.

Fanny (FAN-nee)   A familiar form of Frances, which means "from France." Famous personages with this name include author Fanny Kemble and comedienne Fannie Brice. Variations include *Fan*, *Fani*, *Fania*, *Fannee*, *Fanney*, *Fanni*, *Fannia*, *Fannie*, and *Fanya*.

Flo (FLOW)   A short form of Florence. "Flo-Jo," Florence Griffith-Joyner, is a track-and-field legend.

Frankie (FRAN-kee)   A familiar form of Frances, which means "from France." Variations include *Francki*, *Frankey*, *Franki*, *Frankia*, and *Franky*.

Gennifer (JEN-ih-fer)   A form of Jennifer, meaning "white wave." Variations include *Gen*, *Genifer*, *Genny*, and *Ginnifer*.

Geri (JER-ree)   A familiar form of Geraldine. Singer Geri Halliwell, formerly known as Ginger Spice, is a well-known Geri. Variations include *Gerri*, *Gerrie*, *Gerry*, and *Jeri*.

Jackie (JACK-ee)   A familiar form of Jacqueline. Among the notable people with this name is romance author Jackie Collins. Variations include *Jackee*, *Jackia*, *Jacky*, and *Jacki*.

Jacklyn (JACK-lin)   A form of Jacqueline, meaning "the supplanter." Variations include *Jacalyn*, *Jacleen*, *Jacklin*, *Jackline*, *Jacklyne*, *Jacklynn*, *Jacklynne*, *Jackalyn*, *Jaclin*, *Jacline*, *Jaclyn*, *Jackee*, *Jackia*, *Jacky*, and *Jacki*.

Jammie (JAY-mee)   A feminine form of James, from the Hebrew for "the supplanter." Variations include *Jammesha*, *Jammi*, *Jammice*, *Jammise*, and *Jammisha*.

Jas (JAZ)   A short form of Jasmine.

Jaycee (JAY-see)   A blend of the initials J. and C. Variations include *Jacee*, *Jacey*, *Jaci*, *Jacie*, *Jacy*, *Jaycey*, and *Jaycy*.

Jaydee (JAY-dee)   A blend of the initials J. and D. Variations include *Jadee*, *Jadey*, *Jadi*, *Jadie*, *Jady*, and *Jaydi*.

Jenelle (ja-NELL)   A blend of Jenny and Nell. Variations include *Jenel*, *Jenell*, *Jennel*, *Jennell*, *Jennelle*, and *Jennille*.

Jennilee (JEN-ee-lee)   A blend of Jenny and Lee. Variations include *Jennalea*, *Jennalee*, *Jennielee*, and *Jennilea*.

Jennilynn (JEN-ee-lin)   A blend of Jenni and Lynn. Variations include *Jennalin*, *Jennalyn*, *Jennilin*, *Jennilyn*, and *Jennilyne*.

Jeri (JER-ee)   A short form of Jeraldine. Variations include *Jeree, Jeriel, Jerilee, Jerilyn, Jerri, Jerriann, Jerrie, Jerrilee, Jerrine, Jerry, Jerrylee,* and *Jerryne.*

Jizelle (jiz-ELL)   A form of Giselle, which means "pledge." Variations include *Jisell, Jisella, Jiselle, Jissell, Jissella,* and *Jisselle.*

Jo (JO)   A short form of Joanna, Jolene, and Josephine. Jo was the eldest sister in Louisa May Alcott's *Little Women.* Variations include *Joangie, Joetta, Joette,* and *Joey.*

Jodie (JO-dee)   A familiar form of Judith. Jodie Foster is an Academy Award-winning actress. Variations include *Jodi* and *Jody.*

Johnna (JAHN-ah)   A feminine form of John. Variations include *Jhona, Jhonna, Jianna, Jianni, Jiannini, Johna, Johni, Johnica, Johnie, Johnique, Johnnessa, Johnni,* and *Johnnie.*

Jonelle (JON-el)   A blend of Joan and Elle. Variations include *Johnel, Johnell, Johnella, Johnelle, Jonel, Jonell, Jonella, Jynell,* and *Jynelle.*

Joni (JO-nee)   A familiar form of Joan, meaning "God's gracious gift." Among the notable people with this name is songwriter and folk singer Joni Mitchell. Variations include *Jona, Jonae, Jonai, Joncey, Jonci, Jonelle, Jonessa, Jonetia, Jonetta, Jonette, Jonica, Jonice, Jonie, Jonika, Jonilee, Jonilee, Jonina, Jonique, Jonis, Jonisa, Jonisha,* and *Jony.*

Josie (JO-see)   A familiar form of Josephine, which means "she shall add." Josie was the leader of the Pussycats, a fictional band in the animated television show *Josie and the Pussycats.* Variations include *Joe, Joesell, Joesette, Joselle, Josette, Josey, Josi, Josiane, Josiann, Josianne, Josina,* and *Jozette.*

Kachina (kah-CHEE-nah)   "Sacred dancer." A variation is *Kachine.*

Kaelyn (KAY-lin)   A blend of Kae and Lynn. Variations include *Kaelan, Kaelen, Kaelin, Kaelynn,* and *Kaelynne.*

Kahsha (KAH-sha)   Meaning "fur robe." Variations include *Kasha, Kashae,* and *Kashia.*

Kameron (KAM-er-on)   A form of Cameron. Variations include *Kamren, Kamrin, Kamron,* and *Kamryn.*

Kanda (KAN-dah)   Meaning "magical power."'

Karen (KAHR-in)   A form of Katherine, which means "pure." Variations include *Karin, Karyn, Karyna, Karyne,* and *Karynn.*

Karlotte (KAHR-lot-teh)   A form of Charlotte, which means "little and womanly." Variations include *Karletta, Karlette,* and *Karlotta.*

Karolyn (KAHR-oh-lin)   A form of Carolyn (see English names). Also *Karalyn, Karalynn, Karalynne, Karilyn, Karilyne, Karilyn, Karilinn, Karilynn, Karilynne, Karylin, Karylinn, Karlyn, Karlynn, Karlynne, Karolynn, Karolynne, Karrolyn, Karrolynn,* and *Karrolynne.*

Karrie (KAHR-ree)   A form of Caroline. Variations include *Kari, Karie, Karri,* and *Karry.*

Kassie (KASS-see)   Familiar forms of Kassandra, meaning "inflaming men with love," and Kassidy, which means "clever." Variations include *Cassie, Kassie, Kassey, Kassla,* and *Kassy.*

Kaycee (KAY-see)   A blend of the initials K. and C.

Kaylee (KAY-lee)   Meaning "pasture by the spring." Variations include *Kaelea, Kaelee, Kaeli, Kaelie, Kaeleigh, Kaeli, Kaelie, Kailee, Kaileigh, Kaily, Kalee, Kaleigh, Kaley, Kalleigh, Kayle, Kaylei, Kayleigh, Kayley, Kayli,* and *Kaylie.*

Kaylyn (KAY-lin)   A blend of Kay and Lynn. Variations include *Kailyn, Kaillynn, Kailynne, Kaylan, Kayleen, Kaylene, Kaylin, Kaylynn, Kaylon,* and *Kaylynne.*

Keneisha (key-NEE-sha)   A blend of the prefix Ke and Neisha. Variations include *Kineesha, Kineisha, Kinesha,* and *Kinisha.*

Khrissa (KRIS-ah)   A form of Christine, from the Greek for "Christ-bearer." Variations include *Chrissa, Khrishia, Khryssa, Krisha, Krisia, Krissa, Krysha,* and *Kryssa.*

Kiana (kee-AH-na)   A blend of the prefix Ki and Ana.

Kiona (kee-O-na)   Meaning "brown hills."

Klaudia (KLAUD-ee-ah) A form of Claudia, a Latin family name meaning "the lame." A variation is *Klaudila*.

Kodi (KOH-dee) A form of Cody, the Irish for "helpful." Variations include *Kodee, Kodie,* and *Kody*.

Kolby (KOL-bee) See Colby in English names. Variations include *Kolbie* and *Kolby*.

Koral (KOR-ul) The name of a dark pink gemstone, coral. Variations include *Korel, Korele, Korrel, Korrell,* and *Korrelle*.

Kourtney (KORT-nee) A form of Courtney, which means "courteous." Variations include *Kourtni* and *Kourtny*.

Kris (KRIS) A short form of Kristine, from the Greek for "Christ-bearer." An alternate form of Chris. Variations include *Khris, Krissy, Krissey, Krissi, Krissie, Krissy, Kristi, Kristie,* and *Krysti*.

Krystal (KRIS-tal) Meaning "clear" or "brilliant glass." An alternate form of Crystal. Variations include *Kristabel, Kristal, Kristall, Kristel, Kristell, Kristelle, Krystl, Krystle,* and *Krystyl*.

Krystalee (KRIS-ta-lee) A blend of Krystal and Lee. Variations include *Kristalea, Kristalee, Krystalea, Krystlea, Krystlee,* and *Krystlelee*.

Lakresha (lu-KREE-sha) A form of Lucretia, from the Roman family name Lucretius. Variations include *Lacresha, Lacreshia, Lacresia, Lacretia, Lacrisha, Lakreshia, Lakrisha, Lekresha,* and *Lekresia*.

Laquita (la-KEE-tah) A blend of the prefix La and Quintana, meaning "fifth." Variations include *Laqueta* and *Laquetta*.

Lashanda (la-SHAN-da) A blend of the prefix La and Shanda. Also *Lashandra, Lashane, Lashanna, Lashanta, Lashante, Lashaunda, Lashonda,* and *Lashondra*.

Lashawna (la-SHAW-na) A blend of the prefix La and Shawna. Variations include *Lashauna, Lashaune,* and *Lashaunna*.

Latasha (la-TASH-ah) A blend of the prefix La and Tasha. Also *Latacha, Latacia, Latai,* *Lataisha, Latashia, Lataysha, Letasha, Letashia, Leteshia, Letasiah,* and *Leteisha*.

Latesha (la-TEESH-ah) Meaning "gladness." A form of Letitia. Variations include *Latecia, Lateesha, Lateicia,* and *Lateisha*.

Lawanda (LA-wahn-dah) A blend of the prefix La and Wanda. A variation is *Lawynda*.

Leotie (lee-O-tee) Meaning "prairie flower."

Lissie (LISS-see) A familiar form of Allison, Elise, and Elizabeth. Variations include *Lis, Lissey, Lissi,* and *Lissy*.

Liza (LIE-zah) Meaning "pledged to God." A short form of Elizabeth. Among notable people with this name is entertainer Liza Minnelli. Variations include *Leeza, Lizete, Lizette,* and *Lyza*.

Lizzy (LIZ-zee) Meaning "pledged to God." Also spelled *Lizzie*.

Loren (LOHR-en) Meaning "crowned with laurel." An alternate form of Lauren. Variations include *Lorin, Lorine, Lorren, Lorrin, Lorryn, Loryn, Lorynn,* and *Lorynne*.

Lyndsay (LIND-say) Meaning "linden tree island." A form of Lindsay.

Mahalia (mah-HALL-yah) A form of Mahala. Among the notable people with this name is gospel singer Mahalia Jackson. Variations include *Mahaliah, Mahelea, Maheleah,* and *Mahelia*.

Malley (MAL-lee) Meaning "unfortunate." A familiar form of Mallory. Also *Mallee, Malli, Mallie,* and *Mally*.

Mamie (MAIM-ee) Meaning "pearl." A familiar form of Margaret. Among notable people with this name is Former First Lady Mamie Eisenhower. Variations include *Mame, Mamee,* and *Maimy*.

Marilee (MAR-ih-lee) A blend of Mary and Lee. Variations include *Marrilee* and *Marylea*.

Marybeth (MAR-ee-beth) A blend of Mary and Beth. Variations include *Maribeth* and *Maribette*.

Maryellen (MAR-ee-ell-en) A blend of Mary and Ellen. A variation is *Mariellen*.

Maryjo (MAR-ee-JO) A blend of Mary and Jo. A variation is *Marijo*.

Marylou (MAR-ee-LU) A blend of Mary and Lou. Gymnast Mary lou Retton. Variations include *Marilou* and *Marilu*.

Mausi (MAUS-ee) Meaning "plucked flower."

Maylyn (MAY-lin) A blend of May and Lynn. Variations include *Maylen, Maylene, Maylin, Maylon, Maylynn,* and *Maylynne*.

Meda (MED-ah) Meaning "prophet" or "priestess."

Melonie (MEHL-ohn-ee) An alternate form of Melanie. Variations include *Melloney* and *Mellonie*.

Micki (MIK-ee) A familiar form of Michaela. Variations include *Mickee* and *Mickie*.

Mikhaela (mik-ALE-ah) From the Hebrew for "Who is like God." Variations include *Makayla, Mikaela, Mikhail, Mikhaila, Mikhala, Mikhalea,* and *Mykaela*.

Minal (min-AL) Meaning "fruit."

Minnie (MIN-nee) A familliar form of Mina, Minerva, Minna, and Wilhelmina. Among notable people with this name is actress Minnie Driver. Variations include *Mini, Minni,* and *Minny*.

Minowa (min-OH-wah) Meaning "singer." A variation is *Minowah*.

Myriam (MEER-ee-am) A form of Miriam, which is Hebrew for "bitter." Variations include *Myriame* and *Myryam*.

Nakeisha (nak-EESH-ah) A blend of the prefix Na and Keisha. Variations include *Nakeesha, Nakesha, Nakeshea, Nakiesha,* and *Nekeisha*.

Nakita (nak-EET-ah) Meaning "victory of the people." A form of Nicole. Variations include *Nakia, Nakkita,* and *Nikita*.

Nichelle (NIH-shell) A blend of Nicole, meaning "victory of the people," and Michelle, which means "Who is like God."

Niki (NIK-kee) A familiar form of Nicole and Nikita. Notable Nikis include Model Niki Taylor and writer Nikki Giovanni. Variations include *Nicki, Nickie, Nikki, Nikkey, Nikkie,* and *Nikky*.

Nitasha (nih-TASH-ah) Meaning "child of Christmas." A form of Natasha. Variations include *Nitasha, Niteisha, Nitisha,* and *Nitishia*.

Nituna (nih-TOO-na) Meaning "daughter."

Nuna (NOO-nah) Meaning "land."

Ogin (OH-jin) Meaning "wild rose."

Olathe (OH-lathe) Meaning "beautiful." A variation is *Olathia*.

Onawa (oh-NOW-ah) Meaning "wide awake." Variations include *Onaja* and *Onajah*.

Oneida (oh-NAY-dah) Meaning "eagerly awaited." Variations include *Onida* and *Onyda*.

Petunia (peh-TOON-yah) A name signifying the flower.

Rayleen (ray-LEEN) A blend of *Ray* and *Lynn*. Variations include *Raylene, Raylin, Raylyn, Raylynn,* and *Raylynne*.

Reanne (ray-ANN) A combination of Ray and Anne. Variations include *Rayan, Rayann, Ray-Ann, Rayanne, Reane, Reann, Reannan, Reanne, Reannen, Reannon, Reeana, Reyan, Reyanna,* and *Reyanne*.

Rexanne (reks-ANN) Meaning "queen." Variations include *Rexan* and *Rexann*.

Ricki (RIK-kee) Familiar forms of Erica, Frederica, and Ricarda. Talk show host Ricki Lake. Variations include *Rica, Rici, Ricka, Rickie, Rickilee, Ricky, Ricquie, Riki, Rikki,* and *Rikky*.

Ricquell (rih-KELL) A form of Rachel, from the Hebrew for "eve." Variations include *Rickquell, Ricquelle, Rikell,* and *Rikelle*.

Ronnie (RON-nee) Meaning "true image." A familiar form of Veronica and names beginning with "Ron." Singer Ronnie Spector and the Ronettes recorded "Da Do Run Run." Variations include *Ronee, Roni, Ronnee,* and *Ronney*.

Rosalyn (ROSE-ah-lin) A blend of Rose and Lynn. Variations include *Rosali, Rosalynn, Roselynn,* and *Roslyn.*

Rozene (rose-EEN) Meaning "rose blossom." A variation is *Rozine.*

Ruthann (rooth-ANN) A blend of Ruth, from the Hebrew for "friendship" and Ann, which means "gracious." Variations include *Ruthan* and *Ruthanne.*

Sakuna (SAK-oo-nah) Meaning "bird."

Sapata (sah-PAT-ah) Meaning "dancing bear."

Satinka (sa-TIN-kah) Meaning "sacred dancer."

Shada (SHA-dah) Meaning "pelican." Variations include *Shadae, Shadee, Shadi,* and *Shadie.*

Shakarah (sha-KAR-ah) A blend of the prefix Sha and Kara, meaning "pure." Variations include *Shacara, Shaccara,* and *Shakkara.*

Shakeena (sha-KEEN-ah) A blend of the prefix Sha and Keena. Variations include *Shaka, Shakeina, Shakeyna, Shakina,* and *Shakyna.*

Shameka (sha-MEK-ah) A blend of the prefix Sha and Meka. Variations include *Shameca, Shamecca, Shameika,* and *Shamika.*

Shantel (shan-TELL) From the French Chantal, meaning "song." A variation is *Shantell.*

Shantille (shan-TILL-ee) A form of Chantilly, the name of a lace from Chantilly, France. Variations include *Shanteil, Shantil,* and *Shantille.*

Shaquilla (sha-KEEL-ah) The feminine form of Shaquille, meaning "handsome." Variations include *Shakila* and *Shaquila.*

Sharlotte (SHAR-lot-teh) Meaning "little and womanly." A form of Charlotte. Variations include *Sharlet, Sharlett,* and *Sharlott.*

Sharmaine (shar-MAINE) A form of Charmaine. Variations include *Sharma, Sharmain, Sharmane,* and *Sharmayne.*

Shelsea (SHELL-sea) Meaning "seaport" or "landing." A form of the English Chelsea. Variations include *Shellsea, Shellsey,* and *Shelsey.*

Sherylyn (SHER-ih-lin) A blend of Sheryl, meaning "beloved," and Lynn, which means "waterfall." Variations include *Sharlyne, Sharyl-Lynn, Sheralyn, Sherilyn, Sherilynn, Sherilynne, Sherralyn, Sherrilyn,* and *Sherrilynn.*

Sindy (SIN-dee) Meaning "much." A form of Cynthia. Variations include *Sindee, Sindie, Syndee, Syndey, Syndi, Syndie,* and *Syndy.*

Sissy (SIS-see) A familiar form of the names Cecelia and Cicely, which derive from the word for "blind." Actress Sissy Spacek. Variations include *Sisi, Sisie, Sissey,* and *Sissie.*

Sora (SOR-ah) Meaning "chirping songbird."

Sugar (SHUG-ar) Meaning "sweet as sugar." A variation is *Shug.*

Susie (SOO-zee) Meaning "lily." A familiar form of Susan and Susannah. Notable people with this name include actress Suzy Amis. Variations include *Susi, Susy, Suzie,* and *Suzy.*

Taima (TAY-mah) Meaning "loud thunder." A variation is *Taimy.*

Takira (tak-EER-ah) A blend of the prefix Ta and Kira, which is Greek for "queen." Variations include *Takeara, Taquera, Taquira, Tykera,* and *Tykira.*

Talla (TALL-ah) Meaning "stalking wolf."

Tamesha (tam-EESH-ah) A blend of the prefix Ta and Mesha. Variations include *Tamisha, Tamishia, Temisha, Timesha, Timisha, Tomesha,* and *Tomisha.*

Tamilla (TAM-eel-ah) A blend of the prefix Ta and Mila.

Taneisha, Tanesha (TAN-esh-ah) A blend of the prefix Ta and Nesha. Also *Tahniesha, Taneesha, Taneshea, Taniesha, Tanneshia, Tanniesha.*

Tanya (TAWHN-ya) A form of Tatiana, from a Roman family name. Variations include *Tawnya* and *Tonya.*

Tawanna (TAH-wahn-ah)   A blend of the prefix Ta and Wanda. Variations include *Tawana, Tewanna, Tewauna,* and *Towanna.*

Teralyn (TER-ah-lin)   A blend of Terri and Lynn, meaning "waterfall." Variations include *Teralyn, Teralynn, Terralin, Terralyn, Terelyn, Terelynn, Terri-Lynn, Terrilynn, Terry-Lynn,* and *Terrylynn.*

Terri (TER-ee)   A form of Theresa, from the Greek for "harvester."

Terriann (TER-ee-ANN)   A blend of Terri and Ann, which means "gracious." Variations include *Terian, Teriann, Terianne, Terrian,* and *Terrianne.*

Tina (TEE-nah)   A short form of Augustine, Martina, Christina, and Valentina. Among notable people with this name are singer Tina Turner and actress Tina Louise. Variations include *Teanna, Teena, Teina, Tena, Tenae, Tine, Tinnia, Tyna,* and *Tynka.*

Trixie (TRIX-ee)   Meaning "she brings joy." A familiar form of Beatrice. Variations include *Trix, Trixi,* and *Trixy.*

Tyfany (TIFF-an-ee)   A short form of Tiffany. Variations include *Tyfani, Tyfanny, Tyffani, Tyffanni, Tyffany, Tyffini, Typhanie,* and *Typhany.*

Wyoming (why-OHM-ing)   The name of a western state in the United States. Variations include *Wy* and *Wye.*

Zabrina (zah-BREE-nah)   An alternate form of Sabrina, a Celtic river name. Variations include *Zabreena* and *Zabrinna.*

Zaltana (zal-TAH-nah)   Meaning "high mountain."

Part II:
Resources and Worksheets

Family Names:
A Genealogical History

Complete the following charts from the perspective of your new baby. The names you write represent not only the rich history of familial names in your baby's background but also the love in store for your special child.

Female Relatives

Great grandmothers

_____   _____
_____

Grandmothers

_____   _____

Mother

_____

Aunts

_____   _____
_____   _____
_____   _____
_____   _____

Sisters

_____   _____
_____   _____

Cousins

_____   _____
_____   _____
_____   _____
_____   _____

Other special relatives

_____   _____
_____   _____
_____

Male Relatives

Great grandfathers

_____   _____
_____   _____

Grandfathers

_____   _____

Father

_____

Uncles

_____   _____
_____   _____
_____   _____
_____   _____

Brothers

_____   _____
_____   _____

Cousins

_____   _____
_____   _____
_____   _____
_____   _____

Other special relatives

_____   _____
_____   _____
_____   _____

MOM'S
Favorite Names

BOYS	COUNTRY	PAGE
1. _____	_____	_____
2. _____	_____	_____
3. _____	_____	_____
4. _____	_____	_____
5. _____	_____	_____
6. _____	_____	_____
7. _____	_____	_____
8. _____	_____	_____
9. _____	_____	_____
10. _____	_____	_____

GIRLS	COUNTRY	PAGE
1. _____	_____	_____
2. _____	_____	_____
3. _____	_____	_____
4. _____	_____	_____
5. _____	_____	_____
6. _____	_____	_____
7. _____	_____	_____
8. _____	_____	_____
9. _____	_____	_____
10. _____	_____	_____

DAD'S
Favorite Names

BOYS	COUNTRY	PAGE
1. _____	_____	_____
2. _____	_____	_____
3. _____	_____	_____
4. _____	_____	_____
5. _____	_____	_____
6. _____	_____	_____
7. _____	_____	_____
8. _____	_____	_____
9. _____	_____	_____
10. _____	_____	_____

GIRLS	COUNTRY	PAGE
1. _____	_____	_____
2. _____	_____	_____
3. _____	_____	_____
4. _____	_____	_____
5. _____	_____	_____
6. _____	_____	_____
7. _____	_____	_____
8. _____	_____	_____
9. _____	_____	_____
10. _____	_____	_____

FAMILY'S
Favorite Names

BOYS	COUNTRY	PAGE
1.		
2.		
3.		
4.		
5.		
6.		
7.		
8.		
9.		
10.		

GIRLS	COUNTRY	PAGE
1.		
2.		
3.		
4.		
5.		
6.		
7.		
8.		
9.		
10.		

FRIENDS'
Favorite Names

BOYS	COUNTRY	PAGE
1. _____	_____	_____
2. _____	_____	_____
3. _____	_____	_____
4. _____	_____	_____
5. _____	_____	_____
6. _____	_____	_____
7. _____	_____	_____
8. _____	_____	_____
9. _____	_____	_____
10. _____	_____	_____

GIRLS	COUNTRY	PAGE
1. _____	_____	_____
2. _____	_____	_____
3. _____	_____	_____
4. _____	_____	_____
5. _____	_____	_____
6. _____	_____	_____
7. _____	_____	_____
8. _____	_____	_____
9. _____	_____	_____
10. _____	_____	_____

Index

Adoeette
    boy 214
    girl 222
Adofo (boy) 4
Adomas (boy) 74
Adonia (girl) 206
Adonis (boy) 180
Adowa (girl) 5
Adrian (boy) 86
Adriana (girl) 191, 196
Adriane (girl) 106
Adriano (boy) 185, 194
Adrien (boy) 120
Aduke (girl) 12
Adya (girl) 31
Aetios (boy) 180
Afafa (girl) 5
Afansy (boy) 82
Afghanistan, names from
    42
    boys 42
    girls 42
Afi (girl) 21
Afiya (girl) 21
Afra (girl) 49
Afram (boy) 4
Africa, names from
    3–24
    Benin 3
    boys 3
    girls 3
    favorite 20–24
    boys 20
    girls 20–24
    Ghana 4–6
    boys 4–5
    girls 5–6
    Kenya 7–8
    boys 7
    girls 7–8
    Nigeria 9–14
    boys 9–11
    girls 11–14

Rwanda 15
    boys 15
    girls 15
South Africa 16
    boys 16
    girls 16
Tanzania 17
    boys 17
    girls 17
Uganda 18–19
    boys 18–19
    girls 19
Afryea (girl) 5
Afton
    boy 88
    girl 106
Afua (girl) 5, 21
Agamemnonas (boy) 180
Agasga (girl) 222
Agate (girl) 107
Agatha (girl) 73
Agesilaos (boy) 180
Aggeles (boy) 180
Agnese (girl) 191
Agni (boy) 28
Agrippas (boy) 180
Agrippina (girl) 84
Agu (boy) 9
Ahadi (girl) 21
Ahanu (boy) 214
Aharon (boy) 43
Ahava (girl) 49
Ahiga (boy) 214
Ahmik (boy) 214
Ahona (girl) 222
Ahote (boy) 214
Ahuli (boy) 214
Ahwi (girl) 222
Ahyoka (girl) 222
Ai (girl) 26, 36
Aias (boy) 180
Aida (girl) 191
Aidan (boy) 156

Aidos (girl) 182
Aietes (boy) 180
Aigars (boy) 72
Aigisthos (boy) 180
Aija (girl) 73
Aikaterine (girl) 182
Aiko (girl) 36
Aila (girl) 173
Ailis (girl) 162
Aimery (boy) 137
Aimon (boy) 120
Aimonas (boy) 180
Aina (girl) 12
Aine (girl) 162
Aineias (boy) 180
Aischines (boy) 180
Aischylos (boy) 180
Aisha (girl) 21
Aisling (girl) 162
Aisonas (boy) 180
Aisopos (boy) 180
Aithousa (girl) 182
Aiyana (girl) 233
Aiyetoro (girl) 12
Aja (girl) 31
Ajala (boy) 9
Ajay (boy) 28
Ajmal (boy) 42
Akademos (boy) 181
Akako (girl) 36
Akane (girl) 36
Akanke (girl) 12
Akecheta (boy) 214
Aki (girl) 36
Akiko (girl) 36
Akili (girl) 21
Akins (boy) 9
Akira (boy) 35
Akiva (boy) 43
Akosua (girl) 5
Akritas (boy) 181
Aksel (boy) 174
Akua (girl) 5

Amitai (boy) 43
Amitolanne (girl) 222
Amlika (girl) 31
Amory (boy) 138
Amos (boy) 43
Amphiaraos (boy) 181
Amphidamas (girl) 183
Amphitrite (girl) 183
Amram (boy) 43
Amy (girl) 107
An (boy) 25
Ana (girl) 206
Anaba (girl) 233
Anais (girl) 49
Anakreondas (boy) 181
Anala (girl) 31
Anamoha (girl) 222
Anand (boy) 28
Ananda (girl) 31
Anant (boy) 28
Anastasia (girl) 183
Anastasijia (girl) 84
Anatoli (boy) 82
Anaxagoras (boy) 181
Anaximandros (boy) 181
Anaximenes (boy) 181
Anci (girl) 71
Anders (boy) 178
Andor (boy) 69
André (boy) 120
Andreas (boy) 181
Andrei (boy) 62, 80, 83
Andres (boy) 199
Androkles (boy) 181
Andromache (girl) 183
Andronikos (boy) 181
Andros (boy) 69, 76
Andwele (boy) 17
Andy (girl) 233
Aneko (girl) 36
Anela (girl) 212
Anestes (boy) 181
Anetra (girl) 233

Aneurin (boy) 168
Anevay (boy) 214
Anezka (girl) 66
Angavu (girl) 21
Angbetu (girl) 222
Ângela (girl) 196
Angelika (girl) 84
Angelique (girl) 128
Angelo (boy) 186, 194
Angeni (girl) 233
Angharad (girl) 170
Ani (girl) 212
Anice (girl) 107
Anicuta (girl) 80
Anika (girl) 66
Aniky (girl) 71
Anil (boy) 28
Anila (girl) 31
Anjeni (girl) 223
Ankti (girl) 223
Anna (girl) 66, 78, 87,
   149, 179, 183, 191
Annabel (girl) 107
Annalina (girl) 179
Anne (girl) 107
Annelisa (girl) 107
Annemarie (girl) 107
Annette (girl) 128
Annibas (boy) 181
Annie (girl) 107
Annikki (girl) 173
Annjanette (girl) 233
Anno (boy) 138
Annze (girl) 75
Anon (girl) 107
Ansa (girl) 173
Ansel (boy) 120
Anselm (boy) 138
Anson (boy) 138
Antal (boy) 69
Antalkidas (boy) 181
Antigone (girl) 183
Antiochos (boy) 181

Antiphontas (boy) 181
Antisthenes (boy) 181
Antjuan (boy) 199
Antobam (girl) 6
Antoine (boy) 120
Antoinette (girl) 128
Anton (boy) 82
Antonia (girl) 183, 196
Antonina (girl) 84
Antonio (boy) 186, 194
Antonios (boy) 181
Antti (boy) 172
Anuhea (girl) 212
Anunciación (girl) 206
Anya (girl) 84
Aolani (girl) 212
Aphra (girl) 49
Aphrodite (girl) 183
Apiatan (boy) 214
Apisi (boy) 214
Apollonas (boy) 181
Aponi (girl) 223
Aquene (girl) 223
Aquila (boy) 199
Aqwenasa (girl) 223
Arad (boy) 43
Araldo (boy) 199
Aramis (boy) 120
Aran (boy) 41
Aranck (boy) 214
Araxi (girl) 31
Archibald (boy) 138
Archie (boy) 138
Ardal (boy) 156
Arden (girl) 107
Ardi (girl) 49
Ardice (girl) 49
Ardith (girl) 49
Ardon (boy) 43
Arella (girl) 49
Arethousa (girl) 183
Ari (boy) 44
Aria (girl) 149

Avent (boy) 120
Averill (boy) 120
Avery (boy) 89
Avi (boy) 44
Avishalom (boy) 44
Aviv (boy) 44
Aviva (girl) 49
Avner (boy) 44
Avonaco (boy) 215
Avraham (boy) 44
Avram (boy) 44
Avril (girl) 108
Avshalom (boy) 44
Awendela (girl) 223
Awenita (girl) 223
Awi-Equa (boy) 215
Aya (girl) 36, 49
Ayaka (girl) 36
Ayako (girl) 36
Ayano (girl) 36
Ayers (boy) 89
Ayinde (boy) 9
Ayita (girl) 223
Ayize (boy) 16
Ayla (girl) 49
Aymon (boy) 120
Ayo
  boy 9
  girl 12
Ayobami (girl) 12
Ayobunmi (girl) 12
Ayodele (girl) 12
Ayofemi (girl) 12
Ayoluwa (girl) 12
Ayoola (girl) 12
Ayuhwasi (girl) 223
Azarya (boy) 44
Azi (boy) 9
Azikiwe (boy) 9
Aziza (girl) 21

B

Baba (girl) 6
Babette (girl) 128, 149

Babur (boy) 42
Baby (girl) 233
Baden (boy) 138
Baderinwa (girl) 12
Badria (girl) 42
Badu (boy) 4
Bahati (girl) 21
Bahram (boy) 60
Baiba (girl) 73
Bailey
  boy 120
  girl 108
Baird (boy) 156
Baker (boy) 89
Bakula (girl) 31
Bal (boy) 28
Baldemar (boy) 138
Balder (boy) 174
Baldric (boy) 138
Baldwin (boy) 138
Balin (boy) 28
Ballard (boy) 138
Balogun (boy) 9
Balondemu (boy) 18
Bancroft (boy) 89
Bandele (boy) 9
Banjoko (boy) 9
Bankole (boy) 9
Barak (boy) 44
Barasa (boy) 7
Barbara (girl) 183
Barbie (girl) 233
Barbra (girl) 233
Barclay (boy) 89
Bardolf (boy) 139
Barker (boy) 89
Barlow (boy) 89
Barnaby (boy) 89
Barnes (boy) 89
Barney (boy) 89
Barnum (boy) 139
Baron (boy) 139
Barra (girl) 49

Barrett (boy) 139
Barric (boy) 89
Barrie (girl) 162
Bartlet (boy) 89
Barto (boy) 200
Barton (boy) 89
Bartram (boy) 89
Barukh (boy) 44
Basia (girl) 50
Basilike (girl) 183
Bassett (boy) 89
Bastien (boy) 139
Bathilda (girl) 149
Bathsheba (girl) 50
Batini (girl) 21
Baxter (boy) 89
Bayard (boy) 89
Bayo (girl) 12
Bea (girl) 233
Beaman (boy) 89
Beamer (boy) 89
Beasley (boy) 89
Beata (girl) 78
Beatrise (girl) 73
Beatriz (girl) 196
Beau (boy) 120
Beaufort (boy) 120
Beaumont (boy) 120
Beauregard (boy) 121
Beaver (boy) 89
Bebe (boy) 200
Becca (girl) 50
Beck (boy) 89
Becky (girl) 233
Bedelia (girl) 162
Bedrikh (boy) 64
Bejide (girl) 12
Bela
  boy 64
  girl 66
Belden (boy) 121
Belicia (girl) 206
Belinda (girl) 206

Boone (boy) 121
Booth (boy) 90
Borden (boy) 121
Borgny (girl) 176
Boris (boy) 82
Boseda (boy) 9
Bosley (boy) 90
Bourne (boy) 121
Bowen (boy) 168
Boyce (boy) 121
Brad (boy) 90
Bradburn (boy) 90
Bradford (boy) 90
Bradley (boy) 90
Bradon (boy) 90
Bradshaw (boy) 90
Brage (boy) 174
Braham (boy) 28
Brainard (boy) 90
Bramwell (boy) 90
Branca (girl) 197
Branden (boy) 90
Brandon (boy) 90
Brandy-Lynn (girl) 233
Brant (boy) 90
Braxton (boy) 90
Brazil. *See* Portuguese-
    speaking regions
Breck (girl) 162
Brede (boy) 174
Breena (girl) 162
Brencis (boy) 72
Brenda (girl) 162
Brenda-Lee (girl) 233
Brendan (boy) 156
Brennan (boy) 90
Brent (boy) 91
Brenton (boy) 91
Brewster (boy) 91
Brian (boy) 156
Briana (girl) 162
Briar (girl) 129
Brice (boy) 168

Bridger (boy) 91
Bridget (girl) 162
Brie-Ann (girl) 233
Brigham (boy) 91
Brigid (girl) 162
Brigitte (girl) 129
Brisa (girl) 206
Britany (girl) 108
Britta (girl) 179
Brock (boy) 91
Brody (boy) 156
Bromley (boy) 91
Bronislaw (boy) 76
Bronson (boy) 91
Bronwyn (girl) 170
Brook (boy) 91
Brooke (girl) 108
Brooklyn (girl) 233
Brooks (boy) 91
Brown (boy) 91
Bruna (girl) 149
Brunhilda (girl) 149
Bruno (boy) 139, 186,
    194
Bryce (boy) 168
Bryga (girl) 78
Bryon (boy) 139
Bubba (boy) 231
Buck (boy) 139
Buckminster (boy) 91
Bud (boy) 91
Buddy (boy) 231
Buell (boy) 139
Buffy (girl) 234
Buford (boy) 91
Bulgaria, names from
    62–63
  boys 62
  girls 62–63
Bunmi (girl) 12
Bupe (girl) 17
Burgess (boy) 91
Burke (boy) 121, 139

Burne (boy) 91
Burney (boy) 91
Bursar (girl) 21
Burton (boy) 91
Buster (boy) 231
Butcher (boy) 91
Buzsi (girl) 71
Byford (boy) 91
Byhallia (girl) 223

C

Cable (boy) 121
Cachet (girl) 129
Caddock (boy) 168
Cady (girl) 108
Cai (boy) 168
Cailey (girl) 234
Cailin (girl) 234
Caio (boy) 194
Caitlin (girl) 163
Calder (boy) 168
Cali (girl) 50
Calida (girl) 206
Calvert (boy) 91
Camilla (girl) 192
Camille (girl) 129
Candi (girl) 234
Cannon (boy) 121
Cantrelle (girl) 129
Capri (girl) 234
Cara (girl) 163
Caressa (girl) 129
Cari (girl) 170
Carl (boy) 139
Carla (girl) 197
Carlene (girl) 108
Carlisle (boy) 91
Carlissa (girl) 234
Carlo (boy) 186
Carlos (boy) 194, 200
Carlotta (girl) 192

Denali (boy) 215
Denham (boy) 93
Denise (girl) 130
Denisha (girl) 235
Denley (boy) 93
Dennison (boy) 93
Denton (boy) 93
Derek (boy) 140
Derika (girl) 150
Derry (girl) 163
Derward (boy) 93
Deryn (girl) 170
Deshawn (boy) 231
Desiderio (boy) 200
Desiree (girl) 130
Desmond (boy) 157
Dessa (girl) 130
Destin (boy) 122
Destiny (girl) 130
Detrick (boy) 140
Deva (girl) 32
Deven (boy) 28
Devi (girl) 32
Devin
  boy 157
  girl 163
Devlin (boy) 157
Devonna (girl) 110
Devora (girl) 51, 62
Dewi (boy) 168
Dezba (girl) 223
Di (boy) 25
Diana (girl) 197
Dibia (boy) 9
Dic (boy) 80
Dichali (boy) 215
Dick (boy) 140
Didier (boy) 122
Diego (boy) 200
Dietbald (boy) 140
Dieter (boy) 140
Dietrich (boy) 140
Dija (girl) 130

Diji (boy) 9
Dillon (boy) 157
Dilwyn (boy) 168
Dilys (girl) 170
Diná (girl) 197
Dinah (girl) 51
Ding (girl) 26
Dingane (boy) 16
Dinka (girl) 21
Diodoros (boy) 182
Dior (girl) 130
Dirk (boy) 140
Diwali (boy) 215
Dixie (girl) 130
Dixon (boy) 93
Diza (girl) 51
Dmitri (boy) 82
Dmitro (boy) 86
Do (girl) 6
Dobry (boy) 76
Dofi (girl) 6, 22
Dohasan (boy) 215
Dohate (boy) 215
Dol (girl) 80
Doli (girl) 223
Dolly (girl) 235
Dolores (girl) 207
Dolph (boy) 140
Domina (girl) 110
Domingo (boy) 201
Dominika (girl) 78
Dominique
  boy 122
  girl 130
Domokos (boy) 69
Donal (boy) 157
Donatas (boy) 74
Donatien (boy) 122
Donato (boy) 186
Dondi (girl) 235
Donnell (boy) 157
Donoma (girl) 223
Donovan (boy) 157

Dooley (boy) 158
Dor (boy) 44
Doralynn (girl) 110
Dorota (girl) 75, 78
Dorotea (girl) 192
Dory (girl) 235
Doto (girl) 22
Dov (boy) 45
Doya (girl) 223
Dror (boy) 45
Drury (boy) 122
Duana (girl) 163
Duane (boy) 158
Dudley (boy) 93
Dugan (boy) 158
Duk (boy) 122
Dulce (girl) 207
Dumaka (boy) 20
Dunley (boy) 93
Dunsimi (boy) 10
Dunton (boy) 93
Durko (boy) 64
Durojaiye (boy) 10
Durward (boy) 93
Dushan (boy) 64
Dustin (boy) 93, 140
Dustine (girl) 150
Dustu (boy) 215
Duval (boy) 122
Dwight (boy) 93
Dyami (boy) 215
Dyani (girl) 223
Dyer (boy) 93
Dyke (boy) 93
Dylan (boy) 168
Dyre (boy) 174
Dziko (girl) 16

E

Eamon (boy) 158
Earl (boy) 158

Florent (boy) 122
Florentyna (girl) 78
Florida (girl) 207
Floyd (boy) 95
Flynn (boy) 158
Fola (girl) 13
Folade (girl) 13
Folami (girl) 13
Folashade (girl) 13
Folayan (girl) 13
Folke (boy) 141
Foluke
  boy 10
  girl 13
Foma (boy) 62
Fonso (boy) 141
Fontaine (boy) 122
Fontanna (girl) 131
Fonzie (boy) 141
Ford (boy) 95
Forogh (girl) 42
Fortuné (boy) 122
France, names from
      120–136
  boys 120–128
  girls 128–136
Frances (girl) 111
Francesca (girl) 192
Francesco (boy) 187
Franchot (boy) 122
Franci (girl) 71
Francine (girl) 131
Francisca (girl) 197
Francisco (boy) 195, 201
Francise (girl) 81
Fransçois (boy) 122
Françoise (girl) 131
Frank (boy) 95
Frankie (girl) 235
Franklin (boy) 95
Frans (boy) 172, 178
Frantisek (boy) 64
Franz (boy) 141

Fraser (boy) 122
Frayne (boy) 122
Freddie (girl) 111
Frederica (girl) 111, 150
Frederick (boy) 141
Frederico (boy) 195
Frederique (girl) 131
Fremont (boy) 141
Freya (girl) 179
Frieda (girl) 150
Friedrich (boy) 141
Fritz (boy) 141
Fritzi (girl) 150
Frode (boy) 174
Frøya (girl) 176
Fu (boy) 25
Fujo (girl) 22
Fulbright (boy) 141
Fyodor (boy) 83

G

Gabby (boy) 231
Gabor (boy) 69
Gabriel (boy) 195
Gabriela (girl) 197
Gabriele (boy) 187
Gabrielle (girl) 131
Gad (boy) 45, 216
Gada (girl) 51
Gadi (boy) 45
Gaetano (boy) 187
Gage (boy) 122
Gahiji (boy) 15
Gail (girl) 51
Gakere (boy) 7
Gakeri (girl) 7
Galbraith (boy) 158
Galeno (boy) 201
Galiena (girl) 150
Galina (girl) 84
Galvin (boy) 158

Gamli'el (boy) 45
Ganesa (boy) 28
Gannon (boy) 158
Ganya
  boy 16
  girl 51
Gao (boy) 25
Garcia (boy) 201
Gardenia (girl) 111
Garek (boy) 76
Gareth (boy) 168
Garfield (boy) 95
Garland
  boy 122
  girl 131
Garman (boy) 95
Garner (boy) 122
Garnet (girl) 111
Garnock (boy) 168
Garrett (boy) 95, 158
Garrick (boy) 95
Garrin (boy) 96
Garrison (boy) 122
Garson (boy) 96
Garvey (boy) 158
Garvin (boy) 96
Garwood (boy) 96
Gary (boy) 96, 141
Garyn (girl) 111
Gaspar (boy) 122
Gaston (boy) 122
Gaute (boy) 174
Gautier (boy) 122
Gavin (boy) 168
Gavri'el (boy) 45
Gavriella (girl) 51
Gawain (boy) 168
Gawonii (boy) 216
Gay (girl) 131
Gayle (girl) 111
Gaylord (boy) 122
Gayna (girl) 111
Ge (boy) 25

Horton (boy) 97
Hosheya (boy) 46
Hoshi (girl) 36
Hotah (boy) 216
Hototo (boy) 216
Houghton (boy) 97
Howard (boy) 97
Howe (boy) 143
Howell (boy) 169
Howi
  boy 216
  girl 224
Hoyt (boy) 159
Hua (girl) 27
Huata (girl) 224
Hubbard (boy) 143
Hubert (boy) 143
Huberto (boy) 202
Hubie (boy) 97
Huey (boy) 97
Hugh (boy) 97
Hugo (boy) 195
Hui (girl) 27
Hulbert (boy) 143
Hulda (girl) 179
Humbert (boy) 143
Humita (girl) 224
Humphrey (boy) 143
Hungary, names from
    69–71
  boys 69–71
  girls 71
Hunter (boy) 97
Huntington (boy) 97
Huo (boy) 25
Huritt (boy) 216
Huseina (girl) 22
Huslu (boy) 216
Hute (boy) 216
Huyana (girl) 224
Hyacinthe (boy)
    123
Hyatt (boy) 97

I

Ian (boy) 159
Iasonas (boy) 182
Ida (girl) 151
Ide (girl) 164
Idemudia (boy) 3
Idogbe (boy) 10
Idowu
  boy 10
  girl 13
Idris (boy) 169
Ifama (girl) 13
Ife (girl) 13
Ifetayo (girl) 13
Igasho (boy) 216
Ige (girl) 13
Igilka (girl) 62
Ignace (boy) 76
Ignazio (boy) 188
Igor (boy) 83
Ihor (boy) 86
Iiniwa (boy) 216
Ijaba (girl) 13
Ikeinan (girl) 224
Ikia (girl) 52
Ikuseghan (girl) 13
Ilan (boy) 46
Ilana (girl) 52
Ilario (boy) 188
Ilima (girl) 212
Ilise (girl) 151
Ilisha (girl) 52
Ilona (girl) 71
Ilse (girl) 151
Ilya (boy) 83
Ima (girl) 36, 151
Imala (girl) 224
Imani (girl) 22
Imarogbe (boy) 10
Imelda (girl) 151
Imena (girl) 22
Immanu'el (boy) 46

Imre (boy) 69
Imrich (boy) 65
Ina (girl) 13, 164
Inácio (boy) 195
Inay (boy) 29
Ince (boy) 69
Inder (boy) 29
India, names from 28–34
  boys 28–31
  girls 31–34
Indira (girl) 32
Indulis (boy) 72
Inez (girl) 207
Inga (girl) 176
Ingalill (girl) 179
Inge (boy) 175
Ingellbert (boy) 143
Ingram (boy) 97
Ingrid (girl) 176
Inna (girl) 84
Innis (boy) 159
Innocenzo (boy) 188
Inoa (girl) 212
Inoli (girl) 224
Inteus (boy) 216
Ioan (boy) 62, 80
Iolana (girl) 212
Iolanda (girl) 197
Iolani (girl) 212
Iolanta (girl) 66
Iolo (boy) 169
Ipyana (boy) 17
Iran, names from 60–61
  boys 60–61
  girls 61
Ireland, names from
    156–167
  boys 156–162
  girls 162–167
Irina (girl) 84
Irini (girl) 81
Íris (girl) 197
Irumba (boy) 18

Jassy (boy) 217
Jatinra (boy) 29
Javier (boy) 202
Javiera (girl) 208
Jay (boy) 123
Jaya (girl) 32
Jaycee (girl) 235
Jayde (boy) 232
Jaydee (girl) 235
Jaylee (boy) 232
Jayme (boy) 98
Jaymes (boy) 98
Jayna (girl) 52
Jazz (boy) 232
Jean (boy) 123
Jeanette (girl) 132
Jecis (boy) 74
Jefferson (boy) 98
Jeffrey (boy) 98
Jehan (boy) 123
Jem (girl) 52
Jemima (girl) 52
Jemma (girl) 52
Jemond (boy) 123
Jenelle (girl) 235
Jenica (girl) 81
Jenka (girl) 66
Jennifer (girl) 112, 170
Jennilee (girl) 235
Jennilynn (girl) 235
Jenu (boy) 70
Jeorek (boy) 77
Jerald (boy) 98
Jeraldine (girl) 113
Jerard (boy) 123
Jeremy (boy) 98
Jeri (girl) 236
Jermaine
  boy 123
  girl 132
Jerome (boy) 98
Jerry (boy) 143
Jerusha (girl) 52

Jessamine (girl) 132
Jessica (girl) 52
Jessie (girl) 52
Jésusa (girl) 53
Jetta (girl) 113
Jetzy (boy) 77
Jewel (girl) 132
Jibade (boy) 10
Jie (girl) 27
Jill (girl) 113
Jilleen (girl) 164
Jimbo (boy) 232
Jimi (girl) 53
Jin (boy) 25
Jindra (boy) 65
Jing (boy) 25
Jiri (boy) 65
Jirina (girl) 66
Jivan (girl) 32
Jivin (boy) 29
Jizelle (girl) 236
Jo (girl) 236
Joan (girl) 53
Joanka (girl) 78
Joanna (girl) 113
Joanne (girl) 113
João (boy) 195
Joaquim (boy) 195
Joaquin (boy) 202
Joaquina (girl) 53
Jobeth (girl) 113
Joby (girl) 53
Jock (boy) 232
Jodie (girl) 236
Joella (girl) 53
Joelle (girl) 53
Johann (boy) 143
Johanna (girl) 151, 179
Johnna (girl) 236
Jojo (boy) 4
Jokha (girl) 22
Jolánta (girl) 78
Jolene (girl) 53

Jolie (girl) 132
Joline (girl) 113
Jolon (boy) 217
Jonas (boy) 74
Jonelle (girl) 236
Joni (girl) 236
Jonina (girl) 53
Jonquil (girl) 113
Joosef (boy) 172
Jora (girl) 53
Jordan (girl) 53
Jordana (girl) 53
Jorell (boy) 232
Jorg (boy) 143
Jorge (boy) 195, 202
Jori (girl) 53
Jorunn (girl) 177
Jose (boy) 202
Josef (boy) 65, 143, 175
Josefina (girl) 208
Joséphine (girl) 132
Josette (girl) 132
Josha (boy) 29
Josie (girl) 53, 236
Josyp (boy) 86
Joy (girl) 113
Juan (boy) 202
Juanita (girl) 208
Juci (girl) 71
Judith (girl) 53
Judy (girl) 53
Juhana (boy) 172
Juho (boy) 172
Jula (girl) 78
Jules (boy) 123
Júlia (girl) 197
Juliana (girl) 66, 208
Juliane (girl) 164
Juliann (girl) 113
Julie (girl) 113
Juliet (girl) 132
Júlio (boy) 195
Jumapili (girl) 7

Lukas (boy) 65, 178
Lulani (boy) 212
Lulu (girl) 23
Luminita (girl) 81
Lunn (boy) 160
Lusela (girl) 225
Lusila (boy) 29
Lusio (boy) 217
Lutalo (boy) 18
Luther (boy) 144
Luvena (girl) 114
Luyu
  boy 217
  girl 225
Luz (girl) 208
Lyla (girl) 133
Lyle (boy) 124
Lyman (boy) 99
Lynch (boy) 160
Lynda (girl) 208
Lyndal (boy) 99
Lyndon (boy) 99
Lyndsay (girl) 237
Lynn (girl) 114
Lynnell (girl) 114
Lyrand (boy) 70
Lyront (boy) 70

M

Macario (boy) 203
Mace (boy) 124
Machas (boy) 77
Machiko (girl) 37
Macia (girl) 78
Mackenzie (girl) 165
Maco (boy) 70
Macy (boy) 124
Mada (girl) 114
Madaha (girl) 23
Maddie (girl) 114
Maddock (boy) 169

Madeleine (girl) 133
Madhar (boy) 29
Madongo (boy) 18
Madu (boy) 10
Mae (girl) 114
Ma'ema'e (girl) 213
Maemi (girl) 37
Maeve (girl) 165
Mafuane (girl) 16
Magaskaween (girl) 225
Magda (girl) 66, 78
Magdalene (girl) 54
Magee (boy) 160
Magena (girl) 225
Magnar (boy) 175
Magnhild (girl) 177
Magomu (boy) 18
Maguire (boy) 160
Mahala (girl) 225
Mahalia (girl) 237
Mahesa
  boy 29
  girl 32
Mahi'ai (boy) 212
Mahila (girl) 32
Mahina (girl) 213
Mahira (girl) 54
Mahkah (boy) 217
Mahkoseseha (girl) 225
Mahon (boy) 160
Mahpeeya (boy) 217
Mahwah (boy) 218
Mai
  boy 26
  girl 37, 225
Maija (girl) 173
Maire (girl) 165
Mairead (girl) 165
Mairtin (boy) 160
Maitias (boy) 160
Maitiú (boy) 160
Maj (girl) 179
Maka (boy) 212

Makala (girl) 213
Makalani (boy) 7
Makana (girl) 213
Makani
  boy 212
  girl 213
Makara (girl) 32
Makaween (girl) 226
Makena (girl) 7
Makini (girl) 23
Makoto (boy) 35
Maks (boy) 70
Maksim (boy) 83
Maksym (boy) 77, 86
Makya (boy) 218
Malaika (girl) 23
Malajitm (boy) 29
Malakhi (boy) 46
Malana (girl) 213
Malena (girl) 179
Mali (girl) 41
Malia (girl) 226
Malie (girl) 213
Malika (girl) 71
Malila (girl) 226
Malina (girl) 54
Malini (girl) 32
Malka (girl) 54
Malley (girl) 237
Mallorie (girl) 133
Mallory (girl) 152
Maloney (boy) 160
Malva (girl) 114
Malvern (boy) 169
Mamie (girl) 237
Mammedaty (boy) 218
Mamo
  boy 212
  girl 213
Mana (girl) 213
Mandara (girl) 32
Mandeep (boy) 30
Mandek (boy) 77

Osman (boy) 42
Osmar (boy) 100
Osmond (boy) 100
Osric (boy) 100
Osvaldo (boy) 204
Oswald (boy) 100
Oswin (boy) 100
Ota (boy) 65
Otadan (boy) 219
Otaktay (boy) 219
Otávio (boy) 196
Otek (boy) 77
Otello (boy) 204
Otewomin (girl) 227
Othman (boy) 145
Otieno (boy) 7
Otillie (girl) 66
Otskai (boy) 219
Ottah (boy) 11
Ottar (boy) 175
Otthild (girl) 153
Otto (boy) 145, 175
Ottokar (boy) 145
Ourayi (boy) 219
Ovadya (boy) 47
Owen (boy) 161
Owney (boy) 161
Øystein (boy) 175
Oz (girl) 56
Ozara (girl) 56
Ozigbodi (girl) 6

P

Paavo (boy) 172
Pablo (boy) 204
Pacho (boy) 219
Pacific Rim. *See* Asia and the Pacific Rim, names from
Padma (girl) 33

Page
  boy 125
  girl 134
Pahana (boy) 219
Paige
  boy 100
  girl 116
Paka (girl) 23
Paki (boy) 16, 20
Pakuna (girl) 227
Pakwa (girl) 227
Pål (boy) 178
Palash (boy) 30
Palliton (boy) 219
Paloma (girl) 209
Pamuya (girl) 227
Pana (girl) 227
Pancha (girl) 209
Pancho (boy) 204
Pandita (girl) 33
Panya (girl) 23
Panyin (girl) 6
Paola (girl) 193
Paolo (boy) 189
Papina (girl) 227
Paquita (girl) 209
Paramesh (boy) 30
Pari (girl) 61
Parker (boy) 100
Parnell (boy) 126
Parry (boy) 169
Pascal (boy) 126
Pascale (girl) 134
Pascual (boy) 204
Pasquale (boy) 189
Pasua (girl) 23
Patakusu
  boy 219
  girl 227
Pataman (boy) 219
Patek (boy) 77
Pati (girl) 227
Patia (girl) 116

Patience (girl) 116
Patrice
  boy 126
  girl 134
Patricia (girl) 116, 166, 198
Patricio (boy) 196, 204
Patrick (boy) 161
Patrizia (girl) 193
Patrizio (boy) 189
Patwin (boy) 219
Paula (girl) 198
Paulena (girl) 184
Paulin (boy) 77, 145
Paulo (boy) 179, 196, 204
Paulos (boy) 182
Pausha (girl) 33
Pavati (girl) 227
Pavel (boy) 83
Pavia (girl) 66
Pavit (boy) 30
Pavlo (boy) 86
Pawel (boy) 77
Pay (boy) 219
Payat (boy) 220
Paz
  boy 47
  girl 209
Pazi (girl) 227
Pazia (girl) 56
Peace (girl) 116
Peadar (boy) 161
Pedro (boy) 196, 204
Peeter (boy) 68
Pegeen (girl) 166
Peji (boy) 220
Pela (girl) 78
Peni (girl) 227
Peopeo (boy) 220
Pepin (boy) 145
Peppe (boy) 189

R

Rachel (girl) 56
Rada (girl) 81
Radburn (boy) 101
Radcliff (boy) 101
Radford (boy) 101
Radhiya (girl) 24
Radka (girl) 63
Radley (boy) 101
Radnor (boy) 101
Radoslaw (boy) 77
Rafael (boy) 204
Rafal (boy) 77
Rafe (boy) 101
Rafer (boy) 161
Raffaele (boy) 189
Ragna (girl) 177
Ragnar (boy) 176
Ragnild (girl) 153
Rago (boy) 11
Raheem (boy) 30
Rahil (girl) 63
Raimonds (boy) 72
Raimund (boy) 145
Raine (boy) 101
Rainer (boy) 145
Raini (boy) 220
Raisa (girl) 85
Raizel (girl) 56
Rajah (boy) 30
Rajak (boy) 30
Raktim (boy) 30
Raku (girl) 38
Ralph (boy) 101
Ralston (boy) 101
Ram (boy) 30
Rama (girl) 56
Ramanan (boy) 30
Rami (boy) 47
Ramia (girl) 24
Ramon (boy) 204
Ramona (girl) 209

Ramsden (boy) 101
Ramsey (boy) 101
Ran (girl) 38
Ranait (girl) 166
Rance (boy) 101
Randall (girl) 116
Randi (girl) 116
Randolph (boy) 101
Randy (boy) 101
Ranger (boy) 126
Rangle (boy) 232
Rani (girl) 33
Ranita (girl) 56
Ranjan (boy) 30
Raoul (boy) 126
Raphaela (girl) 56
Rapier (boy) 126
Rasa (girl) 75
Rashid (boy) 17
Rashida (girl) 24
Ratana (girl) 41
Ratri (girl) 33
Raul (boy) 126
Raula (girl) 135
Raulas (boy) 74
Raven (girl) 116
Ravi (boy) 30
Rawlins (boy) 126
Ray (boy) 126
Raya (girl) 56
Rayburn (boy) 101
Rayleen (girl) 238
Raymond (boy) 101
Raymonde (girl) 153
Raynaldo (boy) 204
Raynard (boy) 126
Razi (girl) 56
Raziya (girl) 24
Reading (boy) 101
Reagan (boy) 161
Reanna (girl) 116, 153
Reanne (girl) 238
Reba (girl) 56

Rebecca (girl) 56
Rebel (boy) 232
Rebi (girl) 56
Red (boy) 232
Redford (boy) 101
Redmond (boy) 145
Redpath (boy) 101
Reece (boy) 169
Reed (boy) 101
Reet (girl) 68
Reganne (girl) 166
Regina (girl) 73, 198
Reginald (boy) 101
Régis (boy) 196
Rehema (girl) 24
Rei (girl) 38
Reidar (boy) 176
Reilly (boy) 161
Reimond (boy) 80
Reina (girl) 38, 209
Reinhart (boy) 145
Reinhold (boy) 179
Rekha (girl) 33
Remi (girl) 135
Remington (boy) 101
Rémy (boy) 126
Ren (girl) 38
Rena (girl) 56
Renaldo (boy) 204
Renato (boy) 189
Renaud (boy) 126
Rendor (boy) 70
René (boy) 126
Renee (girl) 135
Renfred (boy) 101
Renie (girl) 135
Renita (girl) 135
Rennie (girl) 116
Renny (boy) 161
Reno (boy) 232
Renshaw (boy) 101
Renton (boy) 101
Renzo (boy) 189

Roseanne (girl) 117
Rosemary (girl) 117
Roshan (girl) 33
Rosie (girl) 117
Rosina (girl) 117
Rosita (girl) 209
Rostislav (boy) 65
Roth (boy) 146
Rowan (boy) 102
Rowell (boy) 102
Rowena (girl) 166, 171
Rowina (girl) 117
Rowland (boy) 146
Rowley (boy) 102
Roxanne (girl) 61
Roy (boy) 126
Royal (boy) 126
Royale (girl) 117
Royanna (girl) 117
Royce (boy) 102
Royden (boy) 102
Roz (girl) 117
Rozene (girl) 227, 239
Rubert (boy) 65
Ruchil (girl) 33
Ruda (boy) 65
Rudee (girl) 153
Rudo (boy) 20
Rudolf (boy) 146
Rudolph (boy) 102, 146
Rudra (girl) 33
Rudyard (boy) 102
Rue (girl) 153
Rufin (boy) 77
Ruford (boy) 102
Rugby (boy) 102
Rui (girl) 38
Rukiya (girl) 24
Rula (girl) 117
Runa (girl) 177
Rune (boy) 146, 179
Rungrot (boy) 41
Rupert (boy) 146

Ruri (girl) 38
Rusalka (girl) 67
Ruskin (boy) 127
Russell (boy) 127
Russhell (girl) 135
Russia, names from
    82–85
  boys 82–84
  girls 84–85
Rusti (girl) 117
Ruth (girl) 57
Ruthann (girl) 239
Rutherford (boy) 102
Ruza (girl) 67
Rwanda, names from 15
  boys 15
  girls 15
Ryan (boy) 161
Ryanne (girl) 166
Ryba (girl) 67
Ryo (girl) 38
Ryou (boy) 35
Ryouta (boy) 35
Ryutaro (boy) 35

S

Saada (girl) 24
Sa'adya (boy) 47
Saber (boy) 127
Sabiti (boy) 19
Sable (girl) 117
Sabra (girl) 57
Sachi (girl) 38
Sada (girl) 38
Sade (girl) 14, 57
Sadhana (girl) 33
Sadia (girl) 57
Sadzi (girl) 227
Saffron (girl) 117
Safiya (girl) 24
Sagara (girl) 33

Sage (girl) 117
Sahale (boy) 220
Sahkonteic (boy) 220
Sahpooly (girl) 227
Sai (girl) 38
Sajag (boy) 31
Sakae (girl) 38
Sakari (girl) 33
Sakda (boy) 41
Saki (girl) 38
Sakima (boy) 220
Sakti (girl) 33
Sakuna (girl) 239
Sakura (girl) 38
Sala (girl) 33
Salama (girl) 24
Salamon (boy) 205
Salaun (boy) 127
Salina (girl) 135
Salliann (girl) 117
Sally (girl) 117
Salma (girl) 24
Salman (boy) 65
Saloli (girl) 227
Salomeya (girl) 75
Salvador (boy) 205
Salvadora (girl) 209
Salvatore (boy) 190
Samala (girl) 57
Samantha (girl) 57
Sameh (girl) 57
Sami (girl) 57
Samoset (boy) 220
Samuela (girl) 57
Samuele (boy) 190
Sanatan (boy) 31
Sancia (girl) 209
Sandeep (boy) 31
Sandor (boy) 70
Sandro (boy) 190
Sani (boy) 31, 220
Sanjiv (boy) 31
Sankar (boy) 31

Sharice (girl) 135
Sharifa (girl) 24
Sharik (girl) 24
Sharla (girl) 135
Sharlene (girl) 135
Sharlotte (girl) 239
Sharmaine (girl) 239
Sharna (girl) 57
Sharon (girl) 57
Sharonda (girl) 58
Sharrona (girl) 58
Shattuck (boy) 102
Sha'ul (boy) 47
Shayna (girl) 58
Shea
    boy 161
    girl 167
Sheba (girl) 58
Sheena (girl) 58, 167
Sheila (girl) 167
Shelby (girl) 117
Sheldon (boy) 102
Shelley (girl) 117
Shelsea (girl) 239
Shenandoah (boy)
    220
Shera (girl) 58
Sherice (girl) 135
Sherill (boy) 103
Sherita (girl) 135
Sherleen (girl) 135
Sherlock (boy) 103
Sherman (boy) 103
Sherrod (boy) 103
Sherry (girl) 117, 135
Sheryl (girl) 135
Sherylyn (girl) 239
Shi (boy) 26
Shifra (girl) 58
Shika (girl) 38
Shilo (girl) 58
Shiminege (girl) 14
Shimon (boy) 47

Shimshon (boy) 47
Shina (girl) 38
Shino (girl) 38
Shira (girl) 58
Shirlene (girl) 117
Shirley (girl) 117
Shiva (boy) 31
Shiye (boy) 220
Shizu (girl) 38
Shlomo (boy) 47
Shmu'el (boy) 47
Shmuli (boy) 47
Shona (girl) 167
Shoshana (girl) 58
Shou (boy) 35
Shouta (boy) 35
Shuang (girl) 27
Shui (boy) 26
Shukura (girl) 24
Shulamith (girl) 58
Shun (boy) 35
Shyla (girl) 118
Si (boy) 26
Siân (girl) 171
Sibeta (girl) 228
Siboniso (girl) 24
Siddhartha (boy) 31
Sidney (boy) 127
Sidonia (girl) 58
Sidonie (girl) 118, 135
Sidonio (boy) 205
Sidwell (boy) 103
Siegfried (boy) 146
Sigfreda (girl) 154
Sigidi (boy) 16
Sigmunda (girl) 154
Sigolwide (girl) 17
Sigourney (girl) 118
Sigrid (girl) 177
Sihu (girl) 228
Siko (girl) 24
Sikudhani (girl) 24
Sikya (girl) 228

Silje (girl) 177
Silvestro (boy) 190
Silvia (girl) 193
Silvio (boy) 190
Simão (boy) 196
Simcha (girl) 58
Simeon (boy) 127
Simion (boy) 80
Simone (girl) 58
Sinclair (boy) 127
Sindy (girl) 239
Sinead (girl) 167
Sinjon (boy) 103
Sinopa (girl) 228
Siobhan (girl) 167
Sipatu
    boy 220
    girl 228
Siphiwe (girl) 24
Sipho (boy) 16
Sipliwo (boy) 16
Sisi (boy) 5
Sisika (girl) 228
Sissy (girl) 239
Sisya (girl) 24
Sita (girl) 33
Siti (girl) 24
Siv (girl) 177
Sivan (boy) 47
Siwili (boy) 220
Skah (boy) 220
Skeeter (boy) 103
Slade (boy) 103
Slana (girl) 228
Slane (boy) 66
Slater (boy) 103
Slawek (boy) 78
Sloan (boy) 161
Sloane (girl) 167
Smedley (boy) 103
Snaige (girl) 73
Snezhana (girl) 63
So (boy) 26

Tsuna (girl) 39
Tu (boy) 26
Tuako (boy) 20
Tuari (boy) 221
Tudor (boy) 170
Tuesday (girl) 118
Tuketu (girl) 229
Tukuli (girl) 229
Tula (girl) 34
Tulinagwe (girl) 17, 24
Tullia (girl) 167
Tullio (boy) 191
Tulsi (girl) 34
Tumaini (boy) 7
Tumpe (girl) 17
Tumu (boy) 221
Tupi (girl) 229
Tuponile (boy) 17
Tupper (boy) 105
Turk (boy) 105
Turquoise (girl) 136
Tusa (girl) 229
Tusajigwe (girl) 17
Tutskwa (girl) 229
Tuuwa (girl) 229
Tuwalole (girl) 24
Twia (boy) 5
Twyla (girl) 118
Tyee (boy) 221
Tyehimba (boy) 11
Tyfany (girl) 240
Tyler
  boy 105
  girl 118
Tynan (boy) 162
Tyne (girl) 119
Tynek (boy) 66
Tyonek (boy) 221
Tyron (boy) 232
Tyrone (boy) 162
Tyrus (boy) 105
Tyson (boy) 127
Tzakhi (boy) 47

Tzao (boy) 26
Tzefanya (boy) 47
Tzidkiyahu (boy) 48
Tzong (boy) 26
Tzvi (boy) 48

U

Uaine (boy) 162
Uberto (boy) 191
Uche (boy) 11
Uchefuna (girl) 14
Uganda, names from
  18–19
  boys 18–19
  girls 19
Ugo (boy) 191
Uilliam (boy) 162
Uinseann (boy) 162
Uistean (boy) 162
Ukraine, names from
  86–87
  boys 86–87
  girls 87
Ula (girl) 167
Ulan (boy) 20
Ulbrecht (boy) 147
Uldis (boy) 73
Ulf (boy) 147
Ulfred (boy) 147
Ulger (boy) 147
Ulla (girl) 154, 179
Ulli (girl) 68
Ullock (boy) 147
Ulmo (boy) 147
Ulrica (girl) 154
Ulrich (boy) 147
Ululani (girl) 213
Uluwehi (girl) 213
Ulva (girl) 154
Ulzumati (boy) 221
Umberto (boy) 191

Una (girl) 167
Unaduti (boy) 221
Unega (girl) 229
Unice (girl) 119
United States, names
  from the 231–240
  boys 231–232
  girls 233–240
Unity (girl) 119
Unn (girl) 177
Unna (girl) 154
Upton (boy) 105
Urano (girl) 39
Urbano (boy) 191, 196
Urbi (girl) 14
Uri (boy) 48
Urika (girl) 229
Urit (girl) 59
Urk (girl) 59
Urneko (girl) 39
Urson (boy) 127
Úrsula (girl) 198
Ursule (girl) 81
Usdi (girl) 229
Use (girl) 229
Usha (girl) 34
Usti (boy) 221
Uta (girl) 154
Utana (girl) 229
Utina (girl) 229
Uuka (boy) 16
U'una (girl) 229
Uwe (boy) 147
Uwimana (girl) 15
Uzoma (boy) 11

V

Vachel (boy) 127
Vaclav (boy) 66
Vacys (boy) 74
Vadim (boy) 83

Yoanna (girl) 59
Yo'av (boy) 48
Yo'el (boy) 48
Yogesh (boy) 31
Yohann (boy) 148
Yokhanan (boy) 48
Yoki (girl) 230
Yoko (girl) 39
Yoluta (girl) 230
Yon (boy) 26
Yona
  boy 48, 222
  girl 230
Yonatan (boy) 48
Yoni
  boy 48
  girl 39
Yonina (girl) 59
Yoofi (boy) 5
Yooku (boy) 5
Yoomee (girl) 230
Yoram (boy) 48
Yori (girl) 39
Yorkoo (boy) 5
Yosef (boy) 48
Yosepha (girl) 59
Yoshi (girl) 39
Yosi (boy) 48
Yoskolo (girl) 230
Yotimo (girl) 230
Youri (boy) 87
Yovela (girl) 59
Yrjo (boy) 173
Yseult (girl) 155
Yu (boy) 26, 36
Yuana (girl) 210
Yudelle (girl) 119
Yue (girl) 27
Yuka (girl) 39
Yuki
  boy 36
  girl 39
Yukiko (girl) 39

Yulia (girl) 85
Yun (girl) 27
Yuri
  boy 84
  girl 39
Yuta (boy) 36
Yutu (girl) 230
Yves (boy) 128
Yvette (girl) 136
Yvon (boy) 128
Yvonne (girl) 136
Yyevgenia (girl) 85

Z

Zabrina (girl) 240
Zacarias (boy) 196
Zacharias (boy) 148
Zacharie (girl) 59
Zahar (girl) 59
Zahavah (girl) 59
Zahra (girl) 24
Zainabu (girl) 24
Zakia (girl) 24
Zako (boy) 70
Zalika (girl) 24
Zaltana (girl) 230, 240
Zamiel (boy) 148
Zane (boy) 106
Zaneta (girl) 210
Zanna (girl) 73
Zara (girl) 59
Zaramo (boy) 17
Zarita (girl) 210
Zaviera (girl) 210
Zawadi (girl) 24
Zayit (girl) 59
Zekharya (boy) 49
Zelda (girl) 155
Zelene (girl) 119
Zelia (girl) 210
Zelma (girl) 155

Zemirah (girl) 59
Zenon (boy) 87
Zenovia (girl) 87
Zera (girl) 59
Zerlina (girl) 210
Zesiro
  boy 19
  girl 19
Zeta (girl) 119
Zhen (boy) 26
Zhivoin (boy) 62
Zhu (boy) 26
Zhuang (boy) 26
Zigana (girl) 71
Zigfrid (boy) 73
Ziggy (boy) 232
Zilla (girl) 59
Zilpah (girl) 59
Zimra (girl) 59
Zimri (boy) 49
Zintkala (girl) 230
Zipporah (girl) 59
Ziracuny (girl) 230
Zita (girl) 210
Zitkala (girl) 230
Ziva (girl) 59
Zizi (girl) 71
Zocha (girl) 79
Zoe (girl) 193
Zoé (girl) 198
Zohar (girl) 59
Zoltin (boy) 71
Zonta (girl) 230
Zoya (girl) 85
Zsa Zsa (girl) 71
Zsigmond (boy) 71
Zsusanna (girl) 71
Zudora (girl) 34
Zusa (girl) 67, 79
Zuwena (girl) 24
Zuzane (girl) 75
Zvulun (boy) 49
Zytka (girl) 79